BMW

3 Series Enthusiast's Companion™

Jeremy Walton

B BentleyPublishers™
.com

BMW
3 Series

3 Series beginnings, the 1500, see Chapter 1

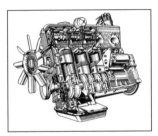

The four-cylinder M10 engine, see Chapter 3

Men and machines: The 1978 racing season, see Chapter 5

Turbo takes on the Porsches! See Chapter 6

Four doors! See Chapter 7

A look inside the M3, see Chapter 9

The author takes the 2.5-liter M3 out for a spin, see Chapter 12

1992's Spa 24-hour race, see Chapter 14

The versatile 318ti can even be used as a planter! See Chapter 21

The latest edition to the M3 family, see Chapter 26

Bentley Publishers, a division of Robert Bentley, Inc.
1734 Massachusetts Avenue
Cambridge, MA 02138 USA
800-423-4595 / 617-547-4170

Information that makes
the difference®

BentleyPublishers™
.com

Copies of this book may be purchased from selected booksellers, or directly from the publisher. The publisher encourages comments from the reader of this book. These communications have been and will be considered in the preparation of this and other books. Please write to Bentley Publishers at the address listed at the top of this page or e-mail us through our web site.

Library of Congress Cataloging-in-Publication Data

Walton, Jeremy, 1946-
  BMW 3 Series Ehthusiast's Companion / Jeremy Walton.
    p. cm.
  Includes index.
    ISBN 0-8376-0220-3 (soft cover : alk paper)
    1. BMW automobiles. I Title.

 TL215.B25 W3482 2001
 629.222'2--dc21

                                                        2001025998

Bentley Stock No. GBM3

08 07 06 05   5 4 3 2

The paper used in this publication is acid free and meets the requirements of the National Standard for Information Sciences—Permanence of Paper for Printed Library Materials. ∞

BMW 3 Series Enthusiast's Companion™ , by Jeremy Walton

Manufactured in the United States of America

Front cover: Photo courtesy of Klaus Schnitzer
Back cover: Exterior car photos courtesy of BMW Historisches Archiv
                Engine illustration courtesy of BMW Grafik Design

Introduction

In 1966, when BMW started to produce the smaller 02 line of cars, they started a revolution by evolution: one that resulted in the sale of more than 6 million 3 Series in 22 years and almost a million of the original 02 pioneers. The best way to overview this evolution is to start with the illuminating perspective of American BMW insider, David Carp. A staffer of Development Design at BMW AG, Carp is a relaxed super auto-enthusiast and, with the practical help of ex-pat Briton Dave Bostin, at Mobile Tradition in Munich, provided a practical "sit and explore" guide through the smallest of BMW production cars, from 1966 through 1999.

Fresh out of Art Center College of Design, Pasadena, California, David Carp joined BMW some years ago. He remembered, "They said there were no vacancies and I was expecting to go back to the US after years of study. In fact, I took a trip to Munich on the hope of helping my career, and it worked out. They looked at my portfolio and took me on in the early nineties. Since that time, my interest in BMW has been fueled by the Roundel US BMW Club magazine and the passion of working inside BMW at Munich.

"I decided to try and collect what was available in design drawings, and—presumably because nobody else wanted them—I ended up with some good stuff, both pre-war and up to today. Looking through these design drawings, I could see BMW themes emerging and realized that a lot of what is held most dear by the purists, especially those who believe only in the round-taillight 02, is actually not reflected in the company drawings. The unseen designs show us BMW was open to a lot more influences than purists realize, and they tried many alternatives...

"As an American, I was surprised at the impact American design had on this most German of companies. When BMW first had a separate

Clockwise from top left: Claus Luthe influenced BMW designs for the 3 Series. Here he is in full 1970s fashion, with a clay model of the 6 Series coupe.

Photo: BMW AG, re-issued by BMW Historisches Archiv, 1999

Dave Carp, our Guide to the American and other outside influences on BMW Designs.

Photo: BMW AG

Parisian Paul Bracq was instrumental in shaping BMW designs for decades after his departure.

Photo: BMW AG, Munich, 1972

Chris Bangle, BMW Design Chief into the new millennium.

Photo: BMW AG

styling department [established in September of 1938], its founder was Wilhelm Meyerhuber, who had been a GM employee at Opel," revealed Carp, adding, "Even in 1938, they were using full-size clay modeling, and that was way in advance of most European rivals."

BMW also checked production designs in a wind tunnel, having learned the importance of aerodynamics in their racing pre-war 328s, which could reach 143 mph on just 136 bhp. Meyerhuber worked on these designs with the assistance of another Opel refugee, Karl Schmuck, who also contributed to the most exciting planned successors to BMW's legendary 328 sports car. Meyerhuber led a team that created perhaps the most beautiful of unseen mass-production sports cars. The intended successors to the 328 were as breathtaking as the Touring-bodied racing 328s that contested Le Mans in 1939 and the Mille Miglia in 1940.

The beneficiary of BMW's design genius was Great Britain, where many post-war British designs were influenced by the same swooping and aerodynamically seductive lines that BMW and the Italian coach houses created to race, then planned to manufacture in street form. The most famous echo of BMW 328 racing themes was the Jaguar XK120, but it has to be said that Williams Lyons and his Coventry employees interpreted such themes with show-business pizzazz.

Carp theorized, "Take the round taillight collectible obsession on 02. I believe round rear lamps came from Ford in the 50s and 60s: certainly Dearborn used that [theme] in everything from the compact Falcon through the Thunderbird, on up to the full-size Galaxie. Then look at Chevrolet Corvair's round rear lamps from 1959: the Americans really had more influence than I expected. Even the dogleg windshield from GM transferred across to some of the smallest contemporary German cars. Then we got the spectacle of a Mercedes with tail fins! Now we can see the transatlantic influences at work on the design of the rare 507 and 503 BMWs of the 1950s. So America had a strong role in shaping modern BMWs. I must add that—as in Britain and many other European manufacturing countries—it was the Italians who had the most direct input to BMW designs of 30–40 years ago. Here, I'd particularly like to mention the work of Michelotti and Bertone, who had influence beyond the BMW designs credited directly to them."

Carp recalls, "The Neue Klasse 1500–2000 family, along with the 02 pedigree look, is usually credited to Wilhem Hofmeister's leadership," but there was a debt to Michelotti that can be seen from the wealth of design drawings Carp has collected.

The E21 3 Series line was created under the hands-on leadership of Parisian Paul Bracq, who established the basic theme with the first 5 Series, before cheating the 1972 Turb show car. Bracq had left BMW by the time the second generation (E30) was being evolved on a 3 Series theme (1976–78). The boss was Claus Luthe, and he also steered the more radical and aerodynamic design direction adopted for the late-1980s 7, 5, and 8 Series, all pre-dating design work for the 4-door E36 sedan of 1990.

The E36 was the most influential BMW design of the 1990s, and was the first to make extensive use of Computer Aided Design (CAD), so there were no technical drawings to create this 3er. Initial design drawings by hand and models were made for E36 and E46, leaving computers with the finalized results to produce precise electronic drawings for production engineering.

The current fourth-generation 3 Series (E46)—actually fifth-generation if you include the 02 line as per current BMW practice—was born of six or seven 1992 sketches submitted by US-based Designworks employee Erik Goplen. These designs competed against those of four or five other design teams, all in house, with overall design direction led by Chris Bangle, BMW design chief.

Along with his summary of the complete 02 to E46 bloodline, Carp highlighted some common 3 Series/02 cues. He explained, "The origins of all 3 Series designs lie with the 02 series cars,

known internally as the Type 114 and commonly referred to as the 2002. To some extent, the first 5 Series sedans, known by their E12 development code, were another primary influence on the 3 Series. The 114 automobiles followed the design lead of their older siblings, the Types 115–118 mid-sized sedans. Essentially, the theme that developed under the design direction of Wilhem Hofmeister consisted of an uncluttered basic form with a short front overhang and outboard wheels. The familiar BMW 'kidneys' crown a dynamically pointed horizontal grille, with a relatively short hood leading to a prominent glasshouse whose rear pillars made a distinctive return at the foot [the trademark C-section swoop at the rearward base of the side rear glass]. A pronounced feature line, pressed into the sheet metal, ran the length and around the car. This feature line is commonly known at BMW as the Sicke."

Carp concluded, "Four generations of 3 Series and 02 document 35 years of BMW thinking for small sporting sedans. Each one witnesses a unique reaction to the realities and wishes of its time, and through exterior design they show their common membership in the 3 Series family."

The 3 Series of 2001 has evolved a very long way from the overly sporting 2002. No matter how the 2002 was dressed or equipped, it was still an out-and-out sport sedan that placed performance far above comfort. Although many BMW traditionalists would renounce the current 3'er as being too big, heavy, and luxurious, it does everything better than its illustrious predecessor— except to stir the soul. The current small BMW is also infinitely more flexible than the 2002. It can be equipped as a competent family sedan, a luxurious convertible, or a fast sporting coupe. In Sport Wagon form, it can carry large loads, and as the Xi, it is a capable four-wheel drive vehicle suited for extreme winter conditions. But most of all, as one quick glance at any 3 Series will confirm, it is, unequivocally, a BMW.

1 Munich's Baby Bestseller

The hits (and some US misses)
of the BMW 3 Series story.

Cult cars pose an incredible problem for an automobile manufacturer. A cult car develops an absolutely rabid enthusiast following. When the automaker attempts to alter it to meet revised regulatory requirements or to appeal to a broader market, the loyal following is the first and loudest to protest.

Companies other than BMW faced such difficulties with new models: MG was met with opposition when it replaced the square-rigged T-Series with the MGA in late 1955, as was Datsun when the 240Z gave way to the 260Z in 1974. BMW found itself in a similar position with the European introduction of the 3 Series in July 1975. In all three cases, the new models were heavier, slower, and less sporting than the superseded car. Yet, the 3 Series—like the later MG and Datsun models before it—consistently exceeded the sales record of its beloved predecessor, for the simple reason that the new model's appeal is intended for a much wider cross-section of the automobile buying public.

American BMW purists were particularly skeptical that the E21 3 Series could ever replace their cherished 02 sports sedans. However, each successive model year E21 and each generation of BMW's 3 Series sold better than its predecessors. This is particularly surprising since the American market, with its fiercer exhaust emissions regulations, ultimately received a product with lower power and sharply inferior handling ability.

Even the original "320i" Federal and California models accounted for more than 66 percent of all US BMW sales. While its percentages did not remain that strong, the 3 Series still accounted for 43 to 44 percent of all US BMW sales during 1997–98.

Then, in July 1998, the introduction of the current E46 took 3'er's sales back above 50 percent. No argument, this is BMW's most impor-

1

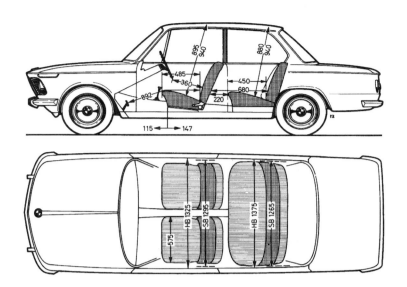

Famous for pace, but not for rear seat space, the original Typ 114 of the 02 family displays the feature line that runs around the car, or *Sicke*.

Line drawing: Issued by BMW AG, 1967

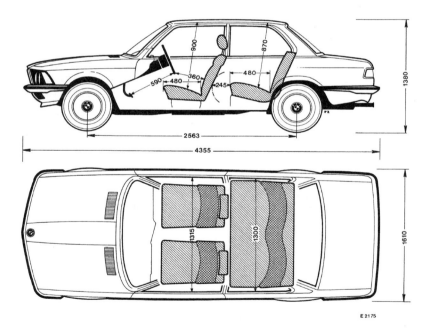

In contrast to the 02, the first 3 Series emphasized interior comforts, especially in the back-seat space.

Line drawing: BMW AG, 1975

The 02's fabled round taillamp that Bimmer purists love so well.

Photo: Author, Monterey, CA, 1999

tant product line in their biggest export market, although the 5 Series makes a case for extra profits and a size that many Americans appreciate.

The sporting reputation of the original BMW 02 line meant that everyday realities, such as limited ventilation and rear accommodation, were often overlooked. Nevertheless, 861,940 units were made during its eleven-year life.

Planning the first 3 Series against a backdrop of world events that included the European fuel crisis, BMW emphasized comfort and civilization over raw 02 sportiness. BMW planned a more

capacious body, initially to be propelled by four-cylinder engines of 90 to 125 bhp.

Unlike the 02 and later 3 Series, the E21 3'er remained a two-door model, and was less versatile than its ancestors and successors. During 1977, it re-opened a fresh post-war European market to BMW, one they had pioneered in the 1930s. Once again, BMW's hallmark was their smaller-capacity, straight six-cylinder for refined sports-saloon motoring.

In Europe, the carburetted 320/6 and the fuel-injected 323i, with 143 bhp, restored enthusiast

The men who were most influential in the transition between bankruptcy and the buoyant BMW of today are (left to right): Wilhelm Hofmeister, Fritz Fiedler, Herr Wolff, and Alex von Falkenhausen.

Photo: BMW AG, 1961, re-issued by BMW Historisches Archiv, 1991

The line-up for four generations of 3 Series and the 02: closest to the camera is the 1998-onward E46. It stands in front of its E36 predecessor (1990–98), the E30, and the 1602 and 2002 family of 1967–75.

Photo: Dougie Firth, Franciacorta, Italy, 1998

interest. The 323i could exceed 124 mph (200 km/h) and reach 62 mph (0-100 km/h) in 8.5 seconds. Although no match for the 2002 turbo, it was a bigger commercial success.

With a total sales figure of 1.36 million, the Bavarians sold almost twice as many of the first 3 Series as they had of the 02 line. BMW also collected excellent profit returns on the 407,552 (around 30 percent) that were sold in six-cylinder form from 1977–82, in Europe only. Few rivals comprehended the BMW philosophy of packing so many quality features in a smaller package. Main rival Mercedes eventually rose to the challenge in 1983, providing the 190 and subsequent C-class to deliver stern opposition to BMW.

However, Mercedes headed the 16-valve M3 to the market with a Mercedes-Cosworth 2.3/16 in 1984. That was almost two years before the first 195/200-bhp M3 was sold in Europe, so BMW was not invincible in this sector, but they certainly established a pattern that home-market rivals Mercedes and Audi followed. By the 1990s, almost every major manufacturer, including those from Japan, seemed to want to enter this market.

Ironically, the closest anyone came to usurping the 3'er in Europe was the pretty and capable front-drive 1998 Alfa Romeo 156. Many critics thought that the Alfa gave a more rewarding drive, which was ironic, because it was Alfa Romeo that inspired the first generations of rear-drive Neue Klasse BMWs. Back then, BMW couldn't afford the Alfa's aluminum twin cams. So a range of iron-block single overhead cam BMWs arrived, proving to be even more versatile than their Italian inspirations.

Whereas competition had been the lifeblood of the BMW 02, the 3 Series had a slower start in motorsports. In the US, Nick Craw, with Miller and Norburn preparation, showed that a 320i could both handle and perform. The 3'er is just as capable, perhaps more so, than an equivalent

The Neue Klasse of BMWs (1500 through 2000) were respected four-door sedans.

Photo: BMW Historisches Archiv, reissued 1999

2002, providing both have equal funding allocated to their track development.

In Europe, Switzerland's Eggenberger concern ran a 320i for a win in the 1980 European Championship. With help from Alpina, it harvested more than 220 bhp and 145-mph potential in endurance races.

The late-1970s BMW Motorsport E21 racing 3 Series were totally re-engineered to accept Formula 2 [M12/7] motors of 305 bhp. This allowed zero to 100 mph in less than 6 seconds, or the more usual German rating of zero to 100 km/h (0-62 mph) in 4.7 seconds.

A turbocharged version of the 3 Series (at 2 liters and up to 654 bhp) was raced in America with Citicorp backing in addition to BMW NA and fac-

tory support. Driven most notably by expat Briton David Hobbs, on occasion the BMW 320-McLaren could beat the Porsche 911 turbos.

In Germany, BMW sedans raced at just 1.4 liters and a mighty 360 to 610 bhp during 1977–80. Schnitzer of Freilasing won the German national title in 1978. Such turbocharged 3 Series programs led to BMW's Grand Prix 1.5-liter turbo motors of 600- to 1,200-bhp capability. Those for the 3 Series were co-developed with the late Markus Hottinger and GS Tuning to provide a German championship turbo contender supported by BMW Motorsport.

The 1982-90 (1991 in the US) second-generation 3 Series stretched the versatility of BMW's

First of a series of BMW studio photographs designed to show us how the 02 fit into the 3 Series story.

Photo: BMW Historisches Archiv, reissued 1999

starter range dramatically. Coded E30, it was received on the home market with the criticism that BMW had not been technically adventurous enough, especially in an age that had spawned both the 4x4 Quattro turbo and a low 0.30 Cd from Audi.

This photo best illustrates the clean appeal of the 2002 at home.

Photo: BMW Historisches Archiv, reissued 1999

Aerodynamically, the 1980s 3 Series hovered just below the 0.40-Cd barrier. It was true that the softened boxy outline remained upright in a world of more aerodynamic designs, but it also remained instantly recognizable.

It was in the field of electronics that the E30 displayed the most technical progress, filtering down features previously only found in the more opulent 6 and 7 Series. The second 3 Series popularized ABS anti-lock braking, the service interval indicator (replacing fixed intervals), and fuel consumption econometer.

The second 3 Series also shared with the 5 Series the job of educating BMW drivers to the benefits of diesel power, developed in association with BMW-owned Steyr in Austria. Fewer than 100,000 diesels were made between 1985 and December 1990, but it had greater potential then an original gasoline alternative, the slow-

Landmarks

Throughout the evolution and refinement of BMW's definitive benchmark, their entry-level sedans saw some sophisticated technology adopted. Still, the basic principles of a slant front engine, driving independently sprung rear wheels in a compact package, remained.

Initially, aerodynamics were not a favored subject at BMW, despite pre-war expertise in racing the 328. The hand-built aluminum coupe body for the Mille Miglia 328 allowed values below 0.30 Cd decades before such figures would be possible in mass production. BMW had no company wind tunnel until the 1980s, and this shows in the recorded aerodynamic drag (Cd) values of all their 1.6-liter models, calculated over more than thirty years.

The original 1966 BMW 1600 punched along with the comparative grace of a brick at 0.48 Cd. By 1998, the 316i (Europe only), which had the smallest engine and skinniest tires yet, would slice through the Autobahn air at just 0.28 Cd. Such Bimmers have little acceleration, but will still run over 100 mph all day without protest.

Aerodynamically, the landmark change was the E36, for the E21 3 Series recorded a bluff 0.45 Cd and

The first 3 Series had only two doors and bore the kidney grille, the "dog-leg" (C-pattern) rear side windows, and the *Sicke* line.

Photo: BMW Historisches Archiv, reissued 1999

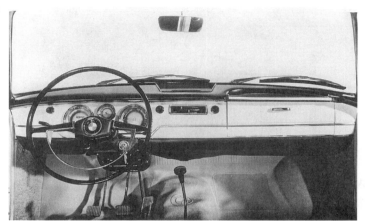

The first 1500 BMW set the format for the generations up to the millennium. A 1500 of 1962–64 had all the period pieces, including sparse (painted) steel and circular dials with minimalist instrumentation.

Photo: BMW AG, Munich, 1961

revving eta six. The 325e (eta) was made in volume (189,267) for Japan and America, between 1983–88.

At the 1982 E30 launch, a major variation was announced: a four-door would join the line in 1983, bringing another bigger-car dimension to BMW's baby. This move certainly escalated the 3 Series's appeal: the four-door accounted for almost half the 2.2 million units manufactured.

BMW specified more profitable options for the 3 Series. The biggest and most expensive bodywork hit was the cabriolet soft-top version of the two-door E30. A massive 143,425 units were made, remaining in production in 1991 even when the E30 had been replaced. The five-door Touring title was exhumed from the 02 period and over 103,704 E30 3 Series units were built from 1988–1991. Not such an enduring idea was BMW's only non-rear-drive 3 Series, the 325iX 4x4 variant, of which 29,589 were made from 1985–91.

The second-generation 3 Series loved motor-

Landmarks, continued

the E30's slight softening of lines left it just above the 0.40 barrier (0.41 Cd). Some derivatives could, however, manage 0.38 Cd; and the original E30 M3, with a radically revised body, rated 0.33 Cd.

To improve the 3 Series range, an entirely new body was designed with immense wind-tunnel input. Using the 1.6 liter motor, an E36 could drop beneath the 0.30 Cd barrier to 0.29. Aerodynamically, the current E46 was only a refinement on this theme, and the best figure recorded for this model is 0.28 Cd.

Given BMW's primary sporting reputation, naysayers are sometimes surprised at the 3 Series's performance in modern safety crash tests. BMW was quick to see how Mercedes treated safety as a core value, so the 3 Series featured crash-tested construction values from the beginning. Automatic belt tensioners arrived in 1974, vented front disc brakes and optional electronic ABS in 1982, driver's-side airbags in 1985, automatic roll-over bar protection for the convertible in 1993, and the ASC+T anti-skid and electronic traction control in 1997.

The archetypal BMW of the 1980s, and *the* BMW 3 Series in many minds, was this 1982–90 rendition. The E30 was not an adventurous design, but it was incredibly successful.

Photo: BMW Historisches Archiv, reissued 1999

sport and the factory homologated the M for Motorsport M3 variant to compete from 1987–92. The M3 surpassed legends like the 328 and the Batmobile coupes. It hauled home the World Championship, the European Championship (twice), and the major national titles of Britain, France, Italy, and Germany.

Inside the 2002ti (a twin-carburetor model not sold in the US), the surroundings were stark: some of the spartan furniture included plastic seating; a large, three-spoke steering wheel; and an extremely simple dashboard layout.

Photo: BMW Historisches Archiv, reissued 1999

There were also myriad M3 wins and championship titles achieved all around the world, in disciplines as different as hillclimbing and rallying. The M3 adapted to the demands of rallying (via Prodrive in Britain) and won a World Championship rally in a Corsica, plus multiple national titles across Europe.

As a sporting road car, the four-cylinder M3 finally eliminated memories of the 2002, winning many more events against harsher opposition. On the street, it evolved from 2.3 liters and 195 bhp in 1986 to the 238 bhp of the final 2.5-liter Evo Sport in 1990, by which time racing M3s put out 360 bhp.

Having doubled the sales figures of the original 3 Series, the sturdy E30 (BMW's highest-quality small car) was a huge commercial hit. The

Landmarks, continued

In the world of power-assisted features, Americans would find nothing remarkable in a small BMW. Even power steering was denied to four-cylinder 3 Series buyers before six cylinders were available. A 1985 start on catalytic converters for the European 3 Series was hardly innovative to US buyers, who had 3-way "cats" in 1976. BMW adopted electrically operated mirrors in 1975, power windows in 1982, and allowed the whir of magic motors to adjust front seating in 1992. Such items usually began as expensive options on the 3 Series.

The *Sicke* feature line, kidney grilles, and C-hook to the rear side window remain, but the E36 3 Series was the first small Bimmer to adopt aerodynamic design.

Photo: BMW Historisches Archiv, reissued 1999

The most recent 3'er iteration is the E46. It retains enough of the old design cues to show its heritage.

Photo: BMW Historisches Archiv, reissued 1999

The input from the 5 Series to its baby brother is not often acknowledged, but this side shot reveals just how closely the two were related, right down to the sculpted side crease.

Photo: BMW AG, Munich, 1974

Scaled down from its larger siblings, the 1979 BMW dash layout for the 3'er was the benchmark for logical clarity. Features that endure include a hazard warning flasher system (top, center console), a four-spoke wheel, and slatted grilles.

Line drawing: BMW AG, Munich, 1979

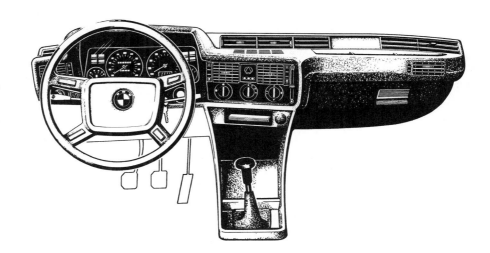

Looking over the styling cues that have formed the face of BMW 1967–98, from 02 to E30, via the E30 racer.

Photo: Author, Monterey, CA, 1999

From 1962–64, the fresh face of 1500 that launched a dominant BMW style.

Photo: BMW Historisches Archiv

3'er's technical features were, however, lagging behind some rivals. It was time to bring BMW's biggest sellers to a new level of aerodynamic and chassis ability, energized by a multitude of four-valve-per-cylinder engines throughout the line.

The E36 generation of the 1990s was again a multi-million seller. By December 1998, over 2.3 million had been sold, with some variants staying in production after the launch of its E46-coded current successor. The chief ingredients in the success of the E36 were a fundamental rethink of BMW small-car engineering, and a massive vari-

ety of body styles and power units. Initially, just a sleeker four-door body was offered. At yearly intervals, a new E36 derivative was debuted thereafter, until there were five main body styles and 31 individual models, the widest choice ever offered by BMW. Yearly introductions began with a two-door coupe, the two-door cabriolet, and the five-door Touring. These choices were totally predictable, until the brave three-door hatchback called Compact, which was 23 cm (9.1 inches) shorter than the four-door, and was made on regular 3 Series production lines.

Remembering BMW's decision to buy Rover Cars and their range of small hatchbacks in 1994, it surprised some that the Compact remains in production. A replacement is planned with opposition set to come from Mercedes as well as

Collector's Choice

Among production totals for the smallest BMWs, we find large numbers and some hot tips for 3 Series collectors, especially of M3 variants.

The 02 in all its guises (1502, 1602, 1802, and 2002) was made from May 1966 to July 1976 and totaled 861,940 units. Of that total, 382,740 were the classic 2002 types, and 112,524 of all 02 series (including some 13,162 of the 1967–71 BMW 1602/1600 US) were exported to the US.

The E21 3 Series was manufactured from June 1975 to September 1983 and production reached 1,364,038 units. Exactly 186,039 units were manufactured to US specifications in four-cylinder guise. Today, the 3 Series is sold in the biggest BMW export market in six-cylinder format only.

The E30 3 Series was made from September 1982

to January 1991 (European production ended in 1990), with production totaling 2,339,251 units. Two-doors accounted for 1,058,562 million units, while 908,789 were four-doors, so the split was almost 50-50 in the first 3'er to offer the choice.

As of December 1998, some 2,373,463 of all E36 variants had been built, so it had already outpaced its predecessor. Of these, some 1.5 million were four-doors, so the percentage of four-door sedans produced had increased, mainly because of rocketing US sales. Even in M3 guise, the four-door could outsell two-doors.

BMW AG records from February 1998 indicated that in E36 guise, the coupes had accounted for approximately 430,000 units, while the three-door Compact hatchback was reckoned at 280,000.

The 5 Series (left) and 3 Series for the millennium were confusingly alike to the general public.

Photo: BMW GB, Brackenell, 1999

Audi. Compact courage repaid BMW, with over 280,000 manufactured by 1998.

The third-generation 3 Series built on BMW's reputation for four-cylinder touring-car expertise, winning 24-hour races at Spa (Belgium) and Germany's Nurburgring with prototype E46 turbodiesel power. The E36 racers scooped many national titles, including those of Japan, Australia, Germany, Britain, Italy, and France.

The M3 six-cylinder was a GT winner in the 1993 Germany series as the GT-R: echoes of this BMW Motorsport program crossed the Atlantic. From 1995 onward, the American PTG-BMW NA team fielded M3 coupes and

Collector's Choice, continued

Convertible 3'ers were far from a tiny niche market, adding 150,000 to E36 production totals.

The least-popular variant—argued over for US sales persistently and not released in either E30 or E36 bodies—was the Touring five-door. Tourings accounted for approximately 130,000 of E36 manufactured.

M3 production figures indicate that 3 Series Ms dominated the 105,260 output of M-cars between 1978 and December 1997, accounting for over 70 percent of all M-sales!

Altogether, some 89,249 of the fastest production 3 Series were made, sub-dividing as 17,970 of the first (E30) M3 and 71,279 of the E36 six-cylinder types. Of the latter, 28,285 were the first European generation of 3-liter coupes, showing that the six-cylinder M3 immediately set new M3 sales records despite the doubts of purists (and some inside BMW), who thought it might have been better-badged as a CSi.

BMW said that 4,364 M3 convertibles were manufactured in E36 format. The rarest E30 M3 sedan was the Europmeister '88, a celebration of winning the final European Touring Car Championship: just 150 were manufactured, all for Continental European consumption.

Also made in batches by the hundred were E30 Evolution I and II, plus special editions Cecotto and Ravaglia (circa 500 units of each), all officially confined to Europe, and the final 2.5-liter M3 Sport Evolution (600 units). The rarest body type was the E30 M3 convertible, and just 786 of these hand-built soft tops were manufactured—not at the Garching Motorsport

four-door sedans tuned to almost 400 bhp. PTG seized three prestige national titles in 1996–98 versus Porsche opposition: a vital general marketing support program as BMW manufactures in the US.

Today, the E46 newcomers offer the highest safety standards: a stiffer body, some "50–60 percent" improved, says BMW, and standard provision of six side and head air bags.

Bayerische Motoren Werke still labors at their engines, often with alternative fuel economy or emission-conscious goals. The first priority for the American market was the redeveloped double VANOS system of E36 M3 to a wider application on all six-cylinder E46s. This promoted pulling power at lower engine rpm for the silky straight six.

For Europeans, there is the 2-liter BMW 16-valve turbodiesel of 136 bhp with a racing pedigree and the presence of counterbalancer shafts for the smaller (1,895 cc) unit for the later 318i. Other important motor developments for E46 cover the two-stage cooling systems with pre-set temperatures (105°C) for ordinary driving demands and a cooler 85°C under the most demanding full-throttle conditions. Note that BMW-branded Digital Motor Electronics (DME), often in association with Siemens, have spread widely in the latest 3 Series, along with many more sophisticated electronic features.

After three generations and 6.1 million predecessors, the latest 3 Series met high expectations. In an era of intense competition within a market niche that BMW created—and initially occupied without opposition—those Munich Millionaires remain the benchmark any rival seeks to beat. Front-runners look to be Mercedes, Audi, Toyota, and Honda, but as they raced for the millennium flag-fall, BMW was still beating most of the 3 Series clones, most of the time in the marketplace. The 3 Series sets a global sales pace and prestige value to die for, whether you are a rival manufacturer or a potential customer.

Collector's Choice, continued

site as previously reported, but fitted in at Regensberg via Wackersdorf, the home of convertible production.

In E36 guise, the rarest M3s were just 50 RHD M3 GT coupes built in 1995 for Britain in British Racing Green, although that color was also used for other short-run M3s in LHD. If you find a 1997-built E36 M3 convertible in the US, it's one of just 12 built that year! Otherwise, the lowest-volume model, unique to the US market, was the BMW M3 Lightweight.

We hold a sales (not production) figure of just 122 in the States for M3L

So, what is likely to be worth collecting among the current E46 line? The least popular body option is likely to remain the five-door Touring, but we speculate that the retained value will be in the convertible and M3 models. Our guess is that an M3 Convertible would just about cover both sectors and is a likely collector's choice. If there is ever a special racing-based model on a limited production run, then experience shows this will return a long-term appreciation. Because of the numbers made, we do not see the two-door coupe as a collectible in respect of rarity values, but it remains a most beautiful and practical expression of Munich's understated affection for elegant coupes.

2 Tracing the Path to the 3 Series

BMW Company history reads like a summary of twentieth-century worldwide warfare, where survival was a major triumph.

Had BMW (Bayerische Motoren Werke) not been supported by its loyal shareholders through its 1959 cash crisis, allowing BMW to re-discover its natural middle-class sports sedan market in the 1960s, today's BMW would amount to nothing more than a production site for Mercedes. In 2001, thirty-two years on from that near-catastrophe, BMW has become internationally based beyond anything the 1960s BMW-watcher could have imagined.

To understand how far BMW and the 3 Series have come, we must trace the company's record of struggle to reach the top of the automotive market. BMW's convoluted history meant it had to regroup in the late 1940s, moving motor car engineering from its East German (Eisenach) headquarters to Munich. That Eisenach site beneath the Wartburg Castle was the butt of many Western jokes because of the smoky two-stroke Wartburg automobile, but it is now the backdrop to increasing GM-Opel production commitment and BMW machine-tool interests.

BMW's original business was building military aviation engines. The BMW initials stand for Bayerische Motoren Werke, formed on July 20, 1917; but the aero-engine company, Bayerische Flugzeugwerke, founded on March 7, 1916, was the initial foundation of BMW. The corporate symbol, the Roundel, was designed around the theme of a whirling white propeller on a blue-sky background. It was first used on October 5, 1917 to register a patent, becoming a recognized symbol during World War I. Although the details on the Roundel badge, especially the lettering, have changed over the years, the emblem is now featured increasingly for BMW manufacture and administration.

World War II aero engine tasks were carried out at Allach, a northwestern suburb of Munich, and at the more central Munich Milbertshofen works, still a 3 Series manufacturing center today. Many of

BMW's aviation landmarks were first tested, or taken to record heights, from the Oberwiesenfeld site that lies beneath the 1972 Olympic stadium complex, opposite the company's headquarters.

Such military engine activity made BMW a target for the Allies during World War II bombing missions. Photographs of destruction around the BMW steel press works in Milbertshofen show the devastating effect of the nonstop bombing campaigns inflicted by USAAF and RAF missions.

It was years before automobile production could be resumed following the postwar American occupation of Munich. The Russians occupied the Eisenach factory in East Germany, the pre-war center of BMW car-production ability. The Communists had the East Germans turning out EMW-badged BMW designs during 1945, but it wasn't until 1952 that BMW delivered a new post-war car to their customers.

BMW in Munich was apparently doomed in the immediate postwar years. All its tangible assets in West Germany were shipped out to sixteen different countries. However, motorcycles (which had taken BMW into road transportation in 1923) hauled BMW in Munich back from the abyss. By the arrival of the 1950s, BMW felt particularly persecuted, as most other leading German manufacturers were long since back in the automotive game. The only company that suffered as badly

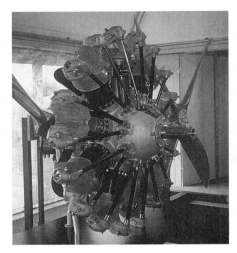

Aero engines were the founding strength behind BMW. This air-cooled, single-row radial dates from the period during which BMW set civilian long-haul endurance standards, taking out a manufacturing license with Pratt & Whitney in Connecticut in 1926.

Photo: Author, Goodwood, West Sussex, UK, 1999

was the Auto Union group, whose major facilities were also behind the Iron Curtain.

BMW displayed a car product before it could mass-manufacture anything. The critical comeback was the Frankfurt Motor Show of 1951, at which BMW displayed a single black saloon. Dubbed the 501, the streamlined four-door contained an update of the 1930s 326 in-line six (1,971 cc with 65 bhp), although an aluminum V8 was to follow. German experts suspect this V8 had links to the aluminum Buick V8, and question how BMW could have afforded to develop its own eight?

It took BMW about a year (November of 1952) to deliver any 501s to customers. At first, the 501 was built around 2000 bodies created by Bauer in Stuttgart (later to produce many BMW variants). However, a tightly financed rebuilding

From left to right, an original 1928–9 Dixi alongside the BMW's first six-cylinder small saloon (303) of 1933–37. Then comes the 700 sedan of 1959–65, and the more familiar Bimmer outlines, with an 02, E21, E30, and the first four-door E36.

Photo: BMW AG, Munich, 1990

program allowed
BMW to have its
production facilities
in operation by 1954.

Building luxury
automobiles would
not support BMW's
fortunes in the
1950s. From 1952–
58, the company
built only 8,936
units of the 501,

After WWI, the
Oberwiesenfeld
airfield, home to
BFW (Bayerischen
Flugzeug Werke),
and the BMW
premises on nearby
Moosacher Street
were surrounded
by fields of green.
Today, the area
is entirely urbanized,
save for the 1972
Olympiapark.

Photo: BMW AG,
1920/Archiv, Munich,
1999

some 9,109 units of the 502, and less than
4,000 units of the saloons in V8 trim. The
sports V8s were even rarer: just 407 of the
1956–59 BMW 503 2 + 2, and only 252 of the
507, were produced.

BMW developed far cheaper models, like the
flat-twin 600. Over 161,000 Isetta-BMW 250 and
300cc microcars were made from 1955–62: they
are now regarded as classics. The licensing agree-
ment with Iso in Italy allowed BMW to develop
35,000 units of the distinctive narrow-rear-track
600 small saloon. The subsequent four-wheeler
700 rear-engine saloons, coupes, and convertibles
earned respect commercially and competitively.
Some 181,121 of the diminutive 700s were made
from 1959–65. It is no exaggeration to say that
they (and their Isetta-BMW predecessors) kept
BMW alive through the V8 years. It was obvious
that BMW needed a popular middleweight to
regain its pre-World War II eminence, but first the
company had to stay in business.

Staying Alive

December 9, 1959, was BMW's blackest Annual
General Meeting on record. Their principal
investor, the Deutsche Bank, had decided to
redeem some of its costly investment in BMW
and consequently revealed a "redevelopment
plan" that amounted to a cut-price takeover by
Daimler-Benz. But Deutsche Bank did not get
its way; the small shareholders and committed

BMW dealers decided to fight the proposition
under the leadership of a Frankfurt lawyer, Dr.
Friedrich Mathern.

Deutsche Bank held more than half the issued
capital of BMW. The white knight came in the
form of the Allach works in Munich, which was
occupied by the profitable MAN truck concern.
Blessed with permission to resume aviation business, MAN management authorized a thirty-mil-
lion-DM loan to the embattled BMW shareholders, who matched the loan.

The inevitable boardroom resignations left
Deutsche Bank with less BMW influence, and
the brothers Herbert and Harald Quandt with
increasing control. Herbert Quandt became the
spiritual as well as financial leader BMW needed.

In 1960, Herbert Quandt took charge of his
new car-building interests, and he maintained a
zealous interest in BMW and their automotive
excellence throughout the remainder of his business career. The General Meeting of November
1960 confirmed that the 700 had already put
BMW back on the road to profit, or at least
reduced losses.

From 1956–59, BMW lost 27.7 million DM.
By 1962, it was back in the black on a modest 2.5
million DM and has marched forward ever since,
although the 1973–74 fuel crisis halved BMW
profits. Yet progress was maintained: the 1979
turnover was 7,387 million DM from a work
force of 41,925, compared to 1,443 million DM

generated by 21,300 employees in 1969, and the loss-making 170 million DM turnover of 1959, when BMW employed fewer than 6,000 workers. Despite 30 years of progress, the 1994–2000 ownership of Rover group cost billions and left BMW vulnerable to aquisition.

The Quandts amassed a fortune estimated at $3.5 billion by the Financial Times on October 23, 1989. Then Herbert's widow (his third wife, Johanna, a former secretary) was judged to be at the "top of the German wealth league." By 1989, almost thirty years after BMW's financial crisis, the original Quandt stake of 15 percent had grown to a reported 47 percent.

A 1995 change in German stockholder law meant that such stakes had to be more accurately disclosed; the real figure appears to have been 49 percent of all BMW stock. Johanna Quandt and her immediate family (Suzanne and Stephan, her children with Herbert Quandt) were left in stockholder control of BMW, through Herbert's seat on the advisory board which passed to his wife.

In 1997, Johanna Quandt passed her shares along to her children. Suzanne and Stephan play a more active role in the BMW background scenes of the 1990s than did their mother, who turned her attention to genetic engineering and "smart" credit card leading-edge technologies.

3 Series Parentage

Limited but crucial financial and investment encouragement during 1960 allowed BMW to invest in just the middleweight that was needed: the Neue Klasse 1500, a grandfather to the 3 Series. The 1500 itself had a comparatively short production life—February 1962 to December 1964—but the 23,557 examples manufactured were enormously influential.

In the 1500, you can see the basic elements of so many BMW generations emerging, including a subsequent (1800) slant installation for a tough SOHC motor; trailing arm rear-end inherited via 600 and 700, driving the back wheels; and the

faithful MacPherson strut front suspension. A mixed disc (front) and drum (rear) braking layout was employed, but with generous 10.5-inch solid front discs. Other period fittings embraced 4.5 x 14-inch steel wheels and cross-ply tires (165 SR radials were optional), as well as worm-and-roller steering, which had a faster lock-to-lock action (3.75 turns) than any 1990 production 3 Series, outside the M3!

With a capacious four-door body of 2,332 lbs (1,060 kg) and an initial 80 bhp, BMW 1500 performance was the first target for subsequent improvement. The ride from 0–62 mph took 16 seconds and the maximum speed was 92 mph. Today's customer would also be disappointed with an average 25.7 mpg. However, the 1500 compares well with a car that influenced BMW engineers—Alfa Romeo's Giulietta saloon. A 1.3-liter Alfa TI from Milan reached 95 mph, hitting 60 mph in 17.5 seconds and returning 24.6 mpg in 1961.

Initially, that extra urge became evident in the four-door saloons, via the inevitable engine enlargements. Its 1,600-cc overbore allowed 83 bhp, and it succeeded the 1500 from 1964–66, but what really restored BMW's performance saloon reputation were the 1800 and 2000 series of the later 1960s.

The 1,773 cc of the 1800 proved as rugged and amenable to extra power as any traditional BMW power unit. Beginning at 90 bhp, it was ultimately developed to 130 bhp in the 1964/5 homologation special 1800 TI/SA, which propelled the M3's Great Granddaddy with a 116-mph maximum, zapping 0–62 mph in 9.0 sec at a 17.7 mpg penalty.

A Godfather for 3'er

The four-door 1500 to 2000 series of saloons, with a long production run of 350,729 units from 1962–1974, was immensely valuable in rebuilding BMW. But the true transformation in BMW's volume fortunes came with a smaller, more

The 1972 BMW Haus, or four-cylinder building, dwarfs the company museum beside a city ring road. Eberhard von Kuenheim was still the dominant force among Quandt family shareholders as well as behind the 1999 dismissals/resignation of the company's two highest-ranking executives.

Photos: BMW AG, 1991; Author Archive, 1999

affordable performance product. The true "Godfather" of the 3 Series was the "02" (for two-door) range that set the sporting and commercial seal of approval on BMW's smallest offering.

First introduced to the public at BMW's 50th Anniversary celebrations of March 1966 as a plain 1600, without the "02" suffix, the design was officially renamed the 1600-2 when it debuted at the 1966 Geneva Motor Show, a day later. The natural contraction to 1602, to distinguish a two-door 1600 from a four-door contemporary, was officially applied starting in April 1971.

The cleanly executed four-seaters were transformed when the American importer Max Hoffman supported BMW's latest engineering inspiration. The notion was to transplant the 2-liter engine from the older 4-door into the new smaller 2-door car. BMW Mobile Tradition reports in its profile, "The BMW 02 Series: The Cult Car" that engineering legend Alex von Falkenhausen was running a prototype 2002s in early 1967. No credit is attached to Max Hoffman's input, but von Falkenhausen did not claim credit for the 2002 combination, instead modestly guiding the author to the 2002 American influence, because the highest-performance 1600 (the twin-carburetor 1600ti) could not comply with US emissions restrictions.

BMW had to find a ethod to offer

American customers better performance if this new-found export market, with such vast potential, was not to be lost. The resulting 2002 combined the nimble, independent suspension flair of the 1600 with an extra 25 bhp and useable mid-range power. If any postwar BMW can be said to have "made" the current BMW reputation for civilized speed, the 2002 (and its ever-faster variants) was that automobile. A 2002 could be driven sideways through circuit corners at 100 mph, just as easily as it could putter to the shop in the high gear, pulling amiably from 18.5 mph and 1,000 rpm. The motor reached 111.1 mph and scrabbled from 0–60 mph in 9 seconds in a June 1968 European example. Its 100 bhp and 116 lb-ft of torque showed the benefit of a slim curb weight (2,240 lbs, or 1,018 kg), demanding only 24 Imperial mpg overall.

The 100-bhp 2002 was a natural backbone to BMW's continuing prosperity in the late 1960s and early 1970s. From January 1968 to the summer of 1975 (July 1976 for Federal US versions), the 2002 was not only a commercial success and a multiple European Touring Car Champion, but also spawned a diversity of variants that foreshadowed how versatile the following 3 Series would become.

Of an official 861,940 units, some 382,740 were

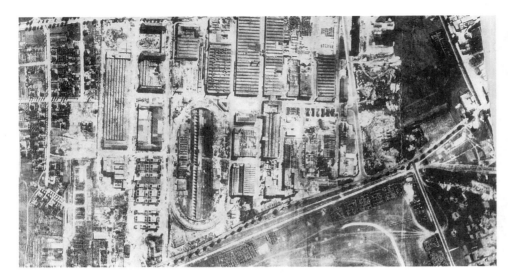

A familiar view to the Allied pilots of WWII, the Munich works were heavily damaged or destroyed. Today, they are a bustling home to the BMW 3 Series.

Photo: BMW AG, 1946/ Archiv, Munich, 1999

of the classic 2002 types. Exactly 112,524 of all 02 series were officially exported to the States, including 13,162 of the 1967–71 BMW 1600 and 1602 USA, of which only 232 were produced. Thus America accounted for 13 percent of all 02 production, but it was closer to 20 percent of annual production once the US got the 2002 message.

In motorsports, both fuel injection and turbocharging were pioneered at BMW by 2002 variants in their successful 1968–69 European Touring Car Championship seasons. The 2002 tii was also used in World class rally events, winning twice and performing with vigor on the 1973 British RAC rally, using an adaptation of a Schnitzer Formula 2 motor.

The 02 range absorbed variants like the Touring and Cabriolet bodies (30,206 and 4,199 respectively were built between January 1971 and December 1975), predicting the 3 Series future. Yet it was the 2002 sedan that provided a race and rally base for further performance, including a 170 bhp turbo, Europe's first turbo in mass production.

Road variants such as the 120-bhp twin-carburetor 2002Ti (not sold in the US) and a 130-bhp fuel injected 2002tii (1971–74 US) were unmatched by European rivals outside Alfa Romeo. Since the Italians were headed nowhere

with heavy financial losses, uneasy industrial relations, and the constant takeover attentions of Fiat, Alfa Romeo was not the commercial rival it should have been. Thus the 3 Series grew to class benchmark maturity, comparatively unopposed.

It proved impossible to replace the 2002 in the hearts and minds of many BMW enthusiasts, particularly in the USA, at least until the 1986 M3. Yet BMW's 3 Series had to succeed its charismatic cousin and continue on the upward sales path for BMW's small-cars. Of course, it did the job beautifully—anything less would have lead BMW to losing its independence.

As it proved, the 3 Series was wildly successful, with each generation of the "Baby Bimmer" selling more than the one before. Even the Gulf War of 1991 did little to depress demand for the first four-door examples of the third 3 Series (E36) generation. By 1992, BMW had overhauled Mercedes automobile output. It was also the year BMW announced that they would build an American factory in Spartanburg, South Carolina. Construction began in Spring 1993, and the facility started to produce 3 Series units in 1994.

Today, Spartanburg is home to an entire Z3-based family of roadsters and coupes, with the X5 SAV (Sports Activity Vehicle) rolling off the lines in late 1999. BMW also has design, engineering and quality control centers in California, the latter checking imported vehicle quality and compliance with ever-stricter emissions regulations.

Throughout the 1990s, BMW appeared recession-proof, setting a new production record in 1992 of 598,000 automobiles, including 100,000 two-door coupes of a then-fresh (E36) 3 Series. But the 1993 sales season proved less easy. Despite appointing a fresh man (Bernd Pischetsrieder) to guide BMW in place of the legendary Eberhard von Kuenheim, a global recession affected luxury car sales. Japan and the Pacific Rim "Tiger Economies," such as Thailand and Indonesia, were particularly damaged. BMW had the compensation of leading Mercedes on auto output, albeit on a slightly depressed 534,000 versus Mercedes' 508,000 yearly total.

A series of British acquisitions also characterized BMW in the 1990s. BMW threw off their Bavarian national car company status to become massively multi-international, including their significant investment in American production, quality control, and design facilities.

On January 31, 1994, BMW made a bold and fatally-flawed acquisition—the quality- and productivity-ravaged Rover Group in the UK. The logic was that the purchase price was about the same as that of developing an SUV/offroader, and Rover had the most famous brand names in that sector.

What BMW did not fully appreciate—as Ford found when they purchased Jaguar—was the depth of British manufacturing problems. For both BMW and Ford, it was like stepping back into the manufacturing dark ages. The root

problem was criminal under-investment combined with the worst of mass-manufacturing management.

Aside from the cut-price cost of Rover, the attractions included a horde of brand names. Paramount were Range Rover, Land Rover, MG, and Mini. Dormant names also included Austin-Healey and Triumph, as well as Riley and Wolseley.

By September 1994 the first American production BMW (a 318i) rolled off a US line at Spartanburg. The following year, the Bimmer Roundel flew over their Designworks purchase in California, and an assembly plant was initiated in Vietnam, but 1995 will be remembered as the year the first new BMW design to be made outside Germany wheeled off a production line. That was the Spartanburg-manufactured Z3 sports car—using many 3 Series parts under that original body. In four sales seasons since then, more than 170,000 sporting Z3s have been sold, hitting almost 20,000 annual sales in the US in 1997. A total of 13,000 RHD units were exported to the UK from 1996–99.

BMW also entered in a joint venture with Chrysler Corporation to build engines in Brazil. The $500 million Tritec Motors Ltd. deal remained intact after Chrysler became DaimlerChrysler. The Brazilian factory supplied motors for the new BMW MINI in 2001–2005

The Regensberg works are a second home to the 3 Series. Beside hosting assembly operations, this plant stamped major body pressings, catered to BMW Individual orders.

Photo: BMW Werkfoto, 1986

production.

By 1996 BMW was claiming big results from their hands-off, separate-company approach to the Rover takeover. BMW set a fantastic 644,100 output level (helped over the 600,000 barrier by Spartanburg). That year, BMW Group bean counters could claim that their 116,112-person workforce made a total of 1.15 million automobiles, including 507,254 Rovers. In 1999, BMW alone made more than 700,000 cars a year and was the world's largest manufacturer of inline six-cylinder engines, pumping out more than 400,000 a year.

In 1998, BMW fought Volkswagen for another UK takeover in the complicated purchase of the most famous luxury-car brand in the world, Rolls Royce. Now, Rolls Royce divorced—once again—from Bentley after a 70-year marriage, and became a BMW brand from 2003 onward. This deal came after a series of moves and countermoves between BMW and Volkswagen that were finalized in 1998.

From the Roman ruins outside, to a complete 3 Series six-cylinder powertrain ready for body assembly, Regensberg dramatically bridged the centuries.

Photos: Author, Germany, 1999

Volkswagen had theoretically acquired the Rolls Royce, Bentley, and Cosworth companies from sellers at UK parent company Vickers Plc. Even legendary Volkswagen Takeover-Meister Dr. Ferdinand Piech was forced to recognize that his new acquisitions did not sit very comfortably with everyday trading realities, such as the critical BMW hardware input to the Bentley and Rolls Royce brands. A Bimmerphile needs to know that most 1999 Rolls Royces and one Bentley automobile model were powered by the BMW 5.4 liter V12 (Rolls Royce Seraph) and the 4.4 liter BMW-Cosworth twin turbo V8 (Bentley Arnage). The V8 is a 64 bhp uprate of the normally-aspirated 4.4 BMW eight seen in the 740 and 540i. The Rolls side of the deal reflects the fact that BMW did not just supply their aluminum V12s to Rolls Royce, but they also provided a raft of electronics and ZF automatic transmission supplies in association with regular BMW suppliers.

The separate aero division of Rolls Royce was not happy about granting the right to use the Rolls "Spirit of Ecstasy" trademark to Volkswagen. The Rolls Royce aero division already had regular joint-company aero-engine business with BMW through the Oberusel and Dahlewitz/Berlin factories established in 1990, creating the Be700 to 750 middle-range power sources.

A traditional country-club golf course deal was struck. Warring BMW Chairmen Bernd Pischetsrieder and Piech called a truce over their earlier takeover battles for Rolls Royce and Bentley, when VW took the bigger prize at £430 million (then around $709.5 million) by outbidding BMW's £340 million ($561 million) offer to Vickers. That July 1998 golfing deal saw Rolls Royce pass to BMW. The "Spirit of Ecstasy" trademark was separately assigned by the aero division of Rolls Royce, who supported BMW because of their joint venture. BMW also took the rights to manufacture Rolls Royces at a greenfield UK site from 2003 on. It all cost BMW AG around $66 million: a bargain, compared to what VW paid to get Bentley.

The BMW of the new millennium is a multi-national company with billion-dollar investment responsibilities, but Britain's Rover Group proved terminally sick. It was sold to the Phoenix Consortium in May 2000 for a nominal £10 with a £500 million ($800 million) dowery. Ford bought the Land Rover business for £1.8 billion ($2.7 billion) which eased the corporate pain.

Spartanburg sales kicked in so successfully for BMW that it forced Mercedes into Alabama for SUV production. Daimler-Benz, the Stuttgart/Untertürkheim parent behind the Mercedes brand, bought Chrysler Corporation in 1998, a move that stunned motor industry observers and has yet to justify itself for both parties. However, Mercedes led BMW on overall US sales in 1998 (including SUVs), although BMW sold more cars (131,559 versus 127,111). The American battleground became so intense between the two German prestige warriors that BMW was forced to announce plans for their own SUV (X5) to be made at Spartanburg.

Rover losses of £650 million (over $1 billion) during 1998 and similarly depressing Rover losses in 1999 changed the face of BMW management. On February 5, 1999, Eberhard von Kuenheim, the Prussian aristocrat who had guided BMW fortunes for almost 30 years, chaired a sensational meeting that saw the services of Chairman Pischetsrieder and ambitious deputy Wolfgang Reitzle abruptly terminated. Piechetsrieder took a reported substantial pay-off (DM 15 million/$8.7 million) for his 25 high-level years with the company, disappearing from corporate view to reappear at VW-owned SEAT in Spain. Reitzle, a 20-year man at BMW, reportedly took more (DM 17.5 million/$10.1 million) and accepted overall management of Ford's premium car division (Volvo, Jaguar, Aston Martin, Lincoln, and eventually Land Rover). Piechetsrieder was replaced by Dr. Ing. Joachim Milberg, who sold Rover off in 2000.

Did Pischetsrieder not recall what the initials BMW (Bayerische Motoren Werke) truly meant? Did his personal taste for British marques—he owned a classic Rolls Royce before the takeover battles with Volkswagen—blind him to some basic truths about industrial Britain? It seemed so, and Herr Pischetsrieder paid for his pro-British stance at the helm of BMW AG with his job.

BMW's 1999 case for Rover was that it needed to grow past the million manufacturing mark to survive without takeover, something Porsche had managed to do without breaking 100,000 units a year. Nevertheless, the Rover situation had attracted predators like Ford and Volkswagen, who circled the BMW encampment, looking for the first signs of fatal hemorrhage.

How simple it all was during the late 1980s and early 1990s! Back then, an unencumbered BMW had reached new peaks of popularity: 1989 was the first year in which they manufactured more than half a million cars. In 1991, some 550,000 BMWs were constructed, while 1992 saw another record (598,000), despite the worldwide recession.

The most salable item in the BMW warehouse was the 3 Series, accounting for over 50 percent of US sales in some recent years and remaining stable

as the biggest contributing line during
1997–98.

Walking around
any of the extensive
3 Series range of the
1990s, it is impossible
to appreciate how
hard BMW struggled
to become a symbol
of late-twentieth-century personal prosperity.
Admiring the shimmering paint, minimalist shut
lines, and high quality
materials BMW brings to
their smallest model line
obliterates the images of
their flattened factories
in the 1940s. This is a
resourceful company that
started building cars officially in 1928, based on
an adaptation of the British Austin 7. It is also
the same BMW that had to make saucepans and
other utilitarian objects to crawl from the postwar
rubble of a destruction made more intense by
BMW's excellence in aero engines engineering.

Further key factors to understanding what
makes the current 3 Series possible include
massive political changes that occurred in East
Germany during 1989–90, followed by German
reunification, replacing Allied control zones
administered by American and British forces.

Production resources

When the Berlin Wall tumbled in 1989, it
brought the past back into BMW's future.
Their pre-war car engineering HQ in Eisenach
emerged into the free world once more. Swiftly,
BMW became involved in that region once more,
but Eisenach never became the hub of the BMW
world again; today, just 300 employees manufacture production tooling.

The Spartanburg
plant began with
small-scale manufacturing of the 3
Series, graduating
to full-scale output
of the Z3, which
incorporated many
components from
the E30 and E36
generations. Today,
the Z3 and X5 are its
main products.

Photos: Steve Fincher/
Courtesy BMW NA,
South Carolina, 1997

By 1999 the BMW facilities were factory-coded
and described as follows:

- Werke 1.1, Munich, Milbertshofen: 3 Series (including M3 sedans, pre-E46), but also a major center
for engines, including a separate high performance-
engine facility of such quality that it has built pure
racing engines when demand exceeded BMW
Motorsport's ability to deliver. Responsible for M3
four and six cylinder engines. Produces parts and
pressed steel panels, plus dynamometers to test
routine production and high-performance (V12,
V8, M3) outputs. 1999 employment level: 23,000
in manufacturing, working two shifts on E46 four-
door and E36/E30 Compact for an output of 750
cars per day. Around 2,000 administrators/managers in adjacent four-cylinder offices, but also factory
administration in original 1920s red brick offices by
main gate (Tor 1.1).

- Werke 2.4, Dingolfing: Acquired from Glas in 1967
and totally redeveloped, working close to 1999
capacity: 5, 7, and 8 Series, latter ended produc-

tion 5/99. Some pressed steel, transmissions (primarily axles), body parts. Winner JD Power quality awards just ahead of Regensburg in 1999. The 1999 employment level: 20,000, making 1,000 cars per day.

- 4.1 Landshut: Also acquired from Glas in 1967, employs 3,000 and makes vital component parts, including plastics for fascias, steering, foot pedals, suspension, and textile components

- 6.1 Regensburg (greenfield, opened 1986, still expanding): Made 3 Series (E46 sedan and E36 convertible, including the last Cabrio M3s of E36 series at 6/99), textiles for 3, and 7-series; glass for 3 and 7-series. Biggest steel press in BMW (named "Jumbo" by its makers) and one of the world's largest, dominates landscape and visiting ears. Its rumbling power stamps complete body sides as well as smaller subsidiary press steel. 1999 employment level: 7,600, working three-shift days, making 210,000 of 3 Series total in 1998, some 28,000 more than 1997 output. Also specific BMW Individual Assembly/conversion areas beside main line for both Individual dealer clients and official police and rescue state orders. Many BMW suppliers employing another 3,000. Total BMW employment on these Regensburg area sites a reported 9,000.

- Wackersdorf: Houses a small BMW body facility and employs 1,600. At 6/99 visit, they were making convertible (E36) bodies in white, but due to end for E46 convertible.

- Werke 5.0, Steyr (Austria): Fully owned BMW subsidiary. Responsible for all diesel engines, including most engines engineering and production. However, new V8 diesel will be manufactured in Munich. A primary center for 3 Series motors, particularly many sixes. 1999 employment level/manufacturing capability: 2,176 employees make 2,000 motors daily.

- Werke 3.1 Berlin: Motorcycles at Spandau, car parts such as 3 Series brake discs. 1998 employment level/manufacturing capability: 1,881 employees made 63,000 bikes in 1998.

Overseas Factories

Spartanburg, US: Greenfield site started with 3 Series production in 1994, but has made Z3 and derivatives using mixture of old and new 3 Series running gear 1995–2003. Commenced X5 Fall 1999. Current employment level/manufacturing capability: 2,000 employees made 260 automobiles daily in 1998. Production rose sharply, with more recent Z4 derivatives and X5 SUV of 1999.

South Africa (Rosslyn): Has assembled BMW products since 1974 from various stages of CKD (Completely Knocked Down) kits, but has become a serious international supplier of both E36 and E46 3 Series. Volumes are low by parent company standards, but the company has a good quality record and has supplied E36 (such as 318iS coupe) to markets such as RHD UK when parent factory production was no longer available.

3 Series Group Facilities

FIZ (Forschrung und Ingenieur Zentrum), the research and development center for all BMW products, is a short car ride north of the Olympiapark and BMW headquarters. BMW employs more than 10,000 engineers of differing disciplines there. FIZ was home to the engineers and designers who created both E36 and E46 generations. Right next door is the Mobile Tradition, housing cars and bikes by the hundred. Unfortunately, it is not open to the public. FIZ has constant electronic and physical interchange links with BMW engines and transmissions engineering at nearby Hufelandstrasse. This street and its marble-stair low rise office blocks has been home to all BMW motor engineering for more than 15 years and is constantly rumored to be integrated at the FIZ. It just hasn't happened, and the motor engineers remain happily ensconced in their rabbit warren with their beloved engine test cells at hand.

Hufelandstrasse has extensive dynamometer resources—more than 100 cells—and is entirely separate from the newly converted buildings for

BMW Motorsport located along the same street. These premises were acquired and custom-built in 1998 to house 200 professionals who work on the Grand Prix racing V10 motor program.

BMW Motorsport, at Garching, contributed all M3 engineering development over the base car in E30, E36 and E46 generations. About 500 people are employed here; and Garching also tackles the BMW Individual program, commercial sports parts sales, and driver training, all of which have very strong customer appeal.

BMW Motorsport was also at work in Preussenstrasse, Munich. Together with an outside contractor and Garching, Preussenstrasse worked on the M42 BMW 2-liter race motor for the championship-winning E36. Preussenstrasse created the original E30 M3 and its S14 motor. Although neither Garching nor Preussenstrasse has ever manufactured 3 Series M-cars, both did become involved in M5 and other 5 Series creation prior to the current V8 M5 era.

To take BMW and the 3 Series to the heights they reached in the 1990s and continue that success into the new millenium, some great motor engineering was required. While the US would not see the best of BMW's motor talents in the 3 Series until the mid 1980s, BMW delivered engines for 3'ers that were worthy of the company emblem and initials, as we see in the next chapter.

3 An Adult Saloon

The 3 Series matured in commercial appeal far beyond anything that the 02 line could have achieved.

Announced in the first week of July 1975 to the German press and European LHD markets, the 3 Series was also sold in RHD comparatively early, arriving in Britain in Autumn, 1975. Subsequently, it was a valuable high-volume seller for BMW in RHD Japan, especially in the economy six-cylinder eta engine guise. Here, we stick to the initial four-cylinder launch. On sale in the US starting in November 1976, this first 3 Series, coded E21, had the toughest of tasks.

BMW AG summarized 3 Series qualities as, "Not a larger small car, but a smaller large car." BMW North America in New Jersey acknowledged just how difficult replacing the 2002 would be. In their introductory press release, when they asked: " How do you replace a legend? It has taken BMW nine years to develop a successor to the popular 2002 series, a landmark car that almost single-handedly created the modern class of compact sedans."

The truth was that BMW had not succeeded—at least, not immediately. Replacing sheer 2002 affordability (last listed at $6,500), never mind the flair of the fuel-injected 2002 Tii (officially imported into the US only from 1971–74) was initially impossible. To emulate such panache under US Federal regulations with a near-$9,000 machine of lower performance and handling capability was not a high point in BMW product engineering. However, the 3'er was an immediate commercial success in the US, as elsewhere.

A former American BMW salesman and subsequent senior BMW CCA (BMW Car Club of North America) official remembered that "The 320i introduction… when the factory had just taken over the import operation, was potentially disastrous. The cars had 110- or 105-bhp (California) engines, a lot less than our 2002s were kicking out, especially when they had been in a keen club member's possession. Worse, the

Front or back, the 3 Series made a huge impact on the consciousness of the world's automobile buyers, who were not prepared to take just another mass-produced two-door.

Photos: Klaus Schnitzer, Virginia, 1999

1977 model year 320 had its suspension set 10 percent softer than in Europe. It felt like it was going to turn over at ridiculously low speeds.

"I turned one over myself, demonstrating it to a customer through a curve that my 2002 always took significantly faster. In fact, I went right back and tried again, several times in the 2002, to make sure I had not imagined the superiority of the 2002. The 320i was a killer car in that original soft-suspension format. Plenty of drivers with track experience turned them right over, and the situation stayed that way, until BMW stiffened up the front suspension and deleted the rear sway bar for the 1978 model year."

In their preview release for the 1978 E21, BMW NA stated, "The suspension of the two-door sports sedan has been modified by stiffening the front springs 10 percent, reducing the size of the front sway bar one millimeter [just 0.039 of an inch!], deleting the rear anti-sway bar, and increasing the damping effect of the shock absorbers." Our knowledgeable contact commented, "You could get the E21 right—plenty of BMW CCA members proved that in racing or on the street. The Three was actually a better car if you spent the kind of money on improving it that so many 02 guys spend anyway."

Even with better hardware from the aftermarket, it took a brave owner to take off the monster 5-mph bumpers, which added over six inches to the overall length, compared to the European 3'er. It was also hard to swallow the fact that, far from matching 2002 power outputs, the

newcomer would have less power thanks to emissions modifications. Crossing the Atlantic cost the 3-er 15 bhp in 49 state trim and 20 bhp for California customers.

The official line was that there were no problems, just a bunch of club diehards who did not want to change over to the future of BMW small-car motoring. Certainly, the 320i—offered as California and 49-State variants, and in both automatic and manual transmission form— offered more creature comforts, but it was also 295 lbs heavier.

The US 320i performance was always going to be less than a Bimmer customer would expect, and Japan tasted California performance levels in October 1976 when their 105-bhp 320i entered production. Despite the restricted power outputs, BMW made solid progress in Japan and—with the Three as its initial backbone—Japan became a major export market. Like the UK, Australia, New Zealand and South Africa, Japan is officially a RHD (right-hand drive) country; but BMW supplied both LHD and RHD steering for this market where customers regarded LHD as a status symbol.

With a curb weight of some 2,600 lbs, the 110-bhp Federal version of the 320i could go from 0–60 mph in 10.8 seconds and nudged 106 mph in fourth (top) gear. Its fuel consumption averaged 21–22 US mpg. By contrast, the 125-bhp European 320i could complete 0–60 mph in 9.6 seconds and sped to almost 115 mph—nearly 10 mph faster than the US equivalent. The fuel-consumption comparison was a little less painful: the European 3 Series flagship returned 25 imperial mpg.

None of this tarnished BMW's burnished reputation in the States. In fact, they sold more cars than ever. The late introduction kept sales under 2,000 in the closing months of 1976, but in 1977, the 320i (49 States or California, manual or automatic) accounted for a third of all BMW sales.

That pattern continued as BMW went past $9,000 pricing for the 320i, selling 22,164 units in 1978 (of a total 30,000 BMWs sold). The original E21 3 Series accounted for more than half of all US sales in 1982, when the company topped 50,000 units for the first time and the 3'er pulled in over 36,000 buyers.

Up until model year 1980, the 2-liter powertrain remained the backbone of all US sales in the 3 Series. For 1980, however, emissions forced another look at US Bimmer performance. The 1.8-liter motor used a 3-way catalytic converter exhaust and Lambda sensor, ditching the thermal reactor and air-injection layout of the 2-liter. The six-cylinder BMWs donated transistorized ignition to the smallest BMW. The 320i badge was retained despite the shrinkage to 1.8 liters, so it was left to the following E30 to adopt an honest 318i inscription.

The 1,766-cc inline four was hitched to a standard five-speed transmission, and horsepower dropped from 110 bhp in 49-State trim to 101 bhp. The rear-end ratio went from 3.64:1 to 3.9:1. A Getrag 245 gearbox with an overdrive fifth and closed-up lower three ratios helped highway gas mileage and gave a boost to initial acceleration alongside that 1.8-liter unit.

Because BMW tackled the excess weight problem in US 320s with vigor, performance of the weaker 1.8 liter actually improved. It

shaved nearly a second from the 0–60 mph time and improved fuel consumption around 4 mpg to total 26 US mpg.

However, it was not all good news from the comfortable driver's seat. The 1.8-liter was at its limits to deliver 101 bhp in Federal trim, and it lost pulling power (torque) in the mid range. On paper, 12 lb-ft does not sound like a major amputation, but when the peak became 4,500 rpm compared to the already-elevated 3,750 rpm, US customers were not happy with the 1.8's driving manners.

How did the company slice curb weights? BMW slashed 30 items to trim 170 lbs from the US 320i's curb weight. Modifications included aluminum fuel lines; lighter disc brake shields, master cylinder housings, brake piston and clutch operation cylinders; thinner gauge steels for some exterior panels; thinner glass; and lighter noise-absorption materials.

Prices for 1980 passed $12,100. Interior identifiers for the 1980 320i included rotary controls for the heating and ventilation, plus a digital quartz clock integrated within the tachometer. Air conditioning was part of a $1,590 "Luxus" Touring Group package, along with a 4-speaker AM/FM stereo cassette player, plus fog lights.

Other options for 1980 included a three-speed automatic transmission for $585, a manual sunroof for $525, and alloy wheels for $470. Customers could also opt for the 320i "S" package (the first 320iS) at $2,475, which brought the Luxus features together with sportier items such as

Clean lines and some framework chrome were hallmarks of the 3 Series, which set more civilized standards for sporty small-car motoring.

Photo: Klaus Schnitzer, Virginia, 1999

Recaro front seats, limited-slip differential, a thicker front anti-roll bar suspension, halogen headlights, and a front air dam. Air conditioning was not offered for the first 320iS and colors were confined to black, alpine white, or silver. The

This factory cutaway drawing of the E21 BMW 3 Series shows the front and rear long-strut suspension, drum rear brakes, and a four-cylinder, carburetted 2.0-liter engine with a standard four-speed gearbox.

Drawing : BMW Presse, 1975

increased driving pleasure, comparative rarity, and subtle equipment enhancements make these "S" package 320s the ones to seek in the US market.

From the start of American sales in 1976, there was a less-visible "Sports Group" option available, which included alloy wheels, Recaro seating, and a BMW sports steering wheel. The 320iS option was available for model years 1981–83. The 1.8-liter powertrain was offered for the same model years, and gave BMW the advantage of being able to sell the same emissions layout across the US.

In its last full year, the 1.8-liter 320 demanded a $13,290 base price and the "S" package cost rose to $2,695 in its ultimate form. This package cost $2,620 without the white wheel rims and mirrors. The Luxus option, with air conditioning, stereo radio/cassette, and fog lights, cost $1,685.

Design hard points

BMW engineers lavished much more time on the 3 Series than on their 1960s saloons—even on an 02 range that had been so enthusiastically sold at home and abroad. The result was that the smallest BMW product was also the most thoroughly developed. The 3 Series inherited some of its "instant maturity," as well as styling cues, from the earlier 5 Series, including what would become the most imitated car-cabin layout of the period.

The first 3 Series outline sounded like that of the 02 series: two-door only, front engine and strut suspension, rear drive with trailing-arm independent layout. A four-door 3 Series was not available until the 1982–1983 release of the E30.

A glance at the larger E21 body, with its more commodious rear-seat, showed the potential for development—especially in an engine bay that BMW admitted would welcome six-cylinder power.

The 1975 (1976 for US) 02 replacement came after a five-year development period and an investment of DM35 million. Whereas the 02 series was originally intended to be a range of smaller cars with engines ranging from 1.3 liters upwards (in fact, European models had nothing smaller than 1.6 liters), the 3 Series was planned to take at least 2-liter engines from the start.

The initial thinking of the design team—led by Bernhard Osswald—centered on loosely retaining the overall dimensions of the 02 line, but considerably enhancing rear seat accommodation. The designers tried a sloping rear window, along the lines of the commercially unsuccessful 2002 Touring, although this solution was soon abandoned.

BMW returned to the conventional wisdom of the clearly defined saloon. Overall length was increased by 105 mm (41 inches) over the 02, totaling 4,355 mm (171.5 inches). Other 3 Series measurement comparisons to the 02 were, according to *auto motor und sport*, as follows: the wheelbase increased from 2,500 mm to 2,563 mm. The front and rear track went from 1,348 mm on the 02 to 1,405/1,399 mm on all 3 Series but the 320i, which ran on a 1,384/1,383-mm stance.

Much of the extra 3 Series length in Europe was accounted for by bumpers with increased defensive capability— each bumper extended 40 mm beyond that of the 02. Thus BMW worked with body dimensions very similar to those of the 02, but managed to extract a full inch (25 mm) in the seating breadth, although the total body fattening was only 20 mm (0.78 inch). The overall height of the E21 was tallish by sports saloon standards, totaling 1,380 mm (54.3 inches).

Such gains imposed a weight penalty. The original 1602 weighed 920 kg (2,024 lbs), but the last test 1502 for *auto motor und sport* weighed 1,020 kg (2,244 lbs). The European market starter model of the new 3 Series range, using the 1.6-liter engine, came in at exactly 1,020 kg. This was a fine engineering achievement for a body that was showing strength gains of close to 20 percent in pre-launch trials.

Bodywork is about so much more than statistics, and BMW set a basic standard for conservative sporting demeanor that also continued its rigid family-class system. The usual BMW identification cues, the kidney grille central section and the hooked surround to the rear side glass, were important to preserve identity. This, along with a general overall feeling of the bigger 5 Series, made it into the compact 3 Series. "A clean industrial design" was the respectful assessment given by *Road and Track* in December 1976.

In Europe, the 316, 318, 320 and 320i badges told the story of three carburetted models and one fuel-injected machine. The adoption of four headlamps on 2-liters and just two headlamps for 1.6- and 1.8-liters ensured that everyone knew where you fitted in the BMW scheme of things. All US models came with quad lamps.

Anti-corrosion work was evident from the first of the 3 Series. BMW described their process: "The chassis is given a corrosion-resistant primer in an immersion bath during the preliminary treatment and the electrophoretic priming. It is then given a number of coats of paint. A careful and practically proven underbody protection and the special BMW system of hollow cavity sealing, which reaches even the furthermost corners, guarantee durability and a high resale value. One example of this high-grade finish: the critical parts of the exhaust system, both inside and outside, are aluminum-coated."

BMW's claims for extended durability are justified, but only with a sympathetic owner. The 3'er needs owner care to keep ahead of winter salt or parking lot paint terrorists. BMW also advertises that its large and small cars share acclaimed paint and anti-corrosion standards. So far as the 3 Series is concerned, this justifiable boast was in transition as this was written, due to the introduction of water-based paints and new facilities at differing times in Munich and Regensburg, the prime sources of 3 Series of E36 and E46 generations.

Body gains

BMW successfully attained four benefits over its 02 line that were most immediately apparent in Europe: safety, comparative silence, space, and aerodynamics. What BMW could not know was that the 3 Series would mature the 02/1500–2000 concepts so successfully that it would claim a complete section of the market, leading to immense profits, plus numerous imitators.

A better cabin that truly set new industry standards, was apparent on both sides of the Atlantic. The first two generations (E21/E30) were of undisputed quality, but many European journalists were disappointed with the 1990/1 interior of the E36 3 Series, calling it shoddy in comparison with its predecessors. The current E46 attracted no such criticism, and it was apparent BMW had learned a lesson.

What were the essentials that seduced so many showroom browsers? An Audi cynic would say, "The badge on the steering wheel." Yet the sturdy four-spoke wheel (with a horn push on each spoke) was carefully dished and raked upon a non-adjustable column to provide a clear view of the elegantly legible instrumentation.

Just four black and white dials were standard issue for the first 3 Series. On the 320, these included a large speedometer (120 mph for RHD UK and 85 mph US; 200 km/h in LHD) and matching 8,000-rpm tachometer, the red-line beginning at around 6,500 rpm for most variants. Dials for water temperature and fuel flanked the main gauges and an analogue clock sat in the center of a dash panel. Orange aircraft-style instrument lighting was widely copied and offered a soft glow that was kind to the eyes.

The quartet of separate quadrant heater/ventilation controls were augmented by a rotary knob for fan speed, while the cigarette lighter and quartz clock were angled towards the driver for convenience. Clive Richardson of Britain's *Motor Sport* summarized the heating and ventilation of the 3 Series "as splendid as that of the 2002 was poor."

The seats, transplanted from the 5 Series and usually covered in cloth with high-quality plastic surrounds, were also praised by many. One journalist commented, "The seats are typically BMW, firm but with support where the body demands it, so relaxing in conjunction with good driving position."

The left-hand steering column stalk controlled main beam/flash for the headlights and flashing indicators, while the right-hand stalk directed the two-speed wipers, which came with powerful washers and an intermittent-wipe function. The combined light rheostat pull/twist switch sat to the left of the steering wheel.

The least spectacular advantage of the 3 Series over an 02 was the combination of increased space and square-rigged frontal area. This change came with a marginal gain on the aerodynamic front: from 0.44/0.45 Cd to 0.43. Fitted with the front spoiler, a 3 Series and a fat-wheeled 02

had virtually the same factor. Those figures are appalling from a 1990s viewpoint, but seen in the 1970 initial-design drawing stage, they hovered slightly below the class average.

The beauty of the BMW body strategy was that the 3 Series really had no direct opposition—the Mercedes 190 was not available until November 1982 when it debuted with four doors rather than two. By 1983, BMW had the second generation 3 Series readied with the promise of four doors.

BMW safety engineers asserted that banishing the split section fuel tank to beneath the rear seat had increased the available crumple zone some 74 percent over the 02. Body-shell resistance to torsional forces increased by 18 percent. These remarks do not apply in the US, where the later "Federal bumper" 2002s had triangulated strengthening beams to beef up areas such as the trunk.

One tradition thankfully maintained was the exceptional tool kit positioned in BMW's under-trunklid compartment. Another BMW tradition that was maintained throughout the first two editions of the 3 Series was the forward-hinged hood which prevented a carelessly latched hood being airlifted over the windshield. A conventional mass-production rear-hinged affair was adopted for the E36 generation of the 3 Series.

The gains in "comparative silence" on the first 3 Series were accompanied by a new heating and ventilation system, which significantly increased cabin comforts compared to the 02. BMW offered a 68 percent increase in sound-absorbent materials for the 3'er and interior noise dropped between six and eight decibels. The biggest contribution to defeating the everyday annoyances of living with the lovable 02 was the effective sealing of the side glass to eliminate the autobahn hiss.

3 Series motor business

Nobody offered such proven and refined engine expertise in a four-cylinder package as BMW. Their transfer of technology from the 02 to the 3 Series was just the beginning of a slant motor

The 3 Series introduced in Europe in the 1970s displayed clean design. The company actually distinguished between four and six cylinders at launch by using single headlamps for the cheaper European four-cylinder derivatives.

Photos: BMW Presse Foto, 1975

dynasty—one that would take BMW's smallest iron-block product, the fabled M10-coded base, from the 1962 BMW 1500 to the 1987 318i.

The original factory engine-type prefixes help identify correct engine/vehicle combinations, and a table in Appendix 3 clarifies which engine did what, and under which badge. Just as the engine is the heart of any BMW, so its code indicates the family to which it belongs. This knowledge can be vital when buying secondhand.

The initial 1.6/1.8/2.0-liter four-cylinders all belonged to the M10 family. The M10 family was replaced by the M40 and subsequent M43 or M43/E46 four-cylinders that motivated the 316i and the 318i. The 318i M40 unit was also the "lower half" of a 16-valve, DOHC cylinder head along M3 principles that powered the 318is, coded as M42. The four-cylinder M3 unit is dealt with in our voluminous M3 chapters, but note that it was coded S14 in all its 2.3-liter/four-cylinder guises. The six-cylinder M3s of both 3 and 3.2 liters, European and American specification, are also discussed in the M3 chapters.

BMW now frequently ignores their series/capacity badging system: i.e., 320 = 3 Series of 2.0 liters. A "315" was actually 1,573 cc in the first generation, while the "316" at the introduction of the second generation had the 1,766 cc engine normally badged as 318. This trend was emphasized in the 1990s E46 generation, right from the introduction of the US 323i (a 2.5-liter) onward.

The M10-based chain-driven fours were to prove tougher over the long run than many of their four- and six-cylinder successors, with the notable exception of the 12-valve, first-generation sixes, which also seemed to shrug off 200,000 miles as routine. Unfortunately, BMW's reputation as master engine-builders suffered with the US public when the quad-valve M42 family stranded owners with unexpected head-gasket failures, which allowed coolant to mix with engine oil.

BMW's enthusiasm for belt drive, which originated with the first M20-designated 12-valve sixes of 1977, waned to such an extent that twin overhead-cam development remained faithful to the chain even as single-cam fours and sixes were utilizing belts. Reviewing BMW power units up to the 1990s, including the largest V12s, we can see that only the four-cylinder 316/318, six-cylinder 320/323/325 gasoline motors, eta-derived SOHC sixes (gasoline), and the first versions of diesel/turbo counterparts abandoned chains for belt-driven operation. The 1983–91 diesel sixes reverted to a chain drive in a normally-aspirated and turbocharged M57 design that replaced the original M21 diesel design.

Chain-driven BMW overhead camshafts reappeared on the 1989 M42 DOHC design of the 318is, although the 316i/318i M40 SOHC unit of 1987 on which it is based utilized a belt-driven overhead camshaft. The belt-drive M40 was made from 1987–1993, when it was replaced by another generation (M43) single camshaft/two-valve-per-cylinder unit that reverted to chain drive. Such a system remains in the current E46 single camshaft family, which was designated M43/E46 and features balancer shafts. This 4-cylinder engine was not available in the US.

All 24-valve twin-cam BMW sixes feature chain drive, but earlier 12-valve diesels and eta derivatives of the original 12-valve, badged 325e, 324d, or 324td, did feature belt drives from 1984–94.

02 Heritage

When it came to power plant engineering for the 3 Series, BMW had a magnificent four-cylinder heritage to draw upon from the 1500 to 2000 4-door family, as well as from the legendary '02' lineage. The company ensured that the new "Three" boasted an engine bay capable of swallowing a new breed of small-capacity sixes, but those were not ready for European consumption before 1977, so the tenacious fours took the initial load.

These 1.5- to 2.0-liter four-cylinders were proven in an M10 line that stretched back to the original 1500. BMW legend Alex von Falkenhausen was the heart of the engines engineering department when the 1500 was conceived in the late 1950s. He he was still in charge when the first 3 Series was presented to the German public in the summer of 1975. Just three years later, von Falkenhausen recalled the conditions under which they created the original 1.5-liter engines. "I had five designers and one engineer for the test bed. The production people say I can go ahead on new engine work, but they say there must be no expense!"

Among the half-dozen engineers who had gathered in that area by 1957 was Paul Rosche, who progressed into Formula

1 and managed BMW Motorsport engines from 1975–99. Rosche remembers the engines engineering department of the 1950s and 1960s well. Dubbed "Camshaft Paul" for his mathematical mastery of camshaft profiling, Rosche recalled the alternative engine studies of the period: "We made designs of single overhead-camshaft engines in sizes from 700 to 1,500 cc. All had four cylinders and water cooling, and all were intended for BMW's smallest sedan lines."

The unique BMW combustion-chamber shape within that crossflow cylinder head (induction on one side, exhaust on the opposite) was dubbed *Wirbelwanne*, which, in German, literally means "swirl bath." The swirling action of the incoming mixture was also promoted by contoured piston crowns. Although the chamber shape would be altered in response to outside pressures such as fuel economy and exhaust emission levels, the principles on which the BMW four-cylinders (and the older six-cylinders) operated went unchanged until the advent of the 1987 M40 series.

Alex von Falkenhausen fought his management for the right to incorporate five main bearings to support the steel crankshaft, the overhead camshaft, and an iron block that was "stiff, very stiff." In fact, the engine team had worked extensively with an aluminum block for their new four-cylinder, but in light of previous experience with alloy V8s, it was not thought worth the additional expense.

The interior of the 3 Series was a better place to be than inside the 02, partly thanks to greatly improved ventilation.

Photo: Klaus Schnitzer, Virginia, 1999

Von Falkenhausen believed that chain drive for the overhead camshaft was an essential, "because a chain will last the life of an engine." What prophetic words considering that many manufacturers, including Porsche with their 944, subsequently encountered camshaft belt-drive/tensioner problems.

From the start of the M10's existence, a 26-degree (to vertical) V-formation of the valves was actuated from that single camshaft by straight aluminum rocker arms. The basics of the 1500 help us to understand the early 3 Series units, as the duplex chain-driven single overhead-camshaft unit was replicated in the 3 Series four-cylinders up to 1987. These engines also included the 30-degree slant of the rigid iron cylinder block (seen from 1800 onward), an alloy cylinder head with V-pattern eight-valves, and a 5-bearing steel crankshaft of phenomenal strength. The crank used five counterweights for the 1500 and eight in the 2-liter development.

The 1500 debuted at the September 1961 Frankfurt International motor show in 75-bhp trim, assisted by an 8.2:1 compression ration. Full production of the 1,499-cc four-cylinder in October 1962 saw its compression elevated slightly (8.8:1) to release 80 bhp. Its power potential, which would realize ten times this horsepower in turbocharged trim, was already being lightly tapped!

Seen through today's lenses, the 2-liter four-cylinders of the first 3 Series seem like ancient history. They were replaced by the small sixes in 1977, having served only as an interim stop gap as the sixes were prepared. But we must understand that the 1,990-cc utilized an 89-mm bore with the 80-mm stroke of the first 1800 generation.

The 2-liter iron four-cylinder entered production in 1965 for the slant-eyed 2000C coupes, which were rated at 100 bhp, or 120 bhp in CS guise. But this engine was most famous in the 2002 and 2002TI, which had the same single- and twin-carburetor outputs. Even better as an all-around sports car was the svelte fuel-injected 2000tii, rated at 130 bhp.

For "02" usage, the von Falkenhausen team certainly explored all possibilities, peaking with 280 bhp from 1,990 cc boosted by a KKK turbocharger (no intercooler!) for the 1969 European racing season. That was the first time a turbocharged saloon car had been raced under international regulations by a major manufacturer in Europe.

Four cylinders for 3 Series

BMW had built a loyal American following with the '02' series, and it had to keep those customers plus attract new ones with greater comfort and the convenience features built into the 3 Series. Lower-lead gasoline was a fact in the US of the 1970s, and was also being introduced in Germany. It was followed by the unleaded era that would become familiar in Europe a decade later, mandating that fundamental engineering changes in combustion chamber design be made. Lowered compression ratios and greater exhaust emission consciousness were inevitable.

In the summer of 1999, BMW engines and transmission development engineering team leader Theo Melcher discussed the engine designs of the 1970s. Looking back on this period, which came within the province of his mentor and predecessor Georg Ederer, he commented, "I think all American enthusiasts of BMW saw was the drop in horsepower from their loved 2002s to the following Federal 3 Series.

"Why was it not possible to give the power equality we have now? Remember, we did not understand the US technical rules so well in that time, and we had not the sophisticated electronics to control the engine. For example, there were no anti-knock sensors, and we were using mechanical fuel-injection systems or carburetors without the engine management computers we have today. Only in the E36 and E46 ranges has it been possible to provide world engines, with the same power on either side of the Atlantic or in Asia."

The primary combustion chamber changes lost the famed "triple hemispherical head" design, a chamber that promoted mixture combustion at compression of 9:1 or 9.5:1 on the bigger-capacity six-cylinders before transference to the high-performance four-cylinders. For example, the 130 bhp of the 2000tii was developed on a 9.5:1 ratio. Aiming for clean combustion on 95-octane fuels, BMW dropped back to 8.3:1 on the 316/318, and just 8:1 on the similarly Solex carburetted 320. Only the 320i was allowed to reach beyond 9:1 thanks to its 9.3:1 K-Jetronic induction unit developed from a 130 bhp Kugelfischer unit that had been made for the 520i since 1972. Again, compression was dropped, as the 520i had originally used the 9.5:1 motor of the 2002tii.

Thus the first four-cylinders for the 3 Series, like the cars, represented a softer and less sporting approach. The lowered compression, revised pistons, and induction equipment had combined to reduce peak torque.

The 1,573-cc four-cylinder was also produced in 75-bhp, low-compression (8:1) trim for the 1502 as a 1975 response to the European fuel crisis. Produced until 1977, the economy 1502 outlasted the rest of the "02" range. The same low-compression approach was also applied to a 1.6-liter 3 Series badged "315" that was made in the E21 body from 1981–82.

Torque news from the 3 Series was better on the carburetted 1.8- and 2-liters (identical for the 320 and the 2002), but again, higher rpm was demanded. Compared to the 2002tii or the earlier (1972–75) 520i, maximum torque was reduced by 5.3

percent, but at least that bucked the trend, as the 320i yielded its best torque figure only 50 rpm below that of its predecessors.

However, peak power was up for the majority of 3 Series in comparison to the "02" equivalents in Europe. The difference was 5 bhp on the 1.6-liter, 8 bhp on the 1.8, and 9-plus bhp for the carburetted 2.0-liter. Whereas all the carburetor units had to rev an average of 300 rpm harder for their horsepower bonus, the 320i initial flagship dropped 100 rpm on the power peak and lost 5 bhp to the 2002tii (125 bhp). That flagship difference at the top of the 3'er line led many to charge the 3 Series with being a less sporting proposition than its beloved "02" forerunners, backed in the US by appalling suspension settings.

New shape, new motor mods

Despite the badging, there were two versions of the 1,766-cc M10 that debuted in the second generation E30 316 and the honestly-badged 318i. For the 316, it had reverted to its old high-compression ways—a Pierburg 2B4 carburetor allied to a 9.5:1 ratio to yield 90 bhp—while the 318i continued as before in LHD guise, but was new to Britain and unavailable in the US. It carried the highest compression yet for a production BMW four-cylinder not intended for competition (10:1). It began September 1982 production in LHD with K-Jetronic fuel injection to

Compared to the 02, the back-seat space increased considerably on a 3 Series, but it was still not competitive with many contemporary front-drive designs.

Photo: Klaus Schnitzer, Virginia, 1999

produce its customary 105 bhp at 5,800 rpm.

For the 1984 model year, the European E30 318i gained the more electronically sophisticated L-Jetronic injection, but horsepower and torque figures remained as before, despite a drop in compression to 9.5:1. Later in the 1980s, the electronic control of cold start was among the benefits conferred by L-Jetronic, but again the power quotes were unaffected.

Both engines incorporated significant features which resulted in quieter running, reduced fuel consumption, and the potential to travel longer between services—"potential" because the unique BMW service interval indicator was introduced, thus intervals depended on usage.

Supporting acts included a new oil pan, viscous coupling for the engine cooling fan, and friction-reduction moves, such as narrowed bearings for the camshaft and lighter valve springs. The 318i also benefited from lighter pistons, and other changes, like extra ribbing for the crankcases, which were allied with stiffer castings for the gearbox to engine bell housing.

Of all the four-cylinder permutations that descended from the 1500, it was the 1800 that came closest to providing BMW with a small-car power unit world-wide. Thus, the 316 and 318i were served by more or less the same motor into the late 1980s. In fuel-injection form, the "1.8" served from Australia to the US and Japan, also meeting the tougher Swiss noise and emission combinations.

Modified for the USA

In July 1976, BMW produced a "49-state" derivative of the original E21 four-cylinder 320i engine for the 1977 model year. Rated at 110 bhp from

Accommodating American standards of in-car entertainment and comfort equipment was not always easy for BMW, especially the standard provision of air conditioning.

Photo: Klaus Schnitzer, Virginia, 1999

the usual 1,990-cc format, maximum power was at 5,800 rpm, while peak torque was 112 lb-ft at 3,750 rpm. It had a reduced (8.2:1) compression and K-Jetronic injection. Of equal significance was the 105-bhp California/Japan development from that base.

Many US 320s were selected in automatic transmission form, which further reduced performance. Of 19,159 US 320i sales in 1977, some 4,561 were automatics (from the 1977 or 1978 model year). BMW was successfully targeting a new breed of customer with the 3 Series. These buyers were more interested in the quality of life than 0–60 mph statistics.

By 1980, continually tightening emission standards had seen the company opt for the 1,766 cc unit in the US, which was also preoccupied with fuel consumption. BMW met both concerns by working a smaller engine harder, both technically and in the task of carrying the 320i badge to much the same timed-performance figures. Equipped with Bosch K-Jetronic, Bosch-developed Lambda probe sensor, and a 3-way catalyst, it had gained a little on compression (8.8:1), yet generated 101 bhp at 5,800 rpm, plus 100 lb-ft of torque by 4,500 rpm, all on low-lead fuels.

When the 3 Series changed its outline to the E30, BMW stayed with the 1.8-liter concept in America and now had the honesty to call it a 318i. American model production started in December 1982 in time for the 1983 showrooms.

As in Europe, the 1,766-cc unit had been reworked, but instead of a 10:1 cr. and K-Jetronic, the Americans received L-Jetronic Bosch fuel injection and 9.3:1 with a 3-way catalytic converter. Power was unchanged at a quoted 101 bhp at 5,800 rpm, but torque was slightly boosted to 103 lb-ft at 4,500 rpm.

Incidentally, internal friction work (slimmer camshaft bearings and lighter valve springs, permitting only 6,300 rpm) was aimed at improving fuel economy further, along with the higher compression ratio. Such work was successful in maintaining a 0–60 mph time of under 10 seconds while improving unleaded fuel economy. Hauling a numerically lower final drive (3.64 versus 3.91), a gain of 2 mpg (to 27 mpg) was recorded over previous US 318/320i models.

The American market was served only by the four-cylinders in the E21 body shape. But in 1984, the E30 hull would bring the six-cylinder 3 Series to that vast market.

US Power and performance

Now, we see how BMW's 4-cylinder engines and transmissions fit into "the scaled-down 5 Series," and the performance they provided in America and Europe.

From its 1976 introduction until model year 1980, a 2-liter served in 49-State (110 bhp) or California (105 bhp) emission trim. Both measured 1,990 cc (121.3 cubic inches) and had comparatively short strokes at 89 x 80-mm (3.5 x 3.15-inch). These were linked to a compression of 8:1, requiring 91-octane fuel grades.

California 2-liters complied with lower emission level regulations, but retained the use of Bosch K-Jetronic fuel injection.

Both power and torque outputs were lower in California specification: the 49-State unit gave 110 bhp at 5,800 rpm while the California model gave 105 bhp at 5,800 rpm. Both delivered maximum torque by 3,750 rpm: the 49-State model at 112 lb-ft and the California version at 108.5 lb-ft.

The motor for a 1980–83 E21 320i measured 1,766 cc (107.7 cubic inches), but allowed shorter stroke dimensions, with a bore and stroke of 80 x 70.9 mm (3.15 x 2.79 inches). This time, all states, including California, were included in one 8.8:1-compression, Bosch K-Jetronic trim that swallowed unleaded 91-octane fuel.

Power suffered, perhaps more than a European could realize, because it was quoted in SAE Net terms at 101 bhp. That was at 5,800 rpm, while peak torque fell to 100 lb-ft at some 4,500 rpm. BMW's diet-conscious moves for model year 1980, as well as clever ratios in the new 5-speed gearbox, allowed acceleration and fuel-consumption gains in steady-speed use.

For the 1975–77 European span, only four-cylinder engines were supplied, and all had been updated from earlier BMW lives. Dominating the development program was the increasing availability of low-lead fuels, with consequently deflated octane ratings. Incidentally, all the 3 Series models were designed with unleaded fuels in mind for their

US market 320i models featured Federally-mandated 85 mph speedometers, while those for Europe read up to 200 kph.

Photo: Klaus Schnitzer, 1975

LHD environment, with low-lead gas becoming available in Germany during 1976.

For Britain, the leaded/unleaded fuel picture is complex because unleaded fuels did not become a serious factor until the 1980s, with the second generation of the 3 Series. So an ignition adjustment is necessary before any of the original 3 Series can safely run cheaper unleaded gasolines.

In the 1970s, BMW Development Chief Bernhard Osswald commented, "We are counting on an increasing price differential between regular and super fuel. With the [price] differences to be expected, the better thermal efficiency of high-compression engines, which require super gasoline, will no longer bring any economic advantage." The injected (320i) Euro engine was actually the only unit to survive with its previous compression (9.3:1) intact, being the product of a later design period.

Germany used a 91 RON grade fuel as their regular grade and 95 RON as their Eurosuper supply. In Britain, the cynically marketed Superplus unleaded fuels were actually a higher octane grade still: 98 RON, but 97 octane was the maximum for year 2000.

BMW European engine development of three single overhead-camshaft (SOHC) carburetted motors (1.6, 1.8, and 2.0 liters), and the ex-BMW 520i K-Jetronic-equipped 2-liter, focused upon reduced compression ratios with modestly elevated power-peak rpm to compensate.

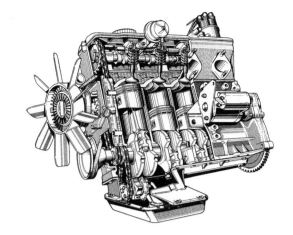

The four-cylinder M10 was the basis for so many affordable Bimmers. This cutaway is of an early E30 single-cam unit for the 316.

Drawing: BMW Engineering, Munich, 1982

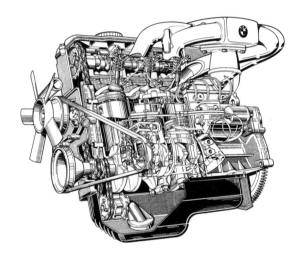

Fuel injection for the European E21 BMW 318i proved to be a production mainstay of the range from 1979–1987. It rated around 105 bhp for the majority of European duties, and 101 bhp on low-lead gasoline in the US.

Drawing: BMW AG, Munich, 1980

The 2002 and its 320 spiritual successor illustrate the extended rpm process for the 3'er perfectly. Both were officially rated at 16 Mkg torque, but the earlier car was peaking at 3,500 rpm, whereas the 320 needed 3,700 rpm. It was much the same story in power, but here the low compression (8:1) 320 was 9 bhp better off than the 2002, hitting a 5,800 rpm peak, compared to the 2002's 5,500. The 320 gained much of its power advantage with a compound Solex 32 33 DIDTA carburetor.

American performance

The original 320i, as imported by then new factory-owned operation, was not worthy of the performance image of BMW, but proved competitive enough on the market to do well in American comparison tests. The worst results came from *Road & Track*. A peek at the data shows why; as tested, the 320i curb weight was nearly 3,000 lbs!

In subsequent test sessions, *R&T* acknowledged that their test gear of the period was heavy and that they ran with two people, compared to a single adult and lighter test gear in the 1980s. This had the effect of making the later low power/lower-weight 1.8-liter of 101 bhp stand up favorably against the 110 bhp originally tested.

To offset anomalies like that above, we have averaged independently obtained figures. Here are the at-a-glance US results:

US 320i vital statistics		
	2-liter	1.8 liter
0–30 mph	3.5 sec.	3.3 sec.
0–60 mph	10.8 sec.	10.5 sec.
0–90 mph	31.0 sec.	27.0 sec.
1/4 mile	18.2 sec @ 75.4 mph	17.6 sec. @ 78 mph
Max speed	106 mph	107 mph

European performance

Full performance figures for all European (including RHD British) 3 Series of the first four-cylinder generation are found in our appendices. Overall, the higher-rpm BMWs were liable to extract a fuel consumption penalty when compared with their predecessors.

The carburetted 320 was a good example with its final drive raised from 3.64 to 3.9:1 (partially to compensate for weight gains of more than 224 lbs over the 2002). This change led some magazines to record 21 to 23 mpg, close to the 22.2 urban mpg recorded by BMW engineers in pre-announcement testing. *Autocar* of London managed nearly 25 mpg overall in the first 320 they tested, recording 0–60 mph in 9.8 seconds and a maximum speed of 111 mph.

The fuel-injected 320i, intended to assuage the performance demand until the six-cylinder 320/323i could be readied (see following chapter), recorded a slight reduction in 0–60 mph elapsed times (9.6 seconds) and a very modest gain in maximum speed (113 mph).

In contrast, *Autocar* recorded maximums of 107 and 116 mph for the 2002 and the 2002tii, coupled to 10.1- and 8.3-second 0–60 mph runs, plus 25.5 mpg (2002) and 25.4 mpg consistency from the 3 Series predecessors. No wonder the first four-cylinder 320i was seen only as a stop-gap by the performance public and BMW.

Soft reasoning

The engineering philosophy for the 3 Series was definitely biased in favor of comfort over handling, but the basic principles of strut front suspension, trailing arm rear, remained in place to be overhauled in conscientious detail. The most obvious handling change was the adoption of the now almost standard mass production feature of rack-and-pinion steering.

BMW recognized the inevitable and switched to a ZF system geared at 21.1:1. This was considerably slower—requiring more than four turns lock-to-lock—than the gearing offered on the 2002 (17.3:1) and became a lifelong feature on all 3 Series except the 1986 M3.

Admittedly, the steering did find support in American road tests and was light enough to park. It could become a twirling chore in sports motoring or tight maneuvers, but (again) US comment from the major magazines was almost all entirely favorable, showing that dynamic tastes differed on either side of the Atlantic.

The 3 Series rack-and-pinion demanded no maintenance, cost a lot less, and required less vital front-end space. However, in higher mileage service over the years, the 3'er did exhibit the kind of front-end shake that has plagued bigger BMWs using their traditional steering box tackle. On the plus side, "the rack" brought increased steering sensitivity and it also performed better in the crash testing that has been part of every Western car manufacturer's routine since the 1970s.

The US fuel-injected four-cylinder behind Bimmer's 320i produced 110 bhp in 49 states, but 105 bhp for California.

Photo: Klaus Schnitzer, Virginia, 1999

The large four-spoke steering wheel was smaller than that of its predecessor, measuring 380 mm (15 inches) compared to the 400 mm (15.75 inches) of the European 2002. Power steering and slightly swifter ratios (19:1) were first offered on post-1977 six-cylinder models in Europe, but no power steering assistance was offered on the US four-cylinders between 1976 and 83.

A glance at the theoretically similar suspension layouts immediately identified some essential design differences between 02 and 3 Series. The 3'er front struts with their eccentrically mounted coil springs were raked rearward at the top mount, and the bottom wishbones were forged instead of pressed steel.

An anti-roll bar was incorporated on all models, instead of the 02 restriction to higher performance models. A simplified bar layout was used that was cheaper than the optional unit of the 02 series, although it was not as effective.

The rear axle progressed from separated coil spring and telescopic damper units (the shock absorbers aft of the springs) to a combined spring strut layout. This was based on considerably stiffened semi-trailing arms, supported by a differential brace that fought the untoward effects of rear-wheel steering.

Elongated springs were a feature of this softened BMW approach to sports motoring. At the front, the springs went from the 2002's 180 mm (7.1 inches) to 192 mm (7.6 inches), while the backs were stretched to 208 mm (8.2 inches) from the previous measurement of 170 mm (6.7 inches). A somewhat vague BMW press briefing attributed these spring changes and unspecified damper setting modifications with a 25 percent overall drop in front-end suspension stiffness allied to a dramatic 40 percent escalation of rear rates.

The German press was kind toward a generally softer suspension character, commenting that it was "a most favorable compromise between sophisticated comfort and optimum driving characteristics." American and British comment was far stronger and led directly to some immediate changes.

Writing in 1978, *Road and Track* summarized the problem. "Since its introduction in 1976, the BMW 320i has been afflicted with a rear suspension problem that has limited the car's cornering ability. The condition, lifting the inside rear wheel, was not only annoying, but was partially responsible for distracting transient oversteer."

In wetter climates than *R & T*'s native California, comments such as this one from Britain's *Motor Sport* in February 1977 were relevant: "The front is now far too soft and the rear too stiff. The 320i wallows soggily at its front end and when pushed really hard exhibits considerable body roll. At the same time the rear roll stiffness, increased over both 2002 and 320, causes the inside rear wheel to pick up far too easily, resulting in pretty abysmal traction in most circumstances."

R & T summarized BMW's reply in the June 1978 issue. "The factory's fix, which represents the only significant change in the newest model, includes removing the car's rear anti-roll bar and increasing the front spring rates to maintain the same total roll stiffness."

The American monthly reported gains in skid-pan g-forces generated from the original 0.726 to 0.743 g in 1978. Engineering editor John Dinkel felt that its skid pad performance was that of "a very balanced and forgiving car to drive." *R & T* commented, "Tromping on the throttle still causes the inside rear wheel to spin, but not nearly as readily or uncontrollably as in previous models."

The magazine acknowledged that the "rather expensive solution" to gain the ultimate response was to order the optional limited-slip differential (part of the "S" package in the USA). It puzzled both German and British sources as to why the limited-slip action was not included on the premier models.

In Europe for 1978, front spring rates also rose, along with firmer damper settings, but front roll-bar thickness was increased. Conversely, back rates were dropped 10 percent, with the accent on bump settings rather than rebound, which was also claimed to "reduce road noise transmission to the bodywork," in BMW's defensive words.

Also new for 3'er was the braking system, but the German press spotted that economics had played a part in this change. In its July 5, 1975

Britain's Triple Choice

In the wake of the winter 1973/74 fuel crisis, the privately-owned BMW Concessionaires GB Ltd. (the factory bought it out in 1981) had been wrong-footed on the gasoline economy front and were advertising "unbeatable performance, unbelievable economy." They supported this new angle on BMW motoring with a quoted 41 mpg at a constant 50 mph for the 2002tii.

A 1602 initiated the UK range at £2,099 and the legendary 2002tii commanded £3,445. These were stiffish prices, considering that a Mini was still less than £1,000 at the time (August 1974) while a Jaguar E-type S3 with V12 power was only £3,743!

By October 1975, the UK concessionaires (then owned by TKM: Tozer Kilbourn, Milbourn) was ready to market three model lines in the common 2-door body. They were the 316 at an initial £3,429, the carburetted 320 at £4,039, and the 320i at £4,749.

As a balance between the sporting purists and the less fanatical customers, *Autocar* summarized a selection of Threes. Here is their assessment:

316/90 bhp, 1.6 liters: "We liked the 316 and found it highly acceptable. It doesn't go like a 320, of course, but it still goes pretty well, and has most of the 320's pleasures in similar measures." (January 17, 1976)

320/109 bhp, 2.0 liters/four-cylinder: "The car is practical and honest, which two virtues on their own could add up to dull—which the quite sparkling performance successfully avoids. It would be better still with more sensible gearing. The price may at first sound high, but for once with this maker it looks quite competitive when seen against the background of its competitors." (November 29, 1975)

320i/125 bhp, 2.0 liters, injection/four-cylinder: "The BMW will still appeal to those who do not want their motoring package to be bigger than necessary. As a compact sporting saloon whose very size is a virtue, it has much to offer in all the important areas where a discriminating buyer will look for refinement and quality." (September 4, 1976)

Right: The traditional full toolkit was preserved in the 3 Series.

Left: Steel wheels and big bumpers were part of the original US Bimmer 3 Series recipe.

Photos: Klaus Schnitzer, Virginia, 1999

issue, *Auto Motor und Sport* reported, "BMW has clearly abandoned the braking system [of the 02]. The expensive system with its double calipers on the front disc brakes has given way to a system with single calipers.

"This economy has consequences only in the event of a failure of a braking circuit. With the old system, the front brakes maintained at least some action. With the new [braking] system of generally common design, damage can render the brakes on one axle set to become useless. BMW acknowledges that [under normal conditions] the new system has advantages.

"It is less sensitive to fading, has less tendency to fading if the brake fluid boils; it reduces unsprung weight and costs less. The saving appears to have been well spent elsewhere. The brake servo unit and the rear drum brakes have become larger, and a pressure-dependent braking force limiter [pressure valve] has been added," summarized Clauspeter Becker in 1975.

There were braking changes "tuned for American conditions," BMW NA reported in the fall of 1977. "Front to rear braking balance has been improved by switching to solid front disc brakes and new rear brake linings which operate at lower temperatures." The braking effort was biased "70 percent front and 30 percent rear."

Despite some criticism, major American magazines of the period generally reviewed the 320i favorably, even when it came to the price tag. *Car & Driver* said, "The BMW 320i is real value for money, no matter how much it costs, because it's beautifully engineered and it's not boring." *Road and Track* published this 1978 verdict: "It's $9,085: not inexpensive but justifiable (by today's standards) to buyers looking for good handling, comfortable ride and joy of driving in a compact but roomy sports sedan."

Customers agreed, for the 3 Series was made in record numbers and established BMW NA's present prosperity. Production minutiae are detailed in the appendices, but it is worth knowing that the first 3 Series entered Munich production under its E21 factory coding in June 1975. Initially, only four-cylinder 316 and 318 (not UK) saloons were made. The 320i came along in October 1975. Factory-supplied production history catalogues list American LHD models from July 1976 (California in September 1976). RHD (UK) manufacture began in November 1975.

The original European E21 shows the slimmer bumpers, similar steel wheels, and heavy rubber inlays needed to protect the flanks.

Photo: BMW GB, Berkshire, 1980

In 1975, less than 44,000 of the smallest BMW were made. Then 1976 saw production get into its stride with more than 130,000 examples. Peak production for the original E21 came little more than a year before its replacement, with 228,832 of the 1.36 million total built during the 1981 season. It would be 1984 before the second-generation 3 Series exceeded that annual output. The most popular first 3 Series model was the 316 (over 337,000 made), but both six-cylinder 320/323i types hit large production numbers too: over 270,000 for 320-6 and 137,107 for 323i.

Some 106,312 other examples of the 3 Series were made in the ex-Glas facility Dingolfing, while 1.25 million of the first generation came from the four-cylinder building in Munich.

Our guide to the Euro-sixes begins in the next chapter, while full production totals can be found in the appendices.

4

A Civilized Baby Six

The M60-coded six-cylinder engines gave BMW's smallest sedans a new muscular character.

Although Americans did not receive the European E21 3 Series six-cylinder engines that are the subject of this chapter, these powertrains foreshadowed combinations that would land in the US years later. When America received the coveted six-cylinders in Spring 1983, they were wrapped in the second generation (E30) bodies and badged 325e, the "e" for eta, greek symbol for efficiency.

Six success

Destined to become the backbone of BMW's US success, American market six-cylinders were initially biased towards economy. The first 12-valve single cam sixes—particularly the 1977 European 323i—were the first step to restore the 2002 performance pace. BMW literally made them by the million.

In August 1977, production began of a new—and far more compact—BMW six-cylinder breed. It was originally coded M60, but retrospectively, all engines from this popular 12-valve family of 1977–91 come under the M20 designation in factory records.

Production was initiated with a carburetted 2-liter (320 and 520) or a fuel-injected 2.3-liter flagship performer for the European 323i. The motor code M20 is now used throughout, although the basic block and architecture evolved into an enlarged range for 1985 that embraced 2.0-liters, 2.5-liters, and eta 2.7-liters.

From 1977 until the 1991 close of production in some of the last E30 3 Series (notably convertible and touring), an astounding 1,763,895 such M20 sixes emerged from two primary factories, Milbertshofen in Munich and Steyr in Austria. The M20s powered an enormous variety of E21 and E30 BMW 3 Series, plus a lesser number of 5 Series.

The M20 family did not reach the US until ten years after its

European debut. It was the first BMW engine to use a belt-driven overhead camshaft, and the first genuinely all-new BMW engine since 1961. For 3 Series, the arrival of a new six-cylinder was crucial to the planned expansion of the range. Thanks to clever production engineering and the use of modern manufacturing methods they actually cost less than the four-cylinders that they replaced.

In the 1980s, derivatives of the inline six would yield both the 2.4-liter diesels (turbocharged, following a normally aspirated unit) and the bold "eta" energy-conservation gasoline unit. This 2.7-liter mated the six-cylinder and the 3 Series together for the first time in American showrooms. Although the eta engine was mass-manufactured in huge numbers for both the American and Japanese markets in the second generation E30 outline (325e), it was not judged a success and did not continue in either the 3 or the 5 Series of the 1990s. Why didn't the eta succeed? In the summer of 1999, Senior BMW engineer Theo Melcher explained that, "The eta did not have the free-revving character people ask of a BMW engine. It did not satisfy what our customers expect of BMW."

The earlier M20 motor, the starting point for all these BMW "small-block" motors, was not a revolution in its iron-block, alloy SOHC head construction, but it set new standards of smooth power delivery.

The slant six (still tilted at 30 degrees to the right) was to feature in the 3 and 5 Series, although in the latter case, it was shared in carburetted 2-liter between 520/320. A 2.3-liter M20 was reserved as the sporting 323i of the 3 Series, intended to "consign even the successful 2002tii to obscurity," as BMW stated in their hopeful

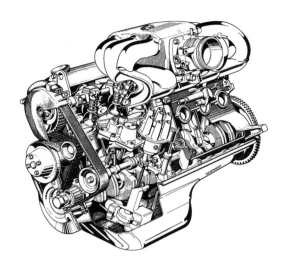

The original small-six design, a 12-valve, single camshaft engine, had a shared belt drive; but this 323i, which reached 143 bhp, marked the point at which fuel injection was utilized in the European range.

Drawing: Niedermeier for BMW AG, 1977

press release.

Developed through the 1970s and calling on a team that included Paul Rosche and Franz Zinnecker, the M60 produced over 60 bhp per liter on super fuel grades and compression ratios of 9.2:1 (320) and 9.5:1 for the 323i. The cross-flow aluminium head retained the V-formation of two valves per cylinder, but the single camshaft, like the spheroidal cast-iron crankshaft, enjoyed the luxury of running in seven bearings. The crankshaft was counterbalanced by the action of twelve counterweights.

Induction for the 320 was performed by a single Solex 4A1 carburetor, while Bosch K-Jetronic served the 323i unit during its initial 1977–82 Euro-span. In a direct comparison, the short-stroke (80 x 66 mm) M60 of 2 liters developed 13 more bhp than its carburetted 89 x 80 mm four-cylinder predecessor, and only 3 bhp less than the fuel-injected 320i/4.

However, that short-stroke bias showed up particularly strongly at 2 liters—the four-cylinder pumped up a bonus of 127 lb-ft on 5,500 rpm versus 118 lb-ft on 4,000 rpm for the same-capacity six. Naturally, the 2,315-cc and its elongated (76.8 mm) stroke disposed of the four-cylinder's torque superiority, yielding 140 lb-ft. Despite

BMW claims at the launch, in comparison to those well-proven fours, there was also a fuel-consumption penalty to be paid for the six-cylinder.

It was this fuel appetite and the need for further emissions development that prevented the small performance six from arriving in the American 3 Series, and promoted the alternative eta six-cylinder cause. BMW NA could not afford to upset the fuel consumption balance of their range in the US, so it was a 325e that belatedly offered North Americans something more than 1.8 liters and four cylinders in the 3 Series, starting in 1984. The 325e engine (also shipped to Japan) was also covered by the opening M60/M20 factory engine codes, but carried a block that allowed 2,693 cc (84 x 81 mm) in a uniquely slow-revving gasoline production engine.

The Greek "eta" tag was applied as an "e" suffix from 1981 onward when it debuted on the 5 Series (525e). Subsequent applications were under the 528e badge in the US (cubic capacity remained 2,693 cc); March 1983 saw the 525e in Europe, and (primarily for Japan and the US) the 325e began production in October 1983.

It was in American catalytic converter form that BMW found most customers for their unusual 2.7-liters, which had been developed to accommodate American preferences for automatic transmission and air conditioning, while consuming low-octane, unleaded-fuel. Over 62,000 US-specification 325e models were manufactured in the best year for the two-door E30 (1986), and more then 189,000 were sold around the globe from 1983–1988. Production of US eta variants ended in 1987.

In Europe, the 325e/525e unit boasted the

highest production compression then seen in a BMW, and the lowest rpm power peak of the company's gasoline-powered range. The figures were 11:1, with some 125 bhp at 4,250 rpm, accompanied by 177 lb-ft of torque by 3,250 rpm.

For the 325e, the engine served "cat" markets on a 9:1 cr that could digest 91-octane unleaded gasoline. Power delivery sagged a little, but remained quoted at 121 bhp, while torque was quoted at 170 lb-ft, all developed at the same rpm peaks as in the 5 Series. The comparison can be seen in the chart below:

	Euro M20	Euro eta	USA/eta
Capacity	1,993 cc	2,693 cc	2,693 cc
Bore x stroke	80 x 66 mm	81 x 84 mm	81 x 84 mm
Compression	9.8:1	11:1	9:1
Octane/type	97/leaded	97/leaded	91/unleaded
Power	125 bhp @ 5,800 rpm	125 bhp @ 4,250 rpm	121 bhp @ 4,250 rpm
Torque	125 lb-ft @ 4,000 rpm	177 lb-ft @ 3,250 rpm	170 lb-ft @ 3,250 rpm
BMW test mpg (US)	25.7	28.4	25.5

The eta was a surprising and innovative departure from BMW and remained unique among commercially developed gasoline engines. It is no longer in production, killed off by the worldwide availability of conventional higher-revving 320i/325i catalytic converter engines. A European appetite for economical and durable diesel and turbo diesel sixes also made eta redundant that side of the Atlantic.

M60 grows into M20

Across generations of the 3 and 5 Series, the M60 (and its M20 successor of 1982) prospered. It expanded to 2.7 liters for gasoline, and 2.4 liters for both turbocharged and normally aspirated diesels. First, let's look at the gasoline derivatives. The table below shows the growth from the European 2.3-liter into a 2.5 that made it across

	M60/2.3-liter	M20/2.5-liter
Capacity	2,316 cc	2,494 cc
Bore x stroke	80 x 76.8 mm	84 x 75 mm
B/S ratio	0.96	0.89
Compression	9.8:1	9.7:1
Power	150 bhp @ 6,000 rpm	170/171 bhp* @ 5,800 rpm
Torque	148 lb-ft @ 4,000 rpm	166 lb-ft @ 4,000 rpm
* rating varies according to application		

the Atlantic.

To emerge as a revised M20 within the 1982 E30 update of the 3 Series, the 1,990-cc unit remained dimensionally intact, but compression was increased from 9.2 to 9.8:1 and Bosch L-Jetronic was adopted. Now, only the 316 would be publicly offered without fuel injection in Europe. As on all 1982-onward E30 machines, the engine benefited from some new castings, including that for the sump and the inlet manifold.

As a six-cylinder 320 became a 320i, there was 3 bhp power increase to 125, the same as for the pre-1977 320i/4. More significantly, the fuel injection and associated manifolding yielded a torque bonus of 7 lb-ft at 4,000 rpm.

The 2.3 liters of the 323i also remained, but there were other significant changes, including a compression rise from 9.5 to 9.8:1 and a switch from mechanical K-Jetronic fuel injection to the L-Jetronic electronic equipment. In making this move, BMW biased output toward enhanced fuel consumption, including an overrun cut-off that was triggered by the descent to below 1,200 rpm. Camshaft profiles were also revised for better low- to mid-range throttle response.

The overall result of these 323i modifications

was a small power loss that would not be tolerated in the longer term. In 1982, the official output was down 4 bhp (now recorded as 139 bhp), but this was obtained at 5,300 rather than 5,800 rpm. Torque—some 148 lb-ft at 4,000 revs—was enhanced a princely 8 lb-ft and delivered 500 rpm earlier.

Within 12 months (effective as of September 1983 in production), BMW had made a series of running changes (including camshaft replacement, inlet manifold diameter and length, and a two-stage distributor) that made a claim of 150 bhp possible at 6,000 rpm. Torque was now reported at 158 lb-ft at 4,000 rpm, and the first examples were with the European press by autumn 1983. Such cars were also listed as having Bosch LE-Jetronic rather than straight-forward L-Jetronic, but the extra "E" introduced cold-start refinements, not power potential.

At first, nobody offered BMW direct opposition for the M60 and M20 families. Even a Mercedes 190E-2.6 became more of a marketing reflex than a balanced combination, as the Mercedes engine was intended for another application and was smooth, rather than powerful. Audi's gasoline-fueled fives were destined for even more performance, while the rest of the world (Volvo, VW, and Lancia, at any rate) adopted various five-cylinder formats. Audi's subsquent 170 bhp V6s failed to offer the refinement or performance of a BMW inline six, but the Audi engineers of Upper Bavaria did start to give BMW serious anguish when they ran four- and five-valve-per-cylinder V6s in the 1990s.

Launch talk

August and September 1977 were reserved for the international launch of a new small six-cylinder engine for the 3 Series, one also shared with the first 520. In order to distinguish the new model from the previous four-cylinder 320 and 320i, it was informally dubbed 320/6 in factory production records.

The factory briefing is intentionally left in the

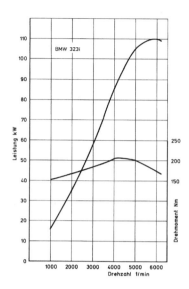

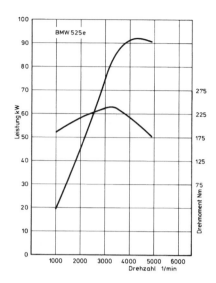

The biggest member of the small-capacity, six-cylinder engine family was the 2.7-liter eta, which also introduced the 12-valve design to American motorists during 1984–87. It was uprated to rev a little more energetically during its life-span, but the low-rpm concept never sat well with BMW engineers or enthusiasts.

Drawing: Issued by BMW Presse, 1983

original text, including spelling. "With its 1978 model program, the Bayerische Motoren Werke—Bavarian Motor Works—are going to be living up to their name particularly well. For a new Motor—engine, if you will, in English—announces a new era at BMW, a 'small' six-cylinder unit of 2 or 2.3 liters, with an overhead camshaft running in 7 bearings and driven by a toothed belt."

BMW revealed that a spheroid cast iron crankshaft also ran in seven main bearings, that it was soothed by no fewer than 12 counterweights, and that the 323i version of the engine featured both K-Jetronic fuel injection and transistorized ignition. They added, "These new engines succeed the 2-liter four-cylinder engine of the BMW 320 (two-door) and BMW 520 (four-door) and put the new model BMW 323i at the top of the compact class. This new type, with its 2.3-liter fuel-injection engine, is a fresh interpretation of the BMW motto, 'For the Joy of Driving' and will surely turn out to be an industry pioneer like the much-imitated 320i and 2002tii.

"Thus the BMW engineers have again made significant progress. With the new small six-cylinder engines, they have made a bridge to the outstanding refinement of their larger 'sixes.' The ability to summon up high performance on

demand will make the enthusiastic driver of this class car newly sovereign. And this is performance on cat's paws," burbled the comfortingly eccentric press package.

The 320/6 was equipped similarly to the 320i/4, but the company started to offer power steering as an option that you might value in any secondhand purchase. The standard layout was a ZF 21:1 rack-and-pinion with a cumbersome 4.05 turn lock to lock.

The 320/6 was never a performance substitute for a 323i, officially yielding 122.4 bhp compared to the latter's 143 bhp and losing almost 30 percent on the torque curve. There were other important specification differences between ostensibly similar in-line six-cylinder 3 Series. The original 320/6 did not offer rear disc brakes (the 323i always did) and the first 320/6 models were carburetted by a complex four-barrel Solex 4 A1, rather than the desirable Bosch K-Jetronic. As a result, both fuel consumption and service bills for 320/6 were frequently higher.

To accommodate the six, a smaller but more efficient crossflow radiator was adopted, carrying a viscous coupled fan which was thermostatically controlled. The electrical system was also upgraded, taking a 65-ampere alternator and 44-

amp/hour battery.

Transmission changes included a larger Fichtel and Sachs clutch and beefier gears for the standard four-speed. In Britain, it was 1979 before an overdrive five-speed was offered, and there is always the later possibility of an optional close ratio set being installed, identified by a direct (1:00) fifth.

An optional ZF HP22 three-speed automatic was available. As for the initially standard manual four-speed, 2- and 2.3-liter small sixes shared the same ratios. An overall difference in gearing was supplied through a 3.64:1 final drive for the 320/6 and a 3.45 for the 323i. Much of the transmission technology could be traced back to 02 ancestry.

The front disc brakes grew approximately half an inch and shared the same 10-inch (255 mm) diameter as the front units of the 323i. The 323i, however, used a fully vented unit with a thickness of 22 mm (0.87 inches), whereas the 320/6 retained a solid unit of 12.7-mm (0.5-inch) depth. The 320/6 used rear drums rather than discs, those drums taking orders from a 9-inch Mastervac servo and sharing their 10.16-inch diameter with all but the 316.

Running gear changes were simply referred to as upgraded springs and dampers, but a closer look at the 320/6 and the 323i showed that the

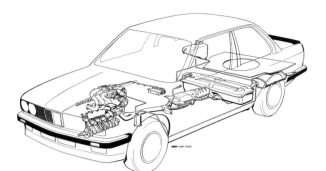

The basic hardware for a catalytic-converter eta motor is shown on the 325e. Note the "saddle" fuel tank and central exhaust chambers, along with the conventional exhaust tail pipe.

Drawing: BMW Grafik, 1985

adoption of replacement 5.5 J x 13 standard steel wheels (as used on US four-cylinders) had boosted rear track a notable 3 mm. More importantly, there were front and rear anti-roll bars (slightly thickened at the back) to restrain body lean on both the sixes.

BMW factory literature deleted a rear anti-roll bar for the four-cylinder models thereafter, reserving it as standard equipment on the 320/6 and the 323i, while noting that the front bar on 320/6 was "stiffened." Standard 185/70 HR rubber—as also used on the 320i—promised more grip than the four-cylinder setup of 165 section tires on the previous 320.

Weight & performance: 320/6

The six-cylinder 3 Series showed natural weight gains, but approximately 50 lbs. of that was owed to the six cylinders up front. This was anticipated by elevated front spring and damper rates. Compared to the 320/4, the 320/6 was plumper by 95 kg (209 lbs.) at the curb.

Full performance figures supplied by *Autocar* are given at BentleyPublishers.com, but note that BMW factory claims were modest, and comprehensive. They are reproduced, in full, in the following table. It's worth comparing them to *Autocar's*

The dusty road to success is illustrated by a 143-bhp 323i pounding gravel in southern Germany. The driver is former PR supremo Dirk Strassl (later found at BMW Mobile Tradition).

Photo: BMW Werkfoto, 1980

results, which could be summarized as: 111-mph maximum speed, 0–60 mph in 9.8 seconds, and 24.6 Imperial mpg overall.

BMW Claimed Performance 320/6 (autumn 1977, 4-speed manual)		
Km/h	Mph	Seconds
0–50	0–31	3.4
0–80	0–50	7.2
0–100	0–62	10.7
0–120	0–75	15.8
0–140	0–87	22.7
0–400 meters: 17.4 seconds		
Maximum speed: 112 mph		
DIN fuel consumption: 29.7 Imperial mpg		

BMW claims—aside from gas consumption—were realistic. The author's notes from the debut of the 320/6 in Southern France included criticisms of "wind noise, concentrated on the driver's side." As for the engine itself, "it had a very accessible torque curve: in fact, 93.5 lb-ft torque, or more, is provided between 2,000 and 6,200 rpm, and it is this flexible power that dominates our drive. I think this small six is a very attractive sporting proposition."

Production & sales progress: 320/6

Without a US sales story, we'll recap pricing in Britain, but begin with the fact that the 320/6 entered LHD production in August 1977. The carburetted model finished its initial run of 101,578 manual gearbox units in September 1979, with a further 13,720 featuring the usual low Continental European take on automatic transmission.

For January 1978, an introductory price of £4,999 was set for the UK's RHD model. At that price, the 320/6 carried a great deal of detailed engineering that enabled it to confidently face British market opposition, which included Alfa Romeo's Alfetta 2000 sedan at £4,800, and the faster Ford Escort RS2000 at £4,168.

The cheapest six-cylinder 320 proved to be an immediate hit in Europe, peaking at 65,369 units in 1979 but also selling within 6,000 units of that summit in 1978 and 1980. It was replaced by the E30 fuel-injected 320i/6 at the close of 1982, when BMW had sold 270,445 in the E21 shell. That made it the second most popular model in the first 3 Series, beaten only by the 316.

The smaller sixes prompted the arrival of the larger (58 liter) fuel tank—under the seats and within a designated crumple zone— on all models. Revised door and seat trims were also introduced at this point. The official start date for RHD production was October 1978, and that means that all UK vehicles should have transistorized ignition, for the 320/6 did not adopt this feature in LHD until August 1978. The ZF automatic transmission proved to be a reasonably popular option in Britain, representing almost 51 percent of all RHD 320/6s.

The 323i reveals the optional multi-spoke wheels and extensive chrome of the early 1980s.

Photo: BMW GB Ltd, Bracknell 1980

By February 1979, BMW was listing the availability of the overdrive (0.813) five-speed gearbox and claiming a bonus of 1.4 Imperial mpg at a constant 75 mph. Performance claims for the automatic were far more pessimistic than usual and included a quote of 0–62 mph in 13.6 seconds. Such sluggardly progress was underlined by quoting 15.8 seconds for the manual four-speed to cover 0–75 mph and more than 19 seconds for its automatic cousin.

By early 1979, digital clocks replaced the neat analogue central clock, with red digits displayed beneath the tachometer of the LHD models. Economy was acknowledged by BMW with a narrowing green section to the low end of the rev counter to encourage fuel-conscious rpm. Black-and-white order was soon back in place, but a formal "economizer" has since been a feature of all 3 Series, except M3, since the E30.

Running changes included the availability in Britain in September 1980 of the Baur convertible body work, one of the models imported by the new management at the now (January 1980) wholly BMW import operation for Britain. Baur factory-approved coachwork roused interest in 3 Series fresh-air motoring when it made its LHD debut in 1977.

An official factory-backed convertible was produced in the second generation of the 3 Series. It amounted to a halfway house between a Targa and a full convertible body (plastic roof panels separated from a fabric rear hood section by a sturdy, safety-conscious hoop), and was no match for the simple elegance of the 1985–90 factory soft top, or the rare full convertible 02s.

Both small sixes finally received the five-speed gearbox as standard. A factory letter from June 1982, announced that "as of works holiday 82, all six-cylinder (manual) models will be fitted with the five-speed overdrive as standard equipment." A five-speed was also available on the less-powerful four-cylinders, but was a standard model year 1980 fit in the US. At this point, the red-line on the 320/6 was reduced by 200 rpm as reflected on the tachometers of vehicles built after August 1982.

The hunger of the UK customer for the highest possible specification was tested by a July 1982 "Special" that foretold the subsequent successful transference of the "SE" extra equipment marketing ploy down the range from its initial 7-Series appearance. These consisted of manual and automatic variants of the 320/6 and 323i. Such extra equipment cost £8,317 on the 320, some £9,063 in automatic guise. The specials represented good value in contemporary terms, for the basic 320/6 exceeded £8,000 during the 1982 UK model year. The special specification of 1982 offered a manual sliding steel roof and multiple-spoke BMW Accessory alloy wheels in an Opal green. These matched the body/interior combination of Opal green metallic hitched to a pine green interior based on the 7 Series' velour. These 1982 specials are an obvious target for collectors, because the

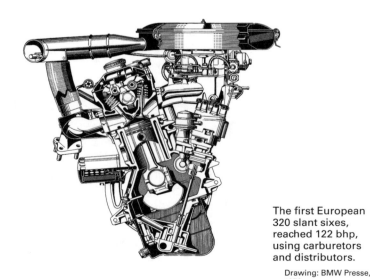

The first European 320 slant sixes, reached 122 bhp, using carburetors and distributors.

Drawing: BMW Presse, 1979

A Baur-built 320 BMW 3 Series convertible poses in front of its factory-built successors in rural Germany.

Photo; Klaus Schnitzer, Germany, 1993

Was this wishful thinking? Well, commercially, BMW was being realistic, but the 323i did not become the all-round motorsport race and rally car of present or past 2002 ability. However, the 323i established a new level of compact, high-quality street performance.

The balance between speed and economy was biased most firmly toward performance. Much of this pace was obtained through the use of K-Jetronic injection and a slight elevation of compression (9.5:1 versus 9.2:1). BMW had dispensed with their laudable low-compression, low-lead-fuel obsession in favor of improved combustion chamber designs which tolerated unleaded fuels and life at 10:1 cr. It was 1981 before the BMW four-cylinders were revised and reverted to higher compression, the LHD-only 318i taking on Bosch K-Jetronic simultaneously.

For the 323i, an extra 325 cc above the 320/6 was obtained via a simple 10.8-mm elongation of

UK order was for just 400 of the 320/6, and less than 200 in 323i trim.

All 3 Series gained extensive interior trim changes and head restraints in time for autumn 1980 sales. For the 320/6 SE, the door mirrors were also color-coded in green, and rear seat head restraints and a sports steering wheel were included, but only automatic transmission specials boasted standard power steering.

The carburetted 320/6 was a very successful derivative in export and home-market guises, one that demonstrated the unique value of placing a purpose-built smooth six-cylinder in a compact car.

Performance & specification: 323i

The 323i was a serious effort to eclipse the sporting legend that was the 2002tii. Indeed, the BMW press briefing in 1977 stated, "The new 2.3-liter six-cylinder develops 143 bhp; it replaces the four-cylinder 320i (125 bhp) and could well consign even the successful 2002tii to obscurity. In any case, its unique conception will soon thrust it into a position of leadership."

323i Claimed performance		
Performance parameter	BMW results	AUTOhebdo results
0–50 km/h (0-31 mph)	2.8 sec	—
0–80 km/h (0-50 mph)	6.4 sec	6.3 sec
0–100 km/h (0-62 mph)	9.5 sec	9.1 sec
0–120 km/h (0-75 mph)	13.6 sec	13.3 sec
0–140 km/h (0-87 mph)	18.5 sec	19.2 sec
0–160 km/h (0-100 mph)	—	28.6 sec
0–400 meters	16.7 seconds	17.2 sec
0–1,000 meters	30.9 sec	31.6 sec
Maximum speed	118 mph	120.1 mph
DIN fuel consumption	30.7 mpg	

stroke, while both cars had an 80-mm bore. BMW's performance claims for a machine that had 143 bhp and 140 lb-ft of torque were modest and were easily surpassed by independent testers in Britain and matched by those in LHD markets. Additionally, we have included the results of the French weekly, *AUTOhebdo*, alongside the BMW claims, but the full *Autocar* statistics are given at BentleyPublishers.com and may be summarized as follows: 0–60 mph in 8.3 seconds; maximum speed, 126 mph; test fuel economy, 19.7 Imperial mpg.

Running gear differences for the 323i were headlined by the move to rear disc brakes (supported by 160-mm [6.25-inch] drums for the handbrake), and vented front rotors, but the suspension was also further enhanced beyond the 320/6 specification. A "sports-tuned" suspension included further stiffening of the front strut damper inserts, on the progressive principles found in 7 Series, plus thicker anti-roll bars. In 1978, *Autocar* reported, "Our preference would be for an even stiffer setup with this type of performance. It was quite common for the car to feel rather soft."

The *AUTOhebdo* 1982 323i had a long list of optional equipment, including sports suspension (covering replacement anti-roll bars, dampers and springs). It also had the close ratio five-speed gearbox, a limited-slip differential set at 25 percent pre-load (this despite the earlier avowed factory intention to switch to a 40 percent figure) and BBS "spider's web" alloys, albeit clothed by the standard 185/70 Michelin XVS tires.

Other running gear changes have been described in our section on the 320/6, but it is worth pointing out that the taller (3.45) final drive allowed nearly 20 mph per 1,000 rpm from the 323i. That meant the maximum speed recorded occupied 6,350 rpm in fourth, rather than the actual rev limit of 6,600 rpm.

External identification for the flagship 323i was confined to front and rear badges, plus twin exhausts (one per side). The 323i came to Britain at £6,249 in April 1978, but there was a long list of options installed on the May 1978 *Autocar* demonstrator, pumping up the price to a significant £8,386 — nearly the cost of a contemporary BMW 528i. The listed options now sound like mundane showroom items for many mediocre saloons: electric mirrors were £222, electric windows added £264, and power steering went to those with another £482 to spare. But there was one intriguing option the factory did not list as available and it was not offered for long in the UK — air conditioning. Was it an aftermarket unit installed on this press car? We think that the E21 was not specifically designed for air conditioning — you can see signs of this in 320i Bimmers exported to the US. Their layout of radio and after-thought air controls was mounted on what *Car & Driver* retrospectively described in July 1983 as "the add-on console hump of yore."

Development & production details: 323i

The 323i entered LHD manufacture in January 1978 and RHD was initiated in March of that year, although1977 saw 35 LHD pilot examples built, plus a pair of RHD forerunners. Output naturally ran somewhat behind the 320/6, but by 1979–81, the factory was "up to full speed" and the sales ratio between 320 and 323 was roughly 2:1.

The best year for the first 323i was 1980, when Munich made 36,424 units, versus more than 65,000 units of the 320 made in 1979. The final totals bear out this approximate 2:1 theory as well, with 137,107 units of the 323 made between 1977 and 1982, compared to 270,445 units of the 320/6. The final commercial difference was that the 323i motor made the change into the next generation of 3 Series with minimal modifications, while the 320/6 required fuel-injection.

The minor change of a brake pad wear indicator was incorporated on the 323i in August 1978. As for the 320/6, a Baur convertible was offered from September 1980, by which time the basic cost of the 323i in the UK amounted to £7,550. The long list of options now embraced central locking at £342 on all 3 Series. It was left to the second-generation 323i, or the special equipment derivatives described below, to crack the £10,000 ceiling. The last of the basic 323i breed in the original body was listed at £8,940, without options.

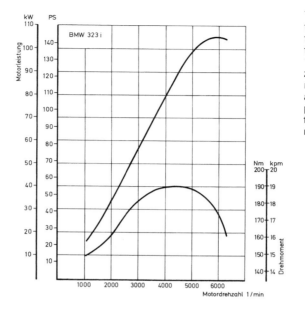

The power and torque curves for the first 323i show that BMW expected 143 bhp only at the zenith of the 6,300 rpm power curve, and that the torque plateau was confined to the 4,000–5000-rpm band.

Drawing: BMW Presse, 1977

The 1982 season was important for the switch in September of that year to a standard five-speed gearbox fitment and the UK "Specials." These cost £9,867 in manual trim and £10,613 for the automatic cousin which, as in the 320/6, incorporated power steering. The original 3 Series did not usually breach £10,000 in the UK, except as a Cabriolet 323i, a combination that retailed at £10,547 in 1980. The 323i automatic saloon listed at £9,300 when it was replaced by the E30 for 1983.

The 323i special version was even more collectible than the 320/6 because just 175 were UK-ordered, and they were very distinctive in two-tone paint. Tints of gray were the order of the day—"Ascot" for the higher levels and "Graphite" for the lower panels. Within, an anthracite cloth was installed and complemented by Recaro sport front seats, seat head restraints, and the inevitable sporty steering wheel.

Production-dynamic changes were more serious than for 320/6, with gas-damped sports suspension listed along with front and rear spoilers—the forward one in matching graphite and the back in standard black. The options list included the manual steel sliding roof and BBS alloy wheels carrying standard Michelins.

In retrospect, the 323i was a fine BMW that was faster than any obvious rival, and built to quality levels emphasized by the six-year anti-rust pledge given in the early 1980s. *AUTOhebdo* summarized its assets neatly, asserting the advantages as: "marvelous six-cylinders; fantastic gear change; steering and driving position; brakes ('durable and powerful'); efficient road holding; sporty and comfortable." The downside? "A sports gear box is an option; too many options."

5 Racing Back to Happiness

Not an obvious racing competitor the 3 Series turned into a regular winner. And that was before they added a turbocharger...

When BMW took a direct interest in contesting American IMSA Camel events, the 1977 German Championship (with the first BMW Junior Team), and the World Formula 1 Championship, it was the 3 Series that delivered some basic hardware and F1-prototype power. BMW Motorsport utilized a 320 engine/chassis platform that was radically re-engineered to succeed at the highest levels.

Was the ability to turn rest into 60 mph in less than 4.5 seconds radical enough? Or the capability to corner that 2-door sedan body like a lightweight Formula car? Then to keep those performances up for hours of global endurance races? BMW Motorsport GmbH achieved all that in the late 1970s, supported by the increasing effectiveness of the Schnitzer concern at Freilassing on the Austro-German border.

BMW Motorsport also benefited commercially, selling over thirty of the BMW 320 racing kits at more than $50,000 apiece in 1978. The M12/7 motor alone represented $13,694 of the package, offering a durable 305 bhp in normally-aspirated form. Demand grew to such an extent (over 500 race engines were made for sedans and formula cars) that there was a period when pedigree M12/7s were built in a corner of the main Munich 3 Series factory. The craftsmen who built these engines in the main factory later turned their hands to BMW's M-power engines and intricacies of the company V12.

Conservative BMW AG admitted that the four-cylinder, plastic-suited, racing 320 was "a mutant." Yet the basic idea of mating the 300-horsepower Formula 2 powerplants with a radically modified 3 Series founded a formula for commercial and competitive success, thanks to BMW's amazing ability to turn out series production racing cars and engines.

A hasty, but well-conceived and tested development program yielded a 765-kg (1,683-lb) package that ran most of the day in World

Championship of Makes events to scoop the 1977/78 FIA titles in the 2-liter category. It managed all this despite the fact that its highly-stressed 1,999-cc M12/7 motor regularly revved to 9,500 rpm.

Junior Team squad members Marc Surer (pictured) and Manfred Winkelhock finished a fine third overall, and were outright class winners at the 1977 ADAC 1,000 kilometer race at Nürburgring.

Photo: Thomas Dirk Heere, 1977, via BMW Presse Archiv, 1989

German magazine figures showed that the 1977 factory BMW 320 with Formula 2 engine energy was capable of 0–62 mph in 4.4 seconds, 0–100 mph in 7.7 seconds, and 0–124 mph in 12.2 sec. An impressive 27 had been delivered by the summer of 1978.

Before the factory-backed 3 Series development in Europe and the US, the "Three" struggled for racing recognition. Obsolete BMW CSL lightweight coupes of the 1968–75 dynasty were simply too successful, and continued to dominate the European Touring Car Championship.

In European races of 4 to 24 hours on the classic continental circuits, from Czechoslovakia to Spa Francorchamps and the Nürburgring, BMW products ruled. This fact led to the abandonment of such a European Series in 1988, when the M3 seized the last of 27 titles.

A 3.2-liter Alpina-BMW was enough to outlast—and often outpace—the fragile and powerful Broadspeed-Jaguar V-12 XJC Coupes. Alpina-BMW secured the European title of 1977, and similar big Bimmers also took the 1978–79 European Championships.

Back in 1976, the author went along to watch the big Jaguar make its European Series debut in the Silverstone September Tourist Trophy. Derek Bell managed to hit the front in the white and blue Jag, but it did not last, providing time to mope around the paddock and meet some former journalistic colleagues from Germany who were out in a smart Heyco-backed 320i.

Kalli Hufstadt (famous for TV commentary in Germany) gently guided us to the German-speaking, Swiss-based, Rudi Eggenberger team which had prepared the sparkling 320i. The Eggenberger rendition of the BMW 320i had to retain a four-speed production gearbox, two valves per cylinder within 2 liters, and was said to make 220 bhp. That four-speed transmission proved to be the Eggenberger 320i's Achilles heel. Swiss Walter Brun dimmed the two-car team's fortunes considerably by subsequently rolling one example into a ball in Sicilian bandit country.

Herr Brun gave the 320i its German Championship debut September 26, 1976, at the airfield track of Hessen, but retired on lap seven. By 1980, Eggenberger had developed the 320/4 into a production-based European Championship winner.

The Eggenberger 320 won the 1980 Euro title with drivers Helmut Kelleners and Siggi Muller. It was a rare occasion, because a four-cylinder car had not won the Championship since 1974. BMW six-cylinders would go on winning in years 1981 through 1983.

323i action: Belgians and Britons

Back in 1976–77, there were a number of other privateer assaults using 3 Series power. These included a French 323i from Georges Benoit for the Spa 24 Hour race and BMW CSL preparation specialists Luigi in Belgium. The latter tapped together a very serious-looking 323i rally car in Martini-racing colors. Backed by BMW Belgium, the 1,106-kg machine sported a 2,344-cc motor with an oversized bore (80.5 mm instead of 80 mm) which operated at 10.8:1 cr. to release 222 bhp at 7,400 rpm. It also had to make do with the four-speed gearbox and was not a success.

The 1978-season test machine, with Surer at the wheel, and the men behind the radical racing 3'ers. From left to right: BMW engines engineering legend Paul Rosche, race engineer and project driving-force Rainer Bratenstein, and infield technical coordinator Dietrich Herzog in the earliest known official photo of the factory turbo installation.

Photos: BMW Werkfotos, 1978

Belgian teams persisted, however, and could take top-six places in their national rallies with the 323i in modified format. Bimmers in showroom 323i trim managed to land in the top ten until 1982. Belgian Patrick Snijers finished third in his country's 1982 Open national Rally Championship, with a 323i that finished fifth and sixth overall at European rally championship levels.

The most potent small-six 323i was also the subject of some expensive race showcasing in Britain with the organization that would become the foundation of Jaguar's sporting rebirth—TWR.

On March 6, 1979, BMW Concessionaires GB Ltd. broke new racing ground with a one-marque racing series for the 323i that was simply entitled "County Championship." Bolstered with £250,000 in prizes, it was the richest one-marque competition seen in Britain up to that point. It was structured on 12 counties racing each other on a medieval jousting basis, for over a dozen rounds.

All the Bimmers were prepared, entered, and serviced by Tom Walkinshaw Racing (TWR). The 323s were interesting, with their natural oversteer traits reversed through the use of double front anti-roll bars. Aerodynamic changes were centered upon a raised rear wing (along the lines of the old CSL) and deepened front spoiler, but one insider remembered, "The first thing you did at a circuit was to knock that front spoiler off. It was so deep, it caught on any curb, and you were always forced across the curbs in the opening laps! Besides, it was a lot faster in a straight line without the front spoiler. Not so good in the corners, but your could live with that. In fact, the spoilers were really there for good looks, because the back one didn't do much for the car in action, either."

The standard front anti-roll bar was joined by an adjustable 24-mm secondary bar, and a 19-mm unit at the back. Replacement springs and dampers were deployed, while the front struts were to TWR specification and both front ride heights and bump and rebound damper settings were adjustable. The chassis changes were aimed at improving safety with drivers of mixed-ability running in one pack.

A limited-slip differential aided traction, along with Dunlop racing tires on the

In 1979, Britain launched the quarter-million-£ County Championship Series for TWR-modified, prepared, and entered 323i sedans.

Photo: Author, Brands Hatch, UK, 1979

optional BBS Mahle 6 x 13-inch alloy wheels. The cars felt stiffly sprung and liked to understeer heavily until massively provoked.

The stripped RHD cabin included a BMW Motorsport wheel, a race seat, an internationally-approved steel roll cage, and a four-point harness. Safety measures also included feeding more air to the disc brakes and the use of unique Ferodo DS11 brake-pads.

Performance was improved through lower weight (the interior was stripped and fiberglass was used for the hood and trunk lid) and signifi-

cant engine modifications. These included a gas-flowed and refinished cylinder head operating at a 9.8:1 cr. and replacement exhaust parts that culminated in a twin-pipe side exhaust that complied with a 115-dba noise-level. Engine output was increased some 20 percent to a claimed 170 bhp.

County Championship drivers for 1979–80 were picked by dealers in the selected counties and included some familiar names to early 1990s Grand Prix spectators: Nigel Mansell and Martin Brundle. Other participants included John Watson, Derek Bell, Winston "Win" Percy, Dieter

320: Factory racing record

The principle achievements of the Group 5 BMW 320s were overall runner-up and 2-liter class honors in world endurance events. The main home market glory came in running a three-car team of normally aspirated 320s in the 1977 German Championship.

Under the title "BMW Junior Team," BMW Motorsport boasted, "For the first time in the history of German motor racing, a car manufacturer now presents a team made up entirely of newcomers to the racing scene." They supported the careers of the already promising Italian-American citizen Eddie Cheever (then 18 years old), Marc Surer (then 25 years old), and Manfred Winkelhock (then 25 years old).

The trio faced intense opposition from

the Zakspeed Ford Escort team and the sibling rivalry of the Schnitzer 320 turbo program: Schnitzer won the German title outright in 1978. It is not an exaggeration to say that the Juniors crashed and bashed their way through the early part of the season, which resulted in Surer having his racing license suspended.

1977 Junior Teammates Marc Surer of Switzerland (in front) and Manfred Winkelhock in typically close 320 racing.

Photo: Unknown photographer, BMW Presse, 1989

Quester, and Barrie Williams. Many of the aces were understandably loath to come and get another drubbing from Barrie "Whizzo" Williams. The Series was discontinued for 1981.

When asked how the 323 was to drive, Williams said candidly, "Depended on who you were, really. They varied quite a lot. There were times when I thought I won too easily—because the car was quicker, rather than me. Then I got beaten in my turn by a car that was obviously faster. We never knew what had happened to them when they were taken away. You just raced what you were given.

"Generally, they were smoother and more powerful than the usual one-make, front-drive, four-cylinder hatchbacks. Not bad cars at all, in fact—just with a lot of understeer dialed in to keep the accidents down," concluded Williams.

Pininfarina used it's windtunnel to co-develop the E21 body for life beyond 160 mph. The extended wheelarches and aggressive spoilers also served as the foundations for 320 turbo racers.

Photo: BMW Werkfoto, Italy, 1976–77

The most famous Juniors of Germany

The 3 Series made a rambling European competition debut in Group 2 and one-marque guise, but when BMW Motorsport and McLaren North America came to grips with its potential, it became a potent racing saloon.

320: Factory racing record, continued

Left: 1977 Junior Team driver, Eddie Cheever (US)

Center: 1977 Junior Team driver, Marc Surer (Switzerland)

Right: 1977 Junior Team driver, Manfred Winkelhock (Germany)

Photos: BMW Werkfoto, 1977

Team manager Jochen Neerpasch disciplined his "boys" by running the comparatively elderly "BMW Senior Team," which was unofficially dubbed, "Gentleman Team." It featured, on occasion, the dynamite combination of Hans Stuck and Ronnie Peterson.

Manfred Winkelhock—subsequently killed racing a Porsche—justified his selection by overcoming the

As has been the case for many of BMW's most effective competition cars, the 3 Series was very rapidly developed. The company was able to use some hardware left over from the glory days of the CSL coupes. BMW also used a very experienced team to test the 3 Series racer, including famed team manager John Wyer, Brian Redman and Grand Prix driver Ronnie Peterson.

Then 37 years of age, Rainer Bratenstein was assigned with the task of technical leadership on the BMW Junior Team project. BMW Motorsport obtained his services directly from Porsche R&D at Weissach. Bratenstein spoke freely about the 3 Series transformation into a competition car. "In three months we had to do the job! It would have been quite simply impossible to develop this car in the conventional way on the drawing board. Even if we had fifty designers, it would not have been possible."

The basic starting points were the steel inner panels of the E21 3 Series and the M12/7 Formula 2 motor. All exterior panels, except those of the roof and associated outline, were replaced by fiberglass components. Plexiglass was used rather than regular window glass on all but the front windscreen, while the aviation business contributed Teflon-insulated wiring harnesses to beat the heat.

The extensive spoiler areas were also done in glass-reinforced plastics; but enlarged back spoilers were a feature of the turbocharged models, especially in German championship trim from Schnitzer or GS Tuning. Some teams only had the resources to fabricate rear spoilers using aluminum rather than the more expensive fiberglass.

The factory racing lightweight panels were all subject to wind-tunnel testing, mostly at the Pininfarina facility in Turin. The main sources of aerodynamic drag were identified in the possible use of ducting in the front "snow-shovel" spoiler and around the air intakes that were needed to feed side-mounted oil and water radiators.

The minimal inner sheet metal had to be

320: Factory racing record, continued

frustrations of the year and securing the class title. Winkelhock was third overall behind the Porsches of Rolf Stommelen and Bob Wollek. Cheever, subsequently seen in American CART/IRL racing and a winner of the Indy 500, plus German-speaking Swiss Surer, amassed enough points to finish in the top six overall.

In the poorly-supported 1977 and 1978 FIA World Championship of Makes, BMW 320 made overall second place to Porsche in both seasons, winning the 2-liter class comfortably on both occasions.

Top: Hans Stuck tackles the 1978 Group 5 World Endurance Championship round at the Nürburgring in the Faltz machine.

Photo: BMW Archiv, 1999

Bottom: At Norisring 1977's German Championship event, Marc Surer has just finished encountering the Heyer Zakspeed Ford, earning him a three-month race-license suspension.

Photos: Eberhard Strahle (Norisring), via BMW Presse, 1989/LAT(grass-cutter), Author Archiv, 1990

extensively reworked to accommodate an engine set back in the frame by 120 mm (4.7 inches) and lowered some 60 mm (2.4 inches). A roll cage with full driver door opening "chicken bars" for maximum side protection took on many of the duties met by the original body, as well as loads far beyond road duty.

Chassis changes

The motivation behind the lowered and re-positioned four-cylinder location in the 320 racer was handling balance. That objective was also achieved by moving some heavier components to the trunk, including the battery and dry-sump oil tank. In the competition E21, brackets were also needed to house the inner driveshaft-driven alternator—a trick learned on the CSL racing coupes. The rear suspension arms were mounted to totally different underbody attachments, requiring further fabrication.

Stupendous braking and basic chassis capabilities literally withstood double the initial

Later to become the SCCA's racing director, Nick Craw was an effective BMW racer of the 1970s in both the 2002 and the 3'er.

Photo: Klaus Schnitzer, US, 1977

competition power. The recipe was based on more CSL lore, including Ate ventilated disc brakes that were cross-drilled in the front and radially grooved in the rear. No servo assistance was required by the massive four-piston calipers. The driver could adjust braking balance fore and aft from the cabin. Commenting on the braking effectiveness at Brands Hatch in 1977, Tom

320: Factory racing record, continued

Right: The Wurth tools-backed normally-aspirated E21 was lucky number 13 for Manfred Winkelhock, who won the Junior class battle in 1977 and finished third overall in the German national title hunt.

Photo: Werner Eisele, 1977, via BMW Presse, 1989

Below: A damp Nurburgring confrontation to remember, with the baby Bimmers, led by Ronnie Peterson, seething around Hans Heyer's lone Zakspeed Ford Escort.

Photo: Unknown German photographer, via BMW Presse, 1989

The non-turbocharged 320s were not quick enough to win outright against turbocharged six-cylinder Porsches, but they recorded a number of third-overall places (notably at Nürburgring and Mosport, Canada) in 1977. These were magnificent achievements for drivers Gilles Villeneuve, Cheever, Surer, and Winkelhock.

Walkinshaw stated that, "They just stop the thing dead, miles before you think it's possible."

Theoretically, suspension carried over the MacPherson strut front layout principles with a trailing arm at the back. But one look swiftly dashes the notion that it had anything more than theory in common with the showroom vehicle. The front Bilstein strut inserts were encased in aluminum (threaded to allow ride height adjustment), and located by purpose-built lower arms and longitudinal links.

The center-lock hubs, for pit-stop speed, were crafted in aluminum, with magnesium used for the upright sections. No rubber bushes were used at all, and formula car bearings served to joint the suspension arms and links. Based on an abbreviated box-section steel CSL racing design, the rear suspension trailing arms were drilled for low weight, and mounted on ball joints to the body. Titanium coil springs were also carried over from the original racing project cars.

Transmission lore

The rear axle was unusual, in that a locked, rather than limited-slip, differential was used. It featured Halibrand drop gears and CSL Group 5 driveshafts. The 5-speed gearboxes of both racing 320 types were by Getrag, but the turbocharged model utilized a heavier-duty Type 265.3.5, as used in the CSL for long-distance events. The 305-bhp Group 5 racers used a then-new Getrag 245/6, which was not quite as much of a heavyweight, featuring non-synchromesh racing gears within a BMW production casing.

Nick Craw in action with the best-known racing 3 Series of its era, the Miller and Norburn 320i.

Photo: Klaus Schnitzer, Lime Rock, US, 1977

Nick Craw was a fine racer, and the BMW's chassis was good enough to support this kind of close encounter with the AMC Gremlin.

Photo: Klaus Schnitzer, Lime Rock, US, 1977

The rearward position of the gearbox necessitated modification to the floorpan and an enlarged transmission tunnel. This move matched the retreat of the powertrain to menace the front bulkhead. Clutch components were of twin-plate Borg & Beck origin on the less-powerful variant, with triple plates for the turbos.

The 3-piece BBS wheels were usually of 16-inch diameter, and could be up to 14 inches wide—11-inches up front—and 19-inches in diameter at the back. For the turbo, "atmo" 320 racers were designed to run 12.5-inch rim widths.

Goodyear supplied the factory-team tires, and the design sizes were 10/22.0–16 for the front of both turbocharged and "atmo" 320 racers. The same size was used on the rear for all but the turbocharged racers, which accommodated 12.5/22.0–19 rubber.

Proven power

The M12/7 Formula 2 BMW motor operated in the upright position, rather than the production slant installation. This modification was inspired by Josef Schnitzer and also applied to the 1970s six-cylinder coupes. The fours were topped by a substantial 16-valve, DOHC cylinder head. Considerable adaptation and fabrication was demanded to accommodate its formula-car exhaust system and dry-sump lubrication within the confines of the production car engine bay. The required fuel was 100-plus-octane gasoline, fed by Kugelfischer mechanical injection to an 11.2:1 cr. chamber with central spark plug. All the electrical systems, including a 0.8-hp starter motor and condenser ignition with electronic rpm limiter, were supplied by Bosch.

The unit measured 1,999 cc, based on an 89.2-mm bore and 80-mm stroke. A steel crankshaft and associated racing components (including 35.8-mm inlet valves and 30.3-mm exhausts) operated "between 7,000 and 9,500 rpm." Peak power was officially reported at 305 bhp on 9,250 rpm, and maximum torque was quoted as the equivalent of 166 lb-ft.

Detail development, particularly around his favored camshaft profiles, allowed BMW engines engineering maestro Paul Rosche to reflect, "By the close of Formula 2 [1984], we could say that the average maximum power had risen from 275 to 315 bhp, equivalent to 157.6 bhp a liter. The best we ever saw was 321 bhp and the normal maximum power zone was 9,500 to 10,000 revs;

1978 Group 5 Racing (non-turbo performance figures averaged from independent German tests)				
Km/h	Mph	Works 320 2.0 Atmo	Schnitzer 2002tii 2.0 Atmo	Ford Escort Zakspeed 2.0 Atmo
0–40	25	1.9	1.8	1.9
0–60	37	2.7	2.6	2.8
0–80	50	3.2	3.5	3.8
0–100	62	4.4	5.3	5.1
0–120	75	5.4	7.3	6.7
0–160	100	7.7	11.8	10.5
0–200	124	12.2	17.5	16.8

the final evolution version (M12/7/1) gave best power on 10,200."

The M12/7 motor in a single-seater was credited by the late Manfred Winkelhock with 307 bhp in 1978, plus 245 Nm (177 lb-ft) at 8,000 rpm. In a works March 782 of 500 kg (1,100 lbs), it returned 0–100 km/h (0–62.5 mph) in 3.5 seconds, 0–100 mph in a scant 6.6 seconds, and 0–124 mph in 10.2 seconds.

The table above shows how the normally-aspirated BMWs performed in the 1970s. A detailed overall comparison, including turbocharged BMWs and their opponents, appears in Chapter 6.

6 The Turbocharged Terror

Turbocharging put this simple sedan on Porsche's pace.

Whereas the normally-aspirated 320 was a straightforward racer of known durability and handling qualities, the BMW we'll call 320T ("T" for turbo) was much more erratic, but an outright winner. Developed on both sides of the Atlantic, it was valuable for its contribution to BMW's Grand Prix engine of the 1980s and its nine-win record in the US, where it was regularly outgunned by the local Porsches.

The 320Ts appeared in three different arenas: German national championships (1.4-liters); World Championship of Makes (the troubled 2-liters); and IMSA/Winston GT in the US, using 2-liters, not the often-quoted 2.1.

Retiring (late 1999) BMW engines engineering chief Paul Rosche acknowledged a number of German championship inputs to the Formula 1 motor program. By 1977, Schnitzer was ready to abandon its 9,400-rpm/292-bhp, normally-aspirated 2002 racers and debuted the turbo 1.4-liter at some 360 to 380 bhp. This was realized on a compression ratio of 6.9:1 within a 1,426-cc concoction (80 x 71 mm), in contrast to the experimental M12/12 short-stroker of 89 x 57.5 mm that Rosche researched in Munich. Schnitzer power allowed the 2002 to screech from rest to 60 mph in less than five seconds and to 100 mph in only 10 seconds.

In 1977, the Schnitzer turbo 2002 immediately proved to be effective: Albrecht Krebs set the first sub-eight-minute lap (7 minutes 58 seconds, with an average speed of 106.8mph!) for a 2-liter class car around the Nürburgring. Schnitzer teammate Peter Hennige scored the first victory for the 1.4-liter Schnitzer 2002 turbo project, conquering the class in the Kassel Calden event of May 8, 1977.

The team had to overcome the inevitable head gasket and transmission problems to make the smaller turbo a regular winner, but in

In 1978, the combination of Harald Ertl and a 1.4-liter Schnitzer-prepared and entered lightweight 3 Series sped away from the opposition.

Photo: BMW Werkfoto, Hockenheim, Germany, 1978: reprinted 1985

1977 they couldn't always manage it. Another win for the Schnitzer 2002 turbo formula in 1977 came from former Ford and Porsche pilot Klaus Ludwig.

Although Josef Schnitzer died in a 1978 road accident, BMW supported Schnitzer's company to swap from 2002 to Group 5 racing 320 technology. The Schnitzer company's cooperation with BMW prospered into 2000, culminating in that magnificent 1999 Le Mans victory for the V12 LMR, and multiple American ALMS series wins.

The 320 Schnitzer assembled for Austrian Harald Ertl to master the 1978 German Championship was very special. Based on the competition 320i, it had to race at 1,426 cc to fall within the 2-liter class when turbocharged. The previous 80 x 71-mm dimensions drew on KKK (Kuhlne Kopp & Kausch) turbocharging and developed 410 bhp (257.5 bhp a liter) at 9,400 revs. Some 441 lb-ft of torque at 7,500 rpm was enough to propel the further modified Group

5 BMW-Schnitzer 320 to 172 mph. All this was achieved on a mild 1.2 bar boost.

BMW increased boost (to 1.5 bar) and modified the breathing of that 1.4-liter, yielding a maximum of 610 bhp, more than enough to be competitive in Formula 1. Paul Rosche affirmed, "The real point about European Formula 2 for all those years, for BMW Motorsport, was that it gave us a basis for a lot of other projects." These included quad-valve technology transfers to the M3 and turbocharged 16-valve DOHC developments, first seen in the E21 racing 3 Series, and then as the M12/13 series, for Grand Prix racing.

Rosche explained, "The Schnitzer car of '78 was interesting, so we got behind the 1979 GS Tuning of Freiburg 320 for Markus Höttinger." Höttinger subsequently died in a Hockenheim racing accident, but this 1979 320T in Jägermeister orange has been beautifully preserved by BMW Mobile Tradition. It remains an important link between sedan racing and Grand Prix technology at BMW.

Back in 1978, motoring journalist Harald Ertl

Harald Ertl gets the jump on the neighboring Ford Capri turbo in the run down to the first corner at Hockenheim.

Photo: BMW Werkfoto, Hockenheim, Germany, 1978.

This side view emphasizes the extended front and rear spoiler sets needed to balance out the 400 bhp generated in the flyweight 1.4-liter Three of 1978.

Photo: BMW Archiv, Germany, 1978, reprinted 1999.

Winning style: Harald Ertl and one of two 1978 Championship-winning Schnitzer 320Ts fielded that season. Note the aluminum rear wing, and the side radiator layout that increased rearward weight bias and boosted traction.

Photo: BMW Archiv, Germany, 1978, reprinted 1999

including a brace of second places.

Ertl won five Division 2 (up to 2-liter) races in the 11-race Deutschenrennsport Meisterschaft (DTM) series of 1978, including the Hockenheim Grand Prix-supporting event. BMW-engined cars won ten of the eleven 2-liter class races that season. Ertl won the title with 162 points, compared to a score of 140 points by Porsche-mounted Dutchman Toine Hezemans. The next best 320 was that of Markus Höttinger, who tied for fourth with two Porsche pilots.

Instantly recognizable by his distinctive beard, Harald Ertl was an affable and articulate character who earned a great deal of respect in single seaters, particularly campaigning at Hesketh as a game Grand Prix privateer, before his untimely death in a light airplane accident in the 1980s.

was able to seize the German national title against fierce Ford and Porsche opposition. Ertl had the pick of two Rodenstock- and Sachs-backed Group 5 Schnitzer 320Ts, both running Dunlop tires. Despite bouts of unreliability that required triple and quadruple water radiators, accommodated in now-bulging side pods, the championship was won with seven podium positions,

In November 1978, Germany's Sport Auto magazine profiled the Champion 320T, making some fascinating comparisons with rival contemporary machinery, as well as with competitors of the past. The latter was represented by the 2-liter Schnitzer 2002, a machine credited with 295 bhp, representing 149 bhp a liter versus 280.3 of the later Schnitzer turbo. Scoured from other

German magazine/ book sources over the years, the figures shown in the table to the right, give us the unique overview.

BMW's British engine associates, Nicholson McLaren engines, worked hard to redevelop the Formula 2 engine and turbocharging for worldwide BMW factory use. Meanwhile, the BMW M1 supercar was prepared to go up against Porsche's mostly unopposed progress in world roofed-racing classes. Unfortunately, this program lacked timing and never blossomed as it should have, and the BMW factory-backed racing effort in the US withered in the early eighties.

Nicholson McLaren at Colnbrook, outside London, and McLaren at Livonia, Michigan, succeeded in making the 320T an occasional American race winner. It had an initial maximum of 620 bhp from a Garrett AiResearch installation, puffing at 1.3 bar on 2 liters. The big problems came when the German factory team tried to run the US McLaren turbo specification in Europe. Whether testing or racing, a spate of piston failures—probably due to fuel octane—resulted. Sunoco routinely produced higher octane numbers that allowed the turbo to reach 7.5:1 or even 8:1 cr. while receiving 1.25 to 1.3 bar (up to 18.5 psi) boost. In Europe, 7:1 was the order of the day, using the same peak boost. The intercoolers were located at the front of the car, as for the production water radiator.

Hans Joachim Stuck and Ronnie Peterson drove the 320 turbo in Europe. A flame-belching sight to behold, this turbocharging alliance did not achieve the results one might have expected from the steamroller record

BMW vs. "The Rest": 1978 Group 5 Racing Performance (in seconds)						
Km/h	Mph	Works 320 2.0 Atmo	Schnitzer 320T 1.4	Schnitzer 2002tii 2.0	Ford Zakspeed 2.0 Atmo	Porsche Kremer 2.9 turbo
0–40	0–25	1.9	3.0	1.8	1.9	1.7
0–60	0–37	2.7	3.7	2.6	2.8	2.5
0–80	0–50	3.2	4.3	3.5	3.8	3.3
0–100	0–62	4.4	5.1	5.3	5.1	4.0
0–120	0–75	5.4	6.0	7.3	6.7	4.7
0–160	0–100	7.7	8.2	11.8	10.5	7.0
0–200	0–124	12.2	12.7	17.5	16.8	10.3

of McLaren-Honda or McLaren-Mercedes in recent Grand Prix. However, it taught BMW Motorsport a lot about 2-liters under the stress of 300 bhp per liter. This performance gave Paul

Markus Höttinger was chosen by BMW Motorsport to drive its development turbo-engined 320 in preparation for its Grand Prix career.

Photo: BMW Archiv, Germany 1978, reprinted 1999

Harald Ertl was a larger-than-life motor journalist as well as a talented driver who briefly reached Grand Prix status.

Photo: BMW Archiv, 1999

Rosche and his team insight into four-cylinder turbocharging lore, before they tackled the Brabham-BMW 1.5-liter GP era.

Turbo trail

The turbocharged variant of the BMW M12 theme was coded M12/9 for the 320, to become 320T. It was plumper, transporting 26.4 gallons of fuel instead of 22 gallons, plus all the ancillary weight created by the turbocharger at the front. In World Championship guise, a 320t weighed 1,936 lbs (880 kg), although it was lighter in US form.

Top: Run under the GS (Gerhard Schneider) Tuning banner, this is the intensively redeveloped front end of the 1979 Markus Höttinger 320 turbo that taught the factory so much about the practicalities of small-bore turbos.

Bottom: The Höttinger BMW 320 of 1979 is perfectly preserved by BMW Mobile Tradition.

Photos: Author, Munich, Germany, June 1999

The best power recorded was from the American version, at 654 bhp, which gave it a power-to-weight ratio of better than 800 bhp a ton in the US. The peak torque was 353.7 lb-ft on higher-octane American fuel, up almost 200 lb-ft from the normally-aspirated racer!

Aside from its lowered compression ratio (7:1 to 7.5:1, according to gasoline octane rating), the M12/9 was dimensionally the same slightly short-stroke 1,999 cc as the M12/7. It was credited with more than 600 bhp from the start, but Paul Rosche said that 500 to 550 bhp was the more realistic endurance racing figure.

A 1978 American move to radiators behind the back wheels brought 20-degree water temperature reductions, better traction, and 610 to 620 bhp. This allowed BMW North America driver David Hobbs to assert in August 1978, "I just don't see how we can wind much more horsepower out of it. Even if we do, we still don't have the torque and that sheer pulling power away from slow corners."

The American specification incorporated much local content, including TRW pistons, Carello connecting rods, and the Garrett AiResearch turbocharger. The camshafts and the valves differed from the Formula 2 specification, although the valves were the same size used in Formula 2/320 Group 5. "Softer" camshaft timing and inherent docility of the turbocharged unit was emphasized by a power range from 6,000–9,500 rpm for the turbo, while 7,000 was the starting point without the turbo.

Talking torque at his British outing in 1977, Ronnie Peterson noted how easy it was to lose time if caught in traffic. By single-seater standards, a 320 had a comparatively heavy body and a small motor to overcome any inherent turbo "lag." This was offset by stunning handling and braking. Peterson proved that talent combined with a manageable car could overcome cubic inches, but it was always an uphill battle against the bigger-capacity Porsches.

Hans Stuck's 1980 Schnitzer 320T had to face intense opposition from the ex-BMW German Champion Harald Ertl in a Zakspeed Ford Capri.

Photo: BMW Archiv, Germany, 1980, reprinted 1999

This Schnitzer turbo motor was among the Munich Legends stock on display at the 1999 Goodwood Festival of Speed in England.

Photo: Author, Goodwood, UK, June 1999

The McLaren BMW alliance was funded by BMW North America and produced some excellent wins against predominantly turbocharged Porsche 911 opposition.

Photo: Author Archive, 1978

David Hobbs' BMW 320T finished fifth at Lime Rock USA, where it was outgunned by the V8s and turbo Porsches.

Photo: Klaus Schnitzer, US, 1978, reprinted 2000

BMW Race Record, 1977–78 320i/320T

The BMW 320T was supplied by BMW Motorsport GmbH, who gave technical support throughout the seasons. Sponsorship in these two seasons came from Citicorp, with additional backing from BMW NA. Ex-pat Englishman David Hobbs drove in the IMSA rounds, while he, Ronnie Peterson, Sam Posey, Tom Klausler and Hans-Joachim Stuck drove in the Internationals. The 320 was turbocharged at Road Atlanta in 1977, the second event.

1977			1978		
Event/circuit	Start pos.	Result	Event/circuit	Start pos.	Result
Daytona	19	DNF, engine	Daytona	3	DNF, piston
Atlanta	28	4th	Sebring	1	DNF, accident
Laguna Seca	1	24th	Atlanta	2	DNF, accident
Mid America	5	DNF, ignition	Laguna Seca	4	4th
Lime Rock	2	DNF, fire	Hallet	2	1st
Mid Ohio	2	1st	Lime Rock	2	5th
Brainerd	20	DNF, gearbox	Brainerd	2	DNF, wastegate
Watkins Glen	2	DNF, accident	Daytona	3	29th
Sears Point	2	1st	Watkins Glen	5	DNF, turbo
Pocono	2	DNF, drive shaft	Sears Point	1	1st
Mosport	2	9th	Portland	2	DNF, turbo
Mid Ohio	2	DNF, throttle	Mid Ohio	3	2nd
Atlanta	1	1st	Atlanta	4	DNF, gearbox
Laguna Seca	1	1st			
Daytona	4	DNF, accident	DNF=Did Not Finish		

Late in 1977, the factory debuted the 320T racer, which was a transatlantic alliance between its own turbo technology and that of McLaren North America, using additional input from John Nicholson in the UK.

Photo: Colin Taylor Productions, UK, September 1977

How did McLaren and BMW come to their first alliance, one to be echoed in the 1990s McLaren F1-BMW V12 ? Teddy Mayer, the American lawyer who ran the Bruce McLaren Grand Prix and USAC team effort in Britain, recalled how McLaren and BMW got together for the 1977 season. Mayer reported, "I knew of Neerpasch for some time before this business came up. It was obvious BMW wanted to continue racing in America and we had the right facilities, especially the engine shop. BMW were looking for the right people, and it just seemed kind of logical that we'd get together."

David Hobbs in search of mid range speed at Lime Rock.

Photo: Klaus Schnitzer, US, 1978, reprinted 2000

The 320T raced from 1977–79 but was always at the edge of durability and chassis ability to make up for mid-range muscle and a comparative lack of cubic inches.

Photo: Klaus Schnitzer, US, 1978, reprinted 2000

American trio

It was tough to make an impression with a 2-liter turbo versus the V8s and larger-capacity turbo Porsche six-cylinders, but David Hobbs always showed total commitment.

Photo: Klaus Schnitzer, US, 1978, reprinted 2000

A trio of 320 racers was imported to get the US racing job done with McLaren NA. Chassis 001 was the normally-aspirated 300 bhp ex-Junior team car raced just once in its original format (at Daytona in February 1977). It was then reworked by McLaren NA around the turbo motor. Body changes included the "cow-catcher" front spoiler and a custom rear item: it stretched a lot further rearward. They expanded side sills/rear wheel-arch extensions to house 19 x 14-inch wide rear wheels in place of the usual 16 x 12.5 inches, plus additional radiators and intercooling.

"001" was crashed at Sebring early in 1978 and rebuilt as a convenient further extension to the European turbo work in progress, an attempt to establish the validity of a 1.5 liter Grand Prix motor. This was the unsponsored, plain-white 320T run at Mid Ohio in 1978 by Tom Klausler and David Hobbs, while the regular car wore Citicorp livery.

The 002 chassis was a turbo 320 and debuted at Mosport in August 1977. IMSA rules changed rapidly,

In December 1969, McLaren established its suburban Detroit premise to have a base for both the Indianapolis and Can-Am operations. The link with BMW came from McLaren engine man Gary Knudsen. Gary gathered a lot of experience with four-cylinder turbocharged American racing engines through McLaren single-seater USAC formula racing cars using Offenhausers. To look after BMW's racing interests, a separate McLaren North America Corporation was established from 1977 onward. By 1978, it had nine employees and its racing team manager was Englishman Roger Bailey.

According to Teddy Mayer, "The 320 seemed just ripe for turbocharging. That Formula 2 engine base was just a super engine, and you've got to hand it to Paul Rosche for one of the best little racing engines around. Our job was strictly about IMSA, but we did some World Championship rounds on the North American continent too—Sebring, Daytona, Mosport—that kind of thing.

"We were able to stiffen the car up a little by making the roll cage do some more of the work, and we stitched the front end together a little. That first season, we found the Porsches weren't quite ready, and you have to say we were unlucky not to win more than the four races we did get.

"In 1978, it was a different game. It's asking a lot for a 2-liter sedan to take on a twin-turbo with 3 liters and more. On the fast tracks, the aerodynamics are not comparable to a Porsche, and it's been uphill all the way. We could have done a little more to the car but it really would get very expensive," concluded Mayer in a 1979 interview.

For 1979, BMW redoubled their efforts, supplying flamboyant Californian Jim Busby with two cars. One of the cars was the Stuck/Peterson World Championship pioneer, and the other was brand new. Busby usually ran one car for himself, but it was very different from the factory car, wearing a "glassback" from roof to tail that considerably altered the outline. This body work was

American trio

David Hobbs in the summer of 1978. Today he is president of a Honda dealership in Wisconsin, but is still seen out in the BMW 320T at major retro events.

Photo: Klaus Schnitzer, US, 1978, reprinted 2000

and that led to the construction of the lightweight 320T, conforming to the more radical GTX category.

The final (003) chassis shipped for BMW North America's most successful road racing program prior to the 1990s was a lightweight. It had a one-piece

nose, a radiator remounted behind the back tires, NACA extraction slots in the rear fenders, and an even boxier profile.

Running in shorter events, the American McLaren 320T was lightened considerably in 1978 (90 kg, or 196 lbs, has been quoted) by the use of a new body and associated plastics, a front subframe assembly, and the substitution of lighter components for those developed in endurance events. Curb weight was estimated at 1,738 lbs (790 kg), boosting the power-to-weight ratio from around 700 bhp a ton to 849 bhp a ton, the best we know of for a racing 3 Series.

That trio of BMW North American McLaren 320T-types recorded nine outright victories. They also took the same number of pole positions, established six fastest laps, and set ten lap records in three seasons.

also seen on the 1979 German Championship contenders and was the principle behind 1986–90 M3's re-profiled rear screen.

Roger Bailey remembered that the Busby BMWs were sold to Frank Gardner's Australian BMW importer racing operation, and BMW NA retains at least one McLaren 320T in its historic fleet.

The valuable 1977–78 Citicorp backing for McLaren/BMW North America expired in 1979. The team usually then ran one car for David Hobbs that year with increased local BMW finance. The Busby cars could be identified by nose-to-tail striping in blue, red and yellow, rather than regular BMW Motorsport livery.

The American effort was the first of the BMW-backed turbos to head into the racing limelight outside Germany, and a first for the 2-liter turbo capacity. McLaren began its year with a normally-aspirated factory car at Daytona, but debuted the 320T for the April 17, 1977 Atlanta

Championship round. Troubled practice, in which they qualified 24th, was overcome with a promising fourth overall finish.

The 320T had potential, demonstrated by the four wins of 1977, but its winning chances were limited by a plethora of Porsches and by less than fantastic reliability. In the 1978 IMSA GT series, the fabled Porsche turbo 935s won 12 of 14 rounds: BMW NA, with Hobbs, won the scraps.

Just two wins was not enough, hence the Busby deal in 1979, when the series title changed to Winston GT and the 320Ts recorded three wins in their final season—all to Hobbs and McLaren. At this stage, the turbo motors came only from McLaren at Livonia, Michigan.

In 1977–79, the BMW-McLaren alliance enlivened American IMSA events among the Porsche army, but victories were within the Mission Impossible zone. One of the nine garnered was a testament to the car's durability, as it allowed nearly five hours of motoring at an aver-

American Trio, continued

Tagged the "Fire and Wind" Bimmers, they were most successfully driven by David Hobbs, who recalled them in 1992 as "quick as hell, easy to set up in corners in a four wheel drift."

Left: The 320T at the 1999 Monterey Historic meeting, when it was in the care of PTG, the Championship-winning operator of more recent race M3s.

Photo: Author, Monterey Historic Weekend (Honored Marque: Auto Union/Audi!), California, 1999

Above: This excellent silhouette study shows the oversize diameter rear wheels sported by the factory turbo in 1997–98 seasons. David Hobbs drives at Lime Rock.

Photo: Klaus Schnitzer, US, 1978, reprinted 2000

age 100.42 mph for Hobbs and Le Mans legend Derek Bell to win at Road America.

BMW never matched those 320T results in European World Championship events. Its UK Brands Hatch debut of September 1977 lasted about six laps before Stuck aquaplaned off the Kentish circuit. True, it had battled with the Ickx Porsche for pole position, but its ability to turn a fast lap never seemed to be accompanied by the durability of the North America car.

The best FIA World Championship of Makes result for the 320T was in 1978 when the North American operation had a ninth place finish in Canada, while Gilles Villeneuve and Eddie Cheever were third overall in a normally-aspirated 320.

The 320T's best-ever European performance had been at Silverstone, England, in April 1978. Hans Stuck and Ronnie Peterson managed four very competitive hours in the 6-hour international and were lying second overall behind Porsche's factory 3.2-liter twin-turbo when the differential failed.

7 Second Edition: More of Everything

From an ultra successful convertible to the Europe-only Touring and the M3, the E30 became the master of a thousand 3'er disguises.

The debut of the 318i in the US in 1983 certainly sparked comment. Some BMW watchers did not rate the 1,766-cc, 101-bhp package that was the only choice for American buyers during its first sales year. This change-over year must have created a few worried faces at the BMW NA offices, because 3 Series sales fell (by 1,843 units) for the first time in its American market history . BMW NA must have wondered if $16,430 was simply too much to charge for a two-door without a radio—especially since the price of the 320i had been held at $13,290 since October 1981. Here's what the critics said:

> After a six-year model run in which each year saw more sales than the year before, BMW's popular 320i sports sedan steps aside to make way for its successor: the BMW 318i.
> —BMW NA OFFICIAL PRESS RELEASE, 1983 LAUNCH OF E30

> Some cars have it rough. The birth of any new automobile is an important event, but when it's a baby BMW, expectations run significantly higher than normal. After all, the littlest BMWs have reigned as the definitive sports sedans for nearly twenty years now.
> —CAR AND DRIVER, 318I TEST INTRODUCTION, JULY 1983

> The new small BMW is better in almost every way: more efficient, quieter, better-riding, better handling, a tad roomier and significantly more comfortable. On

*the other hand, performance is
off and the price is up.*
—*Road & Track,*
318i test verdict,
July 1983

*I've always felt the 320i was
over-priced and over-rated,
coasting on a reputation of
automotive excellence....For the
money involved here I'd rather
have last year's Volvo GLT than
this year's 318i. I'd rather have
a SAAB 900 turbo. I'd rather
have an Audi Coupe. I'd rather
have....*
—*Car and Driver,*
"Counterpoint,"
Jean Lindamood,
July 1983.

Despite the shaky start, BMW NA need not
have worried. As standard equipment they had
included air conditioning, alloy wheels and fog
lamps from the earlier 320i option list, not to
mention power steering, Service Interval indicator, and analogue fuel economy indicator. BMW
NA sales were back on track for 1985, when the
second-generation 3 Series accounted for over

53,000 units (almost 65 percent) of the record
84,008 units BMW NA shifted that season. The
new 3'er quickly became the backbone of the
mid-1980s BMW line in the US, and sold a
record 61,822 examples in 1986. This benchmark
would not be exceeded for almost ten years,
when the E36 sold nearly 65,000 units in 1993.

The second-edition 3'er was a commercial
if not a complete critical success, but to understand the model properly, we need to trace its
evolution. It is annoying to read about the many
models not sent to the US, but things did get
better in America during 1983–90. The fact
that the high-performance M3 was officially
imported to the US was a major breakthrough,
demonstrating that there were profits as well as
prestige to be generated by performance cars in
North America.

October and November 1982 saw the BMW
test-track launch (at Ismaning) of the E30 3
Series. Like so many other "new" BMWs, it looked
very much like its predecessors, despite the fact
that everything but the power train was new.

The E30 was an exclusive, yet just-affordable,
car of palpable prestige and heritage. It was a sedan
designed around simple, rear-drive mechanical
principles, and would accommodate multiple

 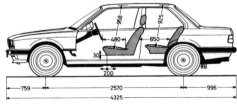 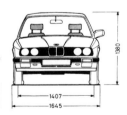

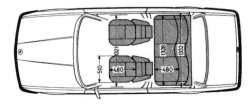

The 3 Series for the
1980s, rested on a
quarter-inch wheel-
base extension and
a 30-mm (1.2 inch)
reduction in overall
length. Width was
increased by 35 mm
(1.4 inches) over the
original 3 Series.

Drawing: BMW
Engineering Document,
Germany, released 1982

body and engine variants, most built in mass production numbers to attain high profit levels.

It's doubtful that such high-quality bodies, paint, and interiors were ever offered by BMW at such an accessible price. However, the electrical components were not up to standard, especially the notorious Service Interval Indicator and the on-board computer, plus the leaky and lazy electric windows. All of these ensured a love-hate relationship among experienced E30 owners.

The secret behind massive (2.2 million) production was the versatility of the E30. Nobody else provided a front-engine, rear-drive layout that housed power plants from the 86-bhp diesel to the 238-bhp Evolution Sport M3.

Developed over a six-year period as part of a multimillion-dollar program that saw BMW also investing heavily in the future of the 5 Series, the later Three was presented in autumn 1982. The BMW management team was led by technical director Karl-Heinz Radermacher and his sales counterpart, Hans Erdman Schönbeck. At the time, the four-door E30 was merely a static exhibit, scheduled to make production about six months after the two-doors.

The key development themes for the updated Three were the modest aerodynamic changes ("it would not be a BMW, if we went too far" commented company directors). These changes resulted in a mediocre 0.38 Cd and a significant degree of civilization and refinement, including a considerably more civil suspension and lower noise levels. Items transplanted from bigger Bimmers included a complex computer, analogue fuel economy pointer, and Service Interval indicator. In his presentation, Karl-Heinz Radermacher also forecast the appearance of diesel engines

in the 1984 3 Series for Europe, as well as anti-lock brakes.

Despite these 3 Series advances, the average model shed 40 kg (88 lbs). Abandoned aerodynamic studies, seen at the rear of some Ismaning hangers, supported BMW worries about losing identity through a sleeker outline, which would be unrecognizable without badges and kidney grilles.

Independent observers, such as L.J.K. Setright, questioned BMW's aerodynamic engineering. Knowing that at the time BMW had no wind tunnel, and that Audi had blazed a new benchmark with its 0.30 Cd 100 sedan (5000 in the US) of 1980, Setright commented, "Is not a drag coefficient of 0.38 a disappointing return for six years of development work?"

BMW happily claimed that this was "the first compact car to offer all the technical features and achievements available in large saloons." Initially there were just the two-door BMW saloons for sale starting in January 1983 in LHD Europe . The first E30s available in the US sold starting in May 1983, as did the RHD British models. Later, BMW met Mercedes' compact (190) four-door challenge, albeit as an extra-cost option (the 190 was strictly a four-door). The four-door E30s became available in November 1984 in the US and in autumn 1983 in the UK. The body offerings grew to encompass a factory convertible (though Baur of Stuttgart supplied alternative soft-tops), a five-door Touring, and the radically modified M3 homologation variant, which tripled its original factory production predictions, thanks to American sales.

The initial European two-door line stretched from the carburetted 1.8-liter four of 90 bhp to the electronic fuel injection 323i, now delivering 139 bhp in place of the original 143 horsepower.

Photos: BMW AG, 1982; BMW Archiv, 1989 reprint

Inside left- and right-hand drive E30 cabins, outstanding instrument clarity, high quality finish, and superb cabin layout are highlighted.

Photos: BMW/Author Archive, 1990

The overall measurements for the E30 four-door were the same as for the two-door. That meant a 101.2-inch wheelbase (2,570 mm, up just 7 mm from the original) within a modestly diminished overall length of 170.3 inches (4,325 mm, compared to 4,355 mm for the E21). Thanks to mandatory Federal bumpers, the overall length of an American-market 318i was 176.8 inches, or 6.5 inches longer than European equivalents.

The front and rear tracks of the E30 were within fractions of each other at 55.4 and 55.7 inches, respectively (1,407 and 1,415 mm, compared to 1386 and 1399 mm for the six-cylinder E21). The overall height was set at 54.3 inches (1,380 mm) for Europe and the US, much as before, although US models always appeared taller with lots of wheel-arch air. The width was up by 35 mm, stretching to a 64.5-inch (1,645 mm) girth.

The most critical dimension was weight. The US versions officially weighed 2,360 lbs (manual Getrag 5-speed) and 2,380 lbs (3-speed ZF automatic). The starter weight for a 318i in European trim was 1,000kg (2,200 lbs). When the test 316i

and four-cylinder European 320i were independently tested, they tipped the scales near 1,040 kg (2,288 lbs): *Car and Driver*'s test weight for a 318i was a portly 2,420 lbs (1,100 kg).

Despite that handicap, *C/D*'s test results were better than BMW predicted, turning 0–60 mph in 9.6 seconds, compared to the factory claim of 11.4 seconds. They also managed a standing 1/4 mile in 17.3 seconds, compared to the predicted 18.3 seconds. Only in top speed did the American market 318i fail to meet expectations, running a measured 106 mph compared to the factory projected113 mph.

Regarding aerodynamics, BMW engineers ignored low-drag Audis and cited stability, marque identity, and road-holding as excuses. However, some mild body contours were allowed, resulting in a quoted 15 percent reduction in drag factor, or an overall 0.37– 38 Cd, depending on tire width.

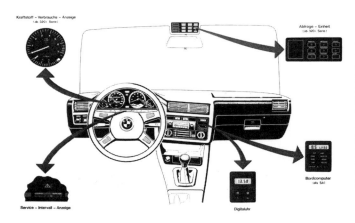

BMW embraced electronic information systems with enthusiasm. The E30 introduced the Service Interval Indicator at the lower end of the range, optional computing, a distracting roof check system of warning lights, an econometer, and digital clock.

Drawing: BMW Engineering Document, Germany, released 1982

Larger wheels—14-inch—and tires were part of the natural evolution. German fours were marketed on 175/70 HR tires, while the smallest tire fitted to a six was 195/60 VR. American 318s were shipped on the 195 sizes, but they were HR-rated.

Rim widths were not fixed by the "fatter is better" philosophy. BMW adopted the 5J x 14-inch fitment for the four-cylinder and the 5.5J x 14-inch for the sixes. All wheels were in steel at the factory level, but most national markets adopted alloys, with 6J x 14 TR as the showroom fitment in the US. In Britain, alloys cost extra (or came packaged in seductive SE models).

Both the front and rear suspensions were significantly altered, but retained MacPherson struts in front and the trailing-arms in the rear. Previously, BMW had employed the front anti-roll bar à la Ford to form part of the lower front wishbone. The re-located roll bar lurked behind the front axle and measured 18.5 mm (0.71 inches), compared to 23.5 mm (0.93 inches) on the first 3 Series. It was asked to cooperate with slightly shorter front coil springs: 130 mm (5.1 inches) compared to the earlier measurement of 152 mm (6.0 inches).

New front wishbones consisted of steel arms formed in the shape of a sickle instead of the earlier single link and were located by a single ball joint mounting. Deployed on two large rubber-bushed mountings, the complete suspension-steering subframe was biased toward low noise levels rather than location.

For the E30, principles of the MacPherson strut front and trailing-arm rear remained. Here, we show the front axle of 320/323i in Europe and the rear layout for the more powerful 323i only. Note the drilled "sickle" crescent lower arm to the front suspension, a major location improvement for the MacPherson strut front-end efficiency.

Drawing: BMW Engineering Document, Germany, released 1982

The rack-and-pinion system was re-worked to increase sensitivity; and suspension modifications cut kickback shocks and reduced steering reactions to adverse cambers. Although the rack-and-pinion ratio did not alter perceptibly from the slow original (moving from 21:1 to 21.45:1), hydraulic power assistance was standard in the US and optional in Europe. The power steering delivered a faster response at 20.51:1, but the feel at the wheel was still that of a four-turn shuffle—without the informative feedback of earlier BMWs.

One fundamental suspension change was the mounting of rear trailing arms at a pivot angle of 15 degrees, rather than at the 20-degree angle on the E21 or the 13-degree angle found on larger contemporary BMWs. The tubular steel arms were attached above the rear transverse subframe at four points, resisting squat forces under acceleration. BMW reverted to mounting the coil spring and damper separately, with the dampers positioned behind the driveshafts. A rear anti-roll bar was listed as a German market option for all but the 323i, which used a 12-mm (0.47 inches) bar and a 16-mm (0.63 inches) bar was fitted to the 318i and 320.

All these changes were said (and proven on the track) to tame the Bimmer's typically untidy loss of grip, especially the rear-end raggedness. Such a benefit was highlighted in four-cylinder models, where the weight over the front was some 537 kg compared to 580 kg for the typical six.

The first four-door 3 Series followed six months behind the two-door and was initially badged 316/318i/320i and 323i in Europe.

Photos: BMW GB, 1983; BMW Werkfoto, Germany, 1987

Anti-lock action

The E30 development news for 1982 was the optional availability of Bosch ABS anti-lock braking for the first time on the 3 Series. It was only offered on the 323i, which came with four-wheel disc brakes as standard equipment. US models did not receive anti-lock braking until 1986, when it was available on even the entry level 325—the four-cylinder 318i had been dropped.

The Mastervac braking servo-assistance now totalled 10 inches in girth, while the servo was supplied by a pressure pump on six-cylinder models. Because of the move to 14-inch wheel diameters, disc brake sizes could be increased, with BMW opting for 260mm (10.24-inch) rotors.

The fronts were served by single-piston calipers described as "fully floating" and "space-sav-

ing," as opposed to the double-piston units previously installed. Only the six-cylinder 320i and 323i had ventilated front discs, a useful improvement for the 320i to complement the addition of fuel injection (the older carburetted 320/6 did not have vented front discs).

Initially, the rear brakes on all but the 323i were of the drum type, with adjustment absorbing any slack activated by reversing. The original 3 Series did not have this useful (but sometime problematic) service feature, but did have 250-mm (9.8 inches) drums compared to the later car's 228.5-mm (9 inches) drums. The later 323i used non-ventilated disc units measuring an unchanged 258 mm (10.2 inches).

Transmissions

New manual gearboxes (drawn from both Getrag and ZF, with the 3HP-22 automatic from ZF) and final drives demanded enlarged casings. The

	E30 (post '82)			E21 (pre '82)		
	316	320/6	323i	316	320/6	323i
BHP	90	125	139	90	122	143
Top speed (mph)	109 [106]	122 [119]	125 [122]	101 [90]	112 [109]	118 [115]
@ rpm	5,740	6,270	6,090	5,890	6,100	6,040
0–31.5 (mph)	3.6 [4.8]	3.1 [4.4]	2.7 [4.2]	3.8 [4.8]	3.4 [4.6]	2.8 [4.3]
0–62.5 (mph)	12.4 [14.2]	10.4 [12.0]	9.2 [10.8]	12.5 [14.7]	10.7 [13.0]	9.5 [11.7]
0–75 (mph)	17.9 [20.5]	14.8 [16.3]	12.8 [14.6]	12.5 [14.7]	15.8 [18.8]	13.6 [15.8]
0–400m (1/4 mile)	18.2 [19.4]	17.2 [18.3]	16.5 [17.5]	18.3 [19.6]	17.4 [18.8]	16.7 [18.1]
Mpg at 56 mph	42.8 [39.2]	45.6 [37.7]	41.5 [35.8]	41.5 [37.2]	39.2 [37.7]	30.5 [26.2]
Mpg at 75 mph	32.5 [29.4]	34.9 [29.1]	35.0 [29.1]	30.4 [27.4]	29.4 [27.4]	31.1 [27.2]

Data in brackets = automatic transmission
Source: BMW Engineering, October 1982

move to larger diameter wheels was accompanied by lowered (numerically) final-drive gear sets. For example, the European 323i went down from 3.45 to 3.25:1 and the 316 went down from the E21's differential of 3.91 to 3.64:1. That 3.64:1 ratio was also shared by the first year American 318s. The effect of these changes, plus the enlarged wheels, increased sound-proofing, and rounded exterior, made for a more pleasant 3 Series experience.

Motors & performance

The major motor change for the European 3'er was to switch all but the basic 1,766-cc, 90-bhp four over to fuel injection. In the US, the introductory 318i came only with Bosch L-Jetronic and a 3-way catalyst. In the German range, the next step after a carburetted starter was a 105-bhp Bosch K-Jetronic 318i, which also reached the UK in October 1983.

The new line then swept into a pair of fuel-injected sixes, the 2-liter and 2.3-liter M20 units sharing L-Jetronic and yielding 125 and 139 bhp. Initially, Britain took all but the fuel-injected 318i, continuing to badge the 1.8-liter misleadingly as a 316, whereas the American 318i became honest about its 1,766-cc capacity.

Independent performance figures are given at BentleyPublishers.com, but BMW provided its own European LHD figures to contrast the E30 and E21. These comparisons emphasize the differences wrought by numerically lowered final drives, bigger wheels and reduced weights. The table above is a summary, signed off as the work of BMW development engineers in a unique German document.

Press reception

We opened this chapter with some American press commentary, but what did the rest of the motor press world make of the E30's arrival? The European media, led by Germany's *Auto Motor und Sport*, admitted that BMW had "no revolution with their new range." They dubbed the newcomer "Meister Proper." AMS recalled that vehicle dynamics, a sporting character, and the harmonious blend of characteristics were key elements of the BMW brand. They felt that the 3 Series upheld these qualities well.

Car of South Africa concluded of their 2-liter, 125-bhp test car, "The 320i is an attractive, distinctive car with sheer drivability which few other cars can match. It is nimble, quiet and refined with a standard of finish and appoint-

The 323i in cost-conscious steel wheel trim—as seen in many European markets—arrived in Britain in 1983 with an official sticker price below £10,000 (equivalent to under $15,000 at that time).

Photo: BMW GB, 1983

ment that will satisfy the discerning motorist used to larger cars in higher price brackets."

Down in Australia, the leading *Wheels* publication was confused by old and new models appearing simultaneously with radically differing specifications. In February 1984, it concluded, "The 323i is a hard car to classify on the Australian market, for it bridges the gap between conventional sedans and coupes. In manual form, at least [it] has brilliant performance with fine road manners. That it is also very high-geared, cramped and expensive, with styling that mirrors the old car, doesn't prevent it from selling well."

Autocar's November 1982 reaction in Britain was as follows: "First impressions are that the cars have achieved new levels of refinement." In its February 1983 summary of the 119-mph 320i, *Autocar* agreed that it offered "incomparable levels of mechanical refinement." "The engine is a jewel," bubbled the weekly, adding, "It is fast, exceptionally efficient, and generally quiet. It is amongst the best built cars in this class, and it now has better (if not perfect) handling."

American model year changes: Four-cylinders

The 318i that arrived in the summer of 1983 as a 1984 model two-door carried a suggested retail price of $16,430 including air conditioning, alloy wheels, and fog lights. The warranty remained at 36 months/36,000 miles, in contrast to the 12

months/12,000 miles offered on the British version until the 1990s.

Other features not previously offered on the 3 Series or available only in Europe included variable assistance power steering and the fuel econometer. Thus, BMW NA was satisfied that it was offering enough to account for the $3,140 price increase over the cost of the 320i. BMW predicted that "over 90 percent" would be delivered with the optional AM/FM radio/cassette player and a manual sunroof, thus taking the sticker price to $17,445.

All 1984 Model Year BMW 318s were shipped into the US with the following standard features: 5-speed Getrag 240/5 (or ZF S 5-16) manual gearbox with overdrive in 5th, 6J x 14 TR alloys with 195/60 HR (often Pirelli P6), disc/drum braking, vacuum servo-assisted, variable ratio power steering, integrated air conditioning (no E21-style console "bump"), rear window defrost, LCD digital clock, econometer, Service Interval indicator, halogen headlamps, height-adjustable front seats, tinted glass/green windshield band, electrically adjustable mirrors, two-speed wipers with flick and intermittent settings, velour carpets, lined trunk, and a traditional full tool kit.

The 1984 BMW 318i options were: an automatic 3 HP22 ZF gearbox ($595), limited-slip differential (LSD) torqued to 25 percent action, 2-way sunroof ($520), AM/FM Alpine stereo radio/cassette player, with electric antenna

($505), Electric central locking (doors, trunk, fuel cap), illuminated key ($195), leather upholstery ($790), metallic paint ($420), and electric front window lifts ($335).

Mechanically, the American 318i was rated at 101 bhp with a 1,766 cc capacity and torque was up 3 percent to total 103 lb-ft. Many motor modifications improved gas mileage, including the switch to L-Jetronic electronic fuel injection, increased compression ratio (9.3:1),

The 1988/89 BMW 325i Sport (*top*) combined a great deal of optional factory equipment to provide a striking RHD package that kept LHD-only M3 sales low. Below that, is the later M-Tech body, which nudged £20,000, equivalent to more than $30,000 at introduction.

Photos: Author, UK, 1989; BMW GB, 1989

lighter pistons, stronger crankcase and bellhousing, viscous-coupled radiator fan operation, and reduced friction losses. Official EPA gas mileage statistics for the manual model were 27 mpg City and 38 mpg Highway, while the automatic was rated at 27/34.

The 318i changed little for 1985, but the big news was the introduction of the 2.7-liter, six-cylinder 325e. BMW did, however, decide to alter the 318i's gearing, looking for improved acceleration in the first four ratios. The final drive ratio went from 3.64:1 to a 3.9:1, and fifth was lowered to 0.82 overdrive. According to BMW NA paperwork, an 0.82 fifth had always been available should a ZF rather than Getrag 5-speed have been shipped—both were listed for Model Year 1984. Despite these changes, EPA fuel economy ratings were unaltered. The interior received electronic climate control, while the option list contained one wrap-up package. Branded "Luxus," it offered electric windows, central locking, and (previously unlisted) cruise control.

For the 1986 Model Year, BMW offered only six-cylinder 325 derivatives. The 318i sales record, supplied by BMW NA, was as follows:

YEAR	SALES
1983	19,198
1984	27,782
1985	12,842
1986	907
1987	18
TOTAL	60,747

In January of 1985, BMW NA announced some important ongoing revisions for Model Year 1985, including the expansion of US BMW choices to nine models, "fulfilling a long-term objective of giving the North American customer a range of models similar to that offered in

Europe." The most important revision was the addition of the four-door 3'er with a base price of $16,925. Standard equipment on the 318i was boosted by electric window operation and central locking. Leather trim was now optional only on the 325e. The Bimmer four-door shared the $795 option of a four-speed version of the ZF 4 HP22 automatic also found on 325e, albeit with wider ratios.

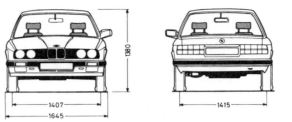

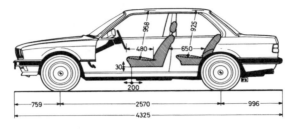

The last model-year E30 BMW in technical detail: note that German models had but one compulsory exterior mirror, even at this late stage.

Drawing: BMW Grafik, released in 1989 for 1990 Model Year 3 Series

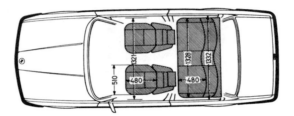

European production diary

Mass output of the E30 began in Europe in September 1982 with two-door LHD 318i and 323i models. The following month saw the 316 and automatic versions coming on stream, but all output was LHD until December 1982, when the RHD 323i and 320i began production, accompanied by the American 318i.

Less than 16,000 of the E30 newcomers were assembled in 1982, but production accelerated, topping 200,000 units a year in 1983. It passed 300,000 units annually by 1987, assisted by the ever-strengthening US market and increasing demand from right-drive Japan and Britain.

It was January 1983 before the RHD 316 was assembled, but that meant a three-model range of two-doors was ready for March 1983 sale in Britain, retailing at £6,995 to £9,935. By 1984 the cost of 323i performance would top £10,000.

All UK models came standard with electrically adjustable mirrors, a Service Interval indicator, and height-adjustable seats. The 320i added

velour carpeting to match the usual cloth trim and tachometer. The 323i delivered improvements detailed earlier, plus twin exhausts, auxiliary fog lamps, and a rear spoiler.

The chief European sales opposition to the BMW 320 was Alfa's Romeo Alfetta, Audi's 80 CD, Ford's Capri 2.8i, Lancia's HPE 2000ie, and Saab's more expensive 900 Turbo. BMW built British sales rapidly because there was no effective opposition from the Rover brands.

In Europe, output of the later 3 Series multiplied rapidly in 1983, with variations on a theme including the important four-door derivative, for which the central (B) post was moved eight inches forward to accommodate the rear door set. More confusing were the Japanese and Australian markets. The Japanese initially took a supply of left-hand drive that saw them through 1983.

It was December 1984 before Japan obtained RHD models. The Japanese specification cen-

Detailing the front in autumn 1987, we can see the ellipsoid headlamps and revised front spoiler with optional auxiliary lamps.

Photo: BMW Werkfoto, Germany, 1987

The most popular badge for many model seasons in the US was that of the slow-revving eta 325e.

Photo: BMW Werkfoto, Germany, 1985

The Federal E30 model range saw American products begin to catch up to their European counterparts, especially with respect to engine power.

Photo: Klaus Schnitzer, US, 1985

Even with upgraded suspension, bigger wheels, and Yokohamas, the understeer could prove to be a powerful pylon-terminator!

Picture: Klaus Schnitzer, US, 1997

tered on a 1.8 injection engine cleansed beyond Californian standards. The Australian RHD formula was again initially based on just the 318i, again to a unique emissions standard.

In August 1983, a BMW (GB) Ltd. dealer circular summarized the four-door specification and prices, plus the introduction of the fuel-injected 318i that had eluded the UK, as follows:

"The 318i falls neatly between the 316 and 320i and shares the 316 specification, except for a standard 5-speed overdrive gearbox. The four-door models share the same standard specification as their two-door counterparts, except that they have fully retractable rear windows and rear compartment heating. The price difference of £350 for these models will ensure very strong demand," wrote current British PR executive Chris Willows in his August directive to the dealer troops. Final production totals for E30 showed an almost fifty-fifty split for the first 3'er to offer the now-traditional two- or four-door choice.

The European BMW range now included cabriolet versions of every 3 Series, but these were the Baur conversions rather than the subsequent (and more elegant) factory convertibles.

Next, we'll deal with the age of the six-cylinder and the multiple motors implanted in the E30 Three, including the first mass-production BMW with quad valve combustion chamber layouts.

8 Power Plays

As the E30 derivatives multiplied, so did power units, with the six-cylinder 325e. An upgraded 323i, a delectably smooth 325i, the 318is, and a diesel.

At first with the 5 Series, and then with the 3 Series, BMW ran into a blind, but profitable alley with their eta economy six-cylinder engine. Strange forces were obviously at work when Bavarians opted for a Greek symbol (eta symbolized "E" for efficiency) and forsook their European high-revving mindset. Instead, America and Japan were targeted as recipients of a lazy (4,700 rpm was the advised maximum) inline six. It offered three characteristic Es: terrific economy and emissions abilities, but limited excitement.

Commercially, the 325e (re-badged 325 as an entry-level 3 Series when the 325i arrived) took BMW NA through lush pastures in the 1980s. They piled on the luxury equipment, and Yuppies stood in line to buy BMWs that got pricier by the model year. Sold strongly from spring 1984 to 1987, the eta concept wilted when a wave of higher-performance Bimmers with 6,400-rpm thrills arrived in 1987. The model remained listed as a plain 325 until 1989, but isolated examples were sold until 1990, although engine manufacture for the US market ceased in 1987.

BMW NA introduced the 325e prior to sales commencing in March of 1984: "Many enthusiasts are keenly aware of the 323i, the highest performing small BMW offered in Europe. Rather than simply adapt this new model to North American emission and fuel economy regulations, BMW created the 325e. Its introduction in America is a world premiere. With its eta powertrain, the 325e offers even great response in the speed ranges where it matters most, along with much higher fuel efficiency than a 323i tuned to American regulations would have achieved."

The eta engine—which had been around since 1981 in the European 525e—was further reworked for American 91-octane unleaded fuel rather the 97-octane leaded grades of contemporary Europe. The 2.7-liter capacity was unaltered with its longer stroke (81 x 84mm), but compression was dropped from 11:1 to 9:1 for the US and a catalytic converter was required.

The 325 motor in America (top) with associated emission gear, and the 325i European motor with (bottom) comparatively uncluttered under-hood layout.

Photos: Klaus Schnitzer, US; Author, UK, 1988

As anticipated by the BMW engineers, such octane changes effected the low-rpm eta less than had been the case with their traditional big sixes. The worst loss was 7 lb-ft from the torque peak, which was down to 170 lb-ft. However, 4 bhp clipped from the European summit of 125 bhp was insignificant

in a market that had become resigned to BMWs losing 20–30 bhp in American emissions trim.

The point of the eta was to provide exceptional fuel economy. EPA figures provided a span from 23 mpg (city) to 36 mpg on the highway, and a combined return of 27 US mpg. *Car and Driver* returned 25 mpg, which was around 3 mpg less than the high-compression European eta.

Did the 325e's performance restore some credibility to BMW's North American reputation? Those 2.7-liters were bound to make a difference over a 1.8-liter four, but the massive torque bonus over 318i was offset by a 350-lb weight gain. A 325e was only 20 bhp up, despite the additional 1.1 liters and two cylinders.

Car and Driver testers power-shifted their way from 0–60 mph in 8.4 seconds on the long (2.88:1) final drive. This obviously dazzled BMW NA, which had predicted a best of 9.4

seconds, and they mentioned the *C/D* feat in their 1984 press release. The magazine's testers also managed 0–100 mph in half a minute or so and observed a 116-mph maximum compared to the forecasted 118 mph.

Seen in the context of the only other US offering—the four-cylinder, 101 bhp 318i—the 325e was bound to look good, unless consumers knew about BMW performance in Europe. To fill in the gaps, the following table shows averaged independent test results alongside those for the US 325e, revealing what those solid European hot shots achieved during the US/UK decade of Yuppiedom.

Dynamically, the 325e picked up a couple of points on the G-force measuring pads of the auto magazines, although the wheel and tires remained as for the 318i. BMW NA had desperately needed something with six cylinders to boost the 3 Series, and they sold it well.

	325e	323i	325i
Liters/bhp	2.7/121	2.3/139	2.5/171
Test weight (lbs)	2,770	2,471	2,524
Maximum mph	116	125	132
0–30 mph (in seconds)	2.7	2.5	2.5
0–60 mph (in seconds)	9.4	8.1	7.4
0–100 mph (in seconds)	31.0	23.5	20.0

In fall 1984, some of the smaller changes in German production made it overseas, including an available four-speed automatic on four-cylinders and more spacious back seats (much appreciated by US testers). "One of the best small-car back-cabins that money can buy," was the media comment highlighted by BMW NA.

In Germany, they were making the first of the LHD-only catalytic converter 3 Series for Europe (318i in two-and four-doors). Tightening German legislation made BMW become serious about upgrading their performers to the catalytic converter form that had been the norm in the US since the 1970s.

An abbreviated first sales season in the US saw the 325e account for over 20,000 of 1984's total sales of the 3 Series (44,433 units). In 1985, the 318 and 325e four-doors both sold some 10,000 units each; but in two-door format, the 325e outsold the 318 with more than 19,000 units to 12,842. The 318i was effectively dropped in 1986, selling under 1,000 units, though 18 stragglers were recorded in 1987.

All told, 161,742 of the 325e models were sold between 1984 and 90, with a record 60,895 units shifted in the 1986 calendar year. The 325e also encouraged high-profit extras like automatic transmission and leather, which were ordered against the self-indulgent backdrop of the 1980s.

Extra horsepower for the 323i

Serious performance from the E30 3'er started in fall of 1984. The 2,316-cc straight six in the 323i was the predecessor to the enlarged motor of the 325i line, one which powered many E30 derivatives on either side of the Atlantic.

In 1984, BMW upgraded the 323i from an official 143 bhp (139 bhp in markets as diverse as Switzerland and Great Britain) to 150 bhp. Principal changes included replacement of the

The sporting cues for 3 Series in the States included alloys, sunroof and auxiliary lamps.

Photo: Klaus Schnitzer US

camshaft, distributor, and inlet manifold. Performance was enhanced a little more than expected, possibly because peak torque was available 500 rpm earlier.

This 323i performance increase was not relevant to US testers, and it also slipped by many of the established British magazines, but it is the missing link in 325i development for the US. *Autocar* tested the 323i in 150-bhp guise, but not in the lower horsepower level for the later body, while *Motor* assessed only the old-shape 323i and the subsequent 325i. *Autocar* recorded 0–60 mph in 8.3 seconds, 122 maximum mph, and 23.1 Imperial mpg overall. Fuel consumption aside, these were not improvements on their results for the first of the 323i 3 Series in the E21 body.

Performance returns: 325i

A year after the upgraded 323i came the public acknowledgment from BMW that European emission regulations were beginning to bite. Tackling emission regulation and extracting a power increase would inevitably involve a displacement increase.

September 1985 saw the European production debut of the 325i, a machine based on a power unit enlarged by 7.7 percent for a gain of 21 bhp (an extra 14.5 percent). A 1984 BMW internal briefing stated their goal as "to once again become the absolute leader in terms of performance in the compact saloon class…. Another objective was to have a genuine successor to the 2002 Tii, or the E21 323i, and to establish a greater lead over the 320i."

BMW congratulated itself heartily: "In terms of its performance, the 325i is matched only by sports cars such as the Porsche 944 with the same engine size, or by larger cars such as the 2.8-liter Toyota Supra. Comparing top speeds, we see that the 325i is definitely the fastest of all comparable saloons."

Subsequently, BMW referred to the Mercedes 2.3/16 and felt that the 325i was "far superior" to the Mercedes in its acceleration below 100 km/h. "Only the Maserati BiTurbo, an exotic with 18 bhp more engine power, is a bit faster. The 325i also leads the field in terms of acceleration. Only the 175-kg [386 lbs] lighter 16-valve Scirocco and the Maserati BiTurbo can out-accelerate the 325," asserted internal documentation.

1984 BMW factory performance comparisons

	BMW 325i	BMW 323i	BMW 2002Tii	VW16v Scirocco	AUDI 90	PORSCHE 944	FORD Escort RST
Capacity (cc)	2,494	2,316	1,990	1,781	2,226	2,479	1,597 (turbo)
Power (bhp)	171	150	130	139	136	163	132
0–62.5 mph	8.3	9.0	9.4	8.0	8.6	8.4	8.7
50–70 mph in direct 4th	8.9	10.3	8.4 *	—	—	—	—
Max. mph	135	127	116	129	125	131	125

* We could not resist including this British Motor test result to illustrate that the 2002Tii was embarrassingly effective. Other independent Motor tests for Tii showed an a maximum of 120 mph. In the US in 1973, *Road and Track* recorded 0–60 mph in 9.6 seconds, coupled with a 110-mph maximum speed, but the $4,360 US tii of that model year had 120 bhp, not the full European 130 bhp.

Here is the slightly facelifted 1987 European 3'er with slightly cleaner and more rounded front end panels and larger rear lamps. This example has a 115-bhp turbodiesel.

Photo: BMW Werkfoto, 1987

The American 325e/325/325i: A convoluted sales story

Whereas Europe had the 3 Series with six-cylinder power since 1977, America had a strange introduction to an inline six within the smallest BMWs. The eta in the 325e lacked the sweet-running, high-rpm joy that had made the 2002 a legend, and the 126-mph 323i a feared autobahn-stormer.

As introduced at $20,970 in Spring 1983 in America, the 325e appeared to be a 318i with an extra two cylinders and a 1.1-liter engine capacity bonus. In fact, it owed more to European six-cylinders being equipped with four-wheel disc brakes. Having rear discs ensured that when anti-lock braking (ABS) was eventually engineered for America, the 325e would be an immediate recipient.

In 1984, the ZF four-speed automatic transmission with lock-up fourth gear—as used to successfully boost the mpg figures of the big-capacity 5, 6, and 7 Series—

remained on the option list. Over 30 percent of customers chose this alternative, which particularly suited the muscular pulling power of the 325e. Other options were confined to a limited-slip differential, leather, cruise control, and metallic paint.

The cut-away of the 1982 BMW 323i shows the chassis details that were also extended to the 325e/325i and other six-cylinder derivatives.

Drawing: Niedermeier for BMW AG, 1983

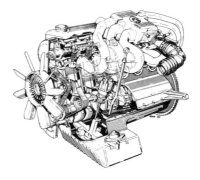

The single (belt-driven) overhead camshaft engine family of "small sixes" grew from this 320i/323i European base into applications for 325e, 325i, and the diesel motors that (for E30) were not exported to either the US or UK.

Drawing: BMW Art, 1983

The first 323i of the late 1970s was the E21. The 143-bhp Three restored performance pride to the line.

Photo: BMW Werkfoto, 1979

Standard equipment was far more generous than for the 318i, including a stereo radio/cassette, along with a 6 Series-inspired 7-way Active Check Control System. The nine-function computer with LCD clock, central locking, and air conditioning in electronic temperature control format were also standard showroom items.

For 1985, there were both four- and six-cylinder 3 Series available in the US. For 1986, that was reduced to just the eta-engined 325e, albeit in three trim levels and in two- or four-door bodies for all but the sportier 325es, which came only as a two-door.

All 1986 Model Year 325s switched to higher-profile 195/65 HR-14s tires from 60 percent aspect ratio rubber. There was a high-mounted rear brake light (Europeans started adopting this safety feature ten years later) and a rear-end ratio shift from 2.79:1 to 2.93.1. The five-speed manual box was said to be "quieter and easier-shifting." BMW trimmed back the Federal bumpers, tightening up the body gaps, but were always fighting serious weight penalties, until 1990s European BMWs adopted common safety measures (door beams, 2.5-mph bumpers).

The 1986 Model Year line for the US featured the base 325, a 325e aimed at the luxury sector, and a sportier appearance for 325es. All models used the certified 121-bhp eta motor. One major gain was standard ABS braking by Bosch for the first time on a US 3 Series. In fact, the electro-hydraulic ABS feature was standard in every 1986 model year BMW.

The starter 325 listed under $20,000 and had a simplified option list that covered just the four-speed automatic ZF "lock-up" gearbox and a limited-slip differential. The five-speed manual gearbox remained the base equipment. Both 325e/es were described as 'upscale' and listed standard leather upholstery, air conditioning, the two-way electric sunroof, on-board computer and cruise control, central locking, and alloy wheels. There were also some trinkets like fold-down rear armrest and map-reading lights.

At $22,540 ($22,990 by Christmas 1986), the 325es may not have offered more power, but it delivered a more stirring driving experience. This was achieved through a carefully calibrated M-tech suspension with softened springs and stiffer gas-filled twin-tube dampers. These improvements succeeded in boosting cornering G-forces to a measured average 0.82g, while allowing an excellent ride.

The 325es also offered enlarged roll bars at either end, plus the incorporation of the limited-slip differential as standard equipment. The cabin gained leatherette or "Country Cloth" sports seats (with augmented lateral and adjustable thigh support). Leather was optional, and was standard for the rim of the sports steering wheel.

Externally, the two-door 325es looked a little more purposeful, with a front spoiler that carried integral fog lights and a discreet back spoiler, both keyed to body colors. Exclusive to the 325e were four choices of leather interior colors.

In 1987, the trio of eta models received only detail changes. For Model Year 1988, however,

the 325 took on the 528e's significantly upgraded Eta unit
and was available at $24,350
(two-door) and $25,150 (four-
door). The 8.5:1 compression
six developed 127 instead of
121 bhp and incorporated
seven camshaft bearings in
place of five. Allied to larger
intake valves and less restriction in the catalytic converter

The E30 version
of the 323i initially
featured a slightly
detuned (139 bhp)
motor, but it was
later upgraded to
reach 150 bhp.

Photo: BMW Werkfoto,
1982

exhaust system, the rpm limit was lifted to 5,500
rpm—nearly a thousand rpm higher than the
originals.

Outstanding gas economy was apparently
untouched: 21/26 US mpg was the EPA City/
Highway forecast for the manual transmission.
The pace was enhanced, including 0–60 mph in
under 8.8 sec and a 119-mph maximum speed,
which makes this the year to look for when purchasing a used 325 eta.

Mid-season, the sportier 325i was ready
to market in the US in 325i, 325is and 325i
Convertible versions for the 1987 calendar year.
Now, only the 325 remained from the eta range.

325i: Svelte speed in the USA

*"The 325is is the first genuinely sport-
ing BMW to reach our shores since the
2002tii went out of production in 1975.
In the intervening years, BMW has sent
a long procession of beautifully built
sub-compact sedans our way, along
with a fine fleet of larger touring cars,
but none of them has moved with the
spirit of the original 2002."*

—CAR AND DRIVER,
AUGUST 1987

This quote summarizes the reasons why the
higher-revving (6,400 rpm cut-out) member
of the M60 engine family was so important to

American enthusiasts. BMW NA had claimed at
every new model introduction for the 3 Series
that the spirit of the 2002 was alive, well, and
returning to the marketplace, but the product
had failed to deliver sports qualities. It failed
because engineering resources were not chan-
neled to meet the challenge of competitive
power while complying with ever-tighter emissions laws. When BMW had to meet that clean-
exhaust horsepower challenge at home, things
started happening.

It was not complete power parity, however, as
the US versions delivered 168 bhp and 164 lb-ft
of torque (compared with 171 bhp and 167 lb-ft
of torque in no-cat European trim).

Now BMW NA could serve both the burgeon-
ing "Upwardly Mobiles" and the hard-driving
hardcore of their clientele. The M3 (see next
chapter) came in with a very decent 192 bhp
(European M3 was rated 195 bhp in cat format,
200 without) in the 1987 Model Year season
announcement.

What did US 325 Series consumers get in
the 1987 Model Year deal? They got an all six-
cylinder line—now echoed in the 2005 E90—
and anti-lock braking was standard. However,
you had to play Spot-the-Badge very carefully,
because the slow-revving, eta-engined entry
model of 121 bhp was badged 325, while the "i"
suffix in the 325i , the 325i Convertible, and the
325is brought the high-rpm, 168-bhp motor.

Since both were straight sixes with single overhead camshafts, an engine identity needs to be established in any used-car purchase of a 1987 model.

A few isolated 325i Convertibles (detailed in Chapter 18) were registered during January 1987. In February, sales began in earnest for the Convertible, the four-door 325i, and the two-door 325is. The differing bodies both carried the 2.5-liter, 168-bhp motors, but were assigned luxury (325i) and sports (325is) sales tasks, replacing the 1986 eta-engined 325e and 325es respectively.

Mechanically, the front engine drove the independently sprung trailing-arm rear wheels in familiar fashion and the sickle-supported MacPherson struts remained. Disc brakes of 10.2-inch diameters sat at all four corners, as they had since the 1986 advent of an all-ABS-braked 3'er model line.

All the new 325i breed were better performers than their predecessors, if a little heavier on gas. Performance predictions were 0–60 mph in 8.5 sec for 325i/iS and a scant tenth longer (8.6sec) for the heavier Convertible. Maximum speeds were anticipated at 130 mph for the Convertible and the 325i, while the aero package of the 325is was expected to haul another 3 mph. EPA fuel consumption statistics were put at 18/23 US mpg in City/Highway mileage.

As ever, BMW was conservative on the acceleration claims. In August 1987, *Car and Driver* logged 7.4 seconds for 0–60 mph, with a recorded 21-mpg average and a 128-mph top speed for a 325is. This meant a full performance ration from Germany, as their largest fortnightly magazine—*auto motor und sport*—clipped off 0–60 mph in 7.5 seconds. The American version was heavier than Europe's, but this difference was offset at lower speeds by a numerically higher final drive.

The 325i and the 325is shared common standard equipment like power steering, a quartet of disc brakes monitored by Bosch ABS, cruise control, central locking, air conditioning, two-way sunroof, leather trim, eight-speaker stereo radio/cassette player sound system with anti-theft, and electric antenna, tinted windows with power lifts, and a five-speed manual gearbox. All ran on 195/65VR-14 tires, but alloy wheels varied by model.

Additionally, the 325is offered the sportier gas suspension set-up of 325es (damping was tightened up and the twin-tube feature was omitted, although both the 325i and the Convertible carried such versatile shocks), plus the front and rear spoilers with the integrated front foglamps. A limited-slip differential was standard on this model, along with the shared 3.73:1 final drive for North America (Europe ran 3.64:1).

Leather was standard for sports seating and the rim of the M-striped, three-spoke, steering wheel in the 325is. The 1987 sport model carried a cross-spoke echo of the M3 alloy wheel, sized 6.5 inch x 14 rather than the 6 x 14 measurements of contemporary 325s.

A 325i delivered the range's shared quota of electronic information systems—On Board 9-function computer, Service Interval Indicator, Active 7-Check Control board, and fuel economy meter—alongside its own rendition of the leather interior. That meant it lacked the sports front seats of the 325is or the Convertible, but had height-adjustable cushion adjustment, a rear center armrest and head restraints in the back.

Options for 1987 Threes were confined to four-speed ZF automatic transmission ($595), metallic paint ($335), and a limited-slip differential that was standard on the 325is but cost an extra $370 for the 325/325i and the Convertible. Thus, 325is options were confined to metallic paint and the four-speed automatic.

Introductory prices were set well above the eta model's $23,180 entry point for a two-door. The equivalent, but better equipped and faster, 325i or 325is were set at $27,300. A 325i

Convertible cost a pricey $31,000, more than an entry-level 5 Series.

In America, 1988 was the Model Year that BMW went with 4x4 for the first time. That they chose the 3 Series for the task was interesting, and a loyal band of owners—mostly within the snow belt—still proclaim their loyalty to the adventurous 3'er. Now BMW NA could offer 14 models in a 1990 line up from the V12 750iL to the entry-point 325 (still with eta power). The 325i, 325is and 325i Convertible selections remained the volume sellers in the line. Modest modifications made the intrusion of the 5-mph bumpers on neat body design a little less obvious on all but the Convertible.

Revised detailing included redesigned front spoilers that incorporated brake cooling ducts, ellipsoid foglamps, a deeper rear bumper apron, and the de-chromed side moldings that had proved popular in Europe. Both the 325i and the 325is had revised rear quarter panels, which elongated the body line to the back wheels.

Other 1988 Model Year alterations included black interior door moldings and 7 Series-bequeathed ellipsoid headlamps, plus body-color-keyed mirrors. Less obvious was the installation of a heated throttle body to improve icy start manners, an airfoil blade on the driver's side windshield wiper, and asbestos-free brake linings. As for their European cousins, all models except the M3 gained larger fuel tanks, measuring out at 16.5 US gallons rather than the previous 14.5.

The 325is now adopted the twin-tube shock absorbers of other models. American customers traveled some of the worst urban road surfaces in the world and agreed on the need for a softer ride, even in a sportier model.

For the 1989 Model Year, the eta engines officially departed from the 3 Series, replaced by the 325i for both two- and four-doors, while the 325is remained on the sporting job. That meant the addition of 41 bhp at entry level because all 325s shared the 168-bhp, 2.5-liter catalyst engine.

Prices now began at $24,650 for the two door 325i, while the four-door equivalent was $25,450 and the 328iS base price was $28,950. It often went over $30,000 with dealer prep, plus shipping, metallic paint ($375), and the $645 automatic transmission offered for all 1989 3'ers except the M3.

The option list was confined to automatic, metallics, and the $370 limited-slip differential (standard on 325is) for most customers. Convertible buyers were also offered a hardtop ($3,500) and heated front seats ($200).

This white 325i Sport looks like the European spec Sport or M-Tech-paneled 325, but was actually a South-African-built hybrid that was lighter and quicker than standard. The Alpina-badged E30 is the Buchloe specialist's C2/2.5, a 185-bhp upgrade of the European spec 323i that allowed 185 bhp and almost 140 mph with a claimed 7.6 second 0–60 mph dash.

Photos: 325i Sport, Author, UK, 1991; 1984 Alpina, *Autocar*, UK

There had been some important shuffling of equipment in the line. Leather was no longer available on the entry-level two- and four-doors, but leather trims were standard in the deal for more expensive Threes, except 325iX.

In practical terms, this was a U-turn for four-door buyers, because the previous model year offered more luxury items. These included leather, so buying a direct replacement was impossible. Similarly, the two-way sunroof on the 325i line had no power-assists, while 325is offered electric motivation.

As before, items like air conditioning and the extensive electronic systems (Active Check Control, computer, Service Interval Indicator, and Econometer), along with the sound system, were standard. That, along with cruise control, electric windows, and tinted glass, applied to all 325i, 325is and Convertible models.

Entering the 1990s, the option choices multiplied in the seven-model 3 Series line, but from a safety viewpoint, the most significant feature was the standard SRS airbag. The main models of the 325i in two- and four-door format, plus the 325is for the sportier set, ranged from $24,650 to $28,950.

Now you could opt for leather upholstery ($895) in the entry level 325s, and the power sunroof ($225) also joined the option list, along with heated front seats ($250) and a $160 ski sack for the 325is. A $500 charge on cross-spoke alloys further distinguished the Convertible from the herd. CD players were also listed as an option for $780, but NA only listed cellular phones as a $1,200 item on the 7 Series.

In 1991, you could still opt for the ZF four-speed on a 325i at $725, or leather ($950) with the electric sunroof listing at $275, but the Sport two-door model was dropped in the 325 line. Instead you could opt for a Sport package at $1925 extra on a 2 or four-door 325i. This gave you most of the previous 325is features, including sports suspension, strategically applied leather, sports front seats and the spoiler body kit.

Alternatively, there was a Touring package available on 325s of either body. Costing $1,665, you got leather seats and steering wheel rim, map reading lamps, plus a center armrest for the four-door.

The European option-list disease spread to the US, with 14 extra-cost choices, ranging from the traditional automatic gearbox to a six-disc CD player at $825 on 325i sedans. Since the cheapest 325i was now $25,600 and everyone knew that E36 was imminent in Europe, BMW NA would not have expected serious sales volumes for the departing E30s.

Contrast Big Bumper 325is in the US and steel-wheeled, rear spoiler, 323i for Britain.

Photos: Side view, BMW GB, 1984; head-on, Author, Monterey, CA, 1996

The two- and four-door sedans sold close to 7,000 units in 1991: the inclusion of the Convertible saw a total of 8,576 four-cylinders sold that calendar year, second only to the 325i line of four-doors by model group (10,854). Overall, 3 Series managed 29,002 sales that 1991 year, a fitting swan song for the full E30 line, although some E30 members—like the Convertibles—made it to the 1993 Model Year.

In 1992 over 32,000 of the new E36 were sold, compared to less than 6,000 of all remaining E30 types. Thus, 1991 really was the mass market farewell of the understated but effective E30.

Meanwhile, on the other side of the pond…

Some subtle aerodynamic detailing was evident in 1985–86; fewer grille bars were installed, an engine undertray was added, and the leading edge of the lower front spoiler also had fewer apertures.

Other 3 Series alterations in the autumn of 1985 encompassed a mysterious 4 bhp bonus for the 320i, taking it to a quoted 129 bhp, which continued until the close of production. All 1986 Model Year 3 Series got beefier steering locks and enhanced lateral support for the seats. The red, blinking digits of the clock were dumped for a return to analogue black and white, but the digital readouts (in a softer orange shade) of the options computer remained.

The 325i enhancements, besides the obvious power augmentation, started with hydraulic twin-tube shock absorbing as part of an upgraded suspension specification, and an oil cooler that demanded an opening in the lower front apron/spoiler.

Installation of four-wheel disc braking continued, but ABS anti-lock braking was a $1,600-plus option in some markets. Foglamps and twin exhausts continued to be the external ID of the European 325i, but the back spoiler now became the body color on those machines with metallic paint.

Another minor, but useful, change was the upgraded capacity of the battery, up from the 320i's 50 amp-hour rating to 66Ah, plus an 8-Ah alternator kicking out 1,120 watts. Because the battery was mounted in the trunk, luggage capacity dropped from 425 liters to 404 liters. The compensation was a modest redistribution of the curb weight which assisted rear-axle traction.

Important minor mechanical changes to the running gear of the 325i also included a replacement twin-pipe exhaust system of larger diameter, increased clamping loads for the clutch plate (derived from 325e and diesel), and heavy duty driveshafts and wheel bearings. Also on the transmission side, the automatic transmission was chosen by many 325i owners, and it now offered three individual settings (including those biased toward either sports or economy motoring).

The steel-wheeled 325i (UK and European standard specification) gained a new wheel cover. As in the US, production 325i tire size was changed from 60-series 195s to 195/65 following the factory summer holidays of 1985.

The good news for September 1986 sales was the inclusion of ABS anti-lock braking as standard on all 325i derivatives in UK and other European markets. The Trans-Atlantic power gap narrowed to 2 bhp. September 1987 saw the power of the 2.5-liter six dropped slightly (to 170 official bhp) because of the lower compression ratio of 9.4:1 and the Motronic management adjusted for 95-octane European unleaded fuels. In the US, 91-octane was the requirement. The same compression ratio change was also made for 320i derivatives.

1988 European range changes

The 1988 Model Year revamp included more visual maneuvering than usual. Such tactics provided the now aging 3 Series line with a brush-up before its nineties successor could be readied. BMW (temporarily) ditched their beloved chrome in favor of matte black for the wind and rear screen surrounds and the side glass encasements, but the rain channel and outer window capping remained chrome-finished. Side rubbing strips lost chrome highlights, and a black plastic insert was placed between the now enlarged, and raised, rear light clusters.

All models, except the M3 and the Convertibles, gained side rear panels that deepened their approach to the back wheels and tires. Neither the M3 nor the Convertible got the European specification 2.5-mph impact absorbing bumpers (initially in contrasting color to the body) and associated smaller spoiler lips.

Mechanically, the most influential change was the adoption of variable-ratio steering from the 316 upward; this feature had first made its presence felt on the 325i and had seeped downward to the 1988 four cylinders. The objective was

lighter steering, without a power-option necessity at parking speeds.

Another notable mechanical change was the provision of up to 64 liters (14.08 UK gallons) in the fuel tanks of six-cylinder models, which had previously managed a maximum of 55 liters. Also effective was the use of ellipsoid outer headlamps for all 3 Series, which also gained that classy green tinted glass throughout the line.

One worthwhile change to the 320i was the addition of twin-sleeve gas dampers, a feature that had previously smoothed out the ride of sportier BMWs. Incidentally, the sportiest 325i Sport package rested during the UK 1988 Model Year but was reinstated for 1989, and was a far larger seller than the LHD-only M3 in this market.

Munich marketers introduced a choice of 14 engines and a body line-up that covered two- and four-door saloons, the M3 modified two-door, a line of two-door Convertibles and the return of a Touring five-door. Catalytic converter versions of the 320i and the 325i provided "a definite shift in demand," according to BMW in Munich. As a result, the last eta engines came off the line in 1987 and the last eta cars were completed in 1989.

This early 318is was fitted with the optional cross-spokes while the one below wore steel wheels with plastic cappings.

Photos: BMW Werkfoto, 1987

The proliferation of home-market diesel BMWs was also relevant to the 325e's demise. The company made a normally aspirated six-cylinder available from September 1985, achieving a quoted 20 percent of the total production of the BMW 3 Series.

In autumn 1987, they added the turbo-charged version of that same M60-based inline diesel six, plus

the refinement of electronic fuel injection to manufacture an economical 324td of 115 bhp. This engine also popped up in the Touring derivatives.

Quoted 324td performance was pretty similar to that of a gasoline-burning 318i, and the driving smoothness was free from the usual vibrations and discords that spoil lesser diesels. If you have ever pursued one along an autobahn, you know that 116 mph and 0–62 mph in 11.9 seconds were realistic BMW claims for its electronically managed turbo diesel. Diesel mpg figures were excellent, with *auto motor und sport* reporting the equivalent of 31.7 urban mpg (26.4 US mpg) and up to 54.3 mpg (45.3 mpg) at 56 mph.

1990: Four-cylinders return to the US

In 1990, BMW NA also previewed the return of four-cylinder power to the 3'er, commenting that the 318is would "provide much of the engineering fascination of the M3 at a more affordable price level" when it arrived in Summer 1990. The move would (for one sales season) take prices below $20,000 in the US for the first time since 1986.

Some sales were registered in April 1990 for the 318is as a two-door (listing at $21,500), with the cheapest four-door (318i) selling from July of that season at $19,900. There was a counterpart four-cylinder Convertible (318iC in BMW NA registration lists) just squeezing out 38 units sold in December 1990. That meant there were nine basic model choices now in 3 Series specifications for the US customer.

Unlike the Europe 316i and 318i which used the single cam M40 engine families, the North American four-cylinders used the M42, DOHC, 16-valve unit. So, what did Americans get with the new four-cylinders? Four-wheel discs and ABS remained a US showroom feature in the new four-cylinders, along with air conditioning

and power assistance for steering, side windows, mirrors, the AM/FM cassette audio, and the driver's-side airbag. The 318is, which cost $1,600 more, included an M-Technic chassis (thicker front and rear anti-roll bars, revised dampers) and the 325is feature of cross-spoked 6.5 x 14 inch alloys.

From the media's perspective, the four-cylinders were a success:

> *"One of the best four-cylinders anywhere."*
> —*Auto motor und sport*, Germany

> *"Arguably the most entertaining handling you can buy for they money."*
> —*Automobile*, US

> *"The newest and least expensive BMW on the market could easily turn out to be the most fun to drive."*
> —*Autoweek*, US

> *"The 318is does not have an identity crisis—it's a BMW complete with credentials and full member rights."*
> —*Road & Track*, US

With reviews as warm as these, the 16-valve 318s could have endured as long as the 2002. However, the production-line body clock was ticking for the E30 line, and it was in the succeeding E36 sedans and Compacts that big sales of these high-output fours occurred.

Despite many claims by a BMW NA desperate to sell any 02 heritage at every emission-gutted new model year introduction, the peppy 16-valve truly was the small BMW that had the most 02 DNA. Unlike the M3, these 318is types were engineered for mass-production affordability and four-cylinder frugality at the pumps. A 318is was not as fast in competition, as the 2002 and tii were in their day. Yet subsequent six-cylinder small Bimmers didn't have the legendary handling balance of the four-cylinder BMW 02/318 line.

M3s were simply too specialized to make the mass impact of the 02 anywhere, save America and Germany. For BMW's customers outside these prime territories, a 16-valve 318is was a very popular choice in the true BMW tradition.

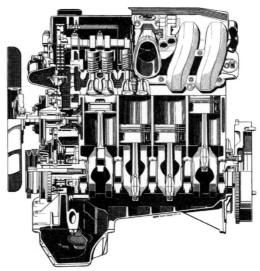

Inside and outside the 136-bhp, chain-drive, double overhead camshaft 318is motor: this is the beginning of a family of 16-valve, high-efficiency units.

Drawing: BMW Grafik Design, 1989
Photo: BMW AG, 1989

Four-cylinder performance

BMW NA anticipated 0–60 mph in 9.8 seconds for the 2,602-lb two-door, or 10 seconds for the 55-lb-heavier four-door, in the 318is line. They reported an electronically limited maximum of 122 mph for the American-market 16-valve 318s, and the EPA prediction was 21/27 US mpg in City/Highway usage.

Road & Track published the only independent US test data we have for 318is. Those 1990 results were further off the European pace than expected for a mere 2-bhp deficit. The benchmark 0–60 mph occupied 10 seconds dead and the quarter mile buzzed by in 17.3 seconds at 81 mph.

In electronically monitored runs, the two-door 136 bhp European model reached 125 mph with 0–60 mph in 9.5 seconds or less. The equivalent of 22.9 US mpg was recorded, whereas the *R&T* guys exceeded expectations with 24 mpg reported in "normal driving."

For Model Year 1991, entry prices did clamber beyond $20,000. The 318i of four-doors listed at $20,300, a 318is retailed for $21,750, and the late-arrival 318Ci carried a sticker of $28,500. Options were restricted on cheaper four-cylinder sedans. Automatic transmission was not available, and the 318s were only allowed metallic paint ($435), limited-slip differential ($465), a manual sunroof ($650), and anti-theft alarms ($540).

New four-cylinder heart for the European 318i

The major change for the 1988 model year was the introduction on the 318i of the 1,795-cc, 115-bhp M40 engine. It was a fine development of existing BMW SOHC themes into a brand new four-cylinder line. The M40 ensured that BMW stayed on the field with the newcomers from Japan, while deploying comparatively simple SOHC/8-valve cylinder heads. This unit also spawned the 16-valve development (M42) that became deeply significant in America and Europe, and was still in production over ten years later as the heart to the Compact 318ti and 318Ci (the latter for Europe only).

In 1990, the 318i sedan with four-doors was notable for taking US Bimmer base prices back under the $20,000 barrier.

Photo: Klaus Schnitzer, US, 1990

That handling and grip were a little more important to BMW in 1987 than they had been in 1977 can be judged from the fact that 318is four cylinder gained previous six-cylinder standard tire sizings of 195/65 dimensions mounted on European-market steel wheels within plastic cappings, unless optionally obliterated.

The M40 engine transformed the best-selling 318i into a far more lovable machine, balancing BMW smoothness with a claimed maximum of 117 mph and a competitive 0–62 mph at 10.8 seconds for manual models, 11.9 seconds for the widely purchased automatic. Independent testing showed the top speed claim was justified and the 0–60 mph potential was under 10 seconds, while returning 27.4 Imperial mpg (22.8 US mpg) for unleaded fuel.

The Road to M3 …

The European perception of the 318is was different than that of Americans. The Hot Hatchback phenomenon (three-door performers with 100 to 150 bhp that followed in the wake of the 1976 Volkswagen Golf GTI) was so strong that it hurt even Bimmer sales in Europe.

BMW, particularly in the UK, denied that they were taking on the Hatch Squad, but pricing (including the deletion of ABS and alloys) indicated that BMW had made a real effort.

The European M42 1.8-liters developed nearly 76 bhp a liter, second only to the fabled M3 in the generation of power per 1,000 cc displacement. Complete with independently assessed 125-mph ability, 0–60 mph in 9.3 seconds, and an overall 27.5 Imperial mpg (fractionally better than the 318i), the 318is became very popular.

BMW made sure the sporting crowd got the message via a front and rear spoiler set, sports seats, M-Technic steering wheel and suspension, and a black satin finish instead of the surviving external chrome. Other showroom equipment included power steering, electric front windows, a rev-counter, central locking, and tinted glass.

Standard colors were Alpine White, Brilliant Red, and the metallic shades of Diamond Black, Laser Blue, and Sterling Silver. A checked interior cloth trim provided a suitably sporty note, but leather was a European option.

9 The Conception of Success

The M3 was a mandatory production item to fulfill BMW's eighties European and global sporting ambitions, but it conquered in the showroom too. Here's how it was done.

Like most major car companies faced with building a run of specialist high-performance vehicles, BMW was pessimistic about the showroom potential of the "M for Motorsport" M3.

The most popular M-car of the 1980s was slated to complete just a 5,000 homologation run for motorsport purposes. Production between 1986 (1987 in the US) and 1990 closed at 17,970 units (including 786 convertibles) with nearly 5,000 bought in the US alone. Just the BMW Motorsport assembly and sales of around 300 competition kits (based around a fully prepared body) exceeded the total 30 year production of some established race car manufacturers.

Established in 1972, BMW Motorsport GmbH is a company that operates within the main BMW AG. Motorsport is charged with creating race or performance mutant Bimmers, and the first (E30) M3 with its S14-coded engine was no exception. In 2001, BMW Motorsport was the umbrella company over a sophisticated multi-department operation that employs over 400 people and handles everything from public driver training to Le Mans and Grand Prix organization.

Daimler Strasse, in a northern suburb of Garching, is home to the commercial activities of BMW Motorsport GmbH.

Photo: Author, Munich, 1999

The first M3 beauty shots were taken at the company test track, where prototypes with either 195 (catalytic converter) bhp or 200 non-cat bhp were taking 0–62 mph in a reported 7 seconds.

Photo: BMW Werkfoto, Ismaning, Munich, 1985

The M-cars and their motors for the street are created in design association with Motorsport, but the M-division no longer builds road cars for the public. That's done by the parent company because of escalating demand. The core to Motorsport's Munich competition business is race motor construction for factory use. Even the Virginia-based PTG racing M3s of the 1990s did not have German factory-built motors. Most racing work outside the 600-bhp Le Mans V12s and the 900-bhp Grand Prix V10s is sub-contracted to outfits such as Heini Mader, located in Switzerland.

Motorsport is so specialized today that Munich also entrusts work outside the engine bay (racing chassis engineering and track aerodynamic development) to the British. BMW Motorsport took the 3 Series higher through the efforts of McLaren North America in the 1970s, Prodrive in the 1980s, and McLaren International in the 1990s. BMW now contracts with Williams Grand Prix Engineering, having also constructed a satellite BMW Motorsport Ltd. building alongside the main Williams Grand Prix site at Grove, Oxfordshire, UK.

BMW Motorsport engineers created a winner of every worthwhile sedan title in the world before settling down to delight BMW performance fans. The M3 also proved to be a worthy performer in tarmac rallying and won across Europe.

Because international sedan racing regulations changed to Group A in 1982, BMW faced a tougher task in their traditional saloon-car killing fields. For 1982, that meant that a manufacturer had to produce at least 5,000 cars a year of the model raced, or obtain a transfer from the previous Group 1 category.

Armed with a Jaguar XJ-S V12 coupe that had been transferred from Group 1, Britain's Tom Walkinshaw Racing (TWR, representing Jaguar and Rover in the early 1980s), along with Volvo's turbo cars, stemmed the flow of BMW saloon-car racing titles.

Because of low production and stricter homologation enforcement procedures in Germany, BMW was forced to race its chunky 528i sedan in 1982. At a consistent 240 bhp, it scored championship-winning points, but lacked straight-line speed. This problem led BMW to switch to the 635 CSi coupes in 1983. These were developed in association with Schnitzer and again lacked front-line M-Power, because the 24-valve (S38) six was not made in sufficient numbers to compete. As a result, BMW had to use the 12-valve 635 rather than the M6. The opposition had 400-bhp aluminum V12s (TWR

The M3 wore its square suit with aerodynamic pride that reflected a number of fundamental sheet metal alterations and plastic composite additions.

Photos: BMW Werkfoto, Ismaning, Munich, 1986

Jaguar), V8s (Rover) or 340-bhp turbo-chargers (Volvo) to counter Bimmer's 285 bhp. Nevertheless, BMW's 635 took three European titles, up to 1986.

The twenty altera-tions/additions to make an original M3 of an E30 body are clearly shown here.

Drawing: BMW Motorsport engineering bulletin, released 1989

When Volvo and Rover withdrew from European Championship racing and TWR concentrated on sports-car racing for Jaguar, only Ford provided consistent sedan opposition to BMW in Europe. Neither the 528i nor the 635i BMWs could effectively oppose Ford's turbocharged Sierras.

M-People

The M3 officially dates back to the summer of 1981. But with the mid-engined M1's production ending at 456 examples, the M3 was actually rendered in one 1985 pre-production example and went into full manufacture starting in the summer of 1986. Some 2,396 M3s were built in 1986, and it was recognized for competition in Groups A and N (5,000 examples built in one year) by March 1, 1987.

Board-level responsibility for BMW's postwar sports activities was initially shouldered by engineering chief Alex von Falkenhausen, who died in 1988. Von Falkenhausen operated with such vigor that he inspired men like engine legend Paul Rosche, who was a key figure in all M-top-ics, race or road. But there were a fair number of other BMW Motorsport personalities who influenced the M3.

Dieter Stappert, who masterminded the Grand Prix victory era with the turbocharged Brabham-BMW, succeeded first M-manager Jochen Neerpasch (1972–80) and held the post until the mid-80s. Wolfgang Peter Flohr was appointed managing director in early January 1985 and was supported by Paul Rosche and ex-Ford competition engineer Thomas Ammerschlager (responsible for M3 production car and Group A racing development). Ammerschlager coordinated the overall conception and production of the race and road M3 until 1989, when he left for a senior management position in the chassis engineering development department of BMW AG.

Karl-Heinz Kalbfell became the managing director of BMW Motorsport on October 1, 1988, and continued to direct its operations until he was required to coordinate all BMW brands. That 1999 appointment covered core BMW 3 to 7

The original M3 displays the side skirts, rear aprons, and extended front spoiler. Competition bodies were manufactured without the sunroof.

Photos: BMW Werkfoto, Ismaning, Munich 1986

So far, the M3 badge has been proudly displayed on three generations of 3 Series BMWs.

Photo: BMW Pressefoto, Italian Press Pack, Mugello, 1986

model lines, as well as the product needed to relaunch the 2001 Mini and 2003 Rolls-Royce. Kalbfell received support on the BMW Motorsport Executive board from Heinz Kolleuberg (Finance) and Paul Rosche, whose effective role was to supply serious track power, with minimal corporate interference.

Every technological strand of the 3 Series that could affordably increase its competitive potential was examined. Braking and handling were magnificent, but not to full competition standards, as that would have been overly harsh for public use. The basics of engines and aerodynamics were mandated and thus incorporated in every car sold to the public. So, we were offered a four-cylinder competition engine with immense strength in a chassis that was more aerodynamically effective than many sleeker shapes.

potential for high rpm, and therefore had more power to weight potential than an in-line six, which has the basic racing drawback of a long and (comparatively) whippy crankshaft.

Paul Rosche explained, "Most important was our experience with four-valve-per-cylinder Formula 2, the M1, and M6. We had proved the large cylinder bore (93.4 mm) for motor racing; the cylinder head design of the M6 looked so good for us that we did the first development work in two weeks by cutting up the head for a six-cylinder and fitting it to a 2-liter four! It worked well, straight away. A six-cylinder would just have been too heavy for the best race handling of a front engine car."

An enlargement to 2,302 cc for maximum effect in the 2.5-liter racing class was made possible via a steel crankshaft and an 84-mm bore. Developed to 8,500 rpm and 300 bhp in Group A racing trim (370 bhp for the modified regulations of Germany and subsequent 95-mm bore/2.5-liter descendant), the M3 could only have been improved for competition with a turbocharger. This was discounted as too expensive in further development costs for what was expected to be a short 3 Series production life.

Questions, questions ...

Why were consumers offered "only" four-cylinders? Why no bolt-on power turbocharger? Conversations with Paul Rosche, Herr Rech, and colleague Franz Zinnecker lead us to conclude that a lightweight four-cylinder was preferable for handling in a front-engine, rear-drive, racing car. Also, a four-cylinder held more

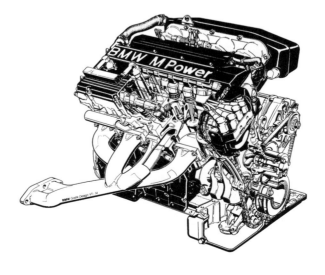

The original four-cylinder M3 motor was bulky, being derived from the S38 six-cylinder head and block.

Drawing: BMW Grafik Design, 1986

This power graph for the original non-catalyzed European motor shows peak power equivalent to 200 bhp/ 147 Kw at 6,750 rpm.

Graph: BMW AG, Munich, 1986

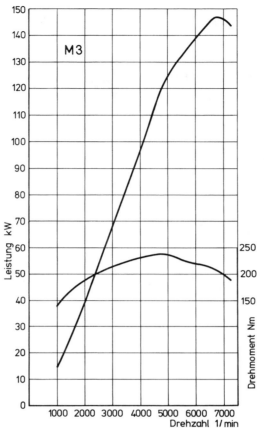

The subsequent 93.4 x 84-mm (2,302-cc) road version of the 16-valve DOHC S14 engine came from literally millions of Deutschemarks and thousands of hours spent in durability and refinement running. It was happy to cover 100,000 durable road miles (and more) at up to 7,250 rpm, with just routine service.

The primary elements of this engine were a traditionally slanted, tough iron block whose honed bores supported central liners cast together. They cooperated with a steel crankshaft that had eight rather than four counterweights. The short stroke shaft served the same bore and stroke dimensions as the contemporary M5 and M6 six-cylinders.

The aluminum cylinder head offered an exceptional 10.5:1 compression, while quad-valve hemispherical combustion chambers and BMW-Bosch ML-3 Digital Motor Electronics (DME) guarded against pre-ignition, even on the lower-octane (91) unleaded gas used in America. The control unit could be manually reset to accommodate from 91-octane unleaded (US) to 98-octane leaded (UK).

The double overhead camshafts were duplex chain-driven, whereas spur gears were used in contemporary BMW racing units. Each cylinder was served by an individual throttle, an approach applied to later six-cylinder M3s. All valving was activated by cup tappets, with the intakes measuring 1.46 inches (37 mm) and

Turbocharging for gasoline engines was also out of BMW managerial favor. This is ironic, since it was BMW who raced Europe's first turbo production car (1969) and built Europe's first production turbo sedan for the public (1973), both in 2002 bodies.

Rosche and Zinnecker were also well aware of turbo potential, as BMW Motorsport had already won the first turbo Formula 1 World title with Brabham's Grand Prix chassis and their iron-block, 1.5-liter four. Motorsport needed management cash to turbocharge the M3, and that was not forthcoming.

Tough motor

BMW stuck to what they knew, breathing new life into the four-cylinder using knowledge acquired from four- and six-cylinder experience.

Some of the primary components that comprised the M3, especially the 10.5:1 compression 16-valve head, tough crankshaft, and carefully baffled wet sump.

Photo: BMW Pressefoto, Italian Press Pack, Mugello, 1986

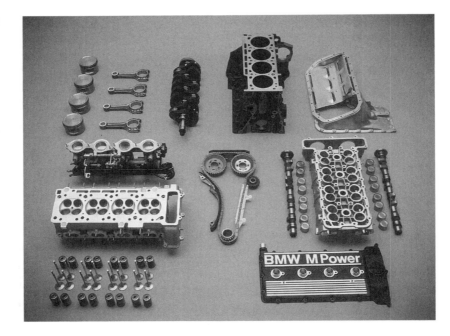

paired with 1.26-inch (32 mm) exhaust valves. The quad-valve chambers were of classic hemispherical contours, served by a central spark plug.

For US trim, welded tubular exhaust mani-folding led to a twin-tract catalytic converter: the introductory 1987 Model Year M3 had a 50-State emission rating. Within a classic finned alloy sump, the wet oil pan enhanced durability in hard cornering via baffles, which also helped restrict foaming at high rpm. Any negligence in checking the oil level prior to a track outing can be punished by terminally expensive death rattles.

The results of all this engine technology were 83.4 bhp a liter in US trim (192 bhp at 6,750 rpm) or 86.8 bhp a liter in non-cat European trim (200 bhp, also at 6,750 revs). For perspective, the 1992–99 European Evo M3 just surpassed 100 bhp a liter (321 bhp from 3.2 liters) and the 1995 American counterpart reached 80.3 bhp a liter (240 bhp from 3 liters). Without the benefit of turbochargers, only Honda automobiles were affordable horsepower per liter opponents.

The maximum torque of the 1980s M3 was 176 lb-ft for catalytic converter specifications and 170 lb-ft for non-cat specifications, both at 4750 rpm. In between, Europe offered its own catalyst model rated at 195 bhp, running octane levels up to 97-octane unleaded.

In practice, the performance gap had closed in Europe with the M3, and curb weights were also getting under control in the US with the adoption of small (2.5-mph) bumpers. BMW reported at the M3's introduction that "just one single type of bumper is required to fulfill all legal standards and regulations worldwide."

The second major innovation that distinguished M3 from its E30 contemporaries was the widened body and enhanced aerodynamics. Radical bodywork changes were allowed by the parent company, including all new steel panels or skins for front and rear fenders and doors. Even the front and rear screens were bonded into the body in search of the last aerodynamic decimal point as well as structural integrity.

The enlarged rear window was slightly tilted, with a fresh top mounting "cap" to provide better airflow to the 40-mm (1.6-inch) raised SMC plastic rear trunk lid and its raised blade/spoiler aerodynamics. Hard plastics also completed the side rocker panels and front spoiler "body kit," but the square wings, similar to those of an Audi Quattro, were in steel. All were immaculately sprayed and matched to underline fine fit and finish, even on pre-production examples.

The body changes reduced the aerodynamic Cd factor to 0.33, improving stability at road speeds beyond 60 mph and track velocities up a further 100 mph. The M3's wheelbase measured 2,562 mm (100.9 inches), or 2,565 mm with the 225/45 VR 16 wheel and tire option. Its overall length came in at 4,360 mm (171.7 inches), while the width measured 1,675 mm (65.9 inches) and the height came in at 1,365 mm (53.7 inches).

American market dimensions differed, particularly in overall length, which was given as 175.6 inches in the 1987 introductory press/brochure material. That was up 3.9 inches on Europe, but in media briefings for Model Year 1988, the figure was corrected to 171.1 inches, along with a simplified 101-inch wheelbase.

Officially, all M3s included the same US standard bumpers: external body-color deformable plastics of polyurethane, reinforced by fiberglass, containing foam impact blocks beneath. Weighed with a full tank of fuel, but no extras, the European model registered a weight of 1,200 kg (2,640 lbs), less than a 100-lb difference from the figure quoted by BMW NA on introduction.

The chassis was fitted with 15 x 7 inch cross-spoke alloys with an initial European tire size of 205/55 VR 15. Shiny wheels hid the

contemporary 5 Series disc brakes, with 284-mm (11.2-inch) vented fronts and 250-mm (11.0-inch) solid rears. Best of all, the ABS braking never panicked, even in track use. Servo-power assistance was provided for both the brakes and rack-and-pinion steering, the latter quoted on a quicker 19.6:1 ratio at launch in Europe, but not in the US.

"Totally Brilliant"

The suspension system was not radically different, retaining MacPherson struts in front and 15-degree trailing arms in the rear, but it was a totally brilliant expression of all that was best in front-engine, rear-drive motoring. Thomas Ammerschlager arrived on the project in 1985, and his Ford racing/Audi quattro street expertise was welcomed by the small M3 project team. Thomas was a key figure in balancing the street compromises of fine handling, acceptable ride, and sheer driving pleasure. He acknowledged that Boge twin-tube gas dampers were

The M3 motor on its wet sump is shown with both the catalyst exhaust system (right) and the non-cat system (left).

Photos: BMW Werkfoto, 1986

helpful in obtaining that acclaimed balance.

Other relevant hardware included two-piece forged steering knuckles and 5 Series wheel bearings in association with five-bolt wheels. The caster action was tripled, along with quicker steering. Sources quote ratios of 19.6:1 in Europe and 20.5:1 in the US, but our Spotter's Guide research agrees with a common 19.6:1 for the USA.

The front anti-roll bar effect was doubled, with an increased thickness and a strut linkage rather than the original attachment to the lower "sickle" wishbone. The rear bar was also thicker, and the M3 squatted an inch lower than its brethren, riding stiffer-poundage coil springs. All these modifications were made with minimal tooling changes to production mounting points.

A limited-slip differential, set to a softish 25 percent for road usage, was standard rear differential, but the final drive ratio was radically different on either side of the Atlantic. America went for an accelerative 4:1, and Europe was more interested

The European M3 reveals that a cooling fan has not been fitted on this preproduction example.

Photo: BMW Werkfoto, 1986

in top-speed cruising at 3.25:1. Subsequently, BMW mated their 220 bhp Evo power train in Europe with a 3.15:1 ratio: this allowed a genuine 148 mph at almost 6,700 rpm in fifth.

The M3 cabin was a good place for the keen pilot to operate. BMW-built sports seats—optional on lesser 3 Series—were included in the European introductory model. The seats were adjustable via levers (three) and knobs to cater for height, thigh support, backrest angle, legroom, and tilt.

A Motorsport-striped, three-spoke steering wheel relieved the graytoned environment, along with bright red needles for the instrumentation and an M-badged speedometer. A European 260-km/h (161-mph) speedometer was matched by an 8,000-rpm tachometer with a 7,250-rpm

The front and rear suspension upgrades abided by E30 principles but contained significant changes, including castor and camber angles and enlargement of both brakes and wheel bearings.

Photo: BMW Werkfoto 1986

red-line. Instead of an Econometer, the rev-counter carried an oil temperature gauge.

Standard equipment for the German model included ABS, the multiplate limited-slip differential, an enlarged 15.4-Imperial-gallon (70-liter) fuel tank, tinted glass, and electric twin mirrors. A Getrag 260 five-speed gearbox featured an isolated first, closest to the LHD pilot.

Getrag ratios for European and American versions were totally different. These statistics were quoted for the Borg Warner synchronized quintet in the original Italian-launch press pack: first, 3.72 (3.83:1, US); second, 2.40 (2.20, US); third, 1.77 (1.40, US); fourth, 1.26 (1:1 direct, US): fifth, 1.0 (083:1 overdrive, US); final drive, 3.25:1 (4:1, US).

European launch options included a simple on-board computer, excellent air conditioning, power windows, central locking, and leather trim.

Launch Fever

The May 1986 press pack told us how BMW felt it had augmented the 3 Series:

"Mugello, May 1986: The BMW M3—four valves per cylinder in typical BMW style. The

The seating was better than before, but the original BMW seats do look simple by today's standards.

Photo: BMW Werkfoto, 1986

BMW 3 Series has a new top model: the M3 with a 2.3-liter, 16-valve, 4-cylinder engine developing no less than 143 kW; 195 bhp with catalytic converter [and 147 kw/200 bhp without catalyst]. Featuring dynamically flared wheelarches, door sills, rear and front air dams, and extra-sloped rakish rear window, this road racer is perfectly designed and fully equipped for motorsport—starting with the 4-valve cylinder head and ranging to the extra-wide wheelarches designed to accommodate 10" wheels in race trim."

BMW reported up to 146 mph and 0–62 mph comfortably under 7 seconds, with or without a cleaner catalytic exhaust. Europeans expected 0–62 mph (0–100 km/h) in the factory's 6.7 seconds and they were also promised that 50–75 mph in fifth (80 to 120 km/h) would not take more than 7.1 seconds.

It was the M3's predictable behavior, even at extremes such as these, that created a loyal following equaling that of the 2002.

Photo: BMW Werkfoto, 1986

Fuel consumption came in at 20.3 US City mpg (24.3 Imperial mpg), and BMW also reported 31.3 US/37.6 Imperial mpg at a steady Highway 75 mph, pretty frugal for a 140-mph bahn-stormer.

Independent tests in Britain showed that the M3 in any trim was by far the fastest 3 Series built to date. *Autocar* in London reported an average 6.5 seconds for 0–60 mph and a little over 17.2 seconds to reach 100 mph. The maximum speed was reported at 142 mph and the magazine recorded fuel consumption at a disappointing 20.2 Imperial mpg (16.8 US mpg) overall (this figure included all performance testing).

During the track introduction at Mugello, Italy, the original 195-bhp and 200-bhp M3s were tested in a side-by-side comparison with a 204-bhp pre-production Ford Sierra RS Cosworth. After many dramas on the journey down from England through France (the Ford had to be repaired twice, once by BMW mechanics!) the results were published in the September 1986 issue of *Performance Car.*

There was no doubt that BMW offered the public the better-developed street car, but turbocharging was always going to give the Ford an edge in motorsports. Surprisingly, the 200-bhp M3 performed almost exactly as predicted over a far-from-flat "drag strip," but the battered engineering/press fleet Ford was seconds adrift of later independent results, once it reached over 60 mph. Here are our back-to-back results for how these 200-bhp track competitors actually measured up in road trim.

Now that we've examined the European M3 foundation, we'll take a look at how the whole M-idea came to America and prospered with the M3 as the star profit-rocket. It was high time for the 2002's magical entertainment ability to be challenged. Even diehard 02 owners in the US could see that this 3 Series would refresh the sporting soul.

	BMW M3	Sierra R S
0-30 mph (in secs)	2.3	2.4
0-60 mph (in secs)	6.9	6.7
0-90 mph (in secs)	16.0	15.3
0-1/4 mile (in secs)	15.3	15.4
0-100 mph (in secs)	20.5	19.3
50-70 mph in 4th/5th (in secs)	7.2/9.9	5.9/7.1
Fuel consumption overall (Imp. Mpg)	26.9	23.4

10 M3 von der USA

BMW got serious about emission-engineered performance cars in the late 1980s, at last giving the US consumer a driving experience to eclipse the apparently immortal 2002.

BMW of North America Product Communications Manager Robert D. Mitchell knows more than anyone about BMW NA's past, with the perspective of the present. So his insight is particularly important, regarding the turning point that saw BMW NA importing the highest performance Bimmers of all to the biggest export market.

"The 1987 Model Year was critical for us," recalled Mitchell. "We always wanted to sell the ultimate high-performance M-cars in the US, and now we had a real opportunity to do so, because further emissions engineering closed the gap between European and American horsepower levels.

"The 325i brought us within 2 bhp of the catalyst European equivalent; and the adoption of common bumpers—there was no mandatory need to have 5-mph units—saw us [using] 2.5-mph common bumpers [on] European BMWs, like the M3. Thus the weight gap diminished. Utilizing appropriate gearing placed a premium on acceleration and we were able to provide driving dynamics that were, for all practical US consumer purposes, the same as Europe."

Mitchell emphasized that it was not just the 3'er line that was involved. "That 1987 Model Year saw an E32 new 7 Series for the States that was substantially closer to its European counterparts. Engineering on that also brought benefits to the 5 and 6 Series lines. Similarly, it was not just the M3 we were bringing in. We were at a stage of huge sales and model expansion in the US, and the decision was [made] to bring in the existing trio of M-cars: M3, M5, and M6."

That meant BMW NA had twelve models to offer in Model Year 1987, compared to nine in 1986. Prices stretched from a $23,180 revised 325 with 127 bhp eta power, through the $27,300 range of 325i and 325is 2.5-liters of 170 bhp, to the M3 at $34,000 for 192 bhp. The M3

The 2.5 Sport Evo lined up alongside the first Federal road warrior.

Photo: Klaus Schnitzer, US, 1998

did not look impossibly expensive, for the 325i convertible was also over $30,000 (actually $31,000 base) and the flagship M6 stickered at $55,950.

Neither the M6 nor the M5 offered such a close pass on European performance as did the M3. The 325i and M3 were the first honest small-scale BMW performers for the US since the 2002s.

So, what did US consumers get for the M3's $34,000 price? The US importers felt it was, "The compact motorsport BMW for avid enthusiasts," and described how it differed from the rest of the M-trio in "several ways. It is the smallest and least expensive—though by no means inexpensive. It is powered by a four-cylinder engine. And it differs the most from its production stablemates."

Technically, the 1987–91 E30 M3s for America were closely based on the technology discussed in the previous chapter. In 50-States emission form it featured the same power rpm-peaks as a European cat model, but 192 bhp and 170 lb-ft of torque represented insignificant losses. This was worth recording, for compression remained at 10.5:1, despite the ability to run 91-octane pump fuel.

Claimed performance was not as close to the European M3 as expected, with 0–60 mph anticipated in 7.6 seconds and top speed was predicted at 143 mph for Model Years 1987 and 1988. EPA certified fuel economy at 17 City/29 US Highway, although an owner could expect 20 to 23 US mpg in enjoyable action. *Motor Trend* reported that driving the M3 was "an absolute hoot," and recorded somewhat sluggish figures of 0–60 mph in 8.1 seconds and the standing 1/4 mile in 16.03 seconds at 88.3 mph.

In his favorite gray quarry, our US photographer dictates the shots for the M3 and decrees that 192 bhp be applied to the slimiest surface he can find within spinning distance of New York City.

Photo: Klaus Schnitzer, US

The M3 quickly became a racing-school favorite, as demonstrated by the Skip Barber school at Lime Rock Park.

Photos: Klaus Schnitzer, US, 1991

Later American M-products all had speed limiters set lower than the European maximums. Many Europeans believed that America still had the universal 55-mph speed limit years after state-by-state limits were restored. We have lost count of the number of German engineers who still shrug their shoulders and say, "What is the point of engineering such performance for the USA? It's only the Double Nickel they do…." For BMW, such attitudes were erased among the motor engineers in the eighties and then revised among the bulk of mainstream executives following the company's American racing experiences and production contact with US realities through the nineties.

In the previous chapter, we noted the technical power train differences in US and Europe specifications. As far as standard equipment for the US showroom model was concerned, metallic paint was the only option in what *Motor Trend* memorably described as the "full-boat" equipment level of the M3. That meant features such as ABS braking,

super suspension, quicker power steering, cross-spoke alloys, the radical body paneling, and the unique US gear sets.

Motor Trend commented, "When sitting in the M3, it's hard to believe it's a competition bred flyer: the seats are as good as they come, six-way adjustable with lots of support." Leather was the

The 192-bhp Federal motor installation bore a few more leads and lines, closing the horsepower gap on Europe.

Photo: Klaus Schnitzer, US, 1987

standard trim, and electronic temperature control (climate control today) monitored the standard air conditioning. A premium sound system (eight speakers, equalizer and amplifier) delivered stereo radio and cassette with anti-theft and an electric antenna, along with central locking and electric window operation. Most of these items were extra cost or unavailable in some European markets, sometimes to lower curb weight in subsequent Evo developments.

The US consumer was getting a fair dollar deal, even if the purchase price made magazine staffers gulp. Console yourself with the knowledge that Britons were not allowed right-drive steering, numbers were limited, equipment was restricted, and they paid approximately 50 percent more than US buyers.

Other US-shipped 3'er period fittings, such as On Board Computer, Service Interval Indicator, and Active Check Control were also features that would not be seen on every European M3. Some markets—including the domestic German arena—charged extra for the electric two-way power roof that was found on every US-bound M3. Air conditioning was regarded as an expensive luxury in Europe—rather than the basic necessity it was in the US—until European traffic and Japanese imports meant that "air" became a more commonplace showroom item through the 1990s.

First year US sales in 1987 accounted for over 1,100 units of almost 6,400 M3s manufactured. Minimally modified, it would sell better in 1988. Unfortunately, when the balance of the 3 Series received a bigger fuel tank, the M3 tank remained at 14.5 US gallons.

One important technical change noted by BMW NA was that the M3's lower arm front wishbones were changed from steel to aluminum for the 1988 Model Year). Subsequently, aluminum wishbones and subsidiary suspension and crossmember components became a selling point on the 5 Series of 1995, and then on the 1998 E46 Threes.

Stickered at $34,800, the M3 sold close to 1,700 units in its strongest sale season of 1988. As before, metallic paint ($375) remained the only option, although every car would exceed $35,000 because destination and handling charges amounted to $325 and dealer prep then listed at $180. Even at that price, the M3 was "only" halfway up the BMW price tree which was topped by the V12 BMW 750iL which sold for $69,000 plus a "gas guzzler" tax of $1,850.

Fewer than 1,000 M3s were sold in 1989, and the sales volume continued to slide for the rest of the model's American sales life. Not surprisingly, the specification did not change in Model Year 1989, and was not to change significantly for the rest of M3's American sales life to 1991.

This side view of the M3 demonstrates that the US-model bumpers were still more pronounced than European model bumpers.

Photos: Klaus Schnitzer, US, 1989

Prices were restrained too. For Model Year 1989, the sticker price was $34,950 and that price was repeated in Model Year 1990. Options were extended to include heated front seats ($250), remote-control alarm system ($515), and the BMW four-season sunroof ($495). Thus equipped, including all dealer and delivery charges, an M3 could retail at $36,736.

The interior of the ultimate production EVO M3 shows the suedette rim steering wheel and red safety belts.

Photo: Klaus Schnitzer, US, 1998

For Model Year 1991, the price of the M3 had climbed by nearly $1,000 and you could now treat yourself to an $825 CD auto-change player, while the anti-theft ($540) and heated seating ($300) were up $50 each. Now, sales were below 400 a year in the US; and the model—out of production in Germany in 1990—was unlisted for 1992. BMW NA sales records reveal that a further 81 BMW M3s sold through their network in that 1992–93 period.

The 1991 US market demonstrated to BMW that sales didn't increase as a God-given right in every calendar year, but that the 3 Series could take almost any commercial punishment. That year, sales shrank back to some 53,343 US units.

Over half of those hard-fought sales—comparatively unaffected by the recession and the impact of Toyota Lexus/Nissan Infiniti on the luxury car market—were 3 Series.

M3 production and US M3 sales: 1985–93

These figures are for the M3 sedan only, excluding Motorsport prototypes, all from the Munich 1.1 plant. All totals have been overhauled since the publication of Unbeatable BMW, using year-by-year sales totals researched and supplied by BMW NA in 1999.

These US statistics do not match the March 1987 to December 1990 production totals of 5,300 supplied by the normally infallible factory's "Produktion Seit 1948" source, but they reveal the main sales trends. These figures show

The most notable features of the Sport Evo M3 are the extended front and rear spoilers, which (with a designated tool) were adjustable, plus oversize wheels and contrasting-color bumper inlays.

Photos: Klaus Schnitzer, US, 1998

how E30 M3 US sales persisted after production ceased, but volumes were negligible, accounting for fewer than 500 units from 1990–93.

The US accounted for 29 percent of all E30 M3 sales in this short period. The subsequent E36 M3 smashed all sales and export records for M3 in the 1990s.

	M3 Sedan Production	US M3 Sales
1985	1	—
1986	2,396	—
1987	6396	1113
1988	3426	1675
1989	2541	979
1990	2424	764
1991	—	384
1992*	—	76
1993	—	5
TOTAL	17,184	4,996

* Previous E30 1990 and 1991 Model Year only available from this point. For Cabriolet statistics see page 121.

American buyer beware! The Model Code (MC) for a US official import car is 1003 and the VIN Code is AK03. European market (therefore gray-market imported if offered in the US) codes were as follows:

M3 Model	Model Code
200-bhp non-cat original	1001 MC with AK01 VIN
195-bhp European cat sedan	1005 MC with AK05 VIN
238-bhp Sport Evolution	1007 MC with AK07 VIN
200-bhp non-cat Convertible	BB01 MC with BB01 VIN
215-bhp cat Convertible	BB05 MC with BB05 VIN

BMW Motorsport also supplied some hints for identifying specific M3 types. Aside from the chassis data, other useful statistics include motor identification codes which are based on 23 4E A, covering initial production from the M3 saloon to Evolution I, upgraded beyond this point to ID-specific rarities.

Because of possible fraud, we'll leave genuine customers to withdraw such valuable details from their BMW network. A genuine 2.5-liter does follow logic in using 25 as the initial engine-number numeral, but the rest of the code is for BMW to reveal on application.

The American market M3 was allowed to stagnate. Given how sales of speciality machines other than the M3—notably, the M5 and 850 CSi coupe—shriveled during the recession, it was not surprising that BMW AG and BMW NA felt no need to continually develop the car.

Recent research shows that it was actually the American E30 M3 that kept those lines alive at Munich during the switch to E36, for production ran all the way to December 1990, totaling around 5,300 units over three years and nine months. The only mystery is that BMW NA Sales figures only add up to a tad short of 5,000, so somewhere, 304 US specification M3s have gone missing.

The E30 was running out of showroom time in the US, but back in Europe, the Evolution pace got a lot hotter before the E30 was done.

11 Evolution of the M3 Species

German, American and British market M3s get regular updates with competition in mind.

The 1983 Mercedes 2.3-liter/16-valve with its Cosworth-engineered DOHC aluminum cylinder head had proved a commercial and competitive bombshell to BMW. It forced BMW to enter the four-cylinder/16-valve arena that its Untertürkheim rival had pried open. That was a good thing for all BMW enthusiasts, for the war to provide efficient 16-valve rear-drive saloons was fought between BMW and Mercedes into the 1990s.

Evolutions on the M3 theme were numerous and encompassed variants from M3 Convertible to the final 238-bhp Evo Sport. This final model had a run of just 600 2.5-liters, completed while the factory ripped out the E30 lines to begin volume production of the E36.

The Convertible M3

BMW Motorsport built a very strictly controlled number of M3 Convertibles from 1988 to June 1991. They used bodies that were created by the adjacent Landshut and Regensberg factories, which were responsible for the reinforced two-door body of the Convertible (Cabriolet in Europe). Fewer than 800 M3 Convertibles were made by the close of production in 1991 and none of them were officially imported to the US.

M3 Cabriolet production at Landshut (body) and Regensberg (assembly)	
Year	Units produced
1988	130
1989	180
1990	176
1991	300
Total	786

The M3 convertible almost did not make it into 1988 production as a four-cylinder at all. The first show car had a 4 x 4 drive train hitched to the usual BMW 325i power plant. This became a one-off when the realists persuaded management to opt for the four-cylinder M3 unit and rear drive. Never sold in large numbers, the model served as a demonstration of the M-division's ability to build niche-on-niche models in the days before BMW Individual was the established entity it is today.

There were essentially three power trains offered in the M3 Convertible: a non-catalytic converter 200-bhp, a catalyzed 195-bhp (October 1988 onward) and a March 1990-manufactured 215-bhp used in Ravaglia/Cecotto special editions. Other power levels could be found in this hand-finished machine, including the 220 bhp Evo II.

The M3 Convertibles were compromised as "Ultimate Driving machines" by the usual loss of structural rigidity resulting from cutting off a steel roof, compounded by the loss of the sedan's bonded screens. The Convertible also sacrificed the sedan's raised rear deck and the M3's trademark back spoiler. At 1360 kg/2992 lbs curb weight was up (160 kg/352 lbs) along with price,

a startling 90,000 DM as compared with a launch price of 58,000 DM for the original M3 sedan.

A few M3 Convertibles (just over 30) were sent to Britain—still in LHD, of course—to see if the natives would pay almost double the launch price of the sedan (£37,250 versus £23,550), which they did. Today, the Cabrio is valued across Europe—the UK included—as worth up to a third more than the sedan.

In Convertible form, the M3 received the 3 Series hood in electrically power-operated form. The roof, however, had no interior headlining, as might have been expected at this price, and the back window was reportedly (*What Car*, June 1989) in plastic. BMW Motorsport reported useful updates, including modifying the soft-top hood release so that it had two hydraulic cylinders for the hood, and fixing the hydraulic cylinder and shift lever for the hood release. The dual hydraulic cylinder system became standard in 1989, and now the power-top operation was flawless, with the top mimicking the disappearing act of more mundane 3'ers.

For reasons staffers doubtless recall—possibly the price proximity—*What Car* critiqued the M3 Convertible alongside Jaguar's 5.3-liter soft-top. They measured the fresh air Bimmer—a 200-

M3 convertibles are among the most desirable of all the E30 variants.

Photo: BMW GB, 1988

Hood raised—and they were all power tops in M3 format—the M3 convertible looks snug in 200-bhp non-catalytic converter specification.

Photo: BMW GB, 1988

bhp example—as capable of 143 mph, 26.2 Imp. mpg (21.8 US mpg), with 0–60 mph completed in 6.5 seconds, and 0–100 mph in less than 18 seconds.

In short, the 2.3-liter BMW was considerably better at accelerating than the 5.3-liter Jag (sold only as an automatic with 142 mph, 0–60 mph in 7.7 seconds, and 0–100 mph in 19 seconds); and the Bimmer consumed a lot less gas. It almost made the BMW look like a thrifty-consumer choice, until you remembered the open-air pleasures of V12 motoring versus four-cylinders.

The best-selling British monthly magazine concluded of their unexpected comparison, "The BMW is an immensely rewarding car to drive and we are very reluctant not to place it top because of this. It also looks very stylish—far more so than its already attractive saloon brother—is cheaper to run than the Jaguar, and the hood mechanism is superb."

Evolutionary evidence

There were so many Evolutions and special editions (2,261 limited-run M-mutants) that they are charted chronologically, adding the perspective of the "normal" production variants. In December 1990 and July 1998, the factory and BMW Sales subsidiaries reported the development of the following M3 variants, and supplied their build dates.

E30 M3 Sedan/Cabriolet output, all models

Type	Bhp	Dates Produced	Units Produced
2.3 M3	200	9/86–8/89	5,187
2.3 M3 (cat)	195	12/86–12/90	6,097 (all types)
2.3 M3 (US)	192	3/87–12/90	5,300
2.5 M3 Sport Evo III	238	12/89–3/90	600, all but three in 1990
2.3 M3 Cabrio (non-cat)	200	5/88–7/89	136
2.3 M3 Cabrio (cat)	195/215	1988–89 (215 bhp ended 6/91)	650
Grand total			17,970

E30 M3 Evolution sedans (Build dates/Production limits within sedan output)			
Type	Bhp	Build dates	Production limit
2.3 M3 Evo I	200	2/87–5/87	505 made
2.3 M3 Evo II	220	3/88–5/88	501 made
2.3 M3 KAT, "Europameister '88"	195	10/88–11/88	150
2.3 M3 Ravaglia/Cecotto	215	4/89–7/89	505
2.3 M3 Cat	215	9/89–12/90	Unlimited
2.5 M3 Sport Evo III	238	12/89–3/90	600, all but three in 1990

Evo power upgrades

BMW Motorsport revealed that the standard 200-bhp (non-catalyst car) could be upgraded some 20 bhp to the level of Evolution II via its parts sales department and a reprogrammed Bosch Digital Motor Electronics (DME) microprocessor. The DME microprocessor is identified as the usual Bosch 0261.200.090, but has a modification to the labeling, to show that Motorsport has re-programmed the standard unit.

Incidentally, the Bosch ID codes for all M3s have the prefix 0261.200. This prefix is then followed by 071 for the 200/195-bhp machines and the 1988–89 Cabrios, 090 for Evolution II, and 091 for all 215-bhp M3s and the last (1990–91) Cabrios. These were the Ravaglia/Cecotto specials, plus M3 KAT saloons (only of the 1989–90 production span shown on the table above). The 092 suffix is reserved for the 238-bhp/2.5-liters.

The same kind of hardware and reprogrammed software approach will increase output of the catalyst M3 from a showroom 195 horsepower to 210 bhp. The Bosch DME programming ID is 0261.200.091. Hardware replacement included new inlet manifolding and heavy-duty valve springs.

Evos in the showroom

Models dubbed Evolutions were necessary for Motorsport, and the Europameister, Ravaglia, and Cecotto special editions were offered to cash in on BMW's admirable Motorsport achievements. Note that Evos were only admitted to FIA International races, such as those Group A events qualifying for the 1987–88 European or 1987 World Touring Car Championship events.

As road cars, the Evo M3s were a mixed bunch. Some earlier 2.3-liters of 220 bhp actually accelerated more slowly than the original 200-bhp models because they were pulling taller gearing. The final 2.5-liter is deservedly a legend, assembling the most desirable features in one spot. Still, the biggest 2.5-liter stretch made what was already a rough motor by Bimmer standards an automobile vibrator that would never have made production, save for the need for speed.

The first modified M3 for motorsports was made between February and May 1987. BMW made slightly more than the 500 required as a 10 percent Evolution on the basic 5,000-unit run originally required for initial homologation. This made an Evo I the basic weapon for BMW's assault on the 1987 World and European Championships, but it was also a winner at home in Germany, with another five assorted national titles falling to the M3 that year. It has collectible pedigree, but little to offer in road use.

The Evolution I ran upgraded aerodynamics, but the power train stayed at 200 bhp with no catalytic converter for the street, and under 300 bhp in race trim. This first Evolution model (200-bhp) had a "E" punched onto the cast eye

This 220-bhp Roberto Ravaglia special edition is identified by black wheel centers on the 7.5 × 16-inch alloys.

Photo: Author, Oxfordshire, UK 1989

of the cylinder head, underneath the fourth cylinder throttle housing. Externally, the car was identified by an extended front (lower leading edge) and two rear spoilers. It also used a lightweight trunk lid, minus the thin-gauge metal roof that caused all the leading M3s to be disqualified at the opening round of the World Championship.

Evolution II (220-bhp) was much more recognizable, both externally and in the upgraded engine bay. Again, a smidgen over 500 were manufactured, this time between March and May 1988. Evo II carried an air collector and cam cover in white, also Motorsport-striped. The motor generated 220 bhp at 6,750 rpm via revised camshafts, pistons, lightened flywheel, replacement air-intake trunking, and reprogrammed Bosch Motronic ECU.

That 2.3 motor ran an elevated 11:1 compression and was mated to a slightly taller final drive (3.15:1). BMW claimed a substantial increase in maximum speed. Their usual M3 figures were 146 mph and 0–62 mph in 6.7 seconds. For the Evolution II, BMW claimed 152 mph and 0–60 mph in the usual 6.7 seconds. *Autocar & Motor* reported 6.6 seconds for 0–60 mph and 17.8 seconds for 0–100 mph, coupled to a 15.2-second quarter mile at 92 mph. The West London

weekly timed the Evo II at 148 mph around the Millbrook bowl, while managing an overall fuel consumption of 26 Imperial (21.7 US) mpg, thanks to the taller final drive.

The Evolution II also sported additional spoilers, which carried front brake ducts and the extra lip on the rear wing, resting on a lightweight boot lid. Further weight savings came from thinner materials used for the rear wing, bumper supports, back screen, and rear side windows. Altogether, the factory expected to save 10 kg (22 lbs) to lower the homologated racing weight.

The 220 bhp Evo II may be the greatest roadgoing M3 of all. It is smoother than the later 2.5 and practically as fast, so long as you kept the revs between five- and seven-thousand rpm. The chassis, running Pirelli P700s of 225/45 section on 7.5 x 16-inch BBS alloys, never seemed to run out of dry road grip, understeering if over-driven. In the wet, the back slid out only if the full 7,300 rpm red-line was employed in second or third.

Later in 1988 (October to November), the factory made the rarest run of any M3 type to see production. Just 150 suitably decorated "Europameister '88" M3s were manufactured to celebrate what turned out to be another BMW win in the final European Touring Car Championship season as of this writing.

Identification clues on 505 of the 215-bhp special edition Ravaglia/Cecotto machines (April to July 1989) included the Evolution II spoilers and the use of body color for the air collector and cam cover (either Misano Red or Nogaro Silver). All the Ravaglia limited editions came with gaudy seat inlays and leather surrounds, and some other interior parts were coated in silver.

Front electric windows and an on-board computer were added to the standard fitments listed earlier for the M3. External identification is aided by black centers for the 7.5J x 16 inch alloys which carry extremely effective Pirelli P700-Z covers in 225/45 sizings. One test car had a plaque inside that read, "M3 73/505 1989 BMW Motorsport GmbH." Cars from these series should be signed either by Roberto Ravaglia (for UK) or Johnny Cecotto.

The 2.5-liter Evolution Sport

The final competition twist to the Evo theme was only briefly produced (3 months and 600 examples between December 1989 and March 1990). A detailed specification, drawn alongside the later 215-bhp M3 of 2.3 liters for instant comparison purposes, can be found in the table to the right.

The primary changes were a capacity increase from 2,302 cc to 2,467 cc, via an elongated crankshaft throw and plumper bores (95 x 87 mm), a consequent gain of 18 bhp and 7.4 lb-ft, and a radical rethink of aerodynamics. Both front and rear spoilers could be adjusted, there was a degree of ground effect, the front whee arches were enlarged, and front suspension was lowered. The interior was overhauled to feature a distinctive Motorsport look, along with a suede finish for the leather steering-wheel rim, gear knob, and hand-brake grip.

The 2.5-liter had been conceived purely as the basis for a more effective weapon against the similar-capacity and more radically aero-developed Mercedes in the German Touring Car Championship. The final M3 Evo bowed against a backdrop of BMW Motorsport's Christmas-time conference which celebrated win-

The limited Ravaglia edition leather/cloth seating was distinctive. Note that manual adjustments remain for front cushion and height.

Photo: Author, Oxfordshire, UK, 1989

Comparative specifications of US 2.3-liter M3 and final 2.5-liter Sport Evo for Europe

		M3 US	M3 Sport Evo III
Engine	Engine type	In-line four-cylinder	In-line four-cylinder
	Construction	DOHC, 16-valve, alloy head, iron block	DOHC, 16-valve, alloy head, iron block
Capacity	Engine capacity	2,302 cc	2,467 cc
	Bore x stroke	93.4 x 84 mm	95 x 87 mm
	Compression	10.5:1	10.2:1
	Peak power	192 bhp @ 6,750 rpm	238 bhp @ 7,000 rpm
	Max torque	170 lb-ft @ 4,750 rpm	176 lb-ft @ 4,750 rpm
	Bhp per liter	83.4	96.5
	Fuel	Unleaded, 91-octane	Unleaded, 95-octane
	Tank	70 liters (14.5 US gal)	62 liters (11.3 US gal)
Transmission	Final drive	4:1	3.15:1
	First	3.83:1	3.72:1
	Second	2.20:1	2.40:1
	Third	1.40:1	1.77:1
	Fourth	1:1	1.26:1
	Fifth	0.81:1	1.00:1
Wheels	Standard tires	205/55 VR 15	225/45 ZR 16
	Standard wheels (alloy)	7J x 15	7.5J x 16
Performance	0–60 mph	7.6 seconds	6.1 seconds
	50–75 mph (5th)	NA	10.7 seconds
	Top speed (claimed)	143 mph	154 mph
	Urban/City mpg (US)	17	18.8
	Mpg at 56 mph	NA	45.6
	Mpg at 75 mph	NA	36.2
Body	Type	Two-door	Two-door
	Length	171.1 in	171.1 in
	Width	66.1 in	66.1 in
	Height	53.9 in	53.9 in
	Front track	55.6 in	55.8 in
	Rear track	56.1 in	56.3 in
	Aerodynamic drag	0.33 Cd	0.33 Cd
	Curb weight	2,735 lbs	2,640 lbs
	Power steering	20.5:1	19.6:1
Suspension	Front	MacPherson strut, anti-roll bar	Lowered 10 mm (0.39 in)
	Rear	Trailing arms (15 degrees trail)	Trailing arms (15 degrees trail)
Brakes	Brakes	4-wheel disc, as original M3 (from 5-series)with changed f/pad material and ABS	As before, plus air ducts from front spoiler and ABS

ning the German national title again in 1989 (quite unexpectedly). Mercedes had been equipped with full-production 2.5-liters (plus subsequent short-stroke Evolutions) for seasons before BMW answered with such a big four-cylinder. While it snowed outside the snug, yet temporary Munich conference halls, inside veteran BMW motor engineer Franz Zinnecker returned to the faithful four and gave it a new lease of life. As German TV broadcast, the menacing black 2.5 M3 Sport Evolution was exposed from under wraps.

The M3 Sport Evo was rated at almost 240 horsepower and could exceed an honest 150 mph.

Photo: Klaus Schnitzer, US, 1998

There was not much to see externally, just the bolt-adjustable wing set and the hint of rogue speed given by the lowered front end and enlarged wheelarches (to take the 18-inch diameter wheels then forecast for Group A). Underneath the forward-hinging hood, there was definitely a tale to tell.....

Franz Zinnecker commented, "At the heart of a really successful BMW engine is the knowledge we have of combustion chamber layout, inlet and exhaust manifolding. If we know more than others, especially in four-cylinders, this dates back to the work of 1967. Then the company had just 12 people in the engine department and we worked with the failures like the Apfelbeck racing engine as well as the four-cylinders that made the company so well known through 02 series and racing. In the department, we had the half-day services of Herr Rech: I tell you, this guy knew more about combustion and four-cylinders than anyone I have ever met. His knowledge was a cornerstone on which we built."

Zinnecker raised a previously forbidden BMW engines engineering topic: "Originally, von Falkenhausen would not let us have Siamese bores. This rule was broken with the bigger six-cylinders and, therefore, we have this feature on all M3 motors as well."

Building on a reputation for ultimate bhp per liter in normally aspirated, catalytic converter-equipped vehicles, BMW Motorsport closed in on the magical 100 bhp per liter, with a final 96.5 bhp per liter. The M3 2.5-liter featured oversize inlet valves (38.5 mm, or 1.52 inches) instead of the usual M3 sizing of 38 mm (1.5 inches), while

This Sport Evo was the biggest capacity—and most powerful— M3 manufactured, at 238 bhp. This example has a strut tower brace to stiffen the front end of the chassis.

Photo: Author, Goodwood race track, West Sussex, UK, 1998

On the M3 Sport Evo, the flap rear wing and extended front spoiler combined with underfloor work were said to increase aerodynamic downforce.

Photo: BMW GB Ltd., 1990

camshaft timing went from a duration of 264 degrees to 282 degrees. The compression ratio was not raised, unlike that of some earlier Evolutions, which could not run catalytic converters. It dropped from 10.5:1 for the series M3 to 10.2:1. Other internal engine changes included sodium-cooled exhaust valves and oil injection jets (an old turbo trick) to spray beneath the pistons.

BMW claimed an entirely believable 154 mph maximum and 0–62 mph in 6.5 seconds, as well as the reduction of the 1-kilometer travel time to 26.7 seconds, rather than the 2.3-liter model's 27.3 seconds. The Evolution final drive did few favors for fifth-gear acceleration (slower than a 2.3), but fourth gear let the engine rev a little and returned a reasonable 7.6 seconds for 50–75 mph. The factory claimed 22.6 urban mpg, equivalent to 18.8 US mpg, which is supported by independent results of 22.68 imperial mpg (18.9 US mpg).

Aerodynamic evolution

From a racing viewpoint, the most significant alteration to the newly refined M3 chassis was a new front and rear wing set that could be adjusted (albeit slowly and carefully for the private owner) to provide three basic positions, fore and aft.

The aerodynamic progression was from fully retracted (front spoiler in, rear laid almost flat) to a full extension of the front "lip" and a distinctly formula "flipper" look to the back blade.

The effect was to maintain the usual 0.33 Cd in the retracted position, cutting front-end lift and allowing slight lift forces on the back. BMW claimed there was "virtually zero lift" in the front and "slight downforces at the rear" when fully extended. They quantified the latter expression, telling us there was "an increase in axle load by a substantial 840 Newton at the front, while at the rear it is still a remarkable 400 Newton."

Backing up the obvious aerodynamic applications was the Venturi principle spoiler, integrated in the front. BMW explained that through its specific shape, "it artificially narrows the flow of air beneath the car by means of a v-shaped wind deflection profile. As a result, the air flowing beneath the car accelerates to a higher speed and creates an under pressure, the car being literally sucked onto the road." The front spoiler also deleted the usual auxiliary lamps in favor of extra brake ducting. Although the front discs and callipers remained unchanged, upgraded heat-resistant pads were selected.

Other front-end changes included lowered ride height (10 mm, or 0.4 inches), a further flare to the wheel arches (to allow 18-inch racing slicks), and yet more attention to compress the lattices of the front kidney grille. All front-end openings were additionally streamlined (headlight mountings, front grille attachment areas, and surrounds to the hood), usually using rubber fillings, which had been seen on racing M3s at the Avus track in 1988.

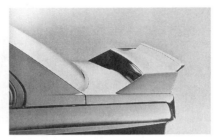

The spoiler and rear wing of the 2.5 Sport Evo had three set positions, "Monza" (high speed, retracted); "Normal" (halfway extended) and "Nürburgring" (fully extended for maximum down-force effect).

Photos: BMW Werkfoto

Curb weight remained as for previous Evolutions at 1,200 kg (2,640 lbs), but that had meant quite a lot of additional lightening to off-set the extra engine capacity effects and generous standard equipment. Specifically, the company attacked the fuel tank capacity, substituting the 320i/325i unit of 62 liters (13.64 Imperial gal-lons) instead of the usual M3 70-liter reservoir. Other slimming maneuvers included lighten-ing front and rear bumpers, rear trunk lid, and the depth of rear and side glass, just as for the original Evolution M3. A further diet regime was implemented through deletion of the roof grab handles and reading lights.

Larger Michelin MXX or Pirelli P700 covers of 225/45 ZR 16 accompanied by 7.5J x 16 cross-spoke alloys with "Nogaro Silver" hub and spoke finish filled the wheel wells, and provided prodi-gious grip on all but the slipperiest of surfaces.

Color combos

The color choices were "Jet Black" or "Brilliant Red," each contrasted by red or black bumper insets. A green band was prominently tinted into the front screen, as had been featured in US M3s. The interior was overhauled with the suedette mentioned earlier, plus red seat belts.

The door trim panels were also unique, and an M3 logo was placed on the door sill. Motorsport seats with seatbelt slots were extremely effective, but no Recaro option was offered on this model. The seats were nor-mally finished in anthracite cloth, and wore Motorsport striping, but black leather was an option and air conditioning was available.

The final M3 Sport Evolution III 2.5 was a magnificent farewell to a fundamentally simple front-engine, rear-drive, four-cylinder format. It had inevitable rough patches as the big four worked through its wide rpm range, but very few rear drive machines from the production saloon-car ranks gave more driving pleasure. It also gave BMW a lot of competition pleasure and its rivals a lot of discomfort.

12 The Ultimate Touring Car: M3 Technology

When the opposition is turbocharged, you'd better have some good ideas in the pits and the driver's seat.

At the media M3 debut in Mugello, Italy, in 1986, Dieter Quester drove a plain white racing M3 prototype, demonstrating that there was more icing to come on the M3 performance cake. According to Munich publicists, this race M3 boasted "nearly 300 bhp" in a weight "close to" the class minimum of 960 kg (2,112 lbs). Pirelli 235/590-16 slicks adorned BBS alloy 16 x 10-inch-wide rims on this 9,000-rpm racing prophet. The test M3 completed a deadly serious hidden agenda, further convincing the BMW Board of Management that the M3 had a world-class racing future.

The M-machine was being prepared to Group A international rules (production of 5,000 per year). All factory preparation was aimed at ensuring customers received a reliable road or race car, as well as some special moves for the factory M3s that would open another era in the BMW Motorsport legend. It was a compressed program, for the road M3 had to make bulk production for homologation in 1986. The M3 subsequently made its factory racing debut at the March 1987 opening round of a new FIA World Championship for Touring Cars.

Details of the 2.3-liter motor were the responsibility of Werner Frowein. Herr Frowein recalled during 1989, "In April 1983, we had the first running prototype of the M3 in place. It had the normal 3 Series body and the four-cylinder engine was derived directly from that of the M88-coded M1 of six cylinders. We had started with the cylinder head and block from an M1, suitably abbreviated to four inline cylinders with the water passages closed off."

In May 1984, an Experimental Vehicle (Versuchtrager, abbreviated to VT) official project number (VT 105) was assigned to the union of the redeveloped 16-valve and what was described as a 3 Series with "Power

In terms of major
titles won, the BMW
M3 was the most
successful touring
car in the world.

Photo: BMW Werkfoto,
1986, Mugello, Italy

Styling." Now the chassis and aerodynamics could progress, initially using the base of a 323i, then the most powerful E30 on offer. Under project numbers 106 to 112, every aspect of the M3, from engine cooling and temperature behavior to crash tests, progressed from that 3-Series foundation.

By October 1984, they were ready to tackle endurance tests on the old 14-mile Nürburgring under the development code VT 113. The M3 test program intensified, including 10,000 kilometers (6,200 miles) around the legendary old race track's humps and treacherous curves, plus 50,000 kilometers (31,500 miles) of high-speed endurance in Southern Italian heat at the Fiat-owned Nardo bowl. Such auto-tortures highlighted Motorsport's needs for lighter, aerodynamically revised bodywork, mostly achieved through plastics. But the cost and path of the M3 project was not so conveniently clarified as a series of development dates and a race debut.

There were fearsome internal company debates, favoring six-cylinders for any street-performance 3 Series in preference to the M3 program. BMW Motorsport extensively tested the domestic rival to M3, the Mercedes 2.3/16, against the 325i. BMW management was seriously worried by the public and press criticism Mercedes had taken for the roughness of their four-cylinder engine with Cosworth-cast 16-valve head, and felt a smooth six was the only answer the buying public would expect of BMW. Even today, when rumors of a "bent Six" (V6) from BMW abound, company engineering and marketing power brokers regard the inline six as sacred, a true BMW-believer's motor-shrine that must not be violated.

Back in the 1980s, there was a rival to the M3 in a road car project labeled E30/7, which took the 3.5-liter power train of the 735i and installed it in a 3 Series high performer of massive, but nose-heavy, potential. The author drove an Alpina E30 BMW concocted along these lines, with over 260 flexible horsepower. It was a great street car with superbly sorted handling that worked well. But as a racing car? Forget it! The weighty engine would have operated under severely restricted European Group A regulations and would not be able to generate enough power to counteract the weight penalty involved. It would obviously require measures such as bigger brakes and transmission components, losing the flyweight agility that was in the M3 bloodline.

As late as June 1985, the M3's future in motorsports was being debated at Board Level via papers submitted by Werner Frowein. It seems that the impetus to compete in the new 1987 FIA World Championship for sedans was prompted by the fact that Bernie Ecclestone was promoting its charms.

BMW had happily dealt with global Grand Prix supremo Ecclestone in both M1 racing and its successful World Championship turbocar victory of 1983, scored with Ecclestone's Brabham team. BMW and Bernie Ecclestone had their Formula 1 fights, but Ecclestone saved corporate face with the M1 supporter races to European Grand Prix. For the Italo-German M1 was so tardy that M1 never completed its planned Porsche-beater sports racing program.

Thus, BMW's historic first world title for a champion (Nelson Piquet) driving a turbocar was both a respected and recent racing memory at the BMW HQ Haus on Munich's pulsing Petuelring. The 1987 World Touring Car Championship race program was agreed upon, devoting DM by the million to becoming the first title-holders.

Race Lore

The S14 slant four-cylinder was built on its DOHC 16-valve layout to create a substantial power bonus. However, the layout of production exhaust manifolding and the restrictions of Group A regulations (standard size porting, standard inlet, and exhaust manifolds) kept power beneath the old 2-liter Formula 2 levels of 310-plus bhp.

BMW factory engines engineering sources reveal the existence of four S14-coded M3 competition motor variants. They started with the S14/1 of 2.3 liters for German, European and World Championship use. We could find no code for the equivalent rally motors, but they grew from the original S14/1. Next, the S14/2 was specifically assigned to German Championship 2.5-liter units, the most powerful slide-throttle, twin-injector, variant to be engineered by Motorsport. The S14/4 was a specific 2-liter for British and many other national championships, derivatives of which were deployed from 1987–92. Italy had a 2-liter street 320is that was powered by a short stroke 72.6 x 69.3mm M3 motor. Built from the usual S14 base, it offered 192 bhp at 6,900 rpm and 122.5 lb-ft of torque by 4,600 rpm, figures that are worth remembering when we get into 2-liter race power outputs.

Before Evo engines were available (roughly March 1987 to July 1988), the S14/1 delivered a quoted 295 bhp at 8,000 rpm, and the PR-predicted 300 bhp was not exceeded until the second (1988) season. Power was always quoted by the Munich press department as increased by 50 percent over standard. This meant 300 bhp at 8,000 rpm: some 128.6 bhp per liter.

The rpm limit in this first season was usually set around 8,500 revs. Maximum torque was far from fabulous in that it was delivered only at a sky-high 7,000 rpm. Yet the Group A M3 boasted 198.5 lb-ft (270 Nm) of torque, some 20 percent higher than the European street value of 176 lb-ft at 4,750 rpm.

A more flexible BMW S14 Motorsport alternative specification for rallying could run legally on

BMW's pedigree twin-cam four was asked to rev higher and higher, escalating from 280 rallying horsepower at 7,500 revs in 1987 to 320 bhp at 9,800 rpm in 1989.

Photos: Author, Munich Mobile Tradition warehouse, 1999

European streets. Centering on less-aggressive camshaft profiles, it was offered from 1987-88. This yielded 270 Nm at 6,500 rpm, some 500 rpm earlier than the pure racing specification: power was a solid 280 bhp at 7,500 rpm, again dropping the peak some 500 rpm. To judge by the results on the tight tarmac tests of Europe, this engine specification was a success. The author's privileged access through Prodrive revealed that it was actually a lot easier to drive than some aftermarket conversions for the street!

The 2.3-liter factory competition units had that breadth of torque and snappy horsepower that BMW street car owners would recognize as a muscular cousin to the pre-emission 2002, right through the street M3s to the 1990s 318is/ti.

The race M3 was slightly overbored (from 93.4 mm to 94 mm) to reach 2,331.8 cc rather than the production 2,302 cc. Another dimensional change was the induction tract width—Motorsport selected 29.5 mm (1.17 inches) over the production 28 mm (1.1 inches).

Running a Bosch Motronic engine management system, further developed by the BMW-Bosch alliance, BMW Motorsport was able to command and monitor a 12:1 cr. in place of the usual 10.5:1, consequently improving power. Subsequently, BMW Motorsport did its own programming.

Some 300 bhp at 8,000 rpm was available courtesy of a new exhaust manifold for the bulk of the 1988 season, but that was not the only motor change. The induction diameter grew to 30.5 mm and larger homologated intake valves with slide throttle operation accompanied that move. Torque was described as similar to the original race motors.

In 1989, the World and European Touring Car Championships were dead, but the white heat of the German home international touring car title hunt meant that BMW had to graft harder to find a winning edge. Utilizing a 12:1 cr., BMW

Motorsport, under the engine direction of Franz Zinnecker, changed most key elements of the 2.3-liter motor. German championship regulations also allowed the use of slide-throttle air admission (as earlier used in Formula 2) and this allowed a small power bonus. The major hunt in 1989 was for higher rpm, to unleash some extra horsepower.

BMW Motorsport engineers overhauled their racing motor with a beefier crankcase, along with lightened camshafts and pistons. A BMW, as opposed to pure Bosch Motronic, Electronic Control Unit (ECU 4) was allied to double injectors to boost rpm and mixture flow. The ECU 4 electronic "brain" prompted both ignition and injection.

The rpm-hunt was effective. At the beginning of 1989, the drivers were allowed 8,800 rpm, while early summer brought them 9,200 rpm, and ended the year with 9,800 rpm at their disposal. Despite this success, the official power peak was given as 8,500 rpm and 320 bhp. Fractionally augmented (+ 3.7 lb-ft, or 5 Nm) pulling power was now rated at 202 lb-ft (275 Nm) for 1989 at the usual 7,000 rpm peak. There was no doubt that the race engine became peakier as well as more powerful. The rally motors received a 10-bhp bonus in 1989, now quoted at 290 bhp at 8,000 rpm.

The continually developed M3 motor was winding toward a 10,000-rpm rev limit and an increasingly narrow power band, but the unreliability of the valve springs affected all of the leading teams. Former Grand Prix and IMSA GTP BMW engines engineer Martin Kolk switched to M3 engine development during 1987–1990 and recalled, "as the revs went up, the springs began to fail. When a spring fails at high rpm, it always makes for other engine damage. We had to do something and I worked through six possible spring solutions before I had the confidence to bet my colleagues that we could go face the 3,500 kilometers of the Nürburgring 24 hours and win with (Roberto) Ravaglia.

"They all laughed at me, but we made it work and the engines became reliable enough to win this race too, not just a sprint 4 hours. I bet them three bottles of champagne per top car, and we had the top six! I tell you, the Christmas party was something that year, because I had won all these bottles of champagne and kept them on one side for the best party we ever had!"

The normally quiet and earnest Kolk recalled wistfully, "Those were good times, racing the M3. Wolfgang Peter Flohr was the manager there, and he knew how to motivate people, how to get 25 hours a day out of each engineer. He was fantastic at leading people, and you need real charisma to lead a department like BMW Motorsport."

Dr. RevMeister!

A 1990 evolution saw the motor grow to 2.5 liters, matching Mercedes in its Evo four-cylinder series of 190Es. Whatever the capacity, experi-enced BMW motor engineers recalled a decade later that the biggest problems were in "making this engine develop power and high rpm" legally.

"It was more difficult than the work we did in Formula," commented one insider, "and the most difficult part of all was to keep up with the stresses inside this engine. It was quite a big four-cylinder, and we got it to rev to the other side of 11,000 rpm, instead of the original design for 7,500!"

This work was applied to the qualification engines, but human nature, or at least the rac-ing driver's perverse nature being what it is, our insider continued, "they all wanted to have the higher revs to race. We could make the engine last just for a qualifying lap at 11,000 rpm, but only if it was put together absolutely perfectly. Then we would change the E-prom ECU and allow the higher rpm.

"I can tell you one funny story that illustrates this about a German driver on the Nürburgring.

Prodrive Performer

Autocar of London hired 1989 RAC Rally of Great Britain winner Pentti Airikkala to drive a num-ber of rally cars in the 1980s, including the 1987 Corsican World Championship-winning Prodrive M3. This winner's performance was electronically tested, something that was easier in a road-registered rally machine with two seats than in the equivalent racer, so these are the most comprehensive figures we have seen for a factory-engined original competi-tion M3.

Equipped with Michelin 8-inch-wide slicks, slicing through racing ratios in the Getrag 5-speeder, this M3 was hauling an exceptionally low curb weight for a fully equipped rally car (2,320 lbs, or 1,050 kg).

The results were a marked improvement on the showroom model, but not so startling as might be expected. Using an 8,600-rpm limit, Airikkala recorded 0–60 mph in 5.3 seconds, and 0–100 mph in a smid-gen over 13 seconds. Maximum speed was 122 mph at 8,600 rpm and the lower gears were obviousy "long" in the race tradition, for first gear allowed over 50 mph!

He was driving for a works-backed team in 1988, but they had little money; I knew they could not afford to blow our engines up. The driver kept asking for us to put a lower axle ratio in his car, to make it accelerate better than all the others. He promised he would back off on

In the UK, the S14/M3 four-cylinder evolved from a 2.3-liter into a unique 2-liter with an 8,500 rpm limit and 274 bhp.

Photo: Author, Silverstone, UK, 1989

the longest straight, which had a dip that always dictated what gear ratio we would use, because you could get the highest revs at this downhill point. So we let him have that axle, but we put a small data logger in the car, without telling him; we looked at the results afterwards. He did not back off at the point he promised: he drove flat out, so the engine just ran against the limiter, which usually would destroy it. Whatever a racing driver says, he will always try and keep a secret advantage over the rest, whatever it costs!"

Insider memories reveal that M3 motors were in such demand at some points in the car's 2.3-liter racing career that a small assembly line was set up to make the motors "almost in series" within the high-performance production engine work hall at Munich Werke 1.1.

Under pre-1993 German regulations, weight could be altered at the whim of the organizers and the success of the drivers. Still, it is worth knowing that the 1989 M3 was forced to race at 1,040 kg (2,288 lbs), which was approximately 100 kg (220 lbs) heavier than the racing weight which the engineers delivered. The wide choice of differentials remained, but 0–62 mph was still quoted at around 4.6 seconds, with top speed elevated to 300 km/h (186.3 mph).

Competition M3 Chassis Progress

Racing cars change specifications from hour to hour, track to track, but BMW produced an average M3 specification for 1987 that is worth recalling.

Placed alongside a production M3, the obvious body changes were the lack of interior trim and an extensive, computer-calculated roll cage. The cage, which had been tested in scale model trim and manufactured by Matter, strengthened the body against twisting and G-forces, as well as crash stress. As testimony to the extraordinary abilities of the 28 meters of lightweight steel welded within a factory M3, the gain in torsional and bending rigidity over a standard 3 Series was increased by a factor of three, according to BMW engineering sources.

Replacement wheels carried racing tires as wide as prevailing regulations would allow. Such 1980s racers predicted production moves, like the 18-inch wheel option on the 1999 328/323 Ci coupes.

The radically-lower ride height, dropped the 3 Series as close to the floor as possible, without popping the tires through the fenders. Rival Ford had such a job getting a realistically-low race ride height (vital for center of gravity and therefore ultimate cornering ability) that it was not unknown for its Sierras to be disqualified for desperate modifications hidden within the wheel arch or flared fenders.

BMW was not whiter than snow on its M3 racing body panels either. All its cars would be disqualified from the opening Monza (Italy) round of the World Championship, and the reason was some imported expertise from Ford! A leading technician within BMW Motorsport had also worked at Ford. He knew of the Ford Motorsport procedure to place thin gauge panels in production outlines.

An argument between BMW and Ford at Monza, in which BMW had pointed out that the leading Eggenberger Sierras should not be running Bosch engine management systems, saw the best Fords disqualified before the event!

Ford personnel retaliated.

Discretely snooping at Matter, suppliers of the BMW M3 racing bodies, Ford Motorsport personnel pointed the technical inspectors at the factory-backed BMW M3 squads. All but a privateer's M3 from Hungary was disqualified, post-race, for having body shells of ultra-thin sheet metal. Such happy squabbles, particularly between Ford and BMW, characterized all European and World Championship touring car racing of the period. Both series were terminated at the close of 1988 and 1987 respectively.

An original Group A Bimmer competed at 960 kg rather than the production 1,200 kg, thanks to a sharply effective diet that slashed 25 percent from the curb weight and immediately boosted power-to-weight ratio. The next body trick was to let the car ride as low as was feasible, dropping the center of gravity as far as possible and postponing the body lean and two-wheeler cornering antics. The M3 roof line touched 1,370 mm in production and 1,330 mm for Group A racing, that 40-mm (1.57 inches) savings also helping the car slice through the air cleanly, with less air drag.

Naturally, more fuel was required by the competition M3, so a larger safety tank made from Kevlar and nylon-reinforced synthetic rubbers (with foam lining to protect the "bag tank" fuel reservoir) was adopted. When compared to a roadgoing M3, another 40 liters was allowed, taking the racer to a total 110-liter (20.2 US gallons, or 24.2 UK gallons) fuel capacity.

The wheelbase was elongated from the usual 2,562 mm to 2,565.5 mm, an insignificant 3.5-mm matter beside the extra inches and millimeters generated by BBS replacement wheels and Pirelli or Yokohama racing rubber. The base set-up was 205/55VR on a 7J x 15-inch wheel. For competition, the rim and overall diameters were permitted a maximum increase of 2 inches, so BMW generally adopted a 9 x 17-inch 3-piece alloy with a magnesium center and 245/610 rubber. Some teams were equipped with 16-inch rollers, which meant the tire sections shrank to 235/590-16. Others used both 16- and 17-inch diameters in 1987, with the smaller size at the front to promote turn-in ability.

Bilstein aluminum tube front struts used encased low-pressure gas damping, concentrically encircled by significantly increased coil spring rates. In British sprint use, well over 1,000 lbs/inch rating were utilized; and the trend for stiffer front-spring rates escalated alongside lap speeds, rear springs running a softer rating in pursuit of rear-drive traction.

The lower suspension arms for the struts were also in forged aluminum and were cross-braced. New hubs and cast-magnesium uprights lay behind the center lock wheel nut. The hubs carried enlarged (332-mm diameter and 32-mm thick) vented disc brakes and facilitated pit-stop wheel change times. Those discs were served by four piston calipers, and were originally supplied by Brembo in Italy.

More teams changed to AP Racing in Britain during 1988, and their later 6-piston calipers made them a regular components supplier to the fastest M3 equipes by 1991. However, we have lost count of the number of factory 3'ers we have seen with mixed brake component suppliers on the same car, especially on the later E36.

ABS anti-lock braking was not used by the 1987–89 factory Group A racers, but was developed during the winter of 1990–91 by a cooperative effort between BMW Motorsport and Alfred Teves GmbH, to contest the German Championship. Development drivers at the crucial Salzburgring progress tests were Steve Soper, Roberto Ravaglia, and Johnny Cecotto. It took some spirited discussion before the system was adopted and even when

The M3 engine started out as a high-performance street motor and evolved into a 365 bhp full race unit with dry sump lubrication.

Photos: Author, Munich Mobile Tradition warehouse, 1999

it was, some T-car back-up M3s for factory-associated teams lacked anti-lock.

A faster steering-rack ratio of 17:1 was recognized in place of the production M3 19.6:1 ratio, and the showroom power steering was deleted. Rose joints and adjustable roll bars completed the competition picture at the front.

For the back end, semi-trailing arms were retained, but the arms themselves were extensively reinforced, along with pivot bearing mounting points and provision for immediate (albeit via wrench) camber and castor adjustment to attune the car to each track. As at the front, adjustable spring plates were also employed to vary vehicle ride height, again in search of ultimate circuit suitability. Once more, a jointed and adjustable roll bar was included, as well as center-lock hubs carrying bigger brakes—vented units of 280 x 20.7 mm that were also served by four piston calipers.

The factory gearbox choice was a five-speed Getrag with close ratios stacked from 2.337 to a direct fifth and choice of final drives that encompassed 3.15 to 5.28:1. The factory picked a 4.41 to demonstrate a 0–62-mph time of 4.6 seconds (the BMW showroom figure was nearly 7 seconds). They reported debut season speeds up to 280 km/h (173.9 mph) in 1987, although those maximums were recorded on the taller 3.25:1 final drive.

The cost of such M3 speed? In his valuable *Tourenwagen Story '89*, author Thomas Voigt quoted typical M3 "on the line" costs at Dm 220,000, equivalent then to £77,200. A senior Prodrive executive quoted £600,000 as the cost of running a pair of M3s in the UK Championship, cheap in comparison with the millions spent on German factory warfare. By 1992, £800,000 per UK team was allocated by BMW (GB) to the UK

Series. Worldwide, BMW Motorsport supplied around 330 racing M3s, or the components to build such competitors. The majority were built to the specification outlined in this chapter, but 60 were built to less-radical (Group N/ Showroom) specifications.

Stepping Beyond

How did the M3 progress over the 1987 specification? Between 1987 and 1989, the 2,332-cc engine capacity was deployed. The only possible progress came from racing fundamentals: aerodynamics, tires, power, and gearing. The four-piston brakes remained at 332-mm/278-mm diameters, but wheel diameters could be increased to 18 inches (still wearing a 9-inch ledge) as a result of the annual Evolution models.

M3 Evolutions also brought with them extended spoilers (1988) and an increasing number of the lightweight panels that had seen the factory M3s outlawed at Monza in 1987. According to factory records, there were three Evolution models (1987, 1988, 1989), and their basics have already been described in our previous road-car chapters.

The biggest change in race-engineering principles for 1988–89 seasons was the occasional adoption of the Prodrive six-speed gearbox in UK-based M3s, but German Touring Car runners frequently reverted to the original five-speed, and an alternative H-pattern Getrag six-speed was widely used. For 1991, other six-speed options had emerged; and Vic Lee Motorsport (VLM) used the Australian ratio sextet from Holinger, introduced for 2-liter British Championship cars and widely used by 2-liter E30 M3 racers in Europe.

1990 2.5-liter Sport Evo Racer

The 2.5-liter stretch of the M3 engine was logical for racing purposes, given the similar-capacity Mercedes opposition. It was important not just for its racing ability, but also for the key role it played in BMW's further understanding of high-performance engines in association with catalytic converters, for the DTM organizers demanded "Kats" for the 1990 season.

This led BMW, and their rivals, into learning practical lessons, namely the departure from ceramic catalytic converter elements, with their limited tolerance of high temperatures, to metallic converters. The metallic converters could take the full blast of these 350-bhp-plus 2.5-liters running at 11,000 revs.

Later, the BMW Motorsport department would apply these metallic "Kat" lessons to the production line. The M5 with the S38/B36 version of the fabled big-block six (where S38 is the usual motor code, "B" stands for Benzene/gasoline, and 36 is for the 3.6-liter capacity) was the pioneer in this respect. The metallic cat breakthrough, along with air pumps and repositioned

In its heyday, the Evolution 2.5-liter M3 was a winning weapon across Europe. Here, it is seen in Italy, when it was equipped with anti-lock racing brakes and a six-speed gearbox.

Photo: Author, Italy, 1992

converters far closer to the top engine manifolding, were the steps that finally brought American BMW market engines toward parity with European output levels during the 1990s.

1990 BMW: More of the Same

Bigger engines, ever-more BMW-supported teams, and much more serious recognition of Group N production racing were the primary messages from BMW at the annual Munich dinner in 1989. Established BMW saloon stars, including multiple champion Roberto Ravaglia, stayed on the German Championship strength in company with Johnny Cecotto and then Monaco-based Briton Steve Soper.

An interesting new recruit was former TWR Rover and Ford contractee, Armin Hahne. who was related to sixties BMW Champion Hubert Hahne. Also driving the latest M3 in 1990 International Group A events were Kris Nissen, recovered from his Porsche crash in Japan, and veteran BMW-contracted Dieter Quester, postponing retirement yet again.

Annette Meeuvissen, former Ladies Fiesta Champion, co-presented the protracted Sportpokal proceeding and was rewarded with a full season in 1990. There was a firm commitment to running a Junior Team again, and three names were nominated: Sandy Grau, Markus Liesner, and Mike Strotman. But their results

were not on a par with earlier Juniors, with only Grau emerging as a serious candidate for international honors.

Yokohama appeared to be the tires to have, but politics precluded running without Pirelli. Schnitzer, the winning team for BMW, agreed in 1990 to terms with the Munich manufacturers; but negotiations were prolonged with Bavarian-based Linder, Nürburgring-based Zakspeed, and Team Bigazzi, which gave victorious Schnitzer-BMW and Johnny Cecotto such a hard time in the 1989 Italian Championship.

Aside from testing a development M3 with a leading German private team, BMW Motorsport pledged that "parts, tuning kits, and concepts" would support both the M3 and the 318iS (the 16v 318). The latter was homologated in Group N and A for January 1, 1990.

In detail, the 2.5-liter stretch meant the racers could use a 95.5-mm bore (production was 95 mm) with the standard 2.5-liter 87-mm stroke to achieve 2,493 cc in place of 2,467 cc. Their use of the traditional 12 cr. and further-reworked BMW-ECU electronic management allowed another 10 bhp, giving a total of 330 at 8,500 rpm. There was a modest 11 lb-ft (15 Nm) boost in torque to a seasonal average of 213 lb-ft (290 Nm). This figure was some 500 rpm higher than that of the older 2.3-liter, peaking at 7,500 rpm.

The author tries out the 2.5-liter M3 from the 1991 racing season in Italy.

Photo: Peter Dron, Italy, 1992

The engineers were worried at the beginning of the year that this ultimate four-cylinder stretch would leave them down 1,000 rpm on the 1989 "screamer," and they set an initial target of 9,200 rpm. This figure was not observed by all the teams, although 9,500 rpm was race-safe by the end of the season, a fine achievement for this large-bore four.

The extra horsepower for the 2.5-liter M3 was vital, as the Mercedes Evolution 190E 2.5/16 had even more radical aerodynamics than the BMW and 333 bhp to propel the same race-weight minimum of 1,040 kg. Despite the extra capacity, Motorsport engineers were still confident that the car could be raced at 940 kg. Unfortunately, that was never allowed on home turf because Mercedes could not get down below the organizers' 1,040 kg.

Despite the modest horsepower and torque bonus, no major performance advances (0-62 mph in 4.6 seconds, 186 mph maximum speed) were reported, the aerodynamic and power advantages most apparent to the drivers in the extra muscle between 50 and 150 mph.

Roberto Ravaglia, the most successful of all E30 M3 drivers, with four international driver's titles to his credit by 1990, commented, "The old motor had its power at 8,000 rpm, the new [2.5-liter] is beautiful at 7,000 rpm. It is the best M3 I have driven." The statistics from Nürburgring Grand Prix circuit backed up that judgment emphatically: the 1987 M3 best upon debut was eight seconds slower than the 1990 best lap!

Contributing to that dramatic rise in lap speed were the replacement aerodynamics (particularly the venturi under the engine bay) and the use of 18-inch wheel diameters as routine for the Yokohamas that proved vital. By 1991, some teams in Italy (CibiEmme) were certainly using 9 x 19-inch diameter rear wheels regularly, usually in association with 18-inch diameter fronts and Pirelli tires.

On the Spot

Your author, writing for the British weekly newspaper, *Motoring News*, was privileged to watch the official unveiling in Munich during December 1989 of the 2.5 Sport Evo E30. Here is the resulting coverage of that memorable event:

"The 1989 BMW Sports Trophy dinner in Munich on Saturday night was also used to unveil a new M3 competition and road car for 1990. Called M3 Sport Evolution, it features a 2.5-liter stretch of the existing 2.3 and advanced aerodynamics, these including front end venturi for limited ground effect and adjustable front and rear spoilers.

"Due for homologation on March 1, 1990 (production of the necessary 500 begins in January 1990), the M3 Sport Evolution is intended primarily to defend BMW's slightly unexpected 1989 German victory over the 2.5-liter Mercedes.

"Although Ford has quit the German series in a turbo huff, Opel will be playing its 24v 3-liter Omega/Carlton hand and Audi will have over 400 bhp in its weighty V8 saloon, so power is at a premium for BMW.

"The racing M3 Evolution (which multiple BMW Champion Roberto Ravaglia has great hopes for) started aerodynamic development in July, 1989. Power will come from 2,467 cc developed by the Preussenstrasse BMW Motorsport engine department, presently managed by Franz Zinnecker. He predicted, 'compared with last year, we will start with another 10 bhp, probably 330 bhp at 8,500 rpm, and there will be more torque.' Racing weight will be 1,040 kg in Germany, 160 kg less than the road car.

"The 1990 Evolution features the manually adjustable front and rear spoiler extensions of the road car to vary downforce, as well as the use of ground effect venturi at the front end. Further lightweight panels are evident, and detail aerodynamic updates extend to reprofiling the traditional front radiator grille and sealing off front-end openings."

Chassis detail changes were headed by the availability of six-piston brakes, and BMW Motorsport specified an increase in vented disc diameters to 13.8 inches in the front and 11.8 inches in the rear.

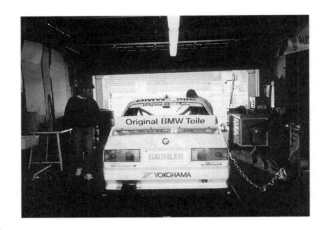

Extended rear wing for the 1992 racing M3 at Nürburgring.

Photo: Author, Nürburgring, 1992

A major technical advance for 1991 was the adoption of an anti-lock (ABS) braking system. This was the cooperative result of work by BMW and Alfred Teves GmbH engineers. BMW was an international pioneer in the use of ABS braking for competition, right back to the 1973-75 CSLs, but such early experiments were inconsistent.

The 1991 season proved ABS to be a BMW success, and the BMW-Teves system seemed particularly adept at overcoming the wheel-locking moments that the rival Mercedes-Bosch ABS deliberately allowed. Mercedes-Bosch allowed the driver to overcome ABS at pre-set pressures.

BMW also included the feature of disabling ABS during high-speed rearward travel (i.e., a spin) so the driver could stamp on the pedal and lock the wheels when homing in on those unfriendly barriers, backwards! BMW drivers could switch out the ABS from the cockpit, if they thought it was hindering progress. At the close of 1991, Steve Soper told the author about lap speed gains measured in seconds for wet conditions. According to factory driver Soper, "I knew the potential of ABS race systems from a track test I did in Britain for *Cars & Car Conversions* magazine in the late 1980s. The Championship-winning Group N Sierra of Robb Gravett had the ABS disconnected, so I tried

hitching it up. I then went faster than Robb with the car; that made me think positively about ABS in racing."

Other leading drivers did not share that view, but BMW Motorsport knew that its rivals would be assessing the system and decided to develop a system of its own. During the 1990–91 winter testing at Salzburgring, Soper could lap over 3 seconds faster with ABS than without ABS. That was enough to convince his fellow front-running drivers, Roberto Ravaglia and Johnny Cecotto, that ABS had potential.

If the factory race M3 rotated, on-board ABS sensors locked out, and the driver could lock the brakes, lessening the consequences. BMW-Teves ABS then automatically reset, but the driver could always dispense with ABS via a cockpit button.

BMW did not win the 1990 or 1991 German titles—those went to 4 x 4 Audi quattro V8s—but the M3 scored some superb results in sprint and long distance races between 1990 and 1992. The 2.5-liter featured enough technical progress to ensure that arch rival Mercedes was frequently defeated in the home series, as we'll see from the hectic M3 race action covered in the next chapter.

13 Tall Tales & Fantastic Results

For five years, the M3 bounded around the globe, scoring startling race results.

This chronicle of the M3's competition achievements is quite a list, and it's just an extract of the M3's complete record, ignoring a multitude of national honors earned by outstanding amateurs. There are still Frenchmen winning tarmac club rallies and embarrassing more modern machinery with their decade old M3s in the premier French Rally Championship.

All over the Bimmer globe, the first M3 continues to compete with honor, but how was it back at the M3's March 22, 1987 debut at Italy's Monza race track? The first 1987 World Championship round in Italy was chaotic. All the leading Fords were outlawed before the race (illegal engine management systems) and all the factory-backed M3s were disqualified from the top six finishing places (plus eighth) for lighter-than-lightweight body plastics and sheet metal!

As a result, BMW started their most expensive program of 1987 with just the privateer points of Austrian veteran BMW campaigner Toni Fischhaber and Czech Jozef Cserkuti. However, Ford got nothing, so it was not a total tragedy for Munich.

The fight against Ford continued in April at Jarama in Spain, and the pattern of the year began to emerge in this race. The Italian crew (Roberto Ravaglia/Emanuele Pirro) and German engineering, with the Austro-German team tactics of Schnitzer, hauled the M3 to the top of this and many more endurance races.

The M3 was not as blazingly fast as a turbo Ford, but it tended to be stronger and faster around the corners. At Jarama, the top three finishers were M3s, while Ford came in fourth and fifth.

BMWs were also 1–2 winners of the third World Championship round at Djion, France, in May, but the Germans knew that they had to keep piling the points on before Ford homologated an enormous gain

Competition E30 M3: Global Highlights

YEAR	DRIVER(S)	CAR	TITLE
1987	Roberto Ravaglia	2.3 M3	World Touring Car Champion (driver)
1987	Winni Vogt	2.3 M3	European Champion
1987	Jim Richards	2.3 M3	Australian Champion
1987	Eric van der Poele	2.3 M3	German Circuit Champion
1988	Roberto Ravaglia	2.3 M3	European Champion
1988	Trevor Crowe (NZ)	2.3 M3	FIA Asia Pacific Champion
1988	Frank Sytner	2.3 M3	British Champion
1988	Jean-Pierre Malcher	2.3 M3	French Champion
1988	Patrick Snijers/ Colebunders	2.3 M3	Belgian Rally Champions
1989	Francois Chatriot/ Michel Perin	2.3 M3	French Rally Champions
1989	Marc Duez/ Alain Lopes	2.3 M3	Belgian Rally Champions
1989	Josep Bassas/ A. Rodrigues	2.3 M3	Spanish Rally Champions
1989	John Bosch	2.3 M3	Dutch Rally Champion
1989	Silvan Lulik	Group N 2.3 M3	Yugoslavian Rally Champion
1989	Roberto Ravaglia	Schnitzer 2.3 M3	German Touring Car Champion
1989	Johnny Cecotto	Bigazzi 2.3 M3	Italian Circuit Champion
1989	Jean-Pierre Malcher	Group A + M3	French Circuit Champion
1989	Harri Toivonen	Group A 2.3 M3	Finnish Champion
1989	Peggen Andersson	Group A 2.3 M3	Swedish Circuit Champion
1990	Roberto Ravaglia	Schnitzer 2.5 Evo M3	Italian Champion
1990	Francois Chatriot	Prodrive 2.3 M3	French Rally Champion
1990	Jean-Pierre Malcher	Group A + 2.5 M3	French Touring Car Champion
1990	Jean-Michel Martin	Group A + 2.5 M3	Belgian Circuit Champion
1990	Cor Euser	Group N 2.3 M3	Dutch Circuit Champion
1990	Hansueli Ulrich	2.3 M3	Swiss Champion
1990	Heikki Salmenautio	2.3 M3	Finnish Circuit Champion
1990	Silvan Lulik	2.3 M3	Yugoslavian Rally Champion
1990	Xavier Riera	2.3 M3	Spanish Hillclimb Champion
1991	Will Hoy	Supertouring 2.0 M3	British Touring Car Champion
1991	Roberto Ravaglia	Schnitzer 2.5 M3	Italian Circuit Champion
1992	Tim Harvey	Supertouring 2.0 M3	British Touring Car Champion

Bernard Beguin wins the 1987 Tour De Corse (Corsica) rally, which was a full World Championship event.

Photo: BMW Werkfoto from undisclosed subcontractor, 1987; Author archive, 2000

vaged a win from a rain-lashed Silverstone with a works M3 for Ravagalia/Pirro as runner up.

Ford didn't allow BMW to win outright again that season, which ranged over a further two events in Australia (Bathurst and Calder) plus an event in New Zealand and a Japanese finale at Fuji in November. It was not all roses for the Sierra turbos, but even when they were disqualified, other Fords won.

It was no surprise when Ford of Europe won the 1987 FIA World Manufacturer's title for Touring Cars, although factory M3 driver Roberto Ravaglia won the driver's title.

BMW and Ford fought for the 1988 European Touring Car Championship, with M3 in a grudge re-match with RS500. That bad black Ford was just too fast for the M3 to beat outright. The evolution Sierra RS500 could be developed to exceed 500 bhp for shorter races, while BMW and its simpler fuel-injected 16-valve could do no more than tinker with the 2.3-liters, exceeding 360 bhp only under German national regulations.

Better BMW reliability and supreme driving talent saw Roberto Ravaglia crowned the

in power and competitiveness with the RS500 Evolution of the original Sierra Cosworth.

The Bimmers didn't win their home event at the Nürburgring in July. Future BMW driver Steve Soper—then a Ford man—took pole. The Ford won that race, but BMWs finished in a block from 2–7, so they kept amassing World Series points.

The RS500 came with all the goodies that Ford didn't have time to develop for the original Cosworth-powered Sierra. Although the chassis wasn't much better than before, the extra 100 bhp put them beyond M3 reach on many circuits.

Eggenberger Ford did not enter the faster Sierra in the 24-hour Spa-Francorchamps endurance classic in the first humid weekend of August, preferring the reliability of the original format. BMW finished 1–2–3, but one Ford had led over 19 of the 24-hours; there was no doubt of the Blue Oval's blistering speed.

In August 1987, Ford took a 1-2 finish in Czechoslovakia using the latest RS 500 evolution of Sierra Cosworth, but a privateer M3 sal-

Winning the first and last World Championship until 2005 for sedan/touring car drivers was the BMW priority in 1987. They succeeded with Roberto Ravaglia, seen here in the Australian Event.

Photo: Author archive, 2000

BMW beat off Mercedes and others to win the 1987 German Championship with a then-new M3.

Photo: Author archive, 2000

last European Champion of the premier-league sedan classes in 1988. Then the FIA controlling body decided they had more than enough of BMW and Ford squabbles, and shut down that European series, too.

BMW tried to hit back at Ford in the later 1980s, but its normally aspirated engines were never going to gain power the way that the Cosworth Ford turbocharged units could instantly generate muscle. Subsequent BMW M3 racing seasons (1988 onward) saw generations of Evolutions to provide extra speed mainly through aerodynamics and a few bonus bhp.

The Evo breed was not allowed in rallying, so Prodrive used the original M3 to win across European tarmac and had restricted access to National Championships. The British 2-liter series obviously did not cater to 2.3- and 2.5-liter Evos, but Germany welcomed them as a natural counterbalance to the Mercedes series of ever wilder 2.3- and 2.5-liter 16-valves. In America, we have recently seen E30 M3s in BMW CCA club events, proving just how fast some of the older M3s can be.

BMW Motorsport manager Wolfgang Peter Flohr commented at the conclusion of that first M3 season, "We knew we could win class victories and hoped there would be success over-

all as well. But we had just won the European Championship (1986) with the 635 coupe from Schnitzer. Herbert Schnitzer and Charley Lamm told us there was no way that our little twerp of a car would be as fast as the 635. Even in the opening development months of the M3, it was immediately 2 seconds a lap faster than the 1986 635."

Pirelli was the initial tire selection for factory-backed M3s, but they went quicker on Yokohamas which became the best choice during the 1987 World Championship season. "Yokos" also appear to be the benchmark tire on US club racing E30s, wherever regulations do not specify a control tire.

The 1987 achievement of Italian Roberto Ravaglia in taking four outright wins with the Schnitzer-prepared M3 was one of the giant-killing feats of modern motorsports. It was a triumph for Schnitzer teamwork and the shining abilities of compatriot co-driver Emanuele Pirro, who accompanied Roberto "Spaghetti" on all his winning runs.

BMW's other success at World Championship level was to prove a one-off result; but since it was the company's first win in the World Rally Championship for fourteen seasons, it was totally unexpected. Prodrive in the UK prepared the M3 that would be victorious in the Tour de

Seen here winning the 1989 German title, Roberto Ravaglia had by then won the 1986 European Championship (BMW 635Csi), the 1987 World title, and the 1988 European Championship.

Photo: Courtesy of Bilstein, Ennepetal Germany, 1989

Corse. This bumpy win against the cream of World Championship rallying machinery from Lancia and Ford was one to salute. The crew comrised Bernard Beguin and J.J. Lenne. Such a road rally victory was totally outside the design brief for the M3 and demonstrates what an exceptionally able and adaptable machine the E30 M3 was.

The international homologation acceptance of the 4WD 325iX for international competition also depended on a Prodrive initiative, but that was nothing compared to the idea of taking the M3 into international rallying. David Richards recalled, "We really forced BMW into it, step by step. BMW was not keen at first, but we have always had fantastic support from the national sales companies, particularly BMW France. They are the best export market for the M3." Thus it was particularly fitting that it was on the French island of Corsica that Prodrive

engineered BMW's first, and so far, only, World Championship Rally win.

Such success had its own commercial rewards. "We built 28 of the 120 competition M3 kits released by Motorsport," asserted Richards in 1988. Besides building the front running M3s for championship honors in France, Belgium, Italy, and the European series that Patrick Snijers led, Prodrive built up M3s, or materially assisted in the national motorsport programs of BMW, in Holland, Spain, Switzerland, Greece, and Norway.

More M3 Rewards

Additional spoils for BMW in that first M3 season included the poorly supported European Championship, which went to now-deceased German Winfried "Winni" Vogt in the Team Linder M3.

Honors were equally shared among the top preparation specialists in the BMW fold, for Belgian Eric van de Poele initiated the Zakspeed move from Ford to BMW with the greatest success a German preparation company can wish for: Der Deutsche Tourenwagen Meisterschaft (German Touring Car Championship) title.

The mild evolution version of the 2.3-liter M3 was enough to win the driver's title in the 1988 British Championship for Frank Sytner.

Photo: Author, Silverstone, UK, 1988

The annual Spa 24-hour racing classic in Belgium was a tough challenge for a high-revving four-cylinder racer, but BMW continued its winning ways in 1989 with this M3 for Roberto Ravaglia, Fabien Giroix, and Altfrid Heger.

Photo: BMW Archiv, Ardennes, Belgium, 1989; released to Author, 1998

Roberto Ravaglia was on a winning run in the 1989 German series, despite fierce DaimlerBenz/ Mercedes opposition from its 2.5-liter Cosworth-enhanced 190.

Photo: BMW Werkfoto, 1989 (BMW Archiv, 1998)

Mercedes fielded their 2.5-liter Evo 190 a year before BMW went oversize on M3. This is the start of the 1989 German season, with Roland Asch in the MS Jet Merc beating Ravaglia to the first corner at the US military airbase circuit conversion of Mainz Finthen.

Photo: Courtesy of Bilstein Ennepetal, Germany, 1989

The simple fuel-injected formula brought BMW the FIA Group A Trophy for makes in the European Hillclimb Championship, plus the national titles of Australia, France, Finland, Holland, and Portugal. It was a stunning list for a newcomer.

Double points should go to the Australian team behind veteran Jim Richards, who were winners against the domestic large capacity V8s. Subsequent heroes for the yellow Benson and Hedges team included former World Grand Prix Champion Alan Jones. They also managed a fine fourth at the Bathurst 1000 in the World Championship round of October 1987. It was an amazing result in a competitive field that included not just the turbo Fords, but native 5.8-liter V8s from GM-Holden. Add a long uphill grade to flog four-cylinders on every lap, and that result enters the realms of the miraculous.

So the M3 was off to a good race and (totally unexpected) rally start. We see in the next chapter how deeply the plot thickens.

14 The Evo Years

How the M3 evolved into a winner

Did you ever catch the original M3 in race action? Did you see those boxy Bimmers carry the fight to every curve against automobiles with twice their power? Maybe you missed out when the factory-backed teams were out-braking turbo leviathans and jockeying for position along every straight-away. You can still get an idea of how the action was then at every BMW CCA club racing event in the USA.

Back in 1988, BMW built on its first season (1987) of daunting success. Between 1988 and 1992, evolutions of the M3 gathered success with every engine capacity from 2.0- to 2.5-liters. The 1988 Evolution M3 had 220 bhp for just 501 road customers; but competitors valued evolved M3s for lighter body panels, extended aerodynamic spoilers, and the ability to pound out more than 300 bhp .

Although the RS500 Ford was an outright winner in the late 1980s, the baby Bimmer was a regular winner in Germany over a longer span. The M3 mastered the German title battle twice, recording 40 wins in 120 German starts before it was retired from front-line factory use in 1992— two years after production had ceased!

EuroSpeed

The second (1988) season for BMW and its factory-supported teams was headlined by the Schnitzer campaign to take the European Touring Championship for drivers. This was the last time that the title was offered until the 21st Century, so it was fitting that an M3 won that 1988 edition. BMW drivers had won the title, or the class contested, 16 times since 1965. In fact, M3 took both 1987 and 1988 honors via drivers Winni Vogt and Roberto Ravaglia.

The 1988 German international series was not the happy hunting ground for the M3 that it had been in 1987. Yet M3s still ran well enough to snatch three pole positions and five wins in a 24-race season. BMW had taken its eyes off the home crown and the factory's best driver (Markus Oestereich) was fourth overall, behind a brace of Fords and a Mercedes.

The 1988 Champion was Eggenberger Ford, whose RS500 was strangled back on turbocharger air supply for 1989 as the authorities vainly tried to equalize the normally aspirated majority with Ford's turbo minority. Ford abandoned the German series in 1990 and returned just briefly with its 2-liter Mondeo in the 1990s.

Outside Germany, the M3 enjoyed a successful 1988 season, scooping up the British (Frank Sytner), French (Jean Pierre Malcher), Dutch (Arthur van Dedem), FIA Asian-Pacific (Trevor Crowe), and Swedish (Lennart Bohlin) Championships.

Even the Portuguese Touring car racing title went the way of the M3, but it was Prodrive in Britain who really excelled on BMW's behalf. Prodrive not only stood behind that Frank Sytner UK victory, but also snatched the Belgian Rally Championship. The same Prodrive crew—Patrick Snijers/ Danny Colebunders—also finished as the runners-up in the European Rally Championship itself, so BMW was on the brink of a unique saloon car double in collecting European racing and rallying titles.

Roberto Ravaglia celebrates his first season with the 2.5 Sport Evo (bottom photo), winning the Italian Championship and his fifth consecutive international title with BMW M-Team Schnitzer.

BMW Pressefoto, Monza, Italy, 1990

The M3 remains a staple in the British BMW Four Plus Championship as well. Here's the field at Thruxton, featuring a typical mix between M3 and modified E30 Threes.

Photo: Author, Thruxton, UK, 1999

1989 Rallying Double

Aside from its German racing win in 1989 (see below), the 1989 BMW M3 season was notable for a unique rallying double when the M3 won both the French and Belgian titles. Again, Prodrive was behind this prestigious coup. To prove it was no fluke, the rally championships of Holland, Spain, and Yugoslavia also fell to M3 drivers.

The Prodrive rally double saw Francois Chatriot and Michel Perin triumphant in France, and Marc Duez and Alain Lopes took their similar 2.3 M3 into the Belgian limelight.

Track Action

Run under Mobil-BMW Finance colors for Frank Sytner, Prodrive also contested some European races in 1988. In a six-month 1988 design-and-development period with three Evolution 2.3 M3s, Prodrive had Xtrac manufacture a non-synchromesh six-speed gearbox by former Williams and Benetton transmission consultant John Piper, today a top-line Grand Prix engineer. The July 1, 1988-homologated six-speed gearbox was baptized in 23 hours of the Spa 24 hour race before an engine failure intervened.

Compared with a Getrag synchromesh five-speed gearbox, the race "Prodrive Six" offered the following ratios (Getrag in parentheses): First, 2.449 (2.337); Second 1.913 (1.681); Third, 1.579 (1.358); Fourth, 1.332 (1.1.50); Fifth, 1.148 (1.00); Sixth, 1.00. That meant a more appropriate ratio for most racetrack cornering quandaries.

Evolution models were not so radical as to force new cars on Prodrive. They displayed new front and rear spoilers, as well as a lightweight trunk deck and rear glass. Prodrive senior race technician, Peter Holley, explained, "power remains around 300 bhp for a really cracking example, with 285 to 295 the norm." Race engineer David Potter added, "The quality of the panels used and the slight glass-thickness reduction do not drop weight appreciably below 1,000 kg, which is still above the M3's class minimum of 940 kg."

Peak power was at 8,200 rpm, but the Bosch Motronic chip in Frank Sytner's car allowed 8,800 rpm. Britain's short tracks delivered Sytner to 150 mph, but the wide choice of axle ratios were claimed to yield up to 175 mph on longer circuits. German magazines electronically timed the M3 to 60 mph in some 4.5 seconds. Prodrive examples with better ratios should have been quicker.

The cabin was functional, but far from stark. The door panels were trimmed and the predominantly white color scheme extended to the Matter built roll cage. The driving position bolted the driver into the car as an integral component, one located by six-point

Sabelts and the clinging embrace of an ultra light Sparco racing seat. The driver was braced by a massive aluminum footrest, while gridded foot pedals prevented slippage.

Instrumentation was extensive, with six dials; and functions such as ignition, lighting, and fuel pumps were supported by nine fused push buttons over the transmission tunnel. The Stack rev-counter was memorable, recalling maximum rpm used and able to supply peak rpms at significant circuit points.

The overbored 2,332-cc engine literally started on the push of a button. Engine management automatically accelerated beyond the 1,150-rpm tickover to produce perfect hot starts on the power of a transplanted Pulsar helicopter battery.

An H-pattern of R-1-3-5, 2-4-6 was daunting, but the instant selection of first was rewarding. There was the inevitable clank of a non-synchromesh box, and the 4-5 downshift took some finding. The deft speed at which every other shift executed was equaled only by motorcycles and formula cars.

The race 2.3-liters disliked full accelerator pedal openings below 4,000 rpm. In practice, 7,000 to 8,800 rpm was the natural habitat of this tough 16-valve. For our test, British championship silencing was fitted; and below 5,000 rpm, the noise emitted really wasn't much more than a performance car. Above 5,000, however, there was a characteristically beefier BMW tone. From 7,000 onward, the whole unit pulled its short-stroke act together, soaring for higher rpm. "You rarely hang onto a gear for more than a couple of seconds," reported Sytner with enthusiasm. With each swift shift the tachometer blinked barely 400–500 rpm and the motor just wanted more....

The resourceful cornering grip was hard to comprehend in such a close relative to a road car, but the steering was not monumentally heavy on the move, even without the standard power steering. Basically, the driver only had to point the M3 at a corner under full throttle and it either screamed through...or not.

Track Action (continued)

Frank Sytner listed the virtues of his 1988 Evolution steed, in comparison with the 1987 M3, as: "more aerodynamic bite and it just turns in terribly well." A set of 16-inch diameter front wheels and 17-inch rears promoted this turn-in speed.

The suspension featured freshly fabricated parts for the MacPherson front struts and vastly stronger rear trailing arms. The layout deployed 1,000-lb/inch front springs (about eight times stiffer than those of a performance road car) with 675-lb/inch rears. Additional rapid adjustment was offered with alternative leverage points for the 27-mm (1.06-inch) front anti-roll bar and 20-mm (0.8-inch) rear, transforming roll stiffness.

Summarizing the race M3, Sytner felt its winning qualities were: "One, robustness—it never feels that you should drive it anything but absolutely flat out. It will run to nearly 9,000 rpm for 24 racing hours. Two, the handling gives it the capability of qualifying in amongst turbo Sierras with nearly twice the power. They brake like hell where we dab and go flat out. You have to work really hard in this car for a lap time, but it's supremely satisfying when you succeed. Three, the brakes are excellent. At 300 bhp, you try not give speed away, but when you do need the brakes, they are brilliant," concluded the 1988 British Champion.

French ace Chatriot was aided by a near repeat of the earlier M3 World Rally Championship victory when he flicked the M3 into second place on the spectacular Mediterranean island of Corsica.

The 1989 Corsican World Championship qualifier saw the Prodrive BMWs of Beguin and Duez snatch fifth and sixth positions. It was at that stage (round 5) that the M3 had elevated BMW to third overall in the World Rally Championship, as Duez had scored an encouraging eighth overall on that year's Monte Carlo Rally.

In 1990, Johnny Cecotto/Fabien Giroix and Markus Oestereich headed a BMW M3 1–2 at the 24 Hours of Spa, the toughest event on the saloon-car calendar. It was an event won on numerous occasions by BMW and Schnitzer. But on this occasion, the "sprint" car distinguished itself by spending only 7 minutes and 30 seconds of the 24 hours in the pits.

The E30 M3 won the Belgian classic over high-speed public roads outright from 1987–92, with one exception. In 1989, Ford managed to get a Sierra Cosworth turbo to the close of 24 racing hours in 1989 and were outright winners, relegating BMW to class honors.

Other notable 1990 M3 achievements outside Germany were the acquisition of the Italian, Dutch, Finnish, Swiss, and Belgian national championships. A fine first and second result in Italy for M Team Schnitzer 1990 drivers Roberto Ravaglia and Emanuele Pirro saw Ravaglia repeat that title win in 1991, the last season of wide-spread international success for the original M3.

British Breeders

Prodrive and Lee may sound like a British pop group, but they were the keys to UK race and rally success with the M3. This prompted the

Johnny Cecotto exercises the extended wing M3 Sport Evo 2.5 at Nürburgring in 1990.

Photo: Courtesy Bilstein, Ennepetal, Germany, 1990

global spread of 2-liter SuperTouring and the eventual selection of Britain as BMW's second motorsport home.

BMW and its M3 were an integral part of a ten-year explosion in touring car racing for restricted 2-liter sedans. At its height, there were national series from Japan to the USA via Australia, Britain and the Common market, plus a World Cup shoot-out in Italy, France, and Britain. BMW was never a winner in these 1993–95 World Cup shoot-outs, but they chased Audi hard in 1995 for a German monopoly over the results.

BMW success in the UK was enough to frighten off opposition initially. The E30 M3 netted the 1988 (Frank Sytner), 1991 (Will Hoy), and 1992 (Tim Harvey) British Touring Car Championships. The last two Championships came from one series confined to 2-liters.

Even the USA tried this four-door, 2-liter, 8,500-rpm format. After the excitement of getting Formula 1 teams involved in the UK (Williams Grand Prix established a division to field Championship-winning sedans for Renault) and up to eight manufacturers contesting the UK Championship, the losers started to desert. Today, 2-liter racing has come back to life with a 2005 World series.

For BMW Motorsport, sub-contractors Prodrive did the UK job solo until Vic Lee Motorsport (VLM) got into a 1991–92 stride that conquered both those UK Championship seasons. The E36 BMW 3 Series continued the 3'er winning Championship trend the following year, but it needed Schnitzer to brave the British climate. Thereafter BMW's UK 2-liter fortunes weakened, although Schnitzer did take a podium position in the 1996 UK title hunt. In 1996, BMW withdrew from the British sedan scene that they had supported since 1979, but they won the 2004 European Championship with a Briton driving a 320i.

The battle between the BMW M3 and Mercedes' 190E Evo was on a level 2.5-liter basis from 1990 onward.

Photo: Courtesy International Tourenwagen Rennen [ITR], Zolder, Belgium, 1990

Britain benefited elsewhere in a massive inflow of BMW (and Audi) Dm to establish UK race-car engineering links. All 3 Series work outside the motor was assigned by BMW to McLaren in 1995–6.

Domestic Glory

In the 1989 season, BMW bounced back on the home front. Its fabulous 2.3-liter M3 won the title by beating the best from Mercedes, even though the 190E boasted 2.5 liters.

The essential 1989 BMW move was allying Roberto Ravaglia with Schnitzer, an apparently unstoppable combination that harvested an unmatched total of internationally-recognized titles, 1986–91.

In that 1989 Championship triumph over 22 qualifying rounds, BMW seized seven wins, five pole positions and a dominant 13 fastest laps. The nearest rival was Ford, not Mercedes, but German championship regulations strangled the Sierra back to some 360 bhp, while the M3 could get almost 330 normally aspirated bhp in its superior chassis.

1990–93 German Politics

Ford felt it had been treated unfairly and dropped out for 1990, signaling the effective end of the turbocharged Sierra's international racing career. Ford was little missed in Germany that year, as Audi joined the fray with its V8 quattro four-door.

In 1989, Franz Zinnecker reported of the racing 2.5-liter M3, pre-season, "for the 2.5-liter M3, I had rejoined BMW Motorsport while Paul Rosche was moved onto another project. Our priorities were to keep on increasing the competition potential of the 2.3-liters, I think it went from 295 bhp to a best of 317 bhp, before we added another 5 bhp with another 500 rpm. That took

us up to 9,800 competition rpm, but we did not think we could gain more under the regulations without an increase in capacity so we make the 2.5-liter. Now I think we may have to come back to an 8,800-rpm limit, but we have more power and new crankshaft balance weights to increase rpm in the future," concluded Zinnecker.

By 1990, the 2.5-liter Sport Evolution III was regularly credited with 330 bhp at 9,500 rpm, which was up from 9,200 rpm earlier in the year. The last official quote for the 2.5 racer was 375 bhp at 8,750 rpm coupled to 290 Nm (213 lb-ft) torque between 7,000 and 8,000 rpm.

Audi took its first German national title in 1990 with Hans Stuck and the V8 limousine, but the BMW battle squadrons put Johnny Cecotto in second (Schnitzer ran him and also collected the Team prize) and placed six M3 drivers in the top ten of the most strongly contested saloon-car series in Europe. BMW utilized additional sub-contractors, such as M Team Bigazzi from Italy, which supported subsequent UK racing teammates Steve Soper and Joachim Winkelhock to fourth and fifth overall in the 1990 DTM.

BMW's 1990 M3, with its enlarged engine, managed more race wins than in its previous championship year (eight). It also record 13 fastest laps recorded in this 22-race German season.

In 1991, the BMW factory line-up included

The 2.5-liter Evo motor in race trim. It first served in 1990 at less than 330 bhp and 9,200 rpm but progressed to a maximum quote of 375 bhp at 8,750 rpm.

Photo: Author, Italy, 1991

Commercial Competitions

The M3 was the European racing sedan success story of the late 1980s, but BMW had more in mind than simply winning races (and, almost by accident, rallies). The company, and particularly its Motorsport offshoot, was ready to commercially exploit the M3 as well.

When the M3 arrived, BMW Motorsport-blessed competition kits were of such a high order that privateers always had a good chance of winning. Individually, or as part of a competition package, the parts supply standards reached with the M3 have yet to be equaled by any other manufacturer for sheer quality and profitability.

During January and February of 1986, a new building at Garching, on the outskirts of an outer Munich industrial estate, was occupied by BMW Motorsport. These premises were transformed into the commercial and engineering heart of BMW Motorsport GmbH, with their own vehicle design and development departments: in 1999, the suburb was humming with at least six E46 M3 prototypes based here.

The majority of engines engineering staff stayed at the traditional Preussenstrasse building. The GmbH payroll went from approximately 100 in 1985 to 400 by December 1987; in November 1991, the figure given was 460 employees and was always put around 450 as we approached the millennium.

Garching expanded the BMW Motorsport subsidiary business of creating very special cars on a professional basis. This included the 400-horsepower V8 and less powerful M5 sixes, the M3 Convertibles, and a number of designer specials. These embraced less glamorous 318i/320i Convertibles with a kiss of M-badged glitz.

Garching also administered the richly rewarded BMW Motorsport Bonus scheme. Regular winners in BMWs, who are not in receipt of more direct factory backing, are invited to compete for points in the annual BMW Sports Trophy. Just before Christmas, a large prize-giving ceremony (which also embraces motorcyclists) is usually held in the Munich area (or Austria), and the top 30 are generously mentioned, with the front-runners appearing on stage. Factory driver attendance was mandatory in past years, so guests socialized with contracted racecar royalty.

The Garching premises also supplied equally thorough competition packages to provide a competitive M3 (Group A or N and subsequent equivalents), although it was left to the individual to decide the engine specialist.

At some £90,000 a car in 1991 (£140,000 with a Motorsport engine and power train) these kits were never cheap. Yet, as one Prodrive professional said, "If you have a single nut or bolt left over, it's your fault.... They never make mistakes!"

Demonstrating the sheer value of business that the competition M3 represented to BMW Motorsport, company press officer Friedbert Holtz confirmed to the author in June 1991 that "around 300" M3 racing cars/kits were supplied to that date.

In November 1991, a further breakdown was supplied by BMW Racing Team Manager Karsten Engel, which revealed that Motorsport GmbH had supplied so many cars that 250 M3s were "racing regularly, all over the world." Further inquiries broke down the number of Group A kits supplied by BMW as 270, with a further 60 supplied in Group N trim to make a total of 330 BMW M3 racing packages supplied from Munich.

How many motor manufacturers have ever managed to turn their racing activities into a profit center? BMW certainly did!

Johnny Cecotto, Dane Kris Nissen, and Joachim Winkelhock for Schnitzer; Bigazzi retained Steve Soper and selected Armin Hahne. The new MM-Diebels Team was awarded former BMW-backed Grand Prix aspirant Christian Danner. Linder was served by the rapid, but unlucky, former F3000 driver Altfrid Heger.

After 14 races, the M3 was once again embattled in the thick of German Championship honors, but it was not to be in 1990–92. Steve Soper for M Team Bigazzi and Johnny Cecotto (M Team Schnitzer) fought the Audi V8 Quattro and Frank Biela. Klaus Ludwig, in the best of the factory-backed AMG Mercedes, demonstrated late-season form and the series resolved into a five-way fight, with Hans Stuck (at PTG with M3 in 2000) filling the third spot.

The final 1991 order in the prestigious driver title fight saw two Audi drivers and one Mercedes driver ahead of the M3 squads. Johnny Cecotto was best of the M-men, leading fifth-placed Steve Soper. The M3 took only one pole position that season, winning and setting fastest lap on seven occasions in a 24-race season that included some overseas associated races in Czechoslovakia (Brno) and Britain (Donington).

The Donington battle before 28,000 spectators turned into a fabulous confrontation between Frank Biela's booming Audi quattro and home hero Steve Soper's agile M3. Around the dips and crests of Donington, Soper was able to squeeze by the Audi, but had to settle for second in the two races, finishing under a second apart on both occasions. It was this kind of racing that convinced many Europeans that the German series was the only way to go.

1992: Obsolete Winner

Now obsolete in the showroom and on the track, the E30 M3 was forced to defend BMW's winning record in Germany while the first of the E36s went to the UK and began a new winning era. The best the Bimmer could do at home in 1992 was a fourth in the final standings for Johnny Cecotto's very special Nürburgring-Warthofer-run example.

In the Championship for teams, things were slightly better, with BMW M Team Schnitzer at least climbing the podium with third overall, leading home Warthofer-Fina and fifth-placed Bigazzi.

Although Mercedes was dominant and Audi withdrew in a huff after losing a V8 crankshaft eligibility argument, the Bimmers had the honor of winning the last E30 M3 factory outing on October 11, 1992 at Hockenheim. Both wins in the double-header weekend fittingly came from Roberto Ravaglia, who never had such success in the E36 2-liter successor.

In 1991, Steve Soper and the Bigazzi M-Team from Italy were among the most effective operators in the German series. Here, Soper wins at the converted Diepholz aerodrome race circuit.

Photo: Courtesy Bilstein, Ennepetal, Germany, 1991

On the home patch at Nürburgring, Johnny Cecotto showed 110,000 spectators his stunning qualifying ability. Mix in some ultra special Anglo-German (Nick Wirth of Simtek) development moves (further gains in cage strength, radical suspension moves, Michelin tires, the best in engines), and Cecotto was on course for fastest laps. He set pole position as well as the fastest lap in the second race. The former motorcycle champion finished second in both high-speed (190 mph reported in places!) confrontations with Mercedes around the combination 25.3-km (15.7-mile) track.

It had been a tough season with a car BMW had not produced in two years, but it was an honorable departure. BMW left the DTM as the most successful marque to that date with 48 victories versus the 42 of Mercedes and 30 of Ford.

The 1990–91 double whammy result of two Audi Championship seasons with a unique V8 4x4 format was to increase pressure for new German regulations. German engineers were unhappy at the racing-by-weight handicap system. Yet the public and TV seemed to be delighted at the resulting close competition.

A new formula was agreed for 1993, abandoning the weight handicaps in favor of a 1,000-kg minimum for all comers, with engines limited to 2.5 liters and six cylinders. All of these rules looked like they suited the new BMW 24-valve M3 down to the ground until the technical arguments resulted in BMW withdrawing from the German series in an abrupt November 1992 announcement.

The fight for honors in the 1991 German Championship eventually resulted in a final at Hockenheim dominated by the V8 Audi quattros. Here we see four of the different marques in Germany that season. They were: BMW 2.5 Sport Evo M3, Audi quattro V8, Mercedes 2.5 Evo, and (to the right in both photos) GM-Opel's troubled straight-six Omega 24-valve.

Photos: Courtesy ITR, Germany, 1991

Here is the 1991 Nürburgring 24 hour-winning team Schnitzer M3 for Germany's Joachim Winkelhock (pictured) and Armin Hahne, supported by Denmark's Kris Nissen.

Photo: Courtesy Bilstein, Ennepetal, Germany, 1991

Back in 1991 the Bigazzi outfit provided two of the hardest-charging M3 operators. Here, Armin Hahne leads Steve Soper in their 1991 Sports Evo 2.5s.

Photo: BMW AG, Munich, 1991

The 1992 Spa 24-hour race was convincingly won by the 2.5 Evo of a typically international BMW team. Steve Soper, Christian Danner, and Jean-Michel Martin (from Britain, Germany, and Belgium, respectively) took BMW's 16th outright victory in Belgium's annual answer to Le Mans.

Photo: Author, Sebring, US, 1992

BMW versus Audi was the on- and off-track preoccupation of what was to be their last DTM racing season. Here the Bigazzi M3 of then points-leader Emanuele Pirro runs outside the 4x4 Audi of 1991 Champion Frank Biela.

Photo: Courtesy ITR, Germany, 1992

Don Dethlefsen's 318is E30 slips through the Pike's Peak International Raceway infield ahead of Arthur Porter's "Art Car" version of the 1800 TI/SA.

Photo: Klaus Schnitzer, Colorado, US, 1999

Former factory racing M3s doze in the Munich sunlight some seven years after the last M-teams fought for home-market glory.

Photo: Author, Mobile Tradition warehouse, Germany, 1999

BMW Motorsport did not repent, and the E36 prototypes—one with four-cylinder power and another destined to become an Art Car, never raced. While Mercedes, Alfa Romeo, and GM-Opel contested increasingly esoteric and expensive versions of the German (finally International) Touring Car Championships of the mid-1990s, BMW stayed with the 2-liter formats. These were dressed in E30 bodies until 1992, when the British were allowed to pioneer the E36 coupe as a 2-liter racer, rendering the E30 obsolete for all but that 1992 final German Championship season.

Goodbye, M3 Racer

In November 1991, the author drove a 2.5-liter Evolution M3 racer in a farewell to the BMW-backed racing E30 M3. This T-car for Altfrid Heger was present at a short track outside Perugia, Italy, and we enjoyed about half an hour in its 9,000-rpm company. The highlight of the day was a subsequent run as passenger to Steve Soper in the same 365-bhp package.

These magic moments underlined that the M3 was the finest four-cylinder racing saloon constructed. It was zestful, strong, and fit to fight any rival in bouts from 10 laps to 24 hours.

15 Body Theme: Fresh Air

The 1986–93 convertible broadened 3 Series appeal and again proved the platform's versatility.

At the March 1993 introduction of the E36 convertible successor to the E30, the company stated, "When BMW introduced the remarkably spacious six-cylinder convertible in 1986, it succeeded in opening up a new market niche in its own inimitable style." Also in inimitable style, Jamie Kitman reported for *Automobile*, "This was the cool car to have in the summer of 1987, nose-bleed price tags be damned."

BMW AG continued logically, "In 1987 alone, 27,000 customers realized their ambition of owning their own open-top 3 Series." Annual sales settled down to just over 21,000 units in 1988 and 1989, before the 318i Convertible (launched at the end of 1990) boosted open top sales of Bavarian-made convertibles to 23,000 units in 1991. "Half were driven by four-cylinder engines and half by six-cylinders," reported the factory.

BMW subsequently confirmed that its production records revealed the output of 143,425 convertibles. The rarest convertible was the Motorsport-blessed 140-mph M3, of which fewer than 800 were manufactured.

BMW added in 1993, "Over 140,000 units of the open-top four-seater convertible, which had become a true classic in the meantime, had been sold by the end of 1992." The factory Convertible—Cabriolet in Europe—was a major step forward in fresh-air motoring and outsold all other specialist E30 derivatives. Introduced in the 1987 Model Year, it was sold with the US catalytic converter version of the BMW small six beneath a 325i badge. The Convertible was so popular in the US that it accounted for more than a third (33 percent) of global convertible sales, totalling 48,412 units from 1987 to 1994 (calendar sales years). All were 325 sixes until 1992, when an intermediate four-cylinder 318iC made the line a little more affordable and added over 1,500 sales beyond the 1991 all-325iC total.

Baur of Stuttgart introduced a 1602 cabriolet conversion in September 1967.

Photo: Author, Concorso Italiano, Quale Lodge, Carmel, CA, US 1999

Pedigree Mutations

There were smaller BMW convertible precedents that stretched back to the 02. Back in September 1967, Baur of Stuttgart had offered a 1602 Cabriolet. This model had a hood that folded fully flat to provide a cleanliness of line that was not echoed by the same company's rather messy 2002 Cabriolet (1971–73) and original 3 Series aftermarket Cabriolets. The latter was available in limited British RHD quantities, but missed the mass market in the US.

The 02 Baur machines were small-run stuff, compared with the factory E30 output of more than 140,000. The first 1602 convertible series totalled 1,681 units and the second, approximately 2,300. They came either with vestigial central "Targa" bar to hide the rollover bar or as the cleanest open BMW this side of the E30 Convertible.

The first 3 Series aftermarket conversions from Baur (late 1977 onward) were equipped with that central rollover section, framed side glass and two separate opening sections. The soft rear folding roof was augmented by a single fiberglass lift-out panel. At the time, the conversion cost was around $4,800/£1,600, above the cost of a new car. By the early 1980s, the British importers used to add more than $9,000/£3,000. That cost was up to $13,000/£4,300 in January 1989, when Baur 3'er conversions were offered for the 316i, 318i, 320i and the 325i in Europe and UK.

Despite the availability of the factory convertible in six cylinders, 16 UK customers chose Baur bodies for their 325i in 1989; 25 went for the 320i; 30 opted for a Baur 318i; and 36 took the cheapest 316i, which exceeded £15,400 in January 1989. In Britain, such Baur conversions were increasingly made available through the 1980s with BMW's blessing, principally to cover the gaps left by the lack of a four-cylinder convertible in the factory line.

The Cabriolet entered European LHD production during March 1986 and the US models belatedly followed in October 1987. Unusually, RHD Britain received earlier supplies, made from June 1986. Convertibles were primarily made at Regensberg, the out-of-town BMW plant that was also home to the E36 successor.

BMW was aware of the coachwork problems associated with a true convertible, particularly the extra strength required to compensate for the lack of any center pillar/rollover hoop. Only the easiest-action convertible tops would be regularly used and therefore attract repeat buyers. BMW tried both Karmann and Baur in the search for a convincing hood, but it took the design efforts of Shaer Waechter of Dusseldorf to come up with a sufficiently ingenious solution to satisfy BMW.

Shaer Waechter dubbed the action "top dead center," and had to support the hood frame with six transverse hood bars and seven links per side. A total of 28 bearings were used to smooth out the action. Those bars exerted sufficient tension on the frame and its triple-layer cloth hood to obviate the need for any studs to secure the hood against water leaks, nor was there any obvious "ballooning" of the soft-top at 100 mph.

The cozy effect was reinforced by the knowledge that the triple-layer laminate structure carried artificial fibers externally, cotton within, and rubber sandwiched in the middle. Not so attractive was the single plastic rear pane, which inevitably clouded or yellowed long before this convertible had served its life span.

For the rarest M3 chop-top, BMW Motorsport engineers added the refinement of electric motor assistance, which was activated at the touch of a button and allowed the top to disappear into the usual rear compartment, complete with "flip top" lid. The power top became universally available on 325iC from 1991 onward.

How did the engineers compensate for the loss of the rigidity normally provided by a fixed roof? The bulk of extra strengthening weight went into basic body building, including deleting spot welding in favor of seam welds. BMW estimated some 131 feet (40 meters) were treated in this manner.

The steel reinforcement of the topless 3 Series body concentrated on the scuttle and structure beneath the dashboard. An extra bar was inserted from steering column to transmission tunnel, with bonus body panels adding muscle to the junction of side sills and front roof pillars. Rear side panels were initially strengthened with an extra plate joining those rear panels to the wheelarches.

There were side sills beneath the doors, plus additional members within those sills. Beefier steel grades were used for the transmission tunnel, with two skins for the rear seat floor panel, extended to the partition between rear seats and the boot.

Even the front wheelarches had reinforcing panels to inject more muscularity to the front end. Meanwhile, the folding roof compartment was anchored to the back wheelarches, but most visible and reassuring was the "windscreen frame made of heavier gauge metal," reported the company.

The better known Baur 2002 (or 1602) Cabriolet/Convertible accounted for most of 4,200 open-air 2002s made between 1971–75. As for the later 3 Series, Baur fitted a rigid lift-out roof panel and fabric rear-hood sections supported on steel pillars.

Photos: BMW Archiv, 1999; Author, UK, 1992

In catalytic converter engine specification, a direct factory curb weight comparison of the 325i two-door versus the 325i Cabrio demonstrated an escalation from 1,200 to 1,310 kg: a gain of 110 kg (242 lbs) in European formats.

To lower the BMW top, one simply ensured the electric side glass was lowered, tweaked two locking levers on the top screen rail through 180 degrees, and pulled the hood away from

The E21 Baur factory-approved version of the convertible theme exhibited a lift-out roof panel/fold-away-rear soft-section design.

Photo: Paul Howard for BMW GB, circa 1979

front and rear tension. A safety catch in the hood compartment released the lid and the hood could then be folded away, out of sight. The BMW solution for hiding the hood beneath a hinged metal lid was exceptionally neat. The only snag was that the trunk lid and hood compartment cover could not be raised simultaneously.

The European and UK 325iC offered reasonable standard equipment at inevitably steep prices. Multiple-spoke alloys, central locking, anti-theft alarm with deadlocks, all electric windows, upgraded suspension, sports steering wheel, green tinted glass, and sports front seats all came standard. The 320i shared all these features, except standard ABS in Europe, and was unlisted in the US.

US Market History

"Combining the silky high performance of the new 2.5-liter engine with the joy of open-air motoring, this sporty—yet luxurious—four-seater brings the quality of a German convertible to a new price class." That was BMW NA's pitch for the soft-top 3'er for 1987, when it was base-priced at $31,000, making it the most expensive 3 Series save the M3. Price was no deterrent, for 1987 proved to be the Convertible's best US sales year, topping 1988 by just under 600 units at a total of 11,609 sold.

It was the first time BMW had officially sold a convertible body in the US in 28 years, dating back to the 1950s 507. As for all 3 Series, except the base 325, leather upholstery and a BMW-branded sound system of six speakers (rather than eight in contemporary sedans) were standard fare.

Showroom equipment was a lot more generous than in Europe, including climate-control air conditioning, cruise control, and an on-board computer, along with 6J x 14-inch cast alloy wheels. Options were initially confined to the popular automatic transmission ($595), metallic paints ($325), and a $370 limited-slip differential.

A specialist hardtop for 1987 onward sold to a minority, as for the subsequent E36 aluminum item. For 1998 MY, the 325iC ignored roofed 3'er changes—to avoid costly retooling costs—except the heated throttle body for cold starts, an airfoil

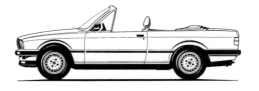

The original clean machine that would sell by the hundred-thousand.

Drawing: BMW AG, 1985

This three-quarter front view emphasized that this was a full four-seater fresh-air experience.

Drawing: BMW AG, 1985

The four-section views from the factory, with dimensions given in millimeters: the roof-line was one of the lowest quoted by the factory for a 3 Series, equivalent to 53.9 inches.

Drawing: BMW Grafik Design, Munich, 1989

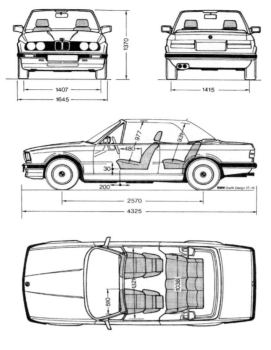

a starter 325i past $80,000 for the flagship coupe. Within that model mix, the 325iC just sprouted sportier cross-spoke 6.5 J x 14-inch alloys on the option list, which grew substantially in 1990. However, base prices had been snipped at $33,850, while options like the automatic hit $700. Those fancy cross-spokes were $500, and a factory-approved autochange CD-player ran $780. There was a dealer-fit remote-triggered alarm/locking system, but this was not priced by BMW NA.

for the driver's side wiper, and asbestos-free brake friction materials. The base price rose by $1,995 to $32,995, and the option list contained some increases, too. An automatic transmission (the usual ZF 4 HP22 ratio quartet) rose to $645. Now the hardtop had a listed option cost at $3,500 and BMW NA decided to offer heated front seats as a $200 option.

The BMW NA excitement of model year 1989 was the introduction of a new 5 Series. The 325iC—dubbed "The Ultimate Tanning Machine" in honor of the "Ultimate Driving Machine" sales logo—merely grew a "slimmer, cleaner-looking, third brake light in its trunklid." Options and their prices remained unchanged, but the base price grew to $34,950 without the traditional Destination and Handling ($345) or Dealer Prep ($145) charges. Sales slid below the 10,000 annual mark and declined every year thereafter, except in 1992.

By Autumn of 1990, BMW NA forecast selling 15 models, including the ill-fated 850i, thus allowing a price span from less than $25,000 for

For 1991, the 325iC was abbreviated by 5.4 inches, losing those ungainly Federal Bumpers (ditched by other 3'ers in Model Year 1989). The acclaimed power top operation (quoted at 20 seconds, up or down) and the 6.5-inch-wide cross-spoke alloys were both part of its elevated $35,950 base tag.

Sales slid to under 5,000 units, but BMW NA already had an answer with the announcement of the 318iC at less than $30,000, also for model year 1991. This $28,500 offering listed few options— the most dynamic was the limited-slip differential at $465—but breathed new life into the 1992 sales stats. Mechanically, the 318iC shared the recently US-debuted 318i/318iS 16-valve motor of 134 bhp, 127 lb-ft of torque, and 1.8-liter displacement. Performance forecasts were 0–60 mph in 10.4 seconds, 122 mph, and EPA estimates of 21 City mpg, 27 mpg on the highway.

Showroom 318iC equipment embraced BMW NA's usual ABS listing (often optional in European markets), six-speaker stereo, and anti-theft. Options were constrained to the limited-

Bimmer's first factory convertible since the 1950s was beautiful as well as practical.

Photo: BMW Werkfotos, 1985

single cam/8-valve 1.8-liter the only model under £20,000 at £18,220. The M3 convertible, of which only 33 were officially sold in Britain, was a wallet-bashing £37,250.

One of the most potentially valuable 3ers of the time was the 1990 BMW 325i Motorsport convertible, which included an electro-mechanical hood assistance system (as opposed to the usual double hydraulic struts). The price was a hefty £28,950, which included £725 for the assisted hood and more than £5,000 for the Motorsport magic.

Only 250 325i M Cabrios were built, and they came with a color choice of Sebring Gray or Macao Blue. They were similarly allied to black or silver leather for the upholstery and black or blue for the hood.

The M-element primarily included a body kit of MTechnic branding that provided a front spoiler, rear skirts and side sills. As on the less-expensive 3 Series convertibles, no rear spoiler was offered, optionally or otherwise. The convertibles differed from their saloon brethren in minor respects: principally in the front and rear aprons, the installation of a black panel between the rear lights, and the use of color coding for bumpers and mirrors. MTechnic branding was also imposed on the upgraded suspension and

slip differential ($465), metallic paint ($435), and heated front seats ($300), while a hardtop was listed—as for 325iC—but not priced.

Convertible sales grew from 3,742 to 5,256 units in 1991–92 sales seasons, boosted by 1,640 sales of the small-capacity model in 1991 and 1,538 units in 1992. For 1992, the big 3'er news was the advent of the E36 325i for the US. The E30 convertible was listed through to 1993 when sales were just over a thousand units (1,391), of which 217 were credited to leftover examples of the 318iC. The last official prices for both models were $28,870 and $36,320 in 1992. In 1993, the 325iC was the sole offering, supported by a 4-year/50,000-mile warranty coupled with a 6-year anti-corrosion deal. A driver's airbag had joined the extensive standard equipment list.

UK/European Market History

The 325i Cabrio began life in the UK at £16,495 in 1986 and took only two sales years to cross the £20,000 barrier. In December 1990, BMW (GB) heralded a price-cutting 1.8-liter derivative. The 325iC was £23,990 on sale alongside the new 3 Series in Britain in September 1991, while contemporary 318i and 320i Cabrios were also still on sale, with a 318i

This is the 2.7-liter Alpina C2 version of the factory convertible, complete with unique front spoiler and the Bavarian specialist's own wheel design.

Photo: Issued by Frank Sytner Limited, Nottingham, UK, 1986

BMW did its best with period technology to make time at the wheel of the E30 convertible as appealing as the appearance.

Photo: Klaus Schnitzer, US, 1989

the steering wheel, supporting 7J x 15 cross-spoke alloys with dark Nogaro painted centers, as for some Evo E30 M3s.

Within, there was a Napa-Tex woven cloth/leather finish for the seating. Extensive leather trim was applied to "outer parts of the seats, doors and side panels, center and tunnel consoles." Further showroom trinkets including a computer, a graduated tint on the windscreen and the extensive use of black satin chrome finishes with body colors applied to mirrors and bumpers.

Aside from the suspension changes, the power train was pure catalytic converter 325i, and the EH-coded automatic gearbox was optional. Specification was fairly generous, comprising four-wheel disc brakes and all-around electric side glass operation, but road wheels for the cheaper 318i derivatives were confined to 5.5 x 14-inch steel rollers carrying miserly 195/65 R 14 rubber. Later designer-label convertibles of 1991 had alloy wheels and upgraded interior trim.

April 1991 was distinguished by a BMW Motorsport exercise named 318i Design

Convertible. The 318i Convertible was £17,840 in late 1990 and an automatic transmission variant cost nearly another £1,000. The Design specification revolved around the usual European 318i power train of 115 bhp and 1,796 cc in both cases. Such 1,220-kg (2,690-lb) machines were rated as capable of 116 mph in a body measured at 0.37 Cd with the roof raised. As for 0–62 mph, that was dismissed in 12 seconds. Mileage expectations were approximately 27 Imperial mpg in urban use.

For 1991, BMW (GB) imported additional 325i Motorsport and 318i Design Convertibles. That season, the 325i was a particularly rare beast, with just 50 planned for importation, all with Lotus white leather upholstery and the

Hood up, or with everything open, the 325iC was an arresting sight.

Klaus Schnitzer, US, 1986

If you don't like the four-seat Bimmer 3 Series approach, there is always the American-built, 3-Series-based, Z3 convertible.

Photo: Author, South Carolina, US, 1997

MTechnic body aerodynamics. The 325iC M had much the same specification as in 1990 but was now creeping towards £30,000 (listed at £29,950).

The 1991 318iC Design featured Neon Blue or green paint, unique striped seat trims, a manual hood (as opposed to the now-standard electro-mechanical device of the 325i), de-chroming and 7J x 15 alloys with 205/55 rubber. After Britain's VAT tax increase to 17.5 percent, the cost of a 318i escalated to £19,240 as a manual, and beyond £20,000 for an automatic.

The factory 3 Series Convertible offered civilized open-air motoring standards which contrasted strongly with most aftermarket conversions. In writing about the 3 Series Convertible in *Car and Driver*, Pete Lyons put it memorably: "Everybody should own a convertible at least once in his life.... Maybe this is one to own all through a lifetime."

16 The 3 Series 4x4: Great Idea, But...

Not every Bimmer owner enjoys the slides and scares that come with winter motoring.

In the beginning of the 1980s, the 4x4 trend caught on, especially with the US market. Audi had done its quattro thing in Spring 1980, prompting European and Japanese opposition to create their own interpretations of a performance 4x4 sedan theme. The result was the production from October 1985 to January 1991 of the 2.5-liter derivative badged 325iX.

BMW obviously could not afford to miss such a major technological advance. Moving quickly to bring a car to market, BMW unwittingly shared a British-engineered Ford 4x4 system. The Ferguson-patented system was effective—and fun to drive on the slipperiest surfaces, with a power bias at the rear wheels—but the clumsy conversion proved significantly heavier than quattro's hollow-shaft gearbox.

The resulting 325iX was the slowest-selling E30 derivative of the Convertible, Touring and iX 1980s permutations. Although BMW 325iX attracted fiercely loyal support from 2,647 buyers at BMW NA showrooms from 1987–94, it was a commercial failure. Production ceased at 29,589 copies, including 12,557 first edition 2-doors on the iX 4x4 theme.

The factory did try 4x4 again with the 5 Series (525iX), which was especially valued in the Touring body. This upscale 4x4 was not repeated at press time with the current 5 Series, but not because it was a failure. Rather, the outstanding 1999 BMW X5 SUV from Spartanburg, South Carolina filled the market slot originally skimmed by 525iX, and the E46 3 Series offered 4x4 optionally from summer 2000 in Europe (328xi) and later in the US as the 325xi and 330xi.

Generation X

During the early 1980s gestation of its 4x4, after a postwar period entirely devoted to heralding the merits of sporting rear-drive cars, BMW engineers faced the challenge of a front- and 4x4-drive majority. The company had experimented with front-drive between the 02 and 3 Series, but dismissed it as out of character with its other products.

But the 1980s challenge of high-performance 4x4 motoring could not be ignored. Audi at Ingolstadt—less than an hour North of BMW at Munich, provoking sharp interstate rivalry—had presented its stunning 4x4 turbo quattro coupe at the March 1980 Geneva Motor Show. That design impacts upon performance motoring today, particularly in a breed of ultra-high-performance Subarus and Mitsubishis bred for the same World Championship stage that Audi dominated some twenty years ago.

In the 1980s, most manufacturers were forced to adopt 4x4 in the wake of the Audi quattro, not for sales volume, but to earn a reputation as technically aware manufacturers. Initially, BMW considered 4x4 most relevant to powerful machinery, and this suggested that forthcoming generations of V12 Bimmers might use a part-time electronically controlled 4x4 system.

To alter an existing front-engine, rear-drive, mid-weight saloon with strut front and trailing-arm rear suspension to a 4x4 configuration, BMW unwittingly had Ford as a traveling companion. The Blue Oval had 1960s and 1970s European competition and prototype police car experience with a Ferguson British-patented 4-wheel-drive system. Ford pressed its European Sierra into 1985 production with a V6 XR 4x4 to replace the "stripes-n-wings" XR4i/Ti breed.

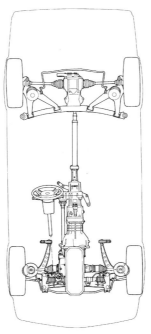

The extent of front-end engineering needed to produce an all-wheel-drive BMW was only made viable by the adoption of the patented Ferguson 4x4 system, also used by Ford.

Drawing: BMW AG Presse, December 1985

BMW also wanted a 1985 production debut and the Ferguson system was released for mass production through a then rare Anglo-German motor-industry cooperative. Thus did Ford Sierra XR 4x4, Scorpio 4x4, Sierra RS Cosworth 4-door, and Escort Cosworth RS share basic 4x4 principles with the BMW 325i. BMW and Ford also demanded a power-split broadly defined as one third front, two thirds rear.

BMW only sold its 4x4 to the public with a Bosch ABS system to slow the plot down on 4-wheel disc brakes of 10.2-inch diameters (the fronts ventilated). Slippery surfaces encourage a 4x4 feeling of invincibility in keen drivers, so this was an important engineering/safety bonus from BMW at that time.

BMW also took basic precautions to improve the slippery surface behavior of ABS. These concerned reprogrammed electronic parameters to reduce yaw momentum, a longitudinal acceleration sensor to distinguish between low and high friction coefficients, and a slight boost to tickover speeds. This was applied directly at the throttle butterfly by an extra electronic control circuit tied to the longitudinal sensor, fighting wheel-lock at low speeds on the iciest inclines.

Based at Schwabisch in Germany, Viscodrive GmbH undertook production runs of more than 5,000 on behalf of the British patent holders in Coventry, who dealt with small-run prototypes and competition requirements of the period under Ferguson or FFD branding. Viscodrive was established as a 50–50 partnership between GKN in Britain and ZF in Germany. This partnership led to a naturally easy path of development for BMW to pursue with the 3 Series, ensuring that the result was a permanent 4x4 device.

The hardware required for the 325i was similar to that of Ford, and added a central differential/transfer box with planetary gears to the base of a normal 325i rear end and a viscous coupling (VC) aft of the gearbox . Rear-drive was fed rearward in the usual manner (though refined by the presence of a VC limited-slip differential) through a 3.91 final drive (standard in the US). This ratio was raised slightly in Europe—to 3.73:1—if the sports five-speed was specified.

The complicated part, as on any front-engine, rear-drive conversion, was to provide the front-drive element, although BMW dispensed with any kind of front locking or limited-slip differential. Power was fed forward by an external shaft from that central differential gear set, the shaft itself motivated by a multiple-row Morse chain.

BMW fed power forward on the opposite side but faced some installation challenges. Thus a new cast-aluminum sump pan had to allow the passage of one drive shaft. So the front end featured many new components, including the provision of equal length driveshafts to successfully fight any tendency to torque steer under harsh acceleration.

Aside from the obvious front differential and two drive-shafts, BMW reworked the suspension around new aluminum lower wishbones and installed a replacement subframe. For the first time, BMW adjusted the front geometry for negative offset, by remounting the front strut and kingpin. Now, an offset of 2.9 mm (0.11 inches) with minor negative camber was adopted in place of positive inclination.

A sharply reduced caster figure—from 9 degrees down to 1.5 degrees—was enforced. Average track was stretched just over half an inch (0.59 inches, or 15 mm) for the iX, according to contemporary reports, which also recorded a ride height raised by 0.79 in. (20 mm).

Note the very narrow wheel offset ledges for the alloys that are unique to the 325iX.

Photo: BMW GB, 1986

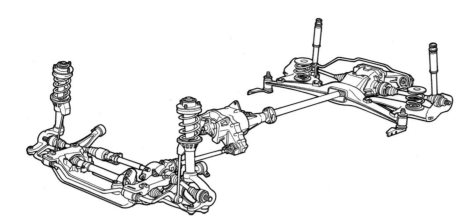

Based at Schwabisch in Germany, Viscodrive GmbH provided the hardware for mass production of Ferguson-patented 4x4 transmissions. The front differential was managed with unequal length driveshafts beneath the motor.

Drawing: BMW AG Presse, December 1985

The wheelbase, overall length, and other vital statistics, apart from extra weight, remained as for the rear-drive models. The standard rear-drivers also provided standard steering and gearbox (European choice of automatic, manual or close-ratio five-speed) and all other items not specifically described as different.

Peripheral changes for the 325iX included the replacement of the spring strut supports, enlarged central transmission tunnel, and wheel-arches to accommodate the revised ride-height.

The standard European wheel and tire combination was a steel 6J x 14 with the usual 195/65 VR tire dimensions, although the optional Michelin 150 TD 365 plus 200/60VR 365 rubber on alloy road wheels was available.

BMW was somewhat puzzled that Ford claimed only 50 kg (110 lbs) as the weight gain of a 150-bhp V6 Sierra over its 2-WD predecessor. The weight gain quoted for the 325iX over the equivalent saloon was 90 kg (198 lbs) in Europe. BMW warned its employees via internal memos of performance losses due to extra weight of additional gear sets, bearings, seals, and joints, as well as the extra air resistance generated by the elevated body height.

On March 6, 1985, a BMW internal memo in Germany quoted the top speed of the 325iX as 212 km/h (131.6 mph) and time for 0–100 km/h (0–62 mph) was recorded by company testers as 9 seconds. That meant a company-estimated loss of 5 km/h top speed, 0.7 seconds on the 0–100 km/h drag, and a 10.3-second time (in fifth) between 50 and 75 mph (80 and 120 km/h) was reckoned to be 1.4 seconds adrift.

X-files: The 325iX in America

The costly 325iX was never a major US seller, except in affluent snow-belt America. It sat in the over-$30,000 class for its 1988 model year introduction, priced at the level of BMW's own Convertible (then $32,995) or the belligerently sporty M3 ($34,800).

Initial supplies of 325iX came only with two doors, which did not help its $33,290 cause. Just 297 were registered in 1987, when only the standard Getrag 260 five-speed manual was offered and metallic paint ($375) was the lone option. Anti-lock braking, leather interior, and electronic cruise control were standard. As were 15 x 7J cross-spoke cast alloys with 205/55VR rubber. America also gained a nine-function on-board computer, air conditioning, and an anti-theft-equipped eight-speaker AM/FM stereo radio/cassette player. All were showroom items, along with mundane but welcome features such as ellipsoid low-beam head and fog lamps, the Service Interval Indicator, and power-operated radio antenna. Externally, the American-market iX could be spotted by its front spoiler and deck-lid air dam, plus widened rocker panels and more notably flared wheelarches.

Public reaction was generally favorable, but a piece in *Motor Trend* for March 1987 might have accidentally triggered some pricing resentment in America. Back then, base cost was translated as $18,500 with $21,500 "Price as tested." More than $10,000 over that prediction was the subsequent reality for a machine with abilities that could not translate via printed performance statistics.

Such factors predicted such slow 325iX sales graphs and the exceptionally low American "take" on a model that should have done better. If it's any compensation to BMW NA, Audi's quattro was not a major US seller either.

It was 1988 before major US motor magazines published test results on the 325iX. An encouraging verdict came from *Motor Trend* in March of that year. After saying $33,000 was "a lot of shekels for a 3 Series," the testers added, "but then it'll do things no other 3 Series has ever done. This is a car that handles in the best BMW tradition, bathes you in low-key luxury, and gets you where you want to go, regardless of the weather. If we were about to head for the high country, we'd be hard-pressed to find a better choice."

In November of 1988, *Road & Track* was able to review its comprehensive findings, pitching the 2-WD (front) and quattro 4x4 drive Audi 90 versus the equivalent 2-WD (rear) and 4x4 BMW 325iX. Conscientiously carrying out five ability tests at Steamboat Springs, Colorado, *R&T* concluded that the front-drive Audi 90 was the best all-round compromise for "hot sun in the summer and freezing white stuff in the winter." For bone-dry southern California, the 325is was *R&T*'s nomination as "such an exquisitely balanced performer when roads are dry that it makes just covering the tar between home and work a joy." The venerable mag's advice for wet or snowy road motoring in the 325is was succinct: "When it snows, park it and drive something else."

Road & Track arrived at the verdict because the 325is stopping distances were so poor in snow, taking 109 ft from 20 mph to zero, versus 75 ft for 325iX. *R&T* concluded, "All-wheel drivers are terrific, if you can handle the extra cost. Which all-wheel driver is best? It depends on handling preferences. If you like the rear-drive handling character of a BMW, a Mustang GT, or a Camaro, the BMW 325iX is the answer. If you prefer a front-driver's ultra-stable feel and good interior packaging, the 90 quattro is the best choice."

For model year 1989, the news was of four-door and automatic transmission availability. Base prices were lowered to get under the $30,000 barrier with the two-door ($29,950), while the four-door listed for $30,750. Both price tags suggested that BMW NA—and the parent factory—realized they had set the prices too high for their pioneer 4x4 sedan.

The option list expanded to cover $645 for the automatic and $200 for heated front seats. Leather upholstery was exchanged for a standard "leatherette" fabric, with no leather option offered that model year. Sales responded during the 1989 calendar year by peaking at 844 units compared to 310 for 1988.

In model year 1990, the 325iX changed little in basic showroom form, with two- and four-doors priced at $29,950 and $30,750 respectively, but the option list bulged. Leather returned at $895, an electric sunroof was now $225 and metallic paint required $375, while heated front seats were up $50 at $250. A CD player optioned out at $780 and you now needed to pay $250 if you wanted the premium sound system, or $515 for a remote-alarm.

Dealer prep was $140 and $245 went for destination and handling shipping. It was possible to spend $35,225 on a fully-loaded 1990 model year 325iX with automatic transmission. Despite the selective pricing, just 699 Bimmer iX variants were sold in the US for 1990. For both two- and four-door model lines, the automatic option was a significant factor, selling more than 50 percent of the two-door line and virtually all of the four-doors.

For model year 1991, the biggest BMW news, across the board, was the adoption of a four-year/50,000 mile warranty. The 325iX received only detail changes, while options were pretty familiar. The most expensive option was the leather upholstery at $950. A CD was $825 and the alarm was $540. A desirable electrically operated sunroof snatched another $275 over the standard manual roof. Incidentally, a ski sack was part of 325iX standard equipment, as it had been for many model years.

Sales in 1991 slipped to 454 units, and it was obvious that the unique 4x4 Bimmer of the E30 was not going to live much longer. Sure enough, BMW NA did not list the model for 1993 or 1994, but it racked up 1,391 sales in 1993 and a few strays (13) found homes in 1994.

Unfortunately, the 325i was not quite good enough and cost too much to make it more than a collector's curiosity. Maybe the later E46 xi with successful X5 hardware will be the 3 series 4x4 answer…

17 The E30 Touring

When is a wagon not a wagon? When it is a BMW Touring

The E30 BMW 325i Touring made its German public debut at the Frankfurt Motor Show in September 1987, but output did not begin until March 1988. Because of the vagaries of introducing so many body styles on one model the E30 Touring body lasted well into the E36 era.

The last E30 Tourings were made in 1994, by which time 103,704 units had been manufactured, none for USA sales. That figure compared with the 2002-based Touring twenty years earlier, which had attracted 30,206 buyers in its brief production life between 1971 and 1974.

Those first 02-edition Tourings were of three-door rather than five-door layout, aimed at European sales. Seeing that both French Renault and some British low-volume designs combined sports coupe flair with a third-door "sports estate" configuration, BMW started looking seriously at interpreting such themes in 1965. There were a number of false starts before Paul Bracq's 1971 interpretation on a 2002tii base achieved BMW Board approval and was displayed at the January 1971 Brussels Show in Belgium.

The first Touring featured not just the simple lift-up tailgate of a modern hatchback, but also the split folding action rear seats that are so common today and was available on platforms from 1600 through 2002 form. Confusing engine-capacity badging and upbeat press reports from *auto motor und sport*, quoting 10 percent of all 02 production as Touring types, could not convince the German public that this prophetic three-door was valid.

The 1970s Touring was unstable under Autobahn sidewind assault and oversteered even more than the traditional tail-happy Bimmers of the period. The Touring became particularly valued by the British establishment, including Grand Prix ace Stirling

177

The 1971 2002 touring was initially badged 2000 tii and was a three-door design, rather than the five-doors configuration used for the E30, E36, and current E46.

Photo: BMW Archiv, Munich, 1971, reprinted 1989

Moss, who had a rather special example with a five-speed gearbox and tuned 2002 motor.

Touring comeback

Some twenty-four years after the 02-based Touring disappeared from production, the company had a new rendition to display on the E30 chassis. The first 16 pre-production Tourings came from the Regensberg in 1987, where production examples were built from 1988–91. The E30 Touring transferred to Dingolfing from 1991–94, where a minority of the 103,000-unit run was produced.

Described by BMW under the heading "Elegant Holdall," the 1988 E30 BMW 3 Series Touring car differed fundamentally from its slow-selling predecessors by being based on a four-door body. Another step forward was that BMW was able to offer such a wide range of motors to haul this five-door. In Europe, customers could pick sixes from 129 bhp (320i) to 170 bhp (325i) on through the useful 324td (turbodiesel) and vastly cheaper—four-cylinder 316i and 318i variants.

Performance was not the point, but to give you an idea of this elegant load-carrier's potential, here are some 1988 quotes from *Autocar*. They said, "The close-ratio Getrag gearbox and

170-bhp engine give performance characteristics which would have been rare in almost any car, saloon or otherwise, ten or even five years ago. It will sprint 60 mph in 7.6 seconds and can squirt from 50 to 70 mph in third gear in just 4.5 seconds. Top speed is a little over 130 mph."

Compared with the six-cylinder models, the 318i Touring was frenetic, with a 4.27:1 final drive necessary to haul 2,601 lbs (1180 kg). Fortunately, the M40 motor was a far smoother, more sophisticated 1.8-liter than its predecessors. Performance for the 318i was adequate in manual-transmission trim, reaching from 0–62 mph in a claimed 11.5 seconds, but the automatic was toward the slowcoach end of the scale at nearly 13 seconds. Top speed was rated at 117 mph (116 mph for the automatic), and the urban fuel consumption was attractive at a listed 27 Imperial mpg for both transmissions.

To preserve the driving pleasure of the 3 Series, BMW concentrated on body strength, aerodynamics, and suspension. Wider side rocker sills and an integral rear spoiler (above the hatchback glass) allowed an 0.36 Cd aerodynamic drag factor, as for the equivalent saloon. BMW also claimed that lift forces on the front and rear axles had been cut significantly.

Body changes beyond the obvious full-depth

Key dimensions
of the E30 Touring
included extra bulk
over the rear wheels.

Drawings: BMW Factory
Brochure, Munich, 1987

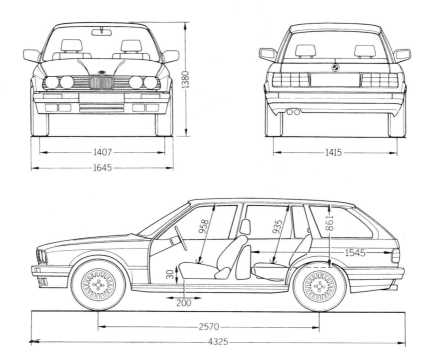

The five-door
Touring became
a desirable buy in
late-1980s Europe.
The idea of creating
such a load carrier
was sparked by the
initiative of a BMW
employee who creat-
ed the first example.

Photo: BMW GB, 1988

fifth-door/hatchback included a considerably
beefed-up rear end. A new roof and modified
side panels were supported by longitudinal and
transverse support members which were "substantially reinforced for extra rigidity. New
intersecting panels and load bearing structures,
as well as bonded side and rear windows also
help to provide greater stiffness," said BMW at
Frankfurt in 1987. However, the 325i Touring
did carry a weight penalty, growing to 1,270 kg
(2,794 lbs) versus 1,180 kg (2,596 lbs) for an

equivalent sedan.

A quartet of disc brakes (vented at the front)
were specified for all Touring models, averaging
10.2-inch diameters as an established minimum
even on the later 318i. Anti-lock braking was an
expensive (over £700, or $1,000) British option
on all but the 325i Touring and many European
Tourings lacked this critical safety feature.

For the 320/325i-based Touring models, a
6J x 14 multi-spoke alloy wore 195/65 rubber.
Suspension changes did not affect the geometry,

The Touring offered useful load capacity but an awkward load entry.

Photo: BMW GB, 1988

with the basic weight distribution remaining at 50 percent front and rear, but the springs and dampers were uprated for the heavier Touring.

At the back, there was the German option of self-leveling suspension, and this was also expensively listed in the UK. The hydropneumatic layout required no additional power source, taking an auxiliary line from the oil circulation system of the power steering, via a tandem pump.

The hatch itself was operated with assistance from two low gas pressure spring struts, and the hand grip was integrated into the license plate surround panel. The fifth door stretched right down between the rear light clusters to provide a small loading sill, but space was limited by the sloping rear window line. The BMW back seats could be folded separately and, the back seat cushion was removable to earn extra depth. Payload was increased to a maximum 1,058 lbs (480 kg).

The luggage compartment was beautifully executed and detailed, including four points at which loads could be lashed down and a roller blind used to cover contents. A safety net between luggage compartment and occupants was originally listed as an option. Stowage spaces were excavated in the side panels, which also helped security, while rear sound speakers could

also be found in this location. That rear end also located the battery on 4x4 Tourings (1988–91) and on LHD diesel Tourings.

Touring production of LHD and RHD examples, plus a 320i version for LHD, was not undertaken until March 1988; and the RHD 320i Touring was made from September 1988 onward. By then, BMW had the 324 turbo diesel on stream. However, like all 3-Series diesel-burners of the 1980s, this model was not offered to America or Britain. Another model that escaped both countries was the 4x4 (325iX) running gear beneath Touring coachwork.

A 318i Touring was manufactured from April 1989, and was offered for sale in Britain in June 1989. Just two gasoline-burning Tourings (325i/318i) remained on sale in the E36 era, lasting until 1993 (325i) and 1994 (318i) respectively in Britain. The UK also received a 320i six-pot Touring that died in 1991 showrooms.

Touring goodies included five-door central locking that also secured the fuel filler cap. A sports steering wheel, halogen auxiliary driving lights, and the BMW headlight wiper-based cleaning system were also standard on six-cylinder British Tourings.

Subtle details like color-coding, the use of green-tinted glass, and the substitution of satin black for chrome were extended to the

The rear bay with the luggage cover rolled out of its retractor reel.

Photo: Klaus Schnitzer, Munich, 1992

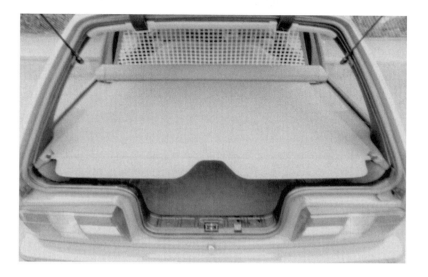

Touring. Introduced at a rare low price, the 318i Touring specification in the UK, compared to a 325i Touring, lost ABS anti-lock braking, alloy wheels, headlight wash and wipe, sports steering wheel, and those halogen front fog lamps. All these items could be made up on the options list.

End Game

The Touring had proved to be a valid concept, as had the progression through E21 to E30 generations of 3 Series. According to BMW, some 1.4 million of the original 3 Series were constructed, defeating commercial criticism of 3 Series potential compared to that of the 2002. The E21 had virtually doubled the figure for "02" sales, but that was just the 3'er start, for E30 almost repeated the sales-doubling process.

The E30 second generation of 3 Series brought an even warmer glow to Munich men of accounts, for its twelve-year span from 1982 to 1994 (1982–90 for sedan majority) brought production of this generation at Munich, Dingolfing, and later Regensberg, to 2,330,251

Alpina offered two power upgrades in the E30 Touring of the later 1980s: the C2–2.5 allowed 190 bhp and near-M3 performance, while the C2–2.7 was slightly more powerful than the European M3 at 210 bhp.

Photo: Author Archives 1990

examples. Once Touring, Convertible, and CKD (completely knocked down) kits assembled at overseas locations are included, the true grand total of all types and modes of E30 production finally tallied up at 2,339,251. This figure is eloquent statistical testimony to one of the most versatile and attractive automobiles manufactured in the late twentieth century.

Now it was time to abandon tradition in the 3 Series, get with the aerodynamic age, and level the transatlantic playing field on the road to power parity between Europe and America, welcoming the sleeker BMW E36.

18 Aerodynamic Age Comes to Planet 3

Aerodynamic body design and the 3'er were strangers in the 1980s, but the E36 sedans began a sleek new 3 Series era.

With a more aerodynamic shape for the 1990s, the E36-coded 3 Series sold strongly from the start, while also providing BMW's lowest contemporary aerodynamic drag (Cd) factor. At the close of the sedan's eight-year life in 1998, over 2.3 million of the third generation 3'er had poured from production lines and CKD assembly plants in Germany, America-Spartanburg and South Africa.

Four-door sedans were the bestsellers, with 1.5 million units made from 1990 to 1998. That was not the ultimate total of E36 production success, for many models continued in production alongside the E46 successor of 1998. The final tally, unavailable from official sources at press time, is likely to top 2.5 million E36-based production vehicles.

While sales charts were dominated by the four-door, the coupe accounted for fewer than half a million units sold (including M3). The "sleeper" surprise was that the Compact hybrid of E36 (see Chapter 22), recorded 330,967 sales by the close of 1998 and was still in production during the summer of 2000.

In the USA, the E36 generation premiered in four-door 325i format for model year 1992. Mere months elapsed before two-door 325i and 318is coupes joined the fun, along with a four-door 318i. Most importantly, this was the first generation of 3'ers that featured engine-power equality with Europe.

Americans actually enjoyed more power in their 16-valve double overhead camshaft 318i sedans than many markets in Europe. Britain was stuck with 8-valve single camshaft motors that yielded at least 21 bhp less.

The 1991 E36 BMW
3 Series takes to
the beach for its
initial beauty shots,
unaware that it
would take a year or
more for it to swim
the Atlantic.

Photo: Author Archive,
1991

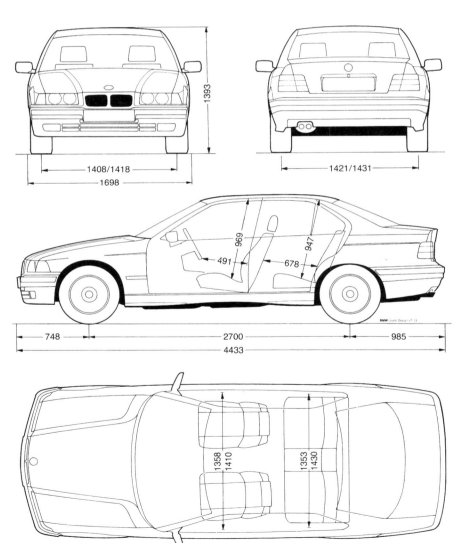

The four-way dimen-
sional drawings of
the six-cylinder E36
generally reflected
an increase in cabin
space over its prede-
cessors, but rear seat
legroom was still
restricted within an
enlarged Three.

Drawing: BMW AG,
Munich, model year 1993

Sales Savior

The new 3'er saved BMW from the direst effects of an early 1990s recession, which included mass lay-offs and discount selling unceremoniously inflicted upon Audi and Porsche in America and Britain. The 3'er American press reception was warm, typified by *Road & Track*'s John Lamm in a March 1991 preview. Mr. Lamm hoped for a sub-$30,000 start price on the 325i (it materialized at $27,990) and concluded, "The new 3 Series is a sweetheart that will likely offer a stiff challenge to Mercedes-Benz 190 sales." It managed more than that, and held its own against the replacement C-Klasse Mercedes.

US E36 sedan sales built rapidly, selling just over 20,000 units in the first year (1992) and exceeding that marker in all sales seasons from 1992–97, save 1996 (19,093). In that year, fuller supplies of both four- and two-door saw two-door sales climb to more than 16,000 units. Sales totals for the E36 BMW 3 Series tallied more than 31,000 units of some 50,000 BMW NA sales in 1993.

The sedan was the mainstay product for BMW in the US, assembled in North Carolina before Spartanburg shifted to full-time Z3 production. Spartanburg contributed 6,195 sedans around a 318i recipe in 1995. The Z3 sports car was to be the primary Spartanburg product until the X5 arrived in 1999.

Technical Tale

The third generation of 3 Series was born into a different Germany than that of its predecessors. The 1989–90 reunification of East and West Germany made no immediate impact on Bimmer engineering philosophy, which

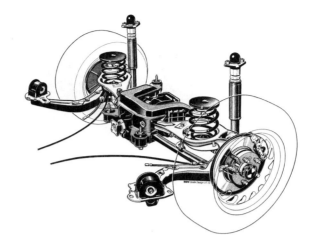

The Z for Zentral control rear axle brought BMW much needed rear end traction.

Drawing: BMW Grafik Design, 1991

remained that of conservative hardware excellence around the hallowed rear-drive layout.

The primary differences for the later 3 Series were listed by BMW as follows: bigger, quieter, more fuel efficient, faster, safer, needs less servicing, handles better and is 80 percent recyclable. The biggest benefit was an aerodynamic drag factor that slid under the 0.30 barrier, boosting fuel economy and lowering cabin noise. BMW recorded 0.29 Cd on the skinny four-cylinder 316i. As the models grew plusher, the Cd values quoted were increased: 0.30 Cd for the 318i and 0.32 Cd for both six-cylinder machines were more typical quotes for well-equipped US models. These revised Cd values were aided by a 61-degree rake to the 5-mm-thick front screen: like its 66-degree rear counterpart, it was bonded into the body, while the side glass sat virtually flush with slightly protuberant rubber seals and sheet metal.

Aerodynamics were further assisted by hiding quadruple headlamps beneath glass panels, as well as by careful air management, including deflectors for all four wheels and underbelly paneling to allow a "flat bottom" effect under the front air dam. Beneath the front bumpers were small strakes placed to deflect the air stream around the front tires, plus the smallest version of the traditional "kidney" grille above the bumper.

A 44-percent reduction in front-end lift and 19-percent reduction on the rear axle were reported. This enhanced directional stability, but the new E36 3 Series wandered at higher speeds, a notable customer complaint in Germany during 1990–91.

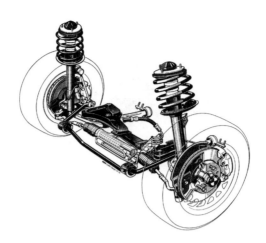

The front end for E36 featured MacPherson strut suspension with strong lower location arms and clever upper geometry.

Drawing: BMW Grafik Design, 1991

The traditional forward-hinging hood was ditched in favor of a conventional front latch and safety catch. BMW claimed a 50 percent reduction in the effect of the external mirrors upon the 3 Series' aerodynamic drag coefficient, but these were subsequently blamed as a source of external wind noise.

An E36 BMW 3 Series incorporated integral spoilers on the back trunk lid and beneath the front bumper. Not so subtle was the extensive use of recyclable gray plastic sections below the bumper line. The sills looked as though they had already been recycled a few times, but BMW said that only the floor mats, trunk lining, and wheelarch liners were made from recycled materials. The company claimed 80 percent recycling potential and that included the polyethylene fuel tank that sat beneath the rear seats. The tank's placement contributed to this Bimmer's low center of gravity and excellent weight distribution—51 percent front, 49 percent back—with half of its 17.2 US gallon capacity filled.

Equally advanced was the share of steel panels coated on both sides by an electrolytic zinc plating treatment, increased to 66 percent (by weight) of all sheet steel panels.

Now, the total length was the same on either side of the Atlantic (also true of the later E30s) at 174.5 inches (4,433 mm). All E36s shared deformable-to-2.5-mph bumpers with low-cost crush tubes, designed to absorb impacts up to 9 mph without transmitting damage to the unitary body structure.

The biggest dimensional difference between the E30 and the E36 was a significant 5-inch (127 mm) elongation of the wheelbase for the E36. Additionally, there was a 4.33-inch (110 mm) gain in overall length, some 1.96 inches (50 mm) on the girth, and just 0.4 inch (10 mm) increase in roof line height. Luggage accommodation was increased by a mere cubic foot. Previously badly-cramped rear-seat accommodation was eased out to allow an additional 1.5 inches of knee room.

Balanced Handling

As a result of its stretched dimensions, particularly the five inch elongated wheelbase, with little front wheel overhang and engine shifted rearward, the newer 3 Series cornered far better than all but its M3 E30 predecessors.

BMW decided that its obsolete limited production (8,000 units manufactured between July 1988 and June 1991) Z1 sports two-seater (based on a 12-valve 325i powertrain) should contribute much of its widely praised rear suspension. The Z1 system, patented worldwide by BMW Technik, was principally adapted to provide extra traction and comfort.

The first official photo released, of the four-door sedan.

Photo: BMW AG, 1991

The rear-end layout appeared to be a simple extension of the independent trailing arm theme, but it was actually a very complex rendition of such an IRS layout. The Z-axle was also a much-needed update.

For the E36, separated coil springs and long-stroke dampers (mounted behind the back wheels) worked in association with double pressed-steel upper transverse and simple cast lower arms. The central arm was placed for maximum longitudinal location, with flexible mountings, surrounding the finned alloy differential. There were longitudinal single trailing arms on each side, located by a large steel subframe.

The subframe was allowed some elasticity to counter the effects of mid-corner braking or deceleration, providing constant tracking under pressure. This was a big contrast to the more "nervous" handling of the earlier "Threes" and particularly reassuring in wet conditions.

The front suspension was a further refined rendition of the MacPherson strut, with slim cast-iron lower arms (similar to E30 in their sickle shape) operating with a combined strut damper and coil spring layout on four-cylinder models. The sixes carried a separated strut and coil spring mounting, "thus improving roll comfort and smoothness by a substantial margin," claimed BMW. Certainly, the European 316i did suffer high roll angles under duress, but it lacked a rear anti-roll bar.

A front anti-roll bar was fitted forward of the axle line on all models. The double-bush-mounted bar had a broad "U-bend" outline. It was linked into the upper reaches of the struts, just below the coil spring bottom mountings on four-cylinder versions. All 3 Series featured twin-sleeve, gas-pressurized shock absorbers, which removed much of the harshness from the ride of earlier sporting "Threes."

Compared with the 1982–90 E30 3 Series, the track increased by up to 0.47 inch (12 mm) at the front and an appreciable 1.18 inches (30 mm) at the back. The biggest increase was on the 316i, its track front measuring 55.83 inches (1,418 mm), compared to the 55.43-inch (1,408 mm) measurement of the other models. The 316i also carried a lighter front anti-roll bar than 318i/320i/325i at 0.75 inch (19 mm), compared to the latter models' 0.89-inch (22.5 mm) bar. The rear roll bar listed at introduction measured 0.67 inch (17 mm) on all models from the 318i upward. The 316i really needed a back bar as well, to take advantage of the generous 15-inch wheel and tire sizes throughout the new range.

Revised MTechnic (optional sports) suspension centered on a reduction in ride height of 0.59 inch (15 mm) and Motorsport-developed rates for springs and dampers. In turn, each MTechnic spring-and-damper combination was tailored to the individual model. A reduction in payload of 20 kg (44 lbs) was quoted on all machines equipped with MTechnic suspension.

The hydraulically-assisted rack-and-pinion power-steering system allowed 3.4 turns, lock-to-lock, instead of the E30 figure of more than four turns. Thankfully, American and British importers standardized power steering throughout the new range.

The standard European E36 steering wheel was a four-spoke affair of 385 mm (15.16 inches) that accommodated two horn buttons around the energy-absorbing hard foam boss. European options for left-hand-drive models included an airbag-equipped four-spoke wheel for the US (similar to the first European M3), or a sports wheel of standard diameter.

Factory wheel and tire equipment followed the general trend of enlarged diameter and little altered rim widths. A 15-inch wheel diameter and five-bolt location was standard throughout the range. In America, the 325i debuted on a cast-alloy 7J x 15 wheel, with Pirelli P600 205/60 HR 15 rubber, a significant upgrade on the previous 6 x 14-inch wheel wear for the earlier 325i.

The UK importers received 316 and 318i models with 6J x 15-inch steel wheels clothed in 185/65 R15H rubber (usually Michelin MXV). For the 320i there was a marginal rim increase to 6.5 x 15 and a 205/60 R15 V cover. The factory optional alloy wheel measured 7J x 15 TR and wore the same size tire in a high-speed V-rating.

The European 325i was delivered on the same tire size as the 320i, but ZR-rated. The 325i brought with it a standard 7J x 15 alloy, but the factory also offered to cover that rim with a 225/55 ZR 15 option, not listed for Britain in 1991 or the USA in 1992, although a 16-inch option soon appeared. Steel rims for poverty models were cleverly concealed behind the plastic wheel covers. Alloy wheels were usually protected via one anti-theft bolt lock per wheel.

BMW chose larger wheel diameters to house upgraded braking components, served by servo-assistance and a tandem master cylinder. A quartet of ample diameter disc brakes was standard in the US and on the six-cylinder models. It also appeared where the customer specified the Teves Mark IV ABS system, which was standard only on the European and US 325i and was an extra-cost item for all other 1991 models.

Single-piston front calipers operated upon generous 286-mm (11.26-inch) discs, ventilated for six-cylinder usage. The fours ordinarily had 228.6-mm (9-inch) back drums in Europe, while the sixes wielded 280-mm (11.02-inch) solid discs, as did the 318i/318is US breed.

Massive development marked E36 body strength for the 1990s, including bonding both front and rear screens into position. There was a reported 60 percent leap in static resistance to torsional bending, and 45 percent under load. Computer analysis and strategic placement of further body braces allowed the 3 Series to surmount a 30-mph head-on impact, a 30-mph rear impact, and the trickier 35-mph values for side collisions—all at speeds above those required by 1990 global legislation.

Such progress allowed the 3 Series to match the 5 Series in future US crash tests. In the US, unlike contemporary Europe, drivers' side air bags were mandated. Europe ramped up their safety requirements during the 1990s and subsequent (E46) designs had an army (well, six) of

Distinctive aerodynamic styling details included twin headlamps behind those streamlining panes and a rounded front end. A small lip, ahead of the front wheels, cuts front-end lift at Autobahn speeds.

Photos: BMW AG, 1993

Safety reinforcement measures are highlighted, particularly the side door beams that boost survival rates and lower injuries in side collisions.

Diagram: BMW AG, 1991

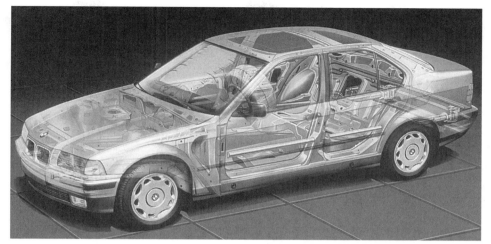

Offering outstanding rear-drive dynamics, the E36 Three is a natural for advanced drivers' courses. The white collection by the church was found alongside the Nürburgring in 1992 and was used by BMW for advanced driver training.

These three E36s were the official 323i saloons of the Brands Hatch circuits.

Photos: Author, Germany, 1992; BMW GB, 1998

bags throughout the closed-roof range. If you are buying an import E36 (perhaps the popular European-motor E36 M3), be aware that air bag standards (and sizes) were different on either side of the Atlantic in the 1990–98 span.

BMW did not rely just on the immensely strong structure and air bags to pass all contemporary Federal Motor Vehicle Safety Standards at 30 and 35 mph. For example, the front seat belts offered a then unique mechanical tensioner that was activated "within milliseconds" of frontal impact, tightening both lap and shoulder belts by 2.36 inch each. Additionally belt snubbers limit spool-out of shoulder belts on locked reels to reduce seat belt slack and improve restraint of front occupants. There was also a neat impact sensor that "automatically unlocks doors and operates the interior lights after accident impact."

Higher curb weights reflected massive gains in body strength. Equipped with the standard Getrag five-speed manual, the new US market 325i weighed 3,021, which swelled by 77 lbs when the THM R1-branded four-speed automatic was fitted. BMW GB quoted the European E36 weight compared to E30 equivalents as up 30 kg (66 lbs) on the four-cylinder 316i, up 35 kg (77 lb) on the 318i, up a formidable 90 kg (198 lbs) on the 320i and some 75 kg (165 lbs) up on the 325i. "Real World" figures

for six-cylinders indicated up to 391 lb as the weight penalty for dramatic safety and luxury equipment enhancements.

Motors

The engines were familiar BMW units, but that did not mean they were hangovers from the distant past. All motors used catalytic converter emissions hardware. The bulk of European production would be in four-cylinder variants of the M40 theme. These 1,596- and 1,796-cc SOHC units shared an 84-mm bore, the 200-cc difference accounted for by a 72-mm stroke in the smaller motor and an 81-mm stroke in the 1.8-liter.

The fours had been prepared to meet the needs of the catalytic converter age and both ran on cheaper unleaded fuel using modest 8.8:1 and 9:1 compression ratios for 318i and 316i respectively. Despite some substantial changes in specification to electronics, pistons, lubrication system, and connecting rods, power quotes were unaffected at 100 and 113 bhp respectively in Europe. For USA, the only four offered was the 138-bhp (M42) version of Europe's 140-bhp 16-valve at 1,796 cc.

Sales Range, Gasket Problems

The M42 four cylinder was the entry engine for the E36 American line, serving both 318i and 318is, subsequently enlarged (1,895 cc) to ener-

The Schnitzer package joined Alpina in being available from BMW dealers in the UK during 1996, these two companies and Racing Dynamics dominating the European aftermarket scene for BMWs, along with Hartge.

Photo: BMW GB, 1995; Bridgestone UK

gize 318i sedan, 318is coupe, 318ti Compact and later Z3 sports cars.

Although it proved a popular and versatile power base, the M42 line, prior to November 1993 build dates, did exhibit an abnormal number of gasket failures. First reports attributed the problem to the head gasket, but an anonymous soul on the Web revealed that the official title was, "timing case profile gasket, one that resides between the cylinder head and timing case." When it failed—and there were reports of this on all M42-engined 16-valve Bimmers from under 30,000 to an average 72,500 miles—coolant leaked from the engine, into the engine compartment. Leaking usually occurred near the passenger side of the steering rack, thence to "the AC compressor, then to ground."

The answer to this problem was an improved rubber compound seal installed on the production line from October 1993, but the higher-mileage failures often left saddened owners with no BMW back-up outside American warranty periods (then 3 years/50,000 miles). Of course, there was also a bill in the region of $1,200 of which labor accounted for a cool $800 at main dealer rates.

Under a magnesium cam cover, the M50-coded 24-valve, DOHC, inline sixes were fresh to the 3 Series in 320i and 325i guise, but had been seen in spring 1990 on the 5-series. Coded M50 [subsequently M52] in the enlarged (2.8-liter) or high torque (2.5-liter) 323i, these engines brought much of the company's four-cylinder, four-valve philosophy to the classic BMW straight sixes. The BMW engine team knew that even the 150 and 192 bhp obtained from the introductory M50 2.0- and 2.5-liter 24-valve units (75.1 and 76.8 bhp per liter respectively) would work hard as curb weights rose inexorably. In the US, only the 2.5-liter 325i was initially sold, with an output of 189 bhp at 5,900 rpm and 181 lb-ft of torque by 4,700 rpm. This performance was achieved on a 10:1 cr. that demanded 90-octane pump fuel in

50-State catalytic converter/Lambda probe and closed-loop mixture-control format.

At introduction, transmission choices were an automatic four-speed or manual five-speed gearbox and a multiple plate ZF limited-slip differential was an initial option. In the US, an LSD was offered on the 1992 325i.

The E30 overdrive fifth-gear manual gearbox was dropped in favor of a direct (1:1) fifth that was designed to cooperate with 3.45:1 final drive on all but the 325i. The 325 also used the 15-inch wheel diameters, but in alliance with a 3.15:1 drive. Reverse gear became a more civilized engagement, benefiting from synchromesh. The forward ratios were also closed up and propeller shaft rates slowed some 20 percent.

A trio of automatics were listed around the world. The debut European four-cylinders took on a conventional four-speed as an option in Britain, while all European sixes were sold from the start with an optional ZF five-speed that had electronic control allowing Sport, Economy and winter driving modes.

The European five-speed was as near flawless as any conventional automatic could be. It was credited with transmitting acceleration and maximum speed demands 14 percent more effectively for the 320i and a whopping 24 percent in the case of the 325i. Note that the five-speed did feature an over-drive top-gear ratio (0.742) which was ruled out in Sport mode, unless the engine was in danger of over-revving.

In the US in 1992, the long-lived option was an electronically commanded four-speed unit also with three mode choices that were labeled Economy, Sport, and Manual.

Cabin Chic

Black and white four dial displays were presented in the effective format that BMW have successfully used for decades since the first 5 Series. The European speedometer for a 316i indicated up to 140 mph (220 km/h) and was matched by a

7,000-rpm tachom-
eter (redlined at
6,250 rpm). The
two remaining
dials displayed fuel
tank contents and
water temperature.
Incorpor-ated into
the tachometer was
the econometer, and
as in prior 3 Series,
the Service Interval
Indicater was fitted. In the States, the first three
years of routine servicing were eventually included in the base purchase price, along with all deliv-
ery/destination/dealer prep costs.

The six-cylinder
became the back-
bone of the US range
in E36 1990s format
and was rated within
three horsepower of
European levels.

Photo: Klaus Schnitzer,
1996

There was the fashionable no-cost option of
ashtrays or extra storage, and the cigarette lighter
replaced by a useful purpose-built power take-off
socket. The seats were all new, formed around
a foam construction in a shell that performed
exceptionally well in crash testing. Standard
adjustment was accomplished via three levers
on the outer seat edge, facing the driver's door.
These were clumsily graduated to govern fore
and aft movement, height, and back-rest angle.

A more satisfactory sports alternative for
front seat occupants was offered, or the customer could opt for electric seat adjustment on
all but the 320i. Leather upholstery was offered
either optionally in Europe or as part of various
packages/straight options in both America and
Britain. Similarly, air conditioning tended to
come with US showroom specs, but was strictly
optional in Europe (sometimes found within
popular SE-branded UK packages).

Performance/Economy

BMW realistically claimed a 233-km/h (145
mph) maximum in Europe, but electronically limited the US to 128 mph for 325i. In
Europe, they expected 0–62 mph in 7.9 seconds
for the new 325i with near original M3 power.

Corresponding figures for the 320i were 214
km/h (133 mph) and 0–62 mph in 9.8 seconds.
Claimed urban fuel consumption was 21.4 mpg
on the larger six and 22.07 mpg for the 320i.
Autocar & Motor returned maximums of 132 and
141 mph for the pair, plus 0–60 mph in 9.1 and
7.3 seconds, coupled to fuel consumption figures
of 20.6 and 22.5 Imperial mpg (17.2/18.6 US
mpg, respectively).

An independent track test of the 325i returned
a time of 7.5 seconds for 0–60 mph, an easily
achieved 141.4 mph on banking, and an overall
average over 2,200 miles of 25.8 mpg (21.5 US
mpg). An automatic European 325i could run 8.9
seconds from 0–62 mph, or 10.8 seconds for the
320i, according to factory figures.

In the US, *Road & Track* reported that the 1992
model year 325i had the capability of running
0–60 mph in 8.3 seconds, the quarter mile in
16.2 seconds at 87 mph, and an excellent 23.5
US mpg overall. BMW NA had predicted 0–60
mph in 7.8 seconds (9.3 with an automatic) and
expected 18/25 mpg from the manual and 18/25
City/Highway in EPA tests for the automatic
transmission 325i.

Sedan Sales Story

Although E30 sedans straggled out of production during 1990, some "Mk2" BMW 3 Series—
most notably Touring and Convertible—survived into the 1990s. A last racing special, the 2.5

Evo M3 E30, was even rushed through as the E36 lines were being established in Munich.

During 1989, BMW factories were learning to production-assemble the third-generation Three. Full E36 production did not begin until the summer holidays of 1990 were over. From September until the end of 1990, some 8,335 units were made. They were all four-door saloons in 318i, 320i, and 325i form.

US models started production in October 1990, although only 660 were made that year. However, in 1991, they made over 8,000 sedan 325s destined for model year 1992 sales in the US. Munich ran 325i through their city production warren until 1995, when they switched to 328i.

May 1995 was the significant date for US Bimmer patriots as Spartanburg first came on line and produced 318is/four-door sedans. They made fewer than 100 in 1994, but assembled and painted 9,224 in 1995, with production shrinking to almost half that (5,204) in 1996 as Z3 became Spartanburg's primary product. BMW records show production of just 1,744 six-cylinder sedans (all 328i sedans) between 1995 and 1996. Total US production of 3 Series totaled 14,590 from 1994–96.

Regensberg joined in the US 3'er production party in 1996 and has been a regular ever since, particularly as the source for Convertible and Touring E36, or subsequent E46 variants. Sales of E36 BMW 3 Series began in January 1991 for LHD Germany, with RHD British models following in April and US four-doors coming on line in June.

Automatic Stability Control? Dynamic Stability Control? Traction Control? Just switch it off for track-side antics like these, away from public roads in the entertaining 328i.

Photo: Klaus Schnitzer, 1997

USA Options

Statistically, BMW NA's perspective on the 325i was unique to the US. Their analysis showed curb weight and wheelbase measurements climbing toward that of the contemporary 5 Series, up 177 lbs and 5.1 inches over the previous 325 and within 463 lbs and 2.4 inches of 525i big brother.

The showroom equipment of the 325 and subsequent 318i/328i cousins is covered by our tables, but it is worth commenting that the six-cylinder 325 and succeeding 328i became the backbone of US sales. Before 1998, if you wanted a new BMW from the 3 Series with a four-pot, it was E36 Compact or nothing.

For its first two US sales years, the 325 stayed under a $30,000 base price, inclusive of a generous 4-year/50,000-mile warranty. It had a short option list headed by automatic transmission and leather upholstery, but standard equipment was far more inclusive than that enjoyed by Europeans. For example, air conditioning was included in the 325i base price, along with a tilt and slide power sun roof and 60 Watt (4x15) amplification through ten speakers.

For successive model years, options multiplied as BMW NA fought to keep the base price attractive and gain the ultimate profit per unit. BMW NA ventured tentatively beyond $30,000 for

US E36 325i sedan/four-door prices, options, and sales, 1992–98

Year	Base price/ Delivery cost	Main options	US Sales
1992	$27,990/$375	Auto, $800; Leather, $1,100; LSD, $510; Metallic paint, $435	17,062
1993	$29,650/$405	Auto, $850; Leather, $1,150; LSD, $510*; Metallic paint, $450	17,977
1994	$30,850/$470	Auto, $900; Leather, $1,150; LSD, $530; ASC+T, $995; Metallic paint, $475	14,027
1995	$32,450/$570	Auto, $975; Leather, $1,450**; AST, $1,100; Metallic paint, $475; Sports Pack, $1,375; Lux Pack, $2,025	13,555

*Package price also available with heated seats & mirrors "inclement weather #1" at $755

**Leather also available as part of Lux Pack's $2,025 with computer and wood trim. The Sports Pack's $1,375 covered 16-inch alloys, 225/50ZR 16 tires, sports seats and suspension, and computer. Limited Slip Differential (LSD) unlisted, All Season Traction (AST) option available instead

US E36 328i sedan/four-door prices, options, and sales, 1996–98

Year	Base price/ Delivery cost	Main options	US Sales
1996	$32,900/$570	Auto, $975, Leather, $1,450*; AST, $1,100; Sports Pack, $2,625; Premium/Lux, $2,025; Metallic paint, $475	13,810
1997	$32,900/$570	Auto, $975, Leather, $1,450*; AST, $1,100; Sports Pack, $2,125; Metallic paint, $475	14,039
1998	$33,670/$570	Auto, $975, Leather, $1,450*; AST, Std; **Sports Pack, $2,125; ***Premium/Lux, $2,125; Metallic paint, $475	N/A

*Leather (1996 MY) also available as part of $2,025 Premium/Lux Pack with computer and wood trim. $2,625 Sports Pack (1996–97) MY included 16-inch alloys, 225 Z-rated tires, leather, sports seats and suspension: a $500 computer was included for 1996 MY but not 1997 MY, when priced dropped to $2,125

**Sports Pack (1998 MY) reduced by $100 and had all 1996–97 MY features, minus computer

***Premium/Lux Pack (1998 MY) featured leather, power sunroof, remote entry and security, wood trim

model year 1994. Bundling popular individual features as Sports and Premium/Luxury packages began a serious 3 Series pricing impact.

Leather remained the most expensive individual extra-cost choice at $1,150, but Sport Package #1 demanded $875 and brought seating and suspension upgrades along with cross-spoke alloys. The electronic All Season Traction Control systems, usually branded ASC (Anti Skid Control), ASC+T (Anti Skid Control + Traction), or All Season Traction (AST) were transferred from larger Bimmers as a $995 option on all six-cylinder Threes .

Technically, all 3'ers were commanded electronically with computer processing power, alongside or integrated with (depending on model) the ABS braking electronics/hydraulics and engine-management electronics. System fea-

US E36 318i sedan/four-door prices, options, and sales, 1992–98

Year	Base price/ Delivery cost	Main options	US Sale
1992	$22,900/$375	Metallic paint, $435; LSD, $510	3,350
1993	$23,710/$405	Metallic paint, $450; Auto, $850; LSD, $510; Cruise, $455; Sports suspension, $160; Rseats, folding, $260	5,936
1994	$28,675/$470	Metallic paint, $475; Auto, $900; LSD, $530; Cruise, $695; Folding rear seats, $260	7,071
1995	$25,600/$570	LSD, $580*; Leather, $1,450**; Metallic paint, $475; Lux Pack, $2,625; Sports Pack, $1,725; Alloys, $850	8,485
1996	$24,995/$570	Metallic paint, $475; Auto, $975; Premium Pack, $2,625***; Sports Pack, $1,725**; Leather, $1,450**; AST, $1,100; Harman Kardon sound system, $675	4,712
1997	$25,950/$570	Metallic paint, $475; Auto, $975; Premium Pack, $2,625***; Sports Pack, $1,725**; Leather, $1,450**; AST, $1,100; Harman Kardon sound, $675; 10-spoke alloys, $585	7,608
1998	$26,720/ Delivery included	Premium Pack, $1,900****; Power roof, $950; Leather, $1,450; Alloy 15-inch wheels, $850; Leather, $1,450; Harman Kardon sound, $975	N/A

*LSD also packaged within Sports Pack, which covered fog lights, alloy wheels, and sports suspension. LSD not listed 1996–98: ASC+T or AST only. AST std., 1998 Model year.

**Leather also packaged with Premium/Lux Pack with Premium Audio system, fog lights, and alloy wheels

***Premium Pack included leather, 15-inch alloys, 205/60 tires on 15-inch rims, fog lights, and color-coded trim

****1998 model year Premium Pack included 15-inch alloys, power roof, keyless entry/security, front armrest, and leather-finish steering-wheel rim and gear knob

tures varied, but the basic principle was to monitor wheel spin under power or wheel locking/skidding under deceleration. AST would counteract potential hazardous driver/weather conditions with a smooth reduction in engine power/judicious rear-brake applications, the latter either individually or simultaneously, according to computer comparison data processed in milliseconds.

The ASC+T system was particularly valuable for automatic transmission users, preventing any sudden shifting while such hazards were encountered. A further refinement was to allow a temporary and minor boost in engine rpm, so that the back wheels rotated smoothly rather than locking under a suddenly closed throttle.

For later model seasons, the more conventional mechanical assistance of a limited-slip differential (LSD in our tables) was deleted for 325i when ASC+T variants were offered. To demanding drivers, an LSD remained a must-have item valued for lower cost (typically around $500).

By 1995, BMW NA felt secure enough to venture beyond a $32,000 base price, and the Premium/Luxury Package debuted at a punishing $2,025, while the Sports Package had escalated to almost $1,400. Taking into account destination and handling charges, plus options, a fully-optioned 328i could command over $38,000 in 1996. The M3 completed the short march to the $40,000 baby Bimmer.

The 328i brought BMW generally acclaimed performance superiority in the everlasting battles against Mercedes, Audi, and key contemporary Japanese cars.

Photo: Jonathan A. Stein

In fact, 1995 was the last hearty year of 325 sales, with the bigger-motor 328i arriving just under $33,000 for the 1996 model year. Offering a significant 14.4 percent improvement in torque (to 207 lb-ft at 4,000 rpm), the 328i also went up to 190 horses (190 at 5,300 rpm) at 600 rpm lower than the 325i. Another relevant dynamic came from the option list, where we found 225/50 ZR-16s wrapped in one-inch larger diameter 16 x 7J cast alloys as part of the $2,625 Sport Package. As that Sport Pack also included MTechnic suspension in replacement dampers and coil springs, plus upgraded front seats with leather trim and a seven-function computer, it is well worth searching out. Luxury lovers, look out for the Premium Pack-equipped 328, because they also included leather, the computer, and wood trim accents at an original $2,025.

The weight was up around 100 lbs in US format (3,120 lbs) with a heavier-duty ZF five-speed (also used in the US M3) replacing the original 325 Getrag, while the 77-lb-heavier automatic nudged 3,200 lbs. BMW NA predicted seven seconds dead for the five-speed's dash from 0–60 mph; automatics took 0.7 seconds longer. Both were electronically limited to 128 mph in the US, but hit just over 140 mph in 193-bhp European specs. Forecast US gas mileages from EPA were 20/29 City/Highway for the manual and 20/27 for the automatic.

In November 1996, *Motor Trend* reported 0–60 mph in 6.5 seconds, just two tenths of a second shy of the earlier US model M3 they tested. This magazine also turned 15 seconds at almost 93 mph in the standing quarter, but the logical surprise was how those 225s lifted cornering G-forces into the 0.90 sector.

The 328i continued to delight testers all the way to the 1998 E46 replacement and sold around 14,000 units a year in 1996–97. The 2,793-cc motor is a wonderful companion, civil through urban streets and ultimately responsive out of town. As good as the original M3 was, the 328 was a better all-rounder.

The 318 Entry-Level

The 1992 model year 318i was notable not just for the $22,900 base price, but for restricting options so severely that no automatic was offered that first sales year. Later, BMW NA went all out to reduce base prices to closer to $20,000, but subsequently used the 318ti Compact at entry levels.

By model year 1996, a 318i sedan hit a base price of almost $26,000. Option packages were deployed, with the Premium Pack quoted at $2,625, a Sports alternative at $1,725, and leather priced at $1,450 if selected separately.

Basic 318 engineering and features progressed quietly but effectively. A dual intake manifold pepped up mid-range performance for 318i sedans from model year 1993 with a 4,800-rpm-activated air flap and dual knock sensors added to engine durability. Although super premium was recommended, these features allowed for the safe use of lower-octane fuels. Combined with the new higher-flow converter, these changes boosted torque from 127 to 129 lb-ft at 4,500 instead of 4,600 revs, and lifted bhp from 134 to 138 at the usual 6,000 rpm. These changes also improved economy to 22/30 mpg City/Highway from EPA sources despite inevitable weight increases (209 lbs) to a total weight of 2,866 lbs.

BMW NA predicted a credible 9.9 seconds as 0–60 mph elapsed time and 128 mph as the limited maximum, as per six cylinders. Note that the 318's standard five-speed transmission was now the Getrag five-speed Type C with a direct fifth.

For 1994, the 318i kept the role of entry-level guardian beneath a $25,000 base price on its comparatively skinny 185/65HR tires and adequate 15 x 6-inch steel rims. In 1995, BMWs 318i arrived on the other side of $25,000 and showrooms sold almost 6,200 small-capacity Bimmers that had been "Made in USA." Mechanically, there was little to report, but color-coded bumpers made them look a little more like their more prosperous six-cylinder brethren.

Inside, either cloth or leatherette upholstery came standard, and six-speaker stereos and cruise control added to the 1995 model year specification. The extras list expanded sharply, so buy one that has the Sport or Premium/Luxury options. These packages addressed "must-have" items like 205/60 wheel and tire combinations from 325, leather upholstery, and even upgraded sound systems.

In model year 1996, sales of the 318i slumped because the 318ti was now the entry-level offering starting at $5,000 less. For the 318i, this meant the slowest sales season so far, with under 5,000 examples sold. Now, all 318-numbered models gained a new 1,895 cc version of the M42 motor, which was fundamentally improved, incorporating roller rockers, replacement Digital Motor Electronics to Bosch ML-Motronic/V12 standards, and stainless steel headers.

The numbers were little-altered at 133 lb-ft torque (up 3 lb-ft) and an unchanged 138 horsepower, but there was more useable torque. The dual induction system now did its changeover trick at 4,200 rather than 4,800 rpm and up to 11 percent fuel economy bonus was anticipated.

Cabin refinements covered fully automatic climate control throughout the Bimmer range, except for the 318ti. The ten-speaker/200-Watt stereo arrived in 318i, and the central locking/security key arrangements were a far better defense against thieving. It also offered full locking from the trunk key, or within (with the exception of the gas flap). As for many model years, Harman Kardon 320-Watt sound systems were an expensive ($675) option.

For model year 1997, a modest boost toward a $26,000 base price was realized. AST electro-hydraulic traction systems were technically unaltered but joined the standard equipment list on all BMW 3 Series. By November 1997, AST was a standard fitment right

In Europe, 3 Series were popular with either four-cylinder or diesel power and steel wheels beneath plastic wheel covers.

Photo: Author, UK, 1999

across the BMW line. In this model year, the 318i lost the option packages and went for individual items like ten-spoke alloys, the tilt and slide sun-roof, and the Harman Kardon sound system; while for 1998, a Premium/Lux Pack re-appeared.

In 1998, its last official model year, there were few changes. The contemporary coupe rang-es—where a 323i six replaced four-cylinder entry models—told the future of the E46 six-cylinder sedan in the US.

Quality Control

As the honeymoon effect of the 3 Series launch faded, and the months ticked by, it was obvious that the factory had basic quality control problems, particularly with cabin quality. BMW attacked these problems vigorously, and acknowledged that remedial work during the 1991–92 European press launches of the two-door coupe. As early as May 1991, major trim changes were required to overcome customer hostility to the shoddy cabin plastics and trim.

On May 15, 1991, BMW (GB) Limited advised their dealers, "The most significant of these changes is the replacement of the current woven cloth with a higher-quality velour-type upholstery for all models. In addition, there will be a range of further product changes as listed [here]: velour cloth door panels (as per revised uphol-stery); color-keyed glovebox panel and air outlets (cur-rently black; will be linked to the interior trim color); cloth trimmed luggage compartment bulkhead; [and] cloth trimmed boot lid lining for 320i/325i models." The com-pany continued, "All of these improvements will take the form of a running change during July production and we are, therefore, not able to identify the vehicle/chassis number point at which the changes will take place."

Our observation of the later cabin specification came in autumn 1991, discovering only that changes were comparatively minor. They helped to obviate only the most glaring deficiencies: by BMW stan-dards, the glove box remained a flimsy affair and the sealing strip between the lip and fascia surround peeled away from full contact. More changes were definitely needed. Then influential Car magazine reported in February 1991, "The new BMW 3 Series—such a wonderful car in so many ways—has caused its maker no end of quality-control headaches. So far, the warranty costs are averaging more than £800 per car." They went on to detail the experiences of a colleague's 320i. "He had the whole door trim come off in his hand. There was a raft of other problems too, most to do with the cabin."

Cynically, Car commented, "BMW, with typical pro-fessionalism, has done a splendid job hushing up the mess." According to that monthly magazine, British dealers replaced complete cars, while German cus-tomers listed their top ten complaints of 1990–91 as: leaking or rattling sunroofs, wind noise (most gener-ated by the wing mirrors), poor door sealing (another potential source of leaks), poor directional stability, squeaks and poor quality of dash, plus inoperative central locking and a gearbox that usually signaled its impending demise by failing to select second.

Car reported that BMW applied an extra 44 lbs (22 kg) of sound-proofing after April 29, 1991, with new seats in the same month and replacement door mirrors starting in June of that year. Better-quality upholstery and headlining were listed from that month on, too, with July 1991 listed as the introduction date for updat-ed door locks and October 1991 for the glovebox.

BMW AG only came to grips with all these prob-lems as they pressed the coupe into 1992 production. BMW never did get the interior of the E36 to match the quality of E30. In terms of materials used, their fit and finish was never completely right, but the cost accountants who asked engineers and designers to save a bit of money around the cabin fittings nearly cost the company its fine quality image. "It looks like a bloody Ford inside," was the forthright opinion of one wealthy dealer from the UK, and that remark was all too close to the truth for far too long.

19 Understated Coupe Style for Three

A new attitude to selling less (two-doors) for more (dollars) was evident in the classy coupe line that moved 3 Series upmarket.

BMW's new attitude for selling the 3 Series was presented to the European public in January 1992 and America that summer. Previously, two-door models started the 3 Series range and indeed, they were the only offering in the first generation of 3 Series. Now, two-doors would have a more seductive body and (initially) a modest price premium.

By the summer of 1992, the sporting shape of the E36 generation 3 Series was developing around the globe, with America eventually taking four (badged 318is/323is/325is/328is) of five engines offered in Europe, the exception being the 150-bhp, six-cylinder 320i. Here, we trace the coupe's development, leaving the astonishing M3 and its ever more powerful European successors to Chapter 23 and its racing story to Chapter 24.

Unlike the "backbone of the range" role allotted to earlier two-door Bimmer 3 Series models, the coupe was only expected to account for a third of total 3 Series output. The first six months' production saw nearly 40 percent of pent-up demand devoted to the subtle two-door. Over the long haul, the crisp coupe Threes of 1992 to 1998 amassed sales of more than 460,000 units. As of mid-1999, the factory did include M3 coupes in their minimum 459,835 production total declared in 1992–98 figures. All but 2,757 came from that 1992–98 period, but some pre-production and pre-sale two-door coups dated to 1990–91.

Thus, M3s and all other coupes accounted for less than 20 percent of a total 2.7 million E36s built in the primary 1990–98 production period, not including the more than 150,000 convertibles made, which were based on the two-door coupe outline. The E36 coupes were primarily made in Regensberg rather than Munich. Late-run factory figures reported 429,974 E36 coupes of all kinds manufactured, including 38,436 M3s.

US E36 325i coupe/two-door prices, options, and sales

Year	Base price/ Delivery cost	Main options	US Sales
1992	$29,100/$375	Auto, $800; Metallic paint, $435; LSD, $510; Computer, $410	7,980
1993	$30,950/$405	Auto, $850; Metallic paint, $450; LSD, $510*; Computer, $420; Sports Pack, $845**; Weather Pack #1 $755***	10,315
1994	$32,200/$470	Auto, $900; Metallic paint, $475; LSD, $530; Computer, $430; Sports Pack $875**	8,693
1995	$33,500/$570	Auto, $975; Metallic paint, $475; Computer, $500^; AST, $1,100; Sports Pack, $1,375**; Premium Pack, $775****	6,359
1996	Not base-priced this model year		248

*Also as part of 1993 Inclement Weather Package #1

**Sports Pack included seats, suspension, and wheels for 1993–94; Sports Pack included 16-inch alloys, 225/50 ZR-16 tires, sports suspension and seating, and computer for 1995

***Inclement Weather Pack included differential, heated seats and mirrors

****Premium Pack 1995 included wood trim and computer

^ Also packaged with Sport and Premium Packs

US E36 318is coupe/two-door prices, options, and sales

Year	Base price/ Delivery cost	Main options	US Sales
1992	$23,600/$375	Metallic paint, $435; LSD, $510	2,817
1993	$24,810/$405	Auto, $850; Metallic paint, $450; LSD, $510; Cruise, $455; Sport suspension, $160	5,892
1994	$25,800/$470	Auto, $900; Metallic paint, $475; LSD, $530; Computer, $430; Cruise ctrl/fogs, $695	5,562
1995	$27,200/$570	Auto, $975; Metallic paint, $475; LSD, $580**; Sports Pack, $700; Premium Pack, $1,750***; Audio, $550	4,131
1996	$27,700/$570	Auto, $975; Metallic paint, $475; Leather, $1,450****; Sports Pack, $700**; Premium Pack, $1,750; AST, $1,100; Premium sound, $675	2,274
1997	$27,700/$570	Auto, $975; Metallic paint, $475; Leather, $1,450; Sunroof, $950; Premium sound, $675; Sports suspension, $350	1,298
1998*	Not listed		171
1999	Not listed		13

*1998 MY: 323is replaces 318is during 1997 @ $29,270 base price, selling 1,159 units in 1997

**Sports Pack for 1995 included upgraded suspension & LSD; for 1996, suspension upgrade and color coded bumpers/side skirts

***Premium Pack for 1995 included leather upholstery and enhanced audio; for 1996, leather and color coding

****Also part of 1996 Premium Package

US E36, 328is coupe/two-door prices, options, and sales

Year	Base price/ Delivery cost	Main options	US Sales
1995	N/A	N/A	6,359
1996	$32,990/$570	Auto, $975; Metallic paint, $475; Leather $1,450*; Computer, $500**; Premium sound, $675; Sport Pack, $2,625***; Premium Pack, $2,025****; AST $1,100	6,375
1997	$32,990/$570	Auto, $975; Metallic paint, $475; Leather, $1,450*; Computer, $500**; Premium sound, $675; Sport Pack, $2,125***; Power sunroof, $950	4,382
1998	$33,670/ Delivery included	Auto, $975; Metallic paint, $475; Leather, $1,450*; Computer, $500**; Premium sound, $675; Sport Pack, $2,125***; Premium Pack, $2,125****; Power sunroof, $950	2,283

Note: 1999 replaced by E46 line but listed @ $ 33,770 base price, selling 1,538 units

*Also part of 1996 Premium Package

**Also packaged with Sport & Premium Packs for 1996

***Sport Pack for 1996 included suspension, computer, 16-inch alloys with 225/Z-rated tires, sports seats, and leather upholstery; for 1997, the same minus computer(!); for 1998, same as 1996 plus double-spoke alloys

****Premium Pack 1996 included leather, computer, wood trim; for 1997, not listed; for 1998, same as for 1996 plus additional security and sunroof

Debut Thinking

BMW AG Board member (Sales) Robert Buchelhofer briefed international media during the 15-day launch of the coupe at Mijas in Spain. Herr Buchelhofer outlined the objectives of the company in designing this model, and reminded us of BMW history in the compact car two-door market.

Buchelhofer began, "Just think of the 02 series and the two 3 Series in years gone by. These were genuine two-door saloons in every respect, the predecessor to the new 3 Series coming both with two, and for the first time, four doors. And they all had something coupe-like about them. Not to mention that BMW actually 'invented' cars of this kind in the first place."

Sales volumes for all US E36 two-door coupes

Year	US Sales
1992	10,797
1993	16,207
1994	14,255
1995	10,669
1996	8,897
1997	6,839
1998	7,154
1999	4,272
Total	79,092

At first glance, there were few styling changes between the saloon and the coupe, but the initial disappointment was soon replaced by customer admiration for the coupe's clean lines. In Britain, the E36 was repeatedly an outright coupe sector leader, once the four-cylinder 318is had joined the 325i launch line.

American coupe sales peaked at 16,200 units in1993. Six-cylinder BMW coupes gradually became the most popular choice as sales shrank to under 10,000 units annually after 1996, when the M3 effect began to kick in and slay the sales of 328is. Even so, over 79,000 coupes were sold in the US, excluding the two-door M3s.

The E36 sedan and coupe used different panels on a shared platform. There was also tricky side glass (it covered the center B-pillar), with automatic part-retraction of the door glass to ease the door-shut procedure, as used in the 8 series. Another unique aspect of the side glass was the electrically-powered rear quarter vents, available as an option in Europe.

The 3 Series coupe was a beautifully balanced design that boosted two-door sales.

Photo: BMW AG, Munich, 1993

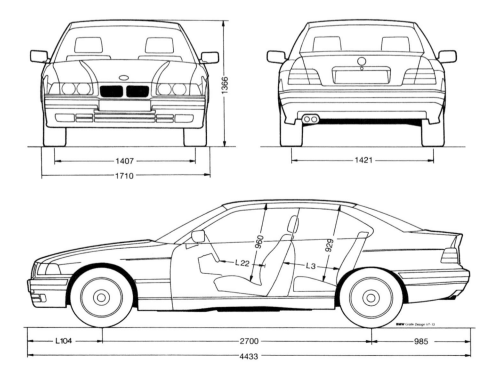

With a lower and shorter roof and more steeply raked windshield, the coupe became undeniably sleeker than the sedan.

Drawing: BMW AG, Munich, 1993

The hatchback-bred rear seats folded individually.

Drawing: BMW Grafik Design, Munich, 1993

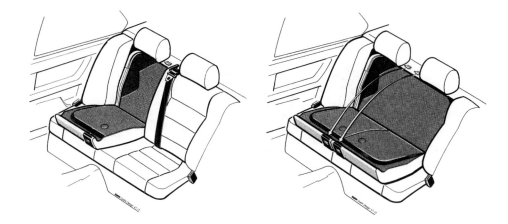

The sedan's back-lights were also replaced with lower and wider panes. The two and four-door models shared wheelbase and length, but the coupe featured an abbreviated (by 30 mm, or 1.2 inches) roofline that was also 30 mm closer to the ground. Hood-to-cabin proportions were significantly altered and the roof pillars—including the glassed-in center post—were more inclined. In addition, both the hood and rear deck lay lower. Most changes were so subtle that, unless both coupe and sedan were parked together, it was not obvious just how committed BMW was to the two-door's individuality.

BMW was back to its old minimalist packaging habits and the rear seats were habitable, but hardly generous. The back seats did have the useful facility of being able to fold forward individually to accommodate extra baggage, although this was treated as an option on the US sedan for some model years.

The effect on aerodynamic stability was said to be beneficial in cutting lift forces, front and rear. In practice, the coupe reduced the sedan's high-speed vagueness between 85 and 130 mph. The quoted aerodynamic drag factor was 0.31 Cd. Thus six-cylinder coupes recorded 0.31 Cd against the 0.32 Cd of their sedan brethren.

Road safety and recycling ability were emphasized with the model. BMW even promised to take back expired European products for digestion at BMW's Landshut site in Germany.

Mechanically, the first European coupes were similar to their saloon counterparts in six-cylinder, 150-bhp (320i) and 192-bhp, 24-valve (325i) guise. This also applied to their five-speed manual and automatic transmissions.

The British arm of BMW realized that all two-door models would benefit from the lower and stiffer MTechnic layout, which offered considerable benefits over winding roads and crests. In the US, sports suspension updates were regularly offered, but too often these were in the option list and amounted only to the standard set-up for some European markets.

American Market Life

The first coupe onto the US stage was the 325is, premiered at the January 1992 International Automobile Show in Detroit. It was well received, winning a place on *Automobile*'s All Star Cars and the *Car and Driver* Ten Best Cars for 1992 lists. With a starting price of $31,355 it sold from spring 1992 until it was gradually replaced by the 328i during 1995.

A few months later, the 318is was available at $6,140 less, and that model sold until the six-cylinder 323i trickled in to usurp the four-pot during 1997. The 318is was not a very tempting

This first official photo of the BMW 3 Series coupe demonstrates how the company got buyers to pay a premium price for removing two doors.

Photo: BMW AG, Spain, 1992

proposition in the US, lacking not just the obvious two cylinders and 51 horses, but also such standard six equipment as leather trim, cruise control or the wider choice of sports packs.

The message now, as it was then, is go for the six, as *Car and Driver's* Arthur St. Antoine commented in August 1992: "I like the 318. It's got some fine moves, it's to-die-for handsome, and its engine is one of the smoothest fours on the road. But the 325's scintillating six truly electrifies the 3 Series package."

Performance did not seem to have suffered in that transatlantic crossing. *C/D* reported an electronically limited 123 mph for the 318i, and 0–60 mph in 8.7 seconds was snappy enough, coupled to 16.6 seconds for the quarter mile at 82 mph.

The EPA numbers for the US were 22 mpg City, 30 mpg Highway, and the magazine managed 28 mpg overall.

In comparison, the American specification 325is emerged from a 1992 *Road & Track*-refereed brawl with Lexus SC300 and Subaru's SVX as a joint winner (with Lexus) for the title of King, Near-Luxury Sports Coupes. The six cylinder coupe took a reported 8.3 seconds to paint the tarmac black over 0–60 mph, and some 16.2 seconds for the quarter-mile at 87 mph. Top speed was not recorded, but 128 mph seemed to be where BMW set the electronic fun-buster in the US.

In time, the coupe line up gave way to a pair of sixes—the 1998 323is and the 1995-onward 328is, both of which were equipped with lighter aluminum, rather than the original cast-iron, cylinder blocks. Independent performance data for an American 323i coupe indicated that 0–60 mph could be obtained in just under seven seconds, with standing quarter-miles in the 15.5-second bracket. Observed fuel economy was 21 mpg and a lowly 0.80g was recorded on stock 205 tires.

By autumn 1992, the 318is 16-valver had joined the six-cylinder launch stock of coupes.

Photo: Author, UK, 1992

The 328i in European Sports Package form featured unique suspension settings supporting cross-spoke 17-inch-diameter BBS alloys that carried 225/45 ZR at the front, 245/40 ZR at the rear.

Photos: Author, UK, 1998

The 170-bhp 323is was a rapid car capable of high speeds and commendable fuel economy. In a 1,513-mile round trip between England and Germany, the swift coupe averaged 77 mph and 28.8 Imperial (24 US) mpg. It is serenely comfortable and fast enough to only be embarrassed by a twin-turbo Porsche on the Autobahn. Just one 215-mile sunny section dropped us to 26.9 Imperial (22.4 US) mpg because the average speed was 95.8 mph. That meant peaking at 135–140 mph regularly, when the 323i coupe continued to progress with an unflustered speed that made mockery of modern speed limits. The torquier 2.8-liter motor popped the 328i Sport (sedan) through 0–60 mph in 6.3 seconds in a *Motor Trend* 1997 trial. That 328i performance was fractions slower than a contemporary US 240-bhp M3! It was quite a car, even by Bimmer standards. Its EPA penalty at the pumps was not unreasonable, at 20 City mpg or 29 Highway mpg.

The 323—another misleading badge that actually covered the 2.5-liter 325i motor, reworked in higher-torque trim—had a specific commercial task. It prepped the American market for the all-six-cylinder E46 line that was imminent.

For the cost-conscious American Bimmer coupe buyer, the 323is replaced 318is in model year 1998, but over 1,100 of the inline six were sold in the 1997 calendar year. The basic appeal was 168 bhp to replace the 138 bhp of the 318, coupled to a 48 lb-ft torque boost to 181 lb-ft. In Europe, the 323i was insignificantly more powerful (170 bhp) than the US model, rating the same 181 lb-ft. Independent performance results reported 323is as capable of 0–60 mph in some eight seconds, leaping to 100 mph in some 20 seconds and—unlimited—recording 141 mph. US EPA consumption predictions were 20 mpg City and 29 Highway, as for the 328i in America.

Our tables tell you most of what you would need to know in selecting a used coupe in the States, but finding a low-mileage 318is in the US can be difficult, as only 2,274 were sold in 1996 and fewer than 1,300 were sold in its final season of 1997.

Among the six-cylinders, E36 325s have been known to happily survive more than 200,000 miles. With it's stronger gearbox, a 328i promises even greater durability and offers near M3 performance at a much lower price.

European Motors and Performance

For the US, the 16-valve M42 motor of 138 bhp and the 24-valve six (189 bhp in 325i) went through the same development stages in our previous sedan saga. However, in Europe, it was not so simple: note that the 318is was not just the old 318is (E30 body) motor carried over. As has been common to both the M40(8v)/M42(16v) European units, a lot of development took place between apparently similar applications.

This time the emphasis was on obtaining low-speed torque from the 1,796-cc (84 x 81 mm) DOHC four. BMW employed an intake manifold it described as ICIS or ICIM (Individual Control Intake System/Manifold), which simply provided different length inlet runners for low and high rpm performance.

Above 4,800 rpm, a butterfly flap opened and all intake pipes were activated for maximum power. The result, compared to an E30 318iS, was a power increase of 4 bhp to 140 at the same 6,000 rpm. BMW expected that customers were more likely to be interested in the spread of pulling power (above 118 lb-ft from 3,300 to 6,200 revs), but peak torque still required a highish 4,500 rpm.

A 318is looked like the BMW coupe bargain of the century in Europe with a top speed of 132 mph, 0–62 mph in 10.2 seconds, and 25.9 mpg over the urban cycle test. This lusty "baby" BMW coupe became a major showroom draw in the UK, particularly as the 318is and its 16-valve/140 horsepower motor was not offered in the four-door sedan line.

The 318is was used to secure BMW's third successive British Touring Car title, in 1992 (see Chapter 25), which did not hurt the 318's commercial appeal in the least.

Performance claims for the European six-cylinders were naturally within fractions of those for the four-door models with the same running gear. However, *Autocar & Motor* obviously had "a good 'un," as its 325i coupe was 3 mph faster, at 144 mph, than its four-door equivalent. It also clipped a tenth off the saloon's 7.3-second 0–60 mph time. Both versions also recorded 22.5 Imperial mpg. *Autocar & Motor* recorded a weight of 1,345 kg (2,959 lbs) for the saloon 325i and an extra 35 kg (77 lbs) for their 1,380-kg (3,036-lb) coupe.

By comparison, the unrestricted European 328i put through the same test procedures saw a storming 143 mph, 0–60 mph in 6.4 seconds and 27.3 Imperial mpg. Weight was recorded as just 5 kg (11 lbs) up on the equivalent 325i.

BMW selected a standard coupe-range 7 x 15-inch alloy wheel (multiple-spoke) that was unique to the model. It wore 205/60 R-rated (for 318/320) and ZR-rated (325i) rubber. Even the 318iS had anti-lock brakes, central locking, the electrically-activated side glass, power steering, and leather for both steering wheel rim and gear lever knob as the standard European specification.

The E36 3 Series coupe surely owed much of its elegance and crisp execution to the increasing American design presence and influence within BMW. The everyday role of computers to precisely monitor, command, and build to the designer's intention also significantly assisted body quality.

The E36 coupe line brought the BMW talent for elegant, individual, durable, civilized speed within a more-affordable price range.

Before the M3 arrived in Europe, this Alpina B6-2.8 liter variant of the 325i coupe was an inspired sporting alternative at a 240-bhp level similar to the final US M3.

Photo: Author, UK, 1992

20 Convertible Joy

The 3 Series Convertible was a fine four-seater
pleasure machine that broke the $40,000 barrier.

The enormous commercial success (over 143,000 sold) of the previous
generation (E30) convertible model implied there would be a drop-top
in the E36 line. What we did not know is that it would be even better
than its predecessor. Its reinforced body was muscular enough to pass
all contemporary and impending crash tests and absorb 321 bhp of
European M3.

The second generation of factory 3 Series soft-tops premiered the
325i powertrain at a French international launch in April 1993. Referred
to in the US as 325iC, it went on sale during the summer of 1993 as a
1994 model at a $39,270 base price.

That the pricey Bimmer was greeted by ecstatic press reviews,
despite its formidable cost, says all you need to know about the E36
Convertible. It was simply the most elegantly practical and enjoyable
four-seater you could buy with this kind of money.

The E36 soft-top was joined by the $28,900 four-cylinder 318iC
($30,370 with destination charges) during the 1994 model year.
Manufacture ceased in the summer of 1999 with an E46 soft-top successor available from summer 2000.

Engineering

The cutaway graphics of the Convertible body in this chapter immediately tell you that the drop-top was far more than a chop-top coupe.
BMW was able to use some external sheet metal in common with the
coupe, but the Convertible was massively reinforced for its topless role.

To meet US standards for 35-mph head-on collisions, plus 30-mph
rear-end intrusions and side-impacts, BMW AG engineered a 30 percent boost in structural strength as compared with its E30 predecessor.
This was achieved through additional strengthening tubes within the

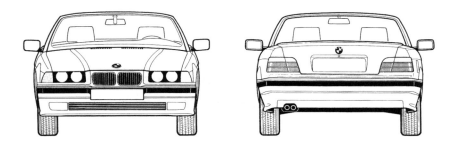

The E36 convert-
ible offered open
top motoring with
greater rigidity than
its predecessors.

Drawing: BMW Grafik
Design for BMW AG
Presse, Munich, 1993

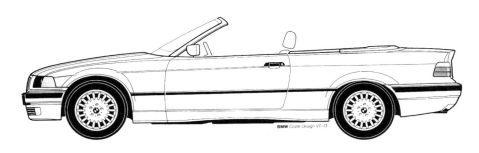

front (A) pillars, while the B-pillars were shorter and stronger, carrying the safety-belt mounts. Additional members between the engine mounts, new longitudinal support arms at the rear, wider door sills, and a cross-member support for the rear seating structure were required.

The inner side panels were re-modeled for Convertible needs, while a longitudinal support brace was welded into position between the outer sills and the floor plate, additionally angled to resist the forces generated by the absence of a steel roof.

An additional brace ran parallel to the front-rear propshaft, while the rear wheel arches had to be modified to accommodate the foldaway hood and a passive rollover bar that would only deploy in reaction to an impending accident. That it was an option in the US (for $1,390)—as well as Europe — is a surprise, given the constant threat of legal action against motor manufacturers.

Nevertheless, BMW was very proud of the passive system, which consisted of individual extruded aluminum bars and was activated by G-force sensors to fully extend within 0.33 of a second. The system weighed 22 lbs (10 kg) and

used components (electromagnetic actuator, butterfly sensor with glass phials and butanol, G-sensor, twin capacitors) that should be safety-inspected for operational integrity. However, if you are lucky enough to find an E36 Convertible for which the original owner invested around $1,400 in this feature, then it makes sense to ensure that it can still function.

All American 3 Series Convertibles came with dual airbags, but initial European production lacked this protection. The passenger-side airbag (130 liters, or 4.6 cu. ft. in Europe) installation was re-engineered around the "basic design from 8 Series." The steering-wheel air bag was available earlier in Europe than the passenger side, and was housed in the usual 3 Series four-spoke tiller.

A lower key device — supporting the trunk-mounted battery on a hydraulic foundation rather than conventional rubber bushes — was intended to cut out the low frequency (15Hz) shakes that characterize so many soft-top bodies.

BMW selected the expense of an aluminum hard-top option at an additional 64 lbs (29 kg) to produce a very different close-coupled winter coupe. This E36 option — color-coded to the body color — was still listed in year 2000 Europe (order code 982). It was priced at $2,295 in model years 1996–98 in America (the only years offered in the US market), or a pricier £2,185 in UK in model year 2000.

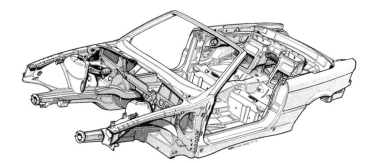

The 3 Series E36 two-door hull was extensively reinforced to compensate for the absence of a fixed steel roof.

Drawing: BMW Grafik Design for BMW AG Presse, Munich, 1993

Convertible rear side panels were elongated to match the lid of the luggage compartment. There was also paneled space to enclose the dropped roof, without an unsightly bulge in the clean-cut silhouette. The folding roof was quicker to operate than its predecessor. Power assistance was an option in Europe, although it was standard on the American 325iC. To drop either top version required the release of manual clamps (two forward on the later power tops, single twist-grip on the original manual fold-away item) as a first step. All came with electric control of the side glass that dropped panes 0.6 inch as the hood compartment cover release was operated. There was a further refinement that allowed raising and lowering of all windows on one switch, as all Convertibles were equipped with power side glass.

The roof itself was constructed in the same materials and layers as E30, which meant triple-layer polyacrylic with a cotton mix. Color choices were confined to three at launch with another three on the option lists. A charcoal gray cloth roof lining covered the rods and linkages, representing a distinct improvement over E30's unlined roof.

A rear poly-glass rear window was zipped in place for easy replacement/removal and—as before—a heater blower mechanism functioned as a defroster. This device was necessary to compete with electric elements in the glass rear windows of some drop-top rivals.

Practical touches included rain guttering, outstanding seals (aided by those automatic open/shut side glass actions), direct roof-rack fitting to carry bikes and skis, plus an entire roof fabric that was instantly removable from the operating structure. Sadly, this was prompted by the number of vandalism cases reported in the US and UK.

Hardware and Efficiencies

The proven power trains shared with existing Bimmers. For the 318iC, there was the earlier 1.8-liter M42 motor of 138 horsepower and 129 lb-ft torque (also used in 318ti, 318i and 318is coupe) hitched to a Getrag Type C five-speed. Optionally, there

The optional alloy hardtop is a desirable option that truly allows a distinctive coupe or a Convertible to occupy the same parking space in your garage.

Photo: BMW AG, 1993

was the usual THM R1 with four-speed automatic and alternative mode settings.

The 189-bhp 325iC with 181 lb-ft pulling power shared units with 325i/325is and featured the same transmission offerings. At this time (model years 1994-95), only the M3 carried ZF five-speed manual and automatic gearboxes.

The original E36 Cabriolet convertible was attractive and cleanly executed, top up or down.

Photos: BMW AG, 1993

Technically, the biggest chassis changes for Convertibles were to retune the shock absorbers to take the additional weight. Wheels and tires remained the production coupe fitment of 15 x 7J with 205/60R-15 tires, but there were 16 x 7J options and 225/50ZR-16s on 325iC from the start.

According to the US importers in model year 1995, the 318iC weighed in at 3,120 lbs, compared to 2,933 lbs for the 318is, while a 325iC waddled along at 3,352 lbs compared to 3,087 lbs for the 325is coupe.

BMW NA expected a manual 318iC to reach from rest to 60 mph in 10.6 seconds, finally attaining 116 mph and recording EPA fuel consumption estimates of 22/31 City/Highway US mpg.

The 325iC was rated by the makers as capable of 0–60 mph in 8.3 seconds (8.9 seconds with the popular automatic transmission), topping out at the usual US-limited 128 mph and EPA-estimated on 19/28 US mpg City/Highway. *Autocar & Motor* returned 0–60 mph in 6.6 seconds for the 193-bhp European-motor 328iC, and found it would capture 139 mph. The British managed 22 Imperial mpg, equivalent to 18.3 US mpg.

American Sales Patterns and Equipment

Right from the start, BMW estimated that 33 percent of all production would be shipped across the Atlantic. BMW was close to the one-third US, two-thirds rest of the world sales result by the close of 1997 when official figures stated production at 148,943 units and BMW NA reported 48,342 . As of December 31, 1999, total sales of the Convertible had grown to 66,175 units in the US (excluding M3).

It is also true that peak production from 1994–97 settled around 30,000 units a year for the E36 Convertible, which was about a third ahead of its E30 predecessor. A final production figure of 196,500 E36 Convertibles was released in 2000, reflecting an autumn 1999 end to production of BMW's most popular convertible 3 Series to date.

As can be seen from the following figures, the ratio of four- to six-cylinder Convertible sales was not initially so biased toward sixes as for the roofed models. However, it did finally go that way with the 328 particularly bashing 318 so hard that BMW NA eventually made the entry model a six-cylinder 323iC.

US E36 325iC two-door Convertible: Sales and equipment, including delivery costs

Year	Base price	Main options	US Sales
1992	$23,975	Metallic paint, $435; LSD, $510	2,817
1993	$36,725	Metallic paint, $450; LSD, $510; Heated F/seats, $360	4,038
1994	$39,270	Auto, $900; Metallic paint, $475; Roll-over system, $1,390; LSD, $530; Computer, $430	7,778
1995	$41,470	Auto, $975; Metallic paint, $475; Computer, $500*; AST, $1,100; Roll-over system, $1,450; Sports Pack, $1,275**; Premium Pack, $775***	7,204
1996	$41,960	Auto, $975; Metallic paint, $475; Computer, $500*; AST, $1,100; Roll-over system, $1,450; Sports Pack, $1,275**; Premium Pack, $775***; Aluminum hard-top, $2,295	762
1997	Replaced by 328iC		6

*Packaged with Sports/Premium, 1995

**Sport 1995–96 included alloy 16-inch wheels, 225/ZR tires, computer, and sports seats

***Premium Pack 1995–96 included computer and wood trim

US E36 318iC two-door Convertible: Sales and equipment

Year	Base price	Main options	US Sales
1994	$30,370	Auto, $900; Metallic paint, $475; LSD, $530; Cruise ctrl, $695*; Roll-over system, $1,390	3,156
1995	$32,570	Auto, $900; Metallic paint, $475; LSD, $580; Cruise ctrl, Std; Roll-over system, $1,450; Premium Pack, $1,750**	3,383
1996	$33,320	Auto, $975; Metallic paint, $475; Leather, $1,450; Hard-top, $2,295; Roll-over system, $1,450; AST, $1,100	2,876
1997	$33,720	Auto, $975; Metallic paint, $475; Leather, $1,450; Hard-top, $2,295; Roll-over system, $1,450	1,629

Note: 1998 Model Year 318iC was replaced by 323iC; 323iC sales in 1997 were 963

*Packaged with fog lights only

**Premium Pack 1995 included leather and uprated audio

US E36 328iC two-door Convertible: Sales and equipment, including delivery costs

Year	Base price	Main options	US Sales
1995	Unlisted		149
1996	$41,960	Auto, $975; Metallic paint, $475; Roll-over system, $1,450; Hard-top, $2,295; Sport Pack, $1,275***; Premium Pack, $775****; Computer, $500*	7,583
1997	$41,960	Auto, $975; Metallic paint, $475; Roll-over system, $1,450; Leather, $1,450**; Sports Pack, $1,725***; Hard-top, $2,295	8,815
1998	$42,070	Auto, $975; Metallic paint, $475; Hard-top, $2,295; Premium Pack, $1,600; Sport Pack, $1,775; Luxury Pack, $6,350	2,661
1999	$42,070	Auto, $975; Metallic paint, $475; Hard-top, $2,295; Premium Pack, $1,300****; Sport Pack, $1,300***	2,892

*Computer packaged in Premium Pack, 1996

**Leather packaged with Sport Pack, 1997

***Sport Pack for 1996 included alloy 16-inch wheels, 225/ZR tires, computer, and sports seats; for 1997, the same, minus computer; for 1999, featured 16-inch alloys, MTech aero equipment, and 3-spoke steering wheel

****Premium Pack for 1996 included computer and wood trim; Premium Pack for 1999 included computer and wood trim

Press Comment

As the third major variant of the 1990 generation, we could have expected a "so what?" factor in the reception for the breezy 3'er. Not so, according to the members of the automotive press.

"BMW seems to have put check marks in more boxes than you could expect from a single car. It can be a sunny convertible, it can be a weather-tight hardtop, it can be a versatile cargo hauler and all the while it earns style points as it goes." *Car and Driver*, 1994, US, of 325iC.

"It's well-balanced, well-mannered and com-fortable. Not to mention attractive." *Autoweek*, March 3, 1997, US, of 328iC.

"If you're in the market for a four seat con-vertible with impressive handling and powertrain credentials, you've just found it." declared *Motor Trend*, in September, 1993.

"This convertible has been worth the wait. The BMW 325 is powerful, handles well and suffers from few of the ride problems found in lesser soft tops. But the price is high when com-pared to those of its closest rivals," according to the June 1993 issue of the British magazine *What Car?*

"We can't find a downside to the less expensive engine. It revs with the same growl and urgency we've come to love in BMW sixes." *Car and Driver*, March, 1998, of the 323iC 2.5-liter versus 328iC 2.8-liter.

"After the highly successful introduction of the new generation six-cylinder 325i last sum-mer comes the new four-cylinder 318i Convertible. With the debut of this second Convertible model comes new affordability for the pleasures of open-air BMW driving: at

This 325i convertible looks particularly sleek from the rear quarter.

Photo: Klaus Schnitzer, Austria, 1993; reprinted in US, 1997

$29,900, the 318i is base-priced fully $8,900 below its six-cylinder stablemate," stated BMW NA in their model year 1994 press briefing.

Referring to our cost/sales charts, you need to know that we have incorporated all Destination, Dealer Handling charges in the base prices of Convertible. This has been done to be consistent with BMW NA's revised pricing policy which incorporated those mandatory charges, allowing a true annual price comparison to be made. Sometimes a quoted base price will therefore not match those quoted by BMW NA pre-1997 model year price lists (issued April 1, 1996).

To get almost a $9,000 difference between four- and six-cylinders was not merely a matter of deleting a brace of cylinders. According to BMW global practice, the value actually gets better the more you spend. This applies especially when packaging up items in the Sport or Premium/Luxury sectors. When launched, for example, the 318iC lacked the 325's power top, premium sound system, and leather upholstery, and featured manual front seat adjustment. If you wanted such features —— not just extra

power — you had to opt for the more expensive model in the first place.

You could make up the leather and sound system deficit with a $1,750 Premium Pack, but an item like the on-board computer — part of the 325's Sports or Premium Packs — was not initially listed for four-cylinder soft tops. Packaged options became more and more influential — and more expensive — for 3 Series sales from 1995 model year onward.

The biggest technical changes came in model year 1996 with new four- and six-cylinder engines. Those for 318iC and the 328i replacement for 325i meant updating throughout the NA range that season. Shared with 318ti, 318i sedan and coupe, the later four-cylinder is strongly recommended for the heavier convertible, having stronger mid-range pulling power out of proportion to its mild boost in cubic capacity from 1,796 cc to 1,895 cc.

For six-cylinders, the 1996 model year was equally important, with 328iC supplanting 325iC, a process started with an initial supply of nearly 150 units in the 1995 calendar year. The newcomer was a much beefier mid-range performer, typified by the production of as much torque at 2,000 rpm for 328 as 325 managed at a peakier 4,200 summit!

The 328's stats were a minimalist 1-bhp gain (190 total) but torque was fattened 14.4 percent and now totaled 206 lb-ft at lower rpm (3,950 versus 4,200 rpm). BMW reckoned on around a second sliced from 0–60 mph capabilities of all models, claiming a conservative 0–60 mph in some seven seconds.

In terms of every day driveablity, 328 is recommended over 325, or even the later high-torque version of the 2.5-liter misleadingly badged 323i. The reason is not outright speed, but the ability to fluidly pull a body weight that was considerably up over sedans and coupes that were getting tubbier by the year. For example, by that 1996 model year, BMW NA revealed 3,120 lbs as the curb weight for sedans and coupes, but the 328iC was reported some 242 lbs heavier still, at 3,362 lbs.

For model year 1997, the big Convertible news was a second-generation power top for 328iC, while 318iC retained the slick manual operation. Now fully automatic via a switch in the center console the 328iC top removed the need to unlock or lock into a final position when the electrical gear had done its job.

You could also raise the 328iC top, along with any windows left ajar, by turning the ignition to "lock" position and holding it there. The top then performed the 20-second auto gyrations, including the open and shut ballet of the fold-away hood compartment.

The news across the 3 Series range in model year 1997 was of a general freshening, plus the standard fitment of All Season Traction Control (AST) which had commonly been an $1,100 option. The Convertibles shared in the detail reshaping of front "kidney" grille, cupholders

arrived in the "console valet," and power mirrors took on heating elements as standard rather than optional status. From a driver's viewpoint, one of the biggest changes was that the clutch had to be depressed before the starter would turn.

For the 318iC, the 1997 calendar year marked the beginning of the end. The 323iC six cylinder replacement sold nearly a thousand units while 318iC sales almost halved. It was also the last year in which new 325i Convertibles were sold — all six of them!

The 323iC demanded only a modest dollar premium for the extra two cylinders. BMW NA said of the "small" six's arrival that the coupe variant put six-cylinder motoring back under $30,000 "for the first time since model year 1993." Also, the 323i convertible's initial "$35,270 was up just $1,550 from the previous 318i Convertible and included ventilated rear disc brakes, where 318 had solid ones."

Because it's a Bimmer doesn't mean there is always Bosch electronics beneath the hood. The "323"-badged 2.5-liter of model year 1998 featured engine electronics from the Siemens MS series, marking a cooperation between BMW and the German electronics giant that became common in the 1990s.

The 1998 model year was also significant because the 323i six-cylinder coupes and Convertibles arrived on the US market supplanting the previous four-cylinder models.

Photo: Klaus Schnitzer, 1997, US

Dynamically, the 323iC weighed in a tad under 3,300 lbs. And its VANOS-valve timing six of 168 bhp/181 lb-ft torque was predicted to punch the 0–60 mph test away in 7.7 seconds (nearly another second for the automatic). It had the predicted capability of returning EPA numbers 20/30 mpg City/Highway as a manual, or one and three mpg worse respectively for City/Highway in the usual four-speed automatic format.

For model year 1999, the E36 convertibles remained on the US and European markets, while an E46 successor was readied for May 2000 release. US prices remained constant, but some of the packages differed in detail, including double-spoke aluminum wheel options along with the three-spoke sports steering wheel lifted from the M3.

The most important option among the dedicated Convertible items was the 323iC availability of a power top within the $2,750 Premium Pack. That 323iC Premium package also covered leather trim, fog lights, heated mirrors, and washer jets for the lamps.

The 328iC option pack route also featured an aerodynamic body kit within a $1,300 Sport Pack. This distinguished 328iC from its 323 counterpart. Sport packaging also included a leather interior, 3-spoke M-wheel, and the 16-inch alloys with 225 tires.

21 Return of the Three-Door

A BMW hatchback for a brave new world

The E36 Compact was a courageous move into cheaper hatchback territory that European giants such as Volkswagen saw as a direct threat. BMW simply saw it as the cheapest automobile that could be offered around a fourth twist on the E36 theme, utilizing some previous E30 hardware to gain a price and packaging advantage from the rear-axle layout.

BMW's approach must have been sound, because it sold over 330,000 Compacts. The then-unique hatchback/rear-drive formula started a trend that continued in BMW's readiness to manufacture a 2001 successor. In Europe Mercedes has followed suit in the C-class replacement to be sold as a 3-door coupe. Now there will be just two rear-drive hatchbacks in the world.

Compact Birth

BMW continually examined opportunities for a smaller range beneath the 3 Series. Their engineers had analyzed front-drive thoroughly, and in the late 1990s, Rover was able to further develop hardware that dated back to BMW's late-1980s research. Mercedes obviously went through the same investigation of the smaller-car potential for a prestige badge. After troubled debuts, the late nineties saw the rear-motor/drive Smart Car two-seater—developed in cooperation with Swatch—and the front-drive A-class four-seater reach mass production. BMW didn't go the whole A-class distance in the Mercedes mold, but they still abbreviated the 3'er by 9 inches (230 mm) without encroaching on major cabin and wheelbase dimensions.

The accountants were happy to produce a fourth E36 major body variant on the same powertrain and floorpan foundations that had served so well for the E36 sedan, coupe and Convertible. The production numbers told them they were right and therefore an E46 successor arrived in Europe in spring 2001.

Technically, the biggest changes were the two-door body with rear hatch with a door aperture that extended down to bumper level, plus the adoption of the previous (E21/E30) 3 Series trailing-arm rear axle. The same hollow-steel arms and independent rear-end layout (separate coil springs forward of long telescopic dampers) are also found in all Z3 derivatives.

The European media often dismisses the older BMW trailing-arm layout as old-fashioned and prone to sudden oversteer tail-slides. BMW failed to publicly refute these consistent criticisms, but this proven trailing rear-axle layout has proven its worth, handling up to 321 bhp in the M Coupe. The same rear-end suspension principles also lived on in all the revered four-cylinder M3s up to the last 2.5-liter Evo of 238 bhp.

The older BMW trailing-arm layout remains capable of delivering enormous amounts of power and pleasure, whatever the power unit. If you feel strongly that efficient transport with consistent understeer is preferable in the daily driver role that the hatchback layout fills so well, maybe you should check out the front-drive majority. However, if you like a dash of fun with current hatchback versatility and a taste of traditional 2002 zest, then 318ti becomes a priority.

The front end, including the bonded screen raked at 61 degrees and its A-pillars, was shared with contemporary E36 sedans. The rest was new, a fact that swiftly became apparent when watching them being built at Munich.

A new and abbreviated 3'er profile. The Compact hatchback measured 13 feet, 8 inches (4.2 meters) and ran on the usual long wheelbase, minus 9 inches of trunk.

Photo: Jonathan A. Stein

The floorpan was shortened and the rear end reshaped to accommodate the more space-efficient simple trailing arm suspension. Not so obvious was the fact that all the side panels—including extended coupe sheet metal for the doors with frames added—had to be reshaped, along with the roof.

The robot-welded sheet-metal surrounds—and the metal itself—that extended to the curtailed rear were reinforced to pass all relevant US tests. These included 30-mph rear end impacts, 35-mph head-on collisions, and European offset crash testing at 55 km/h (34.2 mph).

BMW did not skimp on the safety of the smallest and cheapest (it was under the 30,000Dm barrier at home in February 1994) automobile in their range. Whether it was side impact door-bars, or standard provision of ABS braking and driver's side airbag in all markets, the company ensured a fair safety ration.

The only small compromises in the Compact are the fitment of a smaller fuel tank (13.7 US gallons), a vulnerable filler in the side panels (although the tank was safely located in front of the rear axle) and solid rear disc brakes. An official BMW NA spec listed 11.3-inch solid front rotors coupled to non-vented 11-inch rears. In Europe, however, the front units were vented, as was the case for all other American 3 Series of the period.

Handling was widely admired in the dry, but a little more action-packed in the wet, on the previous-generation (E30) rear suspension layout.

Photo: Anonymous, Austria, 1994

The hallowed 50–50 weight split for ultimate handling balance drifted away from the ideal at 53 percent front, 47 percent rear, according to independent European tests, which also confirmed an actual curb weight of 1,259 kg (2,769 lbs). American importer data reported a weight of 2,734 lbs, distributed 51.4 percent front and 48.6 percent rear alongside a drag coefficient of 0.35.

That curb weight was among the lowest seen for a 3 Series in ten years, and made Compact speed freaks lust all the more for the LHD Europe-only 323ti with 170-bhp six-cylinder power. It was obviously faster than the four-cylinders and reportedly handled well despite extra poundage and a less balanced weight distribution.

Within the Compact was a mixed story of low rent and valuable awkward load space, boosted by that simplified rear suspension. With the rear seats up, the carrying capability was pretty normal—in Europe, they spoke of 11.4 cubic feet (325 liters), while America anticipated an EPA volume of 15.1 cubic feet. Most relevant was that the European figure tripled with the rear seat folded. The downside was that the interior fit, finish, and plastics were not up to previous BMW standards.

BMW boasted of, "a particularly large number of storage boxes and compartments within easy reach of both driver and passenger. The opening button for the glove compartment, for example, faces toward the driver." There were twin vanity mirrors and the substitution of ashtrays and cigar lighter with a power socket and additional storage. The luggage area contained storage recesses plus "fastening lashes and two luggage supports" to help secure the luggage stowed under a blind unique to the Compact.

Road & Track commented in 1996, "Cost reductions include a single-piece molded dash and non-vented brake rotors." The magazine was impressed with the 318ti (in its later 1996 1,895-cc Sport trim, costing $25,850). *R&T* did, however, comment, in comparison with the Volkswagen VR6 Golf (then about $4,000 cheaper in comparable trim): "The interior quality of each hatchback was up to par, but not everything in them was to our liking. The 318ti's headlight switch, for example, has a chintzy feel."

Road & Track creatively summarized, "In an ideal world, we'd put the VR6 engine in the 318ti chassis and create our own hot hatchback. But since this can't be done, we'll pick the BMW 318ti as the winner here. To us, the handling dynamics of a sporty hatchback are a bit more important than its practicality or power."

The tailgate, which stretched down to the rear bumper line, helped handle bulky items, but the rear suspension towers were a load-limiting factor. Lowering the back seats boosted load-haul capability by over 60 percent.

Photo: BMW AG Presse, Munich, 1993

Performance

As originally imported, the American 318ti was claimed to reach 0–60 mph in 9.3 seconds on the original 1,796-cc of 138 bhp and 129 lb-ft of torque. Top speed was restricted to 116 mph and EPA estimated gas mileage for a manual was 22/32 US City/Highway mpg.

A four-speed THM R1 automatic was sold in the US as an option, and was predicted to get 21/29 City/Highway mpg. BMW NA reported that the automatic added a second to the 0–60 mph time.

In the US, launch-year standard equipment included air conditioning, AM/FM six-speaker stereo with wired CD, heated power mirrors, cloth/leatherette trim, manual push/pull side rear glass, power windows, power steering, ABS, and steel 15 x 6J wheels wearing 185/65R all-season tires.

Many Compacts were, however, delivered in sport guise, or had options fitted that substituted alloy wheels with 205 or 225 section tires.

The standard factory suspension called for the usual E36 strut front end (complete with arc lower wishbone) cooperating with an anti-roll bar and twin-tube gas damping. At the back, the 15-degree rake of the trailing arm was pure E30, but twin-tube gas damping and anti-roll bar were part of every 318ti. Sports calibrations and-spring/damper/wheel upgrades were popular, whether as original equipment or from the aftermarket.

In American 138-bhp format, both *Car and Driver* and *Road & Track* published independent performance figures. *C/D* figures were for the original 1,796-cc, while the *R&T* comparison against the Golf VR6 was published using data from the 1,895-cc motor. *C/D* returned 0–60 mph in 8.4 seconds, coupled to a standing quarter in 18.4 seconds at 84 mph. The testers also found that their test car was electronically-limited to 114 mph top speed and measured fuel economy as 25 US mpg. The later and larger BMW four recorded 24 mpg for *R&T*, plus 0–60 mph in 8.3 seconds, with the standing quarter performed in 16.3 seconds at 83.6 mph. Testing a

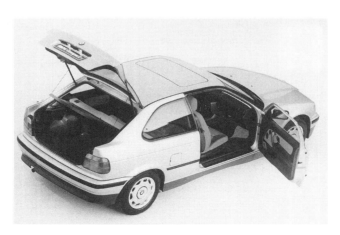

The fourth variant on an E36 theme, the Compact, followed the four-door sedan and the two-door coupe/ Convertible brethren.

Photo: BMW AG Presse, Munich, 1993

UK 1.8ti, *What Car* of November 1996 reported an unrestricted 129 mph for the 1,895-cc unit alongside 0–60 mph in 8.6 seconds and 33.1 Imperial (27.6 US) mpg.

American Sales Life

A base price below $20,000 and a whiff of hatchback sports ability from a then-unmatched three-door, front-engine, rear-drive format were the Big News BMW NA seized upon to make the sales pitch for 318ti in January 1995. That was a year after the 1.6-liter original was introduced to Europe, but only a few months after the autumn 1994 European debut of the 318ti.

In the US introduction, BMW NA commented, "Under the skin, there's the same traditional BMW chassis fine-tuning for a supple ride and agile handling; also traditionally BMW, generously sized 4-wheel disc brakes are standard. Throughout the 318ti, the very same quality standards to which every BMW is built ensures a solidly-constructed finely finished automobile, inside and out."

That factory-owned importer's opinion was backed up by *Motor Trend*'s Bob Nagy, whose first (February 1995) driving impressions for *Motor Trend* concluded, "Excellent power steering, a near-ideal weight distribution, and a taut yet supple suspension make the 318ti a delightful traveling companion, regardless of trim level. Top speed is electronically limited to 116 mph, and even at triple digit velocities, the car felt reassuringly stable. We preferred the extra support of the upline seats in the Sport models, but the standard buckets also deserve high marks for comfort.

"With its aggressive pricing, impressive build quality, exceptional utility, and solid fun-to-drive potential, the new 318ti should have little trouble meeting its modest US sales goals. A jaunty appearance and a BMW pedigree should further help its chances here in America," concluded the *Motor Trend* preview.

There was a serious divergence in opinion on the Compact line. While the German fortnightly *auto motor und sport* was impressed by a body featuring "narrow gaps, precisely closing doors and a lack of any squeaks or rattles when driving," the cockpit was not so widely praised in Europe.

London's *Autocar* reported on November 2, 1994, "The driving position benefits from

Although it added a welcome versatility and affordability to the 3 Series, the interior was widely criticized in Europe as low-rent.

Photos: BMW AG Presse, Munich, 1993

Here are the factory cutaway and dimensions for the 3'er Compact.

Drawing: BMW Grafik Design for BMW AG, Munich, 1994

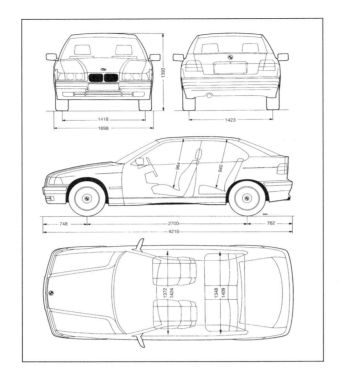

The front suspension and engine-bay layout were the least-changed aspects of the E36-based three-door. However, no front anti-roll bar linkage to the struts was incorporated on this base model (with solid discs).

Drawing: BMW Grafik Design for BMW AG, Munich, 1994

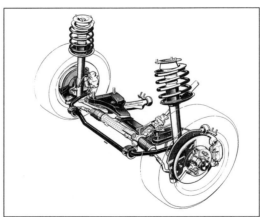

The older, simpler, and lighter rear-axle/suspension layout came from the previous-generation E30.

Drawing: BMW Grafik Design for BMW AG, Munich, 1994

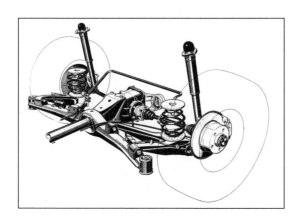

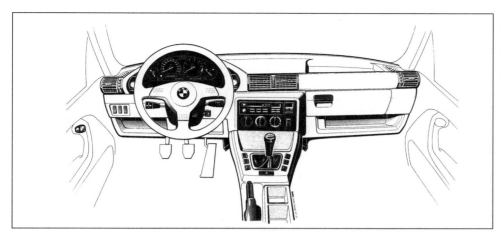

The dash layout was clean, but owed more to previous generations and initially was not finished to the usual BMW standards.

Drawing: BMW Grafik Design for BMW AG, Munich, 1994

low-slung, height-adjustable seats and impeccable ergonomics, although the steering column does not adjust. Our car's optional sports seats provided some compensation but couldn't redeem the redesigned fascia, which looks a shade too downmarket for our tastes because of its chunky push/pull plastic light switches and angled heater controls." This was hardly severe criticism, but the carping about the interior plastics, whether for the dash or minor controls, was a common theme outside the US.

The first 318ti Compacts arrived for a model-year 1996 announcement but sold over 5,100 units in the 1995 calendar year. Much was made of the sub-$20,000 price, but the shipping charge alone put it on the other side of twenty grand.

Many 318ti Compacts were sold in the US at $25,000 to $26,000 with varying optional sports packages, and more than 50 percent of customers (1995-1997) put down nearly $1,000 for the automatic transmission.

Sporting Options

Building on the strongest characteristics of the 318ti, BMW NA and the parent company packaged up some M-branded hardware with more visual appeal. First, there were 200 limited-edition 318ti Club Sports released just in time to catch the close of the 1995 model year. The essential handling ingredients of this package were incorporated into the optional Sports Packs of model years 1996–98.

The pieces that mattered were highlighted by five round spokes within oversize 16-inch alloy wheels carrying 225/50R rubber. Behind that obvious upgrade was the less-obvious MTech suspension, featuring lowered ride heights and stiffened springs alongside twin-tube gas dampers. This combination really

The 16-valve, double overhead camshaft (DOHC), four-cylinder motor featured a peppy 140 bhp in Europe, with much the same performance (138 bhp) in America.

Drawing: BMW Grafik Design for BMW AG, Munich, 1994

Transplanting the 2.5-liter/170-bhp unit to the smallest and lightest member of the E36 range delivered a manufacturer-claimed 0–62 mph in 7.8 seconds for the European 323ti.

Photo: BMW AG for March 1997 release at Geneva Show

A full-length fabric sunroof was a popular fresh-air and plant-hauling feature for the later-1990s 318ti.

Photos: Klaus Schnitzer, US, 1997

BMW CCA's Scott Hughes exercises a 318ti assembled by TC Kline Racing of New Hampshire.

Photo: Klaus Schnitzer, US, 1997

worked, when *Car and Driver* reported observed that, "Lateral grip is up from 0.81 to 0.85g."

Other cosmetic changes which could become appreciated by collectors included a leather-rim steering wheel, an impressive M-branded body kit (including front air dam and sills), and combination leather-and-cloth interior trim for the sports seats and the M-branding (3-color stripe) found inlaid on the gear knob. The Club Sport package also had M-look mirrors.

Under the hood of every model-year 1996 BMW 318ti for the US was the upgraded twin-cam 16-valve engine (now 1.9 liters instead of 1.8) with its many improvements and increased mid-range/low-end torque. Thus the 1996 Compact is the earliest year to buy because of the enhanced motor durability and the most choice.

Sales of the 318ti peaked in the US in 1996 at just over 7,200 units; and the automatic option peaked that year as well, with automatics

US BMW 318ti/Sport Compact three-door: prices, equipment, and sales

Year	Base price*	Main options	US Sales
1995	$19,900	Auto, $975; Sports Pack, $2,400**; Active Pack, $2,400***	5,119
1996	$21,130 (inc. $570 dest. & handling)	Auto, $975; Sports Pack, $2,940**; Active Pack, $2,625***; Power roof, $1,200; Computer, $300	7,238
1997	$21,870 (inc. $570 dest. & handling)	Auto, $975; Sports Pack, $2,940**; Active Pack $2,150***; Power roof, $950; Computer, $300	4,622
1998	$21,960 (inc. $520 dest. & handling)	Auto, $975; Sports Pack, $2,940**; Active Pack, $1,350***; Cruise control, $475; Power roof, $950; Computer, $300	3,735
1999	$23,870	Auto, $975; Calif. sunroof, $1,600; Power moonroof, $950; Computer $300; Cruise control $475; Sat. Nav. C., $1,800****; Moonroof, $950; Metallic paint, $475	656

*All prices include delivery and destination charges.

**Sport Pack: For 1995, included upgraded suspension, 15 x 7-inch alloys/205 tires, fog lights, leather upholstery with additional cloth door inserts over active trim, sports front seats with thigh-adjustable supports (2-way power roof and key-less entry extra); limited edition (200) 318ti Club Sport at $25,850 closed the 1995MY and became the basis for the 1996MY Sport Pack. For 1996, included upgraded suspension, 16-inch alloys (round-spoke), 225/50VR tires, leather trim wheel, gear knob & hand brake, sports seats, fog lights, cloth/leather upholstery, M-design color-coded bumpers and side skirts. For 1997, included upgraded suspension, 16-inch alloys (round-spoke), 225/50VR tires, leather trim wheel, sports seats, fog lights, cloth/leather upholstery, M-design color-coded bumpers, and side skirts. For 1998, included upgraded suspension, 16-inch alloys (round-spoke), 225/50VR tires, leather trim wheel, gear lever and hand brake, fog lights, cloth/leather upholstery, M-aero body kit.

***Active Pack: For 1995, included cruise control, 15x 7 inch alloy wheels with 205/60R tires; remote control key-less entry; leather trim to wheel, gear lever knob and hand brake grip, 4-readout/1-warning-function "compact" computer, 2-way power sunroof (limited slip differential, leather seating, 10-speaker stereo, CD player and choice of two BMW cell phones cost extra). For 1996, included 15-inch wheels/205 all-season tires, power sunroof, leather steering wheel, cruise control, computer, Alpine alarm/key-less entry, metallic paint, color-coded bumpers, and side skirts. For 1997, included 15-inch wheels/205 all-season tires, power sunroof, leather steering wheel, cruise control, computer, Alpine alarm/keyless entry, and metallic paint. For 1998, included 15-inch wheels/205 all-season tires, power sunroof, leather steering wheel & gear lever knob, cruise control, computer, Alpine alarm/keyless entry, and no added charge for metallic paint.

****Listed dealer center only, fit and unpriced by BMW NA: price quoted is for 323i importer option.

accounting for 58 percent of all sales. Sales slipped sharply thereafter, amounting to fewer than 700 units recorded by 1999. By then, it was officially listed as the 318ti Sport and effectively became a limited-edition model at a basic $23,870 with no further options offered. That meant the 1999 model included stiffened and lowered suspension, 16-inch wheels with W-rated tires, fog lights, the M aero-kit pieces, and the M3-style three-spoke steering wheel.

In five years, the 318ti Compacts for the US racked up just over 21,000 sales, making them a little less popular than the six-cylinder, premium-price 328is coupes, which totalled almost 24,000 sales in the same period. Not only was the American preference for six-cylinder BMW 3'ers unmistakable, it was a lot more profitable for BMW NA.

22 Touring, the Sleek Way...

North America never saw the E36 Touring, but it was extremely popular everywhere it was sold.

The E36 five-door Touring was an astonishingly good design, as it had to be in an age when 4x4 SUVs and other permutations of the light-truck 4x4 theme became such significant global sellers. Also remember that BMW launched its X5 into the 4x4 SUV market—one uncomfortably close to the Touring niche—in 1999.

The third-generation Touring eventually had to fight both a Mercedes C-class estate and the Volkswagen Audi group's extremely effective Passat wagon and Audi A4 Avant designs. Nevertheless, BMW's Touring production at Regensberg from 1994–98 ranked heartily above 25,000 units a year (the peak was 34,470 in 1997). When production ended in July of 1999, estimates reported over 130,000 manufactured.

British experience, and subsequent E46 Touring design changes, indicated that the E36 was far from flawless. The following reasons for Audi out-selling BMW comfortably in this sector—with Mercedes closing in—were given in an August 1999 BMW (GB) briefing to media at the French-based launch of the E46 Touring. "The previous E36 Touring was late to the market, fully four years in our case, and diesel motors matter in this sector. So the Audi 1.9 turbodiesel was the key, and it was simply too strong for us. We did not have a competitive diesel in this price sector." In a market segment where fuel economy and utility ranked more highly than a sporting drive, the E30 and E36 Tourings had been at a disadvantage.

Back in the early 1990s, the BMW design team improved the E36 Touring over its E30 predecessor in many ways, fundamentally because this fifth variant on an E36 theme was integrally engineered as part of the plan from the start. Thus the CAD computer techniques could design a substantially larger body with a weight penalty of just 22 addi-

Starting on the left is the original 02 touring in three-door format. Next is the black E30. The silver E36 on the right came from a generation that produced more 130,000 units from 1995–99.

The new E46 Touring is in the foreground.

Photo: BMW GB/AG, released November 1999 for French debut

Engineered alongside the rest of the E36 Bimmers, the Touring was not released until 1995 and therefore carried some features that were not in the original line, including the 2.8-liter six and "323" version of the 2.5-liter.

Photo: Klaus Schnitzer, Germany, 1996

tional lbs (10 kg). Unfortunately, that quote was just for the bare shell—the Touring was among the heaviest E36 models, with the 328i hitting 1,475 kg (3,245 lbs) or more.

The sales performance of the E36 Touring, plus owner comments and US research, led to significant changes in the current E46 model.

Photos: BMW GB/AG, released November 1999 for French debut

For the E36, the load-bay width zoomed from 21.5 to 35 inches, stretching along the flattened sill that lay just above the bumper line. However, retaining the later Z-axle structure intruded on the wheel arch profiles and space between these two vital wide-load

mounting points was slightly down compared to the previous E30.

For E36, the rear-seat split action was undeniably useful in varying load accommodation. A lighter tailgate and a 12 percent gain in volume were also popular, allowing "either a full-size bicycle or four sets of golf clubs" to be carried, according to BMW.

That body incorporated later safety developments such as front and rear crash cells that cost less to repair. Even at the 1995 mass-production launch (69 pre-production examples were made in 1994) the Touring incorporated all the safety features of the range, including side impact door bars, driver's air bag and height-adjustable belts with pre-tensioners.

Equally importantly, torsional strength of the body had been maintained in five-door form. The suspension was stiffened for the anticipated extra weight of both the body and a payload. As with all Touring deviants, this could make them a little

bouncy at the rear when unladen, but the E36 was a big improvement over the E30.

Standard wheel-and-tire combinations for Europe started with a 15 x 6J steel with 185/65R-rubber, but the 328i offered 15 x 7J alloys wearing 205/60R-15 tires. Or there was an extra cost 16 x 7-inch alloy wearing the 225/ZR-16s that were so familiar on the US Sport Packs of the period.

A top speed of 230 km/h for the 328i translated as a better than 140 mph. Even the factory's notoriously conservative performance claims expected 7.4 seconds for the 0–62 mph (0–100 km/h) sprint. Brakes were the usual quartet of vented units for all six-cylinder models, while the four-pot had solid rear discs and vented fronts.

A full range of engines was offered across Europe. The alloy-block 328i topped the line, but there were two economy-conscious diesels (318tds and 325tds) which offered up to 43.5 Imperial (36.3 US) mpg, according to BMW. The

The 170-bhp 323i at
home in a German
market place among
the cobblestones and
shoppers.

Photo: Klaus Schnitzer,
Germany, 1996

The Touring's load
area made maximum
use of a rear-drive
layout.

Photo: Klaus Schnitzer,
Germany, 1996

most economical four-cylinder 318tds still managed to hit 111 mph on just 90 bhp, but wanted
14.6 seconds to haul from 0–62 mph. A 325tds
six-pot demanded only 10.5 seconds for the
European benchmark 0–62 mph (0–100 km/h)
standing-start test. It would run to the 128-mph
US speed-limiter figure for contemporary six-
cylinder gasoline motors on 143 bhp.

A brace of cheaper gasoline engines completed
the Touring powertrains. The Touring came with
the usual European 318i specification

single-camshaft M40 motor. Or there was the
choice of a suave 2-liter six found in 320i, which
was still above the ten second mark for 0–60
mph. A 320i could get down to a disappointing
21.9 Imperial (18.2 US) urban mpg when heav-
ing that substantial body from rest to pace and
back in urban use.

BMW buyer research in 1994 indicated that
UK Touring customers were, on average, 40 years
old, and were likely to be professionals, with
women accounting for more than one third

This 170-bhp powertrain for 323i is about as small as you would want to go in the heavier Touring body's gasoline engine line, but the European diesels were particularly suited to the Touring with their low-end pulling power and economical operation.

Photo: Klaus Schnitzer, Germany, 1996

Here's a 320g, a touring example of one of the ways that BMW is working to produce low emission vehicles, for a cleaner environment. Current company thinking is that hydrogen, not the favored fuel cell, is the 21st century way.

Photo: BMW AG, reproduced for BMW GB, September 1999

of the buyers. There were also a significant 20 percent of buyers listed as retired folk, so this was a BMW that was getting to previously unreached profitable areas.

One pattern that persisted was to specify high levels of equipment as standard. The SE option packages used in Britain were selected by more than 90 percent of buyers in the E30 format (when no diesel option was available in the UK).

Standard British specification at 318i/diesel 318tds level included an airbag sports steering wheel, anti-lock brakes (standard across the range on all E36s), and power assistance for the steering and front glass. Security measures covered central locking with deadlocks, plus the utility of rear wash/wipe and a retractable luggage cover. The 320i/325/tds added alloy wheels, power sunroof, rear electric windows, and a digital clock with an external thermometer.

On the 328i Touring, BMW ran to a bonus eight-function computer, heated mirrors and door locks, headlamp wash/wipe, and rear-seat head restraints. This may sound pretty generous on a quick read-through, but contemporary specifications for the US models were a lot more generous at lower initial prices. Note that a radio was not fitted at the 318 stage, and you could forget items like cruise control or air conditioning, which have popped up regularly in US spec sheets for more than a decade.

The Touring did a stylish job of playing the occasional and distinctly sporting load-carrier, but the fast lane to prestige and manufacturer profit would prove to be the six-cylinder M3.

23 M3 Goes for Six Appeal

The M3 matured into a six-cylinder coupe—with subsequent Convertible and four-door alternatives—in the 1990s.

More than 71,000 owners—triple the number of who bought the original M3—agree that the M3 represents the summit of 3 Series ownership ambition. That customers pay double the cost of a visually similar, but far less dynamic, mainstream 3'er tells us why Munich went back to the M-letter, even though there would be no immediate Motorsport mandate for a second M3. Almost 50 percent of all production was sold in 1994-99 in the United States.

The good thing to know is that we are not alone in this M-obsession. Here is a selection of independent press comments that greeted M3 variants on either side of the Atlantic:

"A swift and efficient express, all wrapped up in a beautiful coupe shell." *Autocar*, December 9, 1992, European 3-liter/286-bhp debut drive story.

"What's so delightful about the audacious BMW is that it punches preposterously beyond its weight. If you want a Ferrari in Savile Row drag, this is your car." *Car*, January, 1994, UK 3-liter/286-bhp.

"Convincing evidence that Munich is now the Automotive Valhalla…. Somehow, it manages to blend a sense of upscale privilege and refinement with flashing good looks, spellbinding performance, and refreshing integrity." *Car and Driver*, July, 1994, US full-test 3-liter/240-bhp.

"The M3 is a formidable piece of work." *Road & Track*, Special edition, 1995, US 3-liter/240-bhp.

"Its low axle ratio and lack of overdrive means the Lightweight needs a little less than a mile to slam into its 6,500-rpm rev-limiter in fifth gear at 137 mph." *Motor Trend*, August, 1995, US 3-liter/240-bhp Lightweight.

"The M3 is simply irresistible in three departments. It has a pretty, practical, and perfectly put-together body; a suspension tuned in paradise; and an engine fit for the Automotive Hall of Fame." *Automobile*, February, 1997, All Stars, US 3.2-liter/240-bhp.

"The M3 Evolution truly regained for the breed the ability to challenge and amuse an appreciative driver on the right roads whilst cosseting and comforting the rest of the time." *Autocar*, October 6, 1999, Farewell to 3.2-liter Evo/321-bhp.

The E36 M-Formula

Moving the M3 tale into the six-cylinder 1990s, we find a complete change of character compared with the four-cylinder M3 of 1986–90. The later M3 delivered a compromised, civilized formula of a searing straight-line punch and high-speed cruising ability that could

not be equaled by its four-cylinder forebearer. Nevertheless, the original M3 retains the right to be called the most enjoyable Bimmer ever to tackle a curve.

The New M3 transformation attracted considerable European press-launch controversy, especially in Britain. Critical comments regarding the handling feedback/numb steering of the newcomer were commonplace after debut drives at the November 1992 launch in Majorca, Spain.

"The truth is—and BMW admits it—this car is no successor to the M3 at all," said the London weekly, *Autocar*. "Overall, the new M3 lacks the edge, the clarity of purpose, that made the original what it was," agreed *Performance Car* in the UK. BMW would meet these disgruntled Brits—and the hard-core Europeans who wanted more—with a 1995 Evolution version, but it was obvious that this was not the path for the US.

E36 M3, US & Europe: Independent performance data

M3 Model	Euro 3.0	US 3.0	Evo 3.2	US 3.2	Lightweight 3.2
Quoted bhp	286	240	321	240	240
Maximum mph	155*	137	158	137	137
0–30 mph (sec)	2.5	2.3	2.2	—	—
0–60 mph (sec)	5.6	6.4	5.3	5.9	5.3
0–100 mph (sec)	13.5	16.0	12.0	15.5	14.0
0–120 mph (sec)	20.0	—	18.5	—	—
1/4 mile (sec/mph)	14.0/101	14.6/97	13.8/104	14.5/98	13.9/100
Overall mpg, Imp or US	24–26 Imp	24–25 US	23–25 Imp	22–24 US	21–23 US
Curb weight (lbs)	3,344 (1,520 kg)	3,230	3,236 (1,471 kg**)	3,170	2,950

*Timed by *Autocar* at 162 mph with the European 155-mph speed-limiter obviously inoperative! In February, 2001 *Autocar* checked the latest E46 M3 (343 bhp) up to 160 mph in sixth, 157 in fifth and zipped 0-60 mph in 4.8 seconds.

**See Evo text: BMW was forced to provide a European Common Market weight of 1,515 kg in 1996 for the Evo coupe, heavier than earlier models despite the weight-saving alloy doors

The new E36 M3 was introduced to the press in Majorca, Spain in 1992.

Photo: BMW AG Presse, Majorca, Spain, 1992

Initially, BMW NA stated that the E36 M3 was not going to be imported. Finally, however, the growing influence of a then-30,000-plus BMW CCA owners club, and BMW NA's natural desire to continue selling profitable models, forced BMW AG to re-examine their cost figures. Some radical technical changes in specification—primarily using an enlarged 328i motor (S50 US) rather than a pedigree S50—allowed a base cost of $36,620 in the US. Power may have dropped by 46 bhp, but US M3 sales heartily exceeded those of any European market. So the American M3 deserves to be seen as a cost-conscious M3 in its own right, rather than a second-rate take on Bavarian brawn.

Thus did the second-generation M3 become truly international, with its own three-body choices (two-door coupe followed by Convertibles and four-doors sedan). A quartet of 3.0- and 3.2-liter 24-valve sixes were installed alongside five- and six-speed manual transmissions, one with a fully automatic five-speed (US only).

A trick SMG (Sequential Motorsport Gearbox) six-speed confined its computer-managed electro-hydraulic selections to Europe. SMG sounded great, but combining mechanical six-speed efficiency with automatic abilities was a slow—and often jerky—shift process.

The table opposite shows how those varying performance formulas stacked up according to contemporary road-test results.

The New M3's Beginnings

Development work for a new M3 started in 1989. Marketing efforts were initially linked with the 2.5-liter, six-cylinder M3 that should have raced in the German National series of 1993 onward. That didn't happen after a row about regulations went unresolved (see Chapter 24), but the E36 M3 showroom product proceeded on its own.

The E36 M3 was not available in production trim for Europe until 1993, but was publicly debuted at the October 1992 Paris Show. It would be model year 1995 before the new M3 came to the US, but nearly 3,000 were sold there in the remainder of the 1994 calendar year, thanks to press hype that only 2,000 would be shipped in the first 12 months.

BMW Motorsport went for an initial static presentation of the M3 coupe during a Nürburgring racing double-header in June 1992. After a seductive "look but don't drive" taste, the November press preview drives in Majorca couldn't come soon enough.

Under the leadership of Otto Pukl, Motorsport GmbH engineers at Preussenstrasse balanced political correctness in exhaust emission and fuel economy with a sledgehammer punch that pitched the M3 into a new prestige-and-performance category midway between Porsche 911 territory and existing mass-production super-sedans.

The 24-valve straight six dominated the engine bay as well as driving impressions, introducing European enthusiasts to VANOS variable valve timing systems.

Photo: BMW AG Presse, Munich, 1992

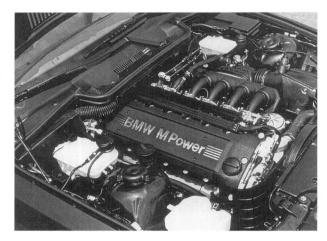

The DOHC development of the M50 325i six was designated simply S50 in Europe (S50 US in America] and was thoroughly re-engineered away from its M50 origins for Europe. It measured 2,990 cc on a unique M3 bore-and-stroke of 86 x 85.8 mm within the cast-iron block.

The aluminum cylinder head came in two sections—"in the interests of superior thermal and mechanical ability," said BMW—and was clamped to the block via a unique asbestos-free head gasket and bolts that "do not require re-tightening at any point in the engine's running life," the factory declared. Some seven bearings were used to support both the cam and crankshafts. The new steel crank, declared safe to a memorable 7,280 rpm, bore twelve counterbalanced weights and cooperated with an oil-damped two-mass flywheel that mated to a 9.45-inch (240 mm) clutch.

A conventional five-speed gearbox was first fitted in Europe. The six-speed manual and clutchless manual (SMG) followed only with the 1995 Evo's power hike in Europe. For the US model, a five-speed manual or automatic was often listed (see page 255).

The engine featured twin overhead camshafts, driven by a double-row chain directly from the crankshaft. The quad-valve combustion chambers featured 1.34-inch (34-mm) intake valves and 1.2-inch (30.5-mm) exhaust valves and a 10.8:1 compression demanded 98-octane Euro-Super-unleaded at an absurdly low quoted 9.1 liters per 100 kms (31.04 Imperial mpg). Without adjustment, but with marginal power losses, the Digital Motor Electronic system (Type 3.3) with selective anti-knock cylinder-sensors (inherited from the contemporary V8s) would allow 95-octane unleaded. A catalytic converter was always part of the E36 specification for all markets.

The M3's camshaft timing was special, and was part of the reason why a European model retained its expensively engineered power and torque advantage throughout the rpm-ranges. Then-commercial Motorsport director Karl-Heinz Kalbfell also revealed that the new M3 motor's VANOS (variable valve timing system) "shares the principles, not all the parts, but the basic idea, with the V12 we supply to McLaren for the F1." Lower-profile electronics also delivered a coil per cylinder (as per other contemporary BMW 24-valve sixes) and a very special Electronic Control Unit (ECU) branded under BMW's traditional Digital Motor Electronics label, but manufactured by the joint BMW-Rolls Royce aviation company.

The VANOS electro-hydraulic high-pressure (100 bar) system operated to optimize inlet camshaft and therefore inlet valve timing according to computer calculations made in milliseconds. The system (also then referred to as VACC) became a lasting feature of the M3 and has now trickled down to the 323i and 328i of both E36 and E46 generations, albeit in double VANOS format which acts on both inlet and exhaust camshafts. VANOS was not part of the US M3 recipe.

Peak power was reported at 286 bhp by 6,900 rpm, equating to a commendable 95.7 bhp a liter. Maximum torque was reported at 320 Nm (235 lb-ft). Torque peaked at 3,600 rpm, but held constant all the way to to 5,900 rpm..

Chassis, Tire and Handling Priorities

The starting points for ride and handling development were the production 3 Series strut front (with pressed-steel lower arm/wishbone) and Z-axle independent rear. Both items needed many detail upgrades to balance the most powerful engines in the range, and 17-inch wheels to carry the package. In fact, there were three alternate road-wheel choices announced at launch.

The usual production wheels were uniquely cast-alloy double ten-spoke 7.5 x 17-inch road rollers, covered by MXX3 Michelins of 235/40 ZR in Europe. The first optional deal was a set of 8.5-inch rims at the rear, retaining the same tire size, while the winter recommendation was another cast-aluminum design, but of 7J x 17-inch carrying 215/45 17 rubber.

In America, the 7.5-inch rims were standard until 1998, when the 8.5-inch rear was offered as standard equipment. The 1998 tire specification therefore changed, allowing a slimmer 225/45 front and 245/45 rear. However, the limited-production Lightweight, which was listed with the 7.5- and 8.5-inch rims, used MXX3s of 235/40s front and back.

US M3 owners often found that the ultra low-profile rubber could not absorb enough impact energy to prevent bent rims due to pot-holed highways. In their 35,000-mile/7-month long-term assessment, *Car and Driver* damaged no less than five such rims, then priced at $441 each! The tires, however, usually survived pothole confrontations intact. The magazine replaced the Michelins at the close of 35,000 miles and anticipated an average tire life of 36,500 miles, having followed BMW M3 policy in not rotating covers to extend front or rear set life.

BMW reported several front and rear chassis modifications for the M3. Front ride height was lowered by 1.22-inch (30 mm) and repositioned strut mountings resulted in improved steering feedback. Stiffer, shorter springs and recalibrated dampers and adjusted auxiliary "helper" springing stiffened the ride. Track control arms took rigid wheel alignment joint and geometry was overhauled; stub axles and associated kinematic characteristics were reinforced; a larger anti-roll bar acted directly on spring/strut layout; and spring mount plates were reinforced.

Front and rear track were both widened, amounting to 56.9 inches (1,444 mm) at the back, and 56.0 inches (1,422 mm) at the front, or up an inch at the back and up just over half an inch at the front.

Revised coil springs, dampers, and a thicker anti-roll bar were fitted to the rear. Also upgraded were reinforced longitudinal control/ trailing

The M3 instrument layout behind the four-spoke steering wheel was a little different than that seen by Americans. In Europe, aside from the 280 km/h (174 mph) speedometer, the 7,300-rev redline of the tachometer also contained an oil temperature scale.

Photos: BMW AG Presse, Munich, 1997

arms, harder rubber bushes, and 850i-specification rear wheel bearings. Suspension geometry, including camber settings, was also modified to suit the new rubber and still retained deliberate elasticity to both offer a civilized ride and to provide a modest toe-in-toe-out trait to counter lift-off oversteer.

Some of the M3 modifications mean that individual bushing replacements may not be available. Up front, if routine replacement of worn front bush is required a complete lower control-arm casting must be purchased.

BMW claimed 1.2 G for the upgraded chassis in handling tests, but no American test appears to have recorded more than 0.92 G.

A 25 percent pre-loaded limited-slip differential—a ZF, multi-plate type—was listed as standard equipment, and this was the traction control of the launch model in Europe. In the US, electronic traction assists were part of the menu. The rack-and-pinion hydraulic power-steering layout also improved via the chassis changes, BMW admitted, adding, "A variable transmission ratio ensures better response." The result was not a critical success to European—particularly British—tastes, and

was the most criticized aspect at the debut drive debriefings. Even for the apparently happy US-bound M3s, both camber angles were increased on cars shipped after 1995, while the 3.2-liter removed a little caster in favor of a sharp increase in caster angles, further promoting feedback to the driver.

One of the most consistently outstanding features of all M3s has been the brakes. Compared to the 325i, the Euro-specification M3 deployed 315-mm (12.4-inch) diameter discs instead of the 2.5-liter's 286-mm (11.26-inch), coupled with a generous 1.1-inch (28-mm) disc thickness. At the rear, it was the same story, with the M3 running 312-mm (13.36-inch) diameters coupled with 20-mm (0.79-inch) depths, while the contemporary 325i wore 280-mm (11-inch) diameters with skinnier 10-mm (0.4-inch) rotors.

Just as important to the consistent stop time of 124 mph in 2.8 seconds at under 130 yards was the upgraded Teves ABS anti-lock system on all models. Add an enlarged master cylinder and a 10-inch brake servo, and you can understand why an M3 could virtually halve its 0–60 mph times in the braking zones.

The winding hilly roads of Majorca provided a perfect environment for journalists to sample the new M3.

Photo: Author, Majorca, Spain, 1992

The most desirable collectors' model for the US: the lightweight M3 for 1995–96 retained the standard 240 bhp, but was the only M3 under a 3,000-lb curb weight.

Photo: Klaus Schnitzer, US

Modest Exterior

Externally, the later M3 was not so radical as its parents, displaying no fundamental body changes. There were, however, extended side sills which helped mask the wider track and fatter rear wheels and thus preserve some decency in the aerodynamic Cd ('drag factor') quotation.

The front-spoiler/under-bumper area was notably reworked to provide an extended vertical air dam in body colors. The M3 also sported quite an aggressive black splitter beneath that dam and enlarged under-bumper air intake. At the rear, there was no counter-balancing trunk spoiler, but the body beneath the back bumper had also gone lower and enveloped a brace of chrome-tipped exhaust stubs. Unseen but effective were underbelly aero-shrouds, which proved to be as vulnerable as the wheels when *Car and Driver* went testing.

According to then-BMW M-Brand product manager Martin Hainge, there was a plan to identify the M3 with a grille badge and a headlight or exhaust motif. An M3 badge insert to the grille only made early "banana yellow" versions of the 1/43rd scale styling model.

"Nothing is allowed to compromise the kidney grille," said Hainge of this pre-production shift in external identity.

That search for a separate identity led to some strong paint schemes: "Dakar Yellow" was best known in the initial European batch, but also popular were "Avus Blue" and "Mugello Red," all named after motorsport events. Less obvious were M3 plaques set into the side rubbing strips and the door kick plates, plus M3 logos on the back trunk panel and either side of the front wings. There were unique aerodynamic "clam" racing mirrors, necessary to claim 0.32 cd with far fatter wheels, and a wider track, than the rest of the line.

Other M3 identification points were most pronounced in the cockpit. The seats were unique, offering extensive shoulder and torso support. They had adjustable backrests that were formed in two sections, catering for differing shoulder widths.

European seats were trimmed in Amaretta (similar to suede-cloth). Leather seating was always a feature of US-shipped E36 M3s, but could be ordered in black, anthracite, silver gray, or (for Europe) Lotus White. Europeans were also offered the far more expensive option of covering every conceivable interior surface with leather.

All E36 M3s were specified with an airbag steering wheel. The special Lightweights came with that dull four-spoke steering wheel, and a three-spoke M Technic leather-rim sports wheel was put firmly on the European option list at launch.

M3 dials carried on the red-needle theme and continued to offer an oil-temperature gauge in place of the econometer in markets outside America. An M-logo was inset in the 8,000 rpm tachometer and an M-stripe decorated the five-speed manual shift lever, but the wheels carried BMW Roundels and were boldly embossed with "BMW MOTORSPORT." The price of all this sophisticated speed in Germany was 80,000 Dm; for the US, the sticker was initially $36,500, while Brits paid over £32,500 for the 1993 RHD derivative.

Evolutionary Production

The variations on an M3 theme almost echoed the proliferation of the mainstream 3 Series variations. The first batch of 470 coupes was made starting in April 1994 at Regensberg, where all E36 M3 production was concentrated. A similar number (463) of M3 coupes were made in June 1993 for right-drive Britain; and the first five American specification M3 coupes were produced in December 1993, with mass-production of more than 3,700 units following in 1994.

Of the major M3 body choices that followed the M3 coupe, both the European Convertible and sedan entered production in 1994 (March and October, respectively); but the American M3 sedan was not manufactured in any volume until

The full M3 line, offering a trio of body styles (left to right, Convertible, sedan, coupe) was not produced until 1994 in Europe. These are the 1995 model year European Evolution examples.

Photo: Klaus Schnitzer, Spain, 1994

1996, and production did not exceed 2,000 units until 1997. The US Convertible did not enter volume production until 1998, but was also the last M3 variant to leave the Regensberg lines, still being manufactured in June 1999.

The most significant M3 in terms of image, impact, and pure driving thrills was the 1995 European Evo coupe, although its 321-bhp powertrain hitched to an H-pattern six-sped gearbox was also sold across Europe in Convertible and sedan bodies.

This coupé did not look different, but the enlarged slant six punched out more than 100 bhp a liter. The coupe lost a little weight with a pair of pricey aluminum doors that were also fitted to the Evo Convertibles but not the four-door sedans, which remained an average 97 lbs lighter than their M3 coupe counterparts. BMW official spec sheet figures for the coupe reported a weight savings of 24 kg (52.8 lbs) per door and a curb weight of 1,515 kg (3,340 lbs). However, US true weights were reported at 3,175 lbs for coupe and sedan.

The stealth version of M3's blitzing 321-bhp European Evo was the four-door sedan. In the US in 1997–98, this four-door, at the usual 240 bhp, was the most popular M3 variant of all.

Photo: BMW GB, 1996

Unlike the lesser sixes, even the Evo retained an iron cylinder block, but it ran 86.4 x 91 mm bore and stroke for 3,201 cc instead of 2,990 cc. Inlet valve sizes went up just a millimeter (from 35 to 36 mm, or 1.42 inches) and the individual throttle body injection retained appropriately matched intake tracts. The compression ratio went up (11.3:1 instead of 10.8:1) and owners were advised to feed it 98-octane unleaded.

The big story was not the hardware but the electronic management, which extended to command the variable valve timing (VANOS) for the Evo. Co-developed by BMW and A. G. Siemens as the MSS50 (Motor Sport S50) system, BMW claimed it was "the first car maker to create its own independent management system."

This was not totally true, but BMW Motorsport had learned enough to program its own wares. Road or track, the main BMW company would become increasingly independent for its electronic systems.

For the Evo M3 customer, MSS50 and the overdrive (0.83) sixth gear meant improved fuel consumption throughout a wide speed range, alongside a 35 bhp bonus. Official Imperial fuel-consumption figures were given as 16.7 mpg Urban through 37.7 Extra Urban , with a combined result of 25.7 mpg.

BMW declared that 100.3 bhp a liter resulted in a total 321 bhp at a rousing 7,000 to 7,400 rpm. That was coupled to 350 Nm (258 lb-ft) of torque by just 3,250 rpm, compared to the origi-

The M3 soft-top was as civilized as the rest of the 3 Series Convertibles.

Photo: BMW GB, 1997

The European Evo coupe delivered 0–60 mph in just over 5 seconds and shaved 1.5 seconds from both 0–100-mph and 0–120-mph times.

Photo: BMW GB, 1997

nal's 3,600-rpm peak. Furthermore, over 340 Nm (250 lb-ft) was delivered between 2,600 and 6,200 rpm, for even better flexibility. The Evo delivered 0–62 mph in 5.5 seconds (5.3 seconds for the 96.8 lb lighter sedan) and the usual 155-mph limited maximum.

In describing some of the Evo's chassis changes, BMW trumpeted that, "Both dampers and springs are all new." BMW had also tightened up the rest of the chassis settings and ditched variable ratio steering in favor of a linear rack that officially cut lock-to-lock from 3.3 to 3.25 turns. More importantly, it made the car feel direct, no longer squirming and rocking unevenly from understeer to oversteer, but pinned-down at the front until the final inevitability of power-driven oversteer took over in the lower gears. BMW commented that the steering geometry changes mentioned earlier would "increase feel," but added that the variable levels of power assistance retained previous values.

The most important Evo change—one that did not make it across the Atlantic for product liability reasons—was the transplant of late-model M5 (E34/3.8) front brakes. These combined an aluminum disc cover and gray cast-iron friction ring, usually labeled "floating" action in racing. The advantages were said to be a longer service life for all brake components through improved heat dissipation.

Externally, only clear indicator glasses and body-color grilles told the European Evo tale. New colors came on stream, including a violent Techno Violet, Byzantium (plum), and the beautiful metallic-tagged Estoril Blue. The 1996 English language/German-sourced M3 brochure offered nine color selections: three were non-metallic (Alpine White, Dakar Yellow, and Bright Red); and Arctic Silver, Cosmos Black, and Boston Green were particularly popular among metallics.

In Europe, where fabrics were still offered, the material was now labeled M-Cross/Amaretta, while the option list now had three leather types (two Nappa selections, one Buffalo) and there were eight interior color choices.

The European Evo went over to unequal widths on both tire and cast-alloy wheel dimensions: the 7.5-inch front and 8.5-inch rear combination would carry the beneficial handling effects of narrower front tires with taller profiles (225/45ZR-17) than the 245/40 ZR-17s of the rear. All coupes came with temporary spare wheels to restore some luggage capacity. In Britain, the standard coupe road wheel was the original M-style Double Spoke II, while Convertibles sat on M Style Double Spokes (five-spoke) and saloons (sedans) came with slotted M Contour II.

In Europe, the standard specification included the third (high-level) brake light imported from the US, along with an auto-dim mirror. Other key standard European equipment included the limited-slip differential, driver's airbag only (passenger side was an option), on-board computer that also controlled the ventilation (air conditioning was strictly a $1,500-plus option), central locking with a sophisticated immobilizer, green tinted glass, adjustable steering column rake adjustment, and visible VIN.

SMG Evolution

Toward the end of the Evolution M3's European sales life (March 1997 onward), after the M3 sedan had been discontinued in Europe, the SMG (Sequentially M Gearbox) was heavily promoted. It had the potential to realize a performance street-driving dream as the perfect alliance between manual gearbox driving pleasure, backed by an automatic action for relaxed city and urban sprawl crawl.

The renamed BMW M GmbH (the commercial arm of the 25-year-old BMW Motorsport) took the H-pattern six-speed normally used on European Evo M3s and mated it with a sophisticated, computer-managed set of high-pressure hydraulics to shift the gears automatically without a clutch, or at the sequential command of a central inline gear lever.

SMG Technical Manager Wolfgang Nehse adapted the usual Getrag six-speed with a unique Fichtel and Sachs clutch under the command of expanded MSS50 engine management electronics. There was a separate SMG control unit, linked via bus data transmission, to exchange data with the engine management system up to 100 times a second.

Using potentiometer and micro switches, the SMG unit could detect whether the center shift lever was in its Sport or Economy mode. As an additional benefit, the factory was also able to tailor the shift programs for specific markets. Shifts were executed by SMG control, comanding magnetic valves within a high-pressure hydraulics system that sent fluid into the clutch master cylinder. Hydraulic cylinders were activated by magnetic valves in the transmission's hydraulic unit. The shift itself came from those cylinders, which turned the main internal gearbox shaft to the relevant shift level, moving the shaft up or down for the appropriate ratio. The hydraulic actuators and valves were attached externally, leaving the Getrag gearbox "almost identical in design and structure to the conventional manual gearbox," said BMW.

Although the ratios remained unchanged, the final drive for SMG was a 3.23:1 ratio, compared to the manual's 3.15:1 (which had been installed in Europe since the start of the 3-liter M3). Declared curb weight at introduction in an alloy-door coupe was 1,535 kg (3,384 lbs), meaning that SMG added around 44 lbs (20 kg).

Although the transmission had driving drawbacks, it was undeniably efficient. Fuel consumption remained unaffected on official figures and in practice.

At that time, the SMG shift cost £1,735 in Britain (around $2,800 at prevailing exchange rates) and was better-liked by customers than by the media, with some 53 percent of all German buyers specifying the SMG system.

BMW claimed that top speed was unaffected and the official acceleration figures (including 0–60 mph in 5.5 seconds for the SMG coupe) were also unchanged.

The additional SMG electro-hydraulic gearbox, lines, controls, and reservoirs added around 44 lbs to the curb weight of the European Evo M3, quoted at a total of almost 3,400 lbs.

Photo: BMW AG Presse, 1998

European Evo M3's pulled over 7,000 rpm and 160 mph top speeds, despite official 155 mph limiters. SMG acceleration would drop by half a second or so compared to the best manual shift drivers, simply because the automated and elongated upshifts occupy around 0.8 seconds each.

American Sales Story

The American M3 started from a different base than that of Europe. For the pricing reasons discussed earlier, the motorized heart of the US M3 had to be a much cheaper, less-powerful unit. But with that motor change—and a subsequent 3.2-liter development—the M3 for the US developed its own character, positioned between the 328is and European M3, but technically based on the iron-block 325is motor (M50) rather than the later alloy-block 2.8-liter M52.

That meant a 2-mm increase in bore and a significant 10.8-mm boost in stroke, which brought the US motor virtually "all square" at 86 x 85.8 mm and 2,990 cc, exactly as for the original 286-bhp Euro M3. Compression fell slightly, however, (10.5:1) to suit 91-octane unleaded premium fuel grades in 50-State format.

Hardware moves included ditching the individual throttles and recalibrating the inlet valve-only version of early VANOS to boost top-end

E36 M3, US six-cylinder sales		
Year	Units sold	M3 types sold
1994	2,953	US 240-bhp E36 debut season, as model year 1995
1995	5,806	Includes 43 Lightweights and 1,311 automatic M3s
1996	3,175	Includes 79 Lightweights and 299 automatic M3s
1997	7,940	New sedan four-door M3 outsells coupe, 4,535 to 3,405
1998	8,762	Four-door sells most at 3,225, while Convertible sells 2,876 and the rest are coupes
1999	6,557	Run-out year, with only Convertible (3,335 sold) fully available
Total	35,193	All M3 types, 1994–1999

The 3.2-liter American M3 engine remained rated at 240 bhp, but was even more flexible to drive than the earlier 3-liter US unit.

Photo: Jonathan A. Stein

The dash layouts between the European Evo in LHD specification (thus the 280 km/h speedo) and the right-drive SMG sequential-transmission model are contrasted. The gear-selection indicator for the SMG box replaced the oil-temperature gauge (where the econometer would be in the US model).

Photos: BMW AG Presse, 1998; BMW GB, 1998

bias. Engine rpm was restricted to 6,500 in all but first and second gears, where 6,800 was allowed. The result was 240 bhp at 6,000 rpm and 225 lb-ft of torque at 4,250 rpm, the latter a near 25 percent increase over contemporary 325is. It also made the unit suitable for the subsequent US-only automatic transmission option and cooperated happily with the Getrag Type C manual five-speed, with direct (1:1) top gear running the European 3.15:1 final drive.

Stated performance claims were confined to a 6.1-second dash over 0–60 mph and the electronically limited 137-mph maximum. Our averaged independent data shows these were fair claims, but one magazine (*Car and Driver*) recorded far

faster figures—including 0–60 mph in 5.6 seconds. The magazines returned anywhere from 22 to 24 US mpg versus EPA/BMW NA figures of 18 City/28 Highway mpg. There were those in Europe who commented that brutal power delivery of their Evo 3.2 could take a 20-bhp slash and be a lot better for street driving. The US translation may have lost too much top-end bhp for European tastes, but the American-spec M3 3.2 was a fine everyday flexible friend.

The basic M3 pattern of upgraded strut front and central-link rear axle with upgraded components survived the trip across the Atlantic, along with "BMW MOTORSPORT"-branded 17-inch diameter ten-spoke alloy wheels in 7.5-inch rim configuration, front and rear. Tires on early 3-liter test cars all seemed to be the Michelin ZRs in the 235/40 size.

Springs and dampers were recalibrated for the US and the revised anti-roll bar location plus thicker bars also made it to the US. Along with a multi-plate ZF limited-slip differential with no electronic traction control assists, the American M3's handling earned praise far beyond the early European response. Measured G-forces on the skid pad—not a feature of European track testing—ran from 0.86 G to 0.90 G on Michelin MXX3 tires.

The big brakes (12.4- and 12.3-inch rotors) also formed part of the US specification and won praise equal to that of the chassis. *Road & Track* measured acceleration and braking at at 0–100–0 mph in a fraction over 20 seconds, formerly the preserve of supercars costing up to three times the M3 sticker price.

Although officially a 1995 model, the M3 coupe was announced by BMW NA at $35,800 (plus $470 destination charges) after its debut at the January 1994 Detroit Auto show. Externally, it was the European model, right down to the location of M3 badges and those cast-alloys with an optional tail spoiler. Of the six colors offered in the US, four were unique to the M3.

Internally, the same multi-adjustable seat frames as for the European model were apparent, but Nappa leather was a big showroom plus. Unlike in Europe, air conditioning was standard, as was the 200-Watt, ten-speaker stereo. The US model was prewired for a six-disc CD autochanger, but the unit itself was not included. At no cost, you could opt for the Amaretta suede cabin finish that was standard in Europe.

In the initial 1995 model year, cruise control ($455 packaged with fog lights) and an electric sunroof ($1,120) were the only listed options. Selling nearly 3,000 units in 1994, the M3 gained many options in January 1995 and the base price was elevated to $37,950. For the first time on any

BMW M-car, $1,200 would add a ZF 5-Speed automatic transmission with choice of manual, economy or sports modes.

BMW NA claimed 0–60 mph in just about a second longer than a manual (6.9 versus 6.1 seconds). It also reported that EPA tests allowed another one mpg around town (19) and the overdrive fifth gear equalled highway returns for the manual at 28 mpg. *Car and Driver* confirmed that an M3 automatic returned "fine fuel economy—24 mpg, the same as the stick-shift M3."

C/D also supplied a chart that is valuable not for their manual-shift M3 times—which they acknowledged were very rapid and were later unable to match with a 700-mile Lightweight—but also provide the only independent readout of the four-door M3 automatic sedan.

Car and Driver US M3 Test Performance Test		
	Manual	**Automatic**
0 to 30 mph	1.9 sec	2.6 sec
0 to 60 mph	5.5 sec	6.7 sec
0 to 100 mph	14.7 sec	17.1 sec
0 to 130 mph	28.7 sec	34.5 sec
1/4-mile	14.2 sec	15.3 sec
	@ 98 mph	@ 95 mph

Other options released in January 1995 and running through that elongated 1995 model year included a massive $3,000 Premium/Luxury package. This parceled up seven major features, from power front seats to M-Contour alloy wheels (forged alloy five-spokes, were sold at $1,450 separately), M-wood trim, leather for door and side panel inserts, cruise control, and the on board computer.

The M3 Lightweight

In 1995 and 1996, American M3 sales totals included the most radical attempt at a low-weight 3 Series to date. Exclusive to the American market, the M3 Lightweight sold 122 units (43 the first year, the balance in 1996), although the anticipated quota was originally 85.

The Lightweight ran exactly the same 3-liter/240-bhp motor and five-speed transmission as its contemporaries but had a "Racer's Edge," stripping out many of its civilized aspects to reach a coupe curb weight—according to *Motor Trend*—2,950 lbs. That weight is some 225 lbs less than the official curb weight claimed for the 1995 model year M3 coupe in US trim.

Out went the air conditioning, sound insulation, radio, and many power assists, including the window lifts. There was no sunroof, the trunk was bare of trim, including the floor panel, and the carpeting got meaner as well as leaner. Leather was ditched in favor of cloth or carbon-fiber trims, and aerodynamics were enhanced.

Gains included alloy skin doors, and the forged five-spoke 17-inch wheels with 8.5-inch rear rims coupled with the usual 7.5-inch fronts and equal tire sizing, front to back. The most noticeable changes were the twin-pylon rear wing and extended front spoiler/splitter. Another hidden benefit was the under-shielding paneling, which cut aerodynamic drag.

A low axle ratio of 3.23:1 and the weight loss noticeably boosted acceleration. *Motor Trend* noted, "It was 0.9 second quicker 0–60 mph than the previous M3 we tested (5.3 seconds versus 6.2 seconds) and 0.7 seconds better over the quarter mile (13.9 seconds at 99.6 mph compared with the regular version's 14.6 seconds at 97 mph)." Top speed, however, remained governed to 137 mph.

Test Lightweights went out without any fine-tuning to meet the lower weight and increased aerodynamic appendages. Strong understeer was reported in handling tests on standard 235 ZRs. Since the diet-conscious Bimmer was made to meet IMSA street/stock racing rules and the first batch of 85 were pre-ordered, there was no reason to sort it out, since everything would be tuned to each track and differing tire/wheel combinations anyway.

US M3, 1996 Onward

For model year 1996, the M3 was back with a larger (3.2-liter) motor, a $38,960 base price, and a substantially upgraded chassis. Much of this handling improvement was inspired by the European Evo. However, the two 3.2-liters were not the same, and the power gap between the two models widened dramatically to 81 bhp.

The American unit retained its 240-bhp rating while Europe went up to 321 horsepower, but the transatlantic torque figures were not so far apart, at 236 lb-ft for the US unit versus 258 lb-ft in Europe. The chart on the next page helps sort out some of the other key differences in the apparently similar 3.2-liter M3s on either side of the Atlantic.

The bigger US engine involved stretching that S50US base into S52US, still with an iron block. There was an 0.4-mm-larger bore and a 4.1-mm-larger stroke, coming in at 49 cc smaller than the European motor. Maximum horsepower was shunned in favor of a 5 percent torque increase at 450 rpm lower than pre-1996 model year 3-liters. Other US motor changes for the 3.2-liters included reduced mass for the valve gear components (lifters, springs, and seats) stainless steel headers in place of the cast-iron manifolding, and finer tolerances for camshaft balance. As before, the 6,800-rpm limit was allowed in the first two manual ratios, with 6,500 retained as the limit otherwise.

A 3.2 US M3 was a very pleasant engine to handle and had enough top-end performance to entertain. BMW NA claimed the torque increase sliced 0–60 mph from 6.1 to 5.9 seconds, but

1997: UK M3 vs. US M3

Prices*	UK M3 coupe £38,446 ($65,358)	US coupe, $40,270 (£23,688)
	UK M3 Convertible £44,015 ($74,825)	US Convertible $46,470 (£27,335)
Motor:	Iron block, alloy head, DOHC, 24v	Iron block, alloy head, DOHC, 24v
	Double Vanos variable valve timing	Variable intake valve timing
	Individual throttles	Conventional 325/328 thermoplastic intake system
	MSS50 BMW Siemens ECU	Siemens DME MS41.2
Compression	11.3:1	10.5:1
Bore x stroke	86.4 x 91.0	86.4 x 89.6mm
Capacity	3,201 cc	3,152 cc
Power	321 bhp @ 7,400 rpm	240 bhp @ 6,000 rpm
Torque	258 lb-ft @ 3,250 rpm	236 lb-ft @ 3,800 rpm
Transmission (rear drive)	Either six-speed manual or SMG six-speed	Either ZF5HP18 auto or Getrag five-speed manual
	Manual 3.15:1 final drive	3.32 and 3.38:1 US automatics
	Multiple-plate limited-slip differential	Multiple-plate limited-slip differential with All Season Traction control (AST) electronics later in run
Curb weight	3,236 lbs (coupes)	3,175 lbs (coupes)
Suspension	Upgraded E36 struts front, multi-link rear principles with replacement springs and dampers, unique anti-roll bars	Upgraded E36 struts front, multi- link rear principles with replacement springs and dampers, unique anti-roll bars
Wheels & tires	M-Style Double Spoke II 7.5 (F) and 8.5 (R) x 17 with Michelin	As Europe, but US Dunlop 225/45 ZR [F] & 245/40 ZR [R]
Brakes	12.4-inch (F) and 12.3-inch vented with Teves ABS	12.4 in. (F) and 12.3 in. vented with ABS anti-lock
Top speed	Electronically restricted to 155 mph	137 mph
0–60 mph	5.2 seconds	6.4 seconds
Fuel consumption	Our results in 1998: 27.3 Imp. Mpg [22.7 US] of 98-octane unleaded	Our results 1998: 23 US mpg of 93-octane

*£-to-US$ rate was £1=$1.70 at this time.

other key figures appeared unaltered, save that the importers reported a 1-mpg gain on the EPA economy estimates at 20 City mpg.

One piece of hardware which took a leave of absence in model year 1996 was the automatic transmission. BMW NA explained, "The M3 is offered only with the five-speed manual transmission, a heavy duty ZF that is unchanged from 1995. The five-speed automatic transmission that was offered in 1995 M3s will return for 1997 in refined form." Another power transmission change was the standard incorporation of traction control.

As noted, the European chassis upgrades for the Evo made it across to the US, including a slightly quicker steering ratio, but the system was still described as a variable ratio, as for the pre-1995 Evo in Europe. Wheels and tires changed to a standard M Double Spoke II with the same unequal 225/45 and 245/40 ZR-17 dimensions noted for the European Evo.

Equipment upgrades for model year 1996 extended to automatic climate control, with the usual individual settings for each side of the cockpit, and larger controls allied to a red LED readout of temperatures and fan boost levels set. The audio system fascia panel was also redesigned at this point with an enlarged display, for radio station presets, and a weather band facility. The sound-system option was a Harmon Kardon super premium system, which upgraded performance of all ten speakers and boosted peak output to 320 rather than 200 Watts at a cost of $675.

There were a number of additional security enhancements (center locking switch on the console, freewheels for the exterior locks, transponder ignition key, simplified remote control), all of which proved effective in dramatically dropping theft rates.

External cosmetic moves for this model year covered black for the central front air inlet (under bumper) and the factory installed—rather than dealer—option of a rear spoiler (carrying third brake light) at $650. A Luxury Pack was introduced at mid-year. For $3,300, there were many of the previous Premium Pack items available. It is most easily identified by the wood trim accents on center console, dashboard, and interior body panels, with chrome interior door handles and leather insert panels in door and side trim. The practical benefits included cruise control, eight-way power front seats, computer, and the M Contour II wheels.

The 1997–98 calendar years saw M3 sales peak at 7,940 and 8,762 units respectively, with a new sedan four-door M3 outselling the coupe and the M3 convertible selling by the thousand in the latter season as well. The 1997 model year M3 was little altered, but the sedan bowed in at the same $39,380 base price as the coupe. *Autoweek* (March 3, 1997) dubbed the latest M3 as, "The best sedan in the world for less than $40,000."

The significant technical introduction in 1997 was of aluminum/cast-iron mixed-compound brake rotors (as featured in the 1995 Evo) with their floating hub action, improved service, and performance efficiencies. The standard wheels remained a 17-inch by 7.5- and 8.5-inch widths, but in M Double Spoke

For the M3 Convertible, the hood was lined, and full power assistance was provided standard along with the automatic rollover protection system.

Photo: Author, Hancock Shaker Village, US, 1998

II. The luxury package continued to be offered at $3,300, with the "high-gloss walnut trim" and more functional items retained.

As promised, the automatic transmission option (still $1,200) returned, but was confined only to the sedan. The ZF

The M3 future was previewed at the 1999 Frankfurt and 2000 Geneva auto shows. This is the 1999 German show car with blacked out windows and no interior.

Photo: BMW Press, Germany/UK, 1999

five-speed with three shift modes was now coded 5HP18 and carried a raised (3.38:1) final drive, as well as retaining the overdriven fifth gear (0.74:1).

For model year 1998, all M3s—and there were now three—clambered over the $40,000 barricade. Whereas the coupe and sedan were only just past forty Gs at $40,270, the ultimate price combination of the Convertible body and M3 running gear came in at $46,470. For that price, you got the usual US 240-bhp power train and overhauled chassis capabilities, but the suspension was not so radically lowered as other models, with just 0.3 reported as "the chop."

The Convertible element was modified over other 3 Series in that the hood was lined, with full power assistance provided (as was the case on later 328iC), and the rollover protection system became standard. Note that the central locking system on the M3 Convertible latched not just the doors, trunk, and fuel flap, but also the glovebox.

The three-spoke M Technic steering wheel made its debut on the Convertible M3, while the option list contained the usual M items plus the

$2,200 aluminum hardtop and minus the $650 rear spoiler of other M3s. The $1,200 automatic transmission option was also available with the soft top.

Despite its sales success, out-ranking the coupe in the US market in the full model years it was offered, the M3 sedan was unlisted for model year 1999. That left the M3 coupe and Convertible on offer at their 1998 model year prices as of August 1998.

By the close of the 1999 calendar year, BMW NA had sold a stunning 35,193 M3s, or around half the total 71,279 units manufactured. Now all the E46 successors were in place, except for the M3 and Convertibles, with the Touring set to form a new (to US) 3 Series choice.

Through 1998–2000, BMW M GmbH developed an even more powerful E46 successor to the M3 (too late for detailed inclusion in this book). The Good News was that the full 3245 cc would come to the US at a minimum of *330* bhp in 2001. We have squeezed caption pictures of the new M3 from page 290 onward, and the author's driving impressions can be found in *Roundel* magazine, November 2000.

24 The US Racing M3: From Under-Developed to Underdog

The PTG-prepared M3 raced in the US for five E36 seasons with mixed results.

The BMW racing M3 ran for five US racing seasons prepared by Prototype Technology Group (PTG) preparation of Winchester, Virginia. From its headquarters in Woodcliff Lake, NJ, on December 22, 1999, BMW NA reflected upon this ultimately happy union:

"The BMW M3 completed its fifth successful season of sports-car racing in North America, despite the challenges presented by a new series and transitions in car specifications.

"Since its introduction in 1995, the BMW M3 has consistently topped the field in GT and GTS sports-car racing. It has amassed 33 pole positions, 32 victories, six podium [1–2–3] sweeps, 82 podium finishes, and 130 top-10 finishes in 52 races. BMW M3s have set 28 track records and 19 fastest race laps.

"BMW has scored 11 sports-car GT championships with the M3 in five years, including four manufacturer championships [1996, 1997, and two in 1998] and three driver titles [Bill Auberlen of Redondo Beach, CA in 1997, Mark Simo of Carlsbad, CA in 1998, and Ross Bentley of Vancouver, BC in 1998]. Tom Milner's Winchester, Va.-based Prototype Technology Group, which runs BMW Team PTG, has topped the team ranks four times [1997, twice in 1998, and 1999].

"This year [1999], BMW competed in the new American Le Mans Series and in the United States Road Racing Championship. Although the BMW M3 was chasing a Porsche built to year-2000 specifications and was constrained by 17 rule changes, it still garnered two pole positions, four victories, a podium sweep, 16 podium finishes and 29 top-10 finishes. BMW Team PTG won its fourth team title, set a qualifying record, and recorded two fastest race laps.

"'We have enjoyed quite a bit of success over the past five years, and look forward to pushing the competition hard in the coming season,'"

251

said Richard Brekus, manager, product planning and strategy for BMW of North America, Inc.

Behind the brave words lay a disappointing 1999 season in which Porsche had finally re-established their supremacy under a constantly changing rulebook. To upset the previous PTG-BMW M3 supremacy, Porsche private teams ran the latest 996 development of the 911 theme, which proved to be unbeatable in a straight fight.

Having stomped over all comers from 1996–98, PTG was left to pick up the 1999 places. The 2000 season saw a more powerful (420 bhp) and lighter E46 from PTG in the US, England, and Germany. Still, the results were usually dominated by Porsches, so for 2001, both PTG and Schnitzer were armed with V8 pacing variants. The Good News is that a showroom V8 3 Series is on the way.

At the 1994 Nürburgring 24 Hours, BMW entered a pair of 340-bhp "Dream Team" M3s for Jochen Neerpasch and Hubert Hahne—neither finished.

Photo: Author, Germany, 1994

Once Upon a Time…

The M3 got off to a very shaky racing start when its intended role as a 2.5-liter, six-cylinder E36 in the 1993 domestic German series abruptly canceled in late 1992. The M3 was a low-key winner in a subdued national German GT series of 1993 prior to restoring the American BMW national racing reputation during 1995–99.

The late February 1992 issue of the 2.5-liter rules, and interminable arguments over engine location, led BMW Motorsport to contest—and win—the lesser ADAC German GT Championship with an M3 GT. BMW abruptly abandoned its national German sedan racing series for the first time in over thirty years. BMW Motorsport engineer Karsten Engel explained, "The first development of the new M3 was made almost completely useless for us by the constant changes in German regulations.

It was late February before we could see the definite rules, and that meant we had to start again on most aspects of the car. This applied especially to the new six-cylinder engine, which was to be completely new, as the road car is 3 liters and we are limited to 2.5 liters."

In 1993 in Germany, an allowed curb weight of just 1,000 kg was mandated, so new M3 racing performance should have been spectacular. Horsepower was expected to top 400 bhp and the later body shape should have boosted maximum competition straight-line speeds beyond 180 mph.

Group N international homologation for the European-motor M3 of 3 liters/286 bhp was achieved by spring 1993. The M3 became an extremely effective privateer 3- and 3.2-liter production racer across Europe. It was a regular winner—even when the factory used 2-liter SuperTourers—in Germany's annual Nürburgring 24 Hours (last winning in 1997).

Most customers went for the Group N version, a very lightly tuned (300 bhp) 3-liter, that could be little modified. The interior trim could be stripped and slick racing tires were allowed,

The spartan, but highly functional M3 cockpit with and without the detachable steering wheel. We also show the mass of alloy and composite fabrication that feeds air to the race-hot brakes and motor Our thanks to PTG for allowing such close candor.

Photos: Klaus Schnitzer, Virginia, US, 1999

but the body had to remain stock and all modifications were either banned or subject to very small production tolerances.

The six-cylinder M3 was an outright winner in so many production races that a Junior 2-liter class for privateers in the production classes became the norm across Belgium and Britain in the late 1990s. This suited Honda's Integra-R and Peugeot's quasi-works 306 GTI S16; and neither of BMW's E36 or E46 factory kits were sufficient to make an lasting impact in this less radically-engineered category. The final insult came when the 1999 Spa 24 Hours did not go to a BMW for the first time in the 1990s and Peugeot scored a 1–2–3 result.

The factory fielded its first M3s in a low-key domestic ADAC (Germany's biggest auto club)

GT Championship. BMW Motorsport entered Venezuelan expat Johnny Cecotto in a wild-looking M3 conservatively engineered at 325 bhp. It was more fuel-efficient and sustained a better pace than turbo Porsche and Ford opposition, but BMW personnel dismissed that 1993 achievement as the result of a proper factory team with a talented driver simply achieving their goals.

The ADAC GT Championship was dubbed "Festival of Great Makes." BMW decided that the six-cylinder M3 was right for the job, and proved the point by securing the initial eight-race ADAC GT title. It took the combination of Johnny Cecotto and a fractionally overbored M3 GTR deviant.

Germany's *auto motor und sport* magazine dubbed M3 GT's appearance the "Schwarzenegger

Rated at 380 bhp, the long-stroke 3.2-liter was revised for the 2000 racing M3 at 420 bhp, both peaking at 8200 rpms. Also on view, the intake system, quad-valve heads, and weight-matched reciprocating parts.

Photos: Klaus Schnitzer, Virginia, US, 1999

BMW M3 five-year US racing summary*

Year	Races	Poles	Wins	1–2–3	Top 3	Top 10	Fastest laps	Records
1995	7	1	0	0	3	7	0	1 qual
1996	10	7	4	1	14	25	4	7 qual, 3 race
1997	11	7	9	4	22	37	3	5 qual, 3 race
1998	13	16	15	0	27	32	10	5 qual, 3 race
1999	11	2	4	1	16	29	2	1 qual
Total	52	33	32	6	82	130	19	28

*Also note: 11 National Championship titles were won, including 1996 IMSA GTS-2 Manufacturer; 1997 SportsCar GTS-3 Manufacturer, Team, and Driver (Bill Auberlen); 1998 SportsCar GT3 Manufacturer, Team, and Driver (Mark Simo); USRRC GT3 Manufacturer, Team, and Driver (Ross Bentley); 1999 American Le Mans Series GT Team; and (non-PTG) 1998 One Lap of America, Fourth overall/class win for Roy Hopkins/Nancy Becker using 318i-badged E36 with Euro-spec 3-liter/286-bhp M3 motor! BMW CCA member Russ Wiles also performed with honor in one-lap events, and remains a club winner in his M3 E.

Look." This body style was applied to a limited-production run of German road-registered, all-white M3 GTRs. They were distinguished by wheel arch extensions and side sills that utilized 18-inch diameter BBS (10-inch-wide fronts, 11-inch rears) with 245/40 or 285/35 ZR tires.

The M3 GT price was DM 250,000 in the winter of 1993, but you needed to pay more to have your street 286-bhp rebuilt as a 325-bhp GTR competition motor, which also boosted torque 6 percent. Although it was a mild 15 percent power boost, the motor featured fundamental changes to suit the power-to-weight formula. The primary move was an 86.35-mm bore in place of the production 86-mm, which bumped displacement to some 3,018 cc. Compression escalated from 10.8:1 to 12:1, the motor drew breath through a competition air filter, and there were new Bosch digital electronics. The power band was moved from the M3's docile 3,600-rpm torque peak to a 5,500-rpm summit, with 8,000 rpm as the upper limit and 7,000 rpm for peak horsepower.

BMW then added a sequential six-speed gear-box for the works GTRs. In total, three optional five-speed and six-speed boxes as well as three final-drive ratios were homologated. BMW used Teves race ABS anti-lock braking, enormous steel disc brakes, and Uniball joints for a suspension that retained production principles but was—like the contemporary race 318i—fabricated for the job. The big brakes were required not so much for the performance of the car, but for the arduous task of repeatedly stopping its 1,300-kg (2,860-lb) allotted race minimum weight. The M3 GTR motor was a little more powerful because the ADAC regulations balanced power-to-weight ratios to bring a wide variety to the grid.

The ADAC GT debut at Avus-Berlin saw wall-to-wall Porsches of varying preparation standards and types meet Honda's NSX, Wolf Racing Ford Escort Cosworths, a swift Abt Audi, and even a Callaway Corvette. All those marques appeared in the final top ten and Honda was just as seriously prepared as BMW. But in the end, 1993 BMW factory drivers Cecotto and Kris Nissen came in 1–2!

The front and rear assemblies showing the Brembo 8-piston caliper at the steering end of things and the stripped-to-the-hub rear.

Photos: Klaus Schnitzer, Virginia, US, 1999

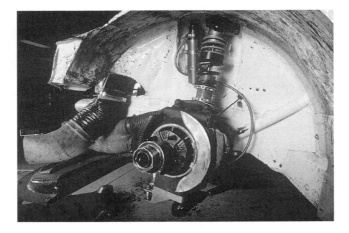

est annual outings to the Nürburgring 24 Hours with the M3 sixes, and 300-bhp customer M3s in showroom (Group N) race stock trim. For the June 1994 Nürburgring 24 Hours, BMW decided to field a brace of modified (around 340 bhp) M3s for what they called "BMW Dream Team Super Oldies" to race around the old 'Ring layout. One such M3 was averaging over 95 mph and was fourth fastest overall—just eight seconds slower than the best of the works drivers could manage in the pole-sitting 318i 2-liter factory entry.

The season was not a walkover, for Honda and Armin Hahne did a consistent job in the normally-aspirated Honda NSX, and the turbo Porsches usually out-qualified or set faster race laps than the works M3s. Still, a factory M3 could race faster for longer than the turbo opposition, as minimum fuel consumption limits had been set at 5.9 US miles per gallon (7 UK mpg). That was hard for a flat-out turbo to manage and in many races the turbo Porsches and Fords were reduced to conserving fuel on the run to the final flag, or out of fuel after a hard charge. Meanwhile, the M3 and NSX (riding along in the M3's double-decker rear-wing air) were more fuel efficient under duress.

That 1993 ADAC title did not signify a major factory competition effort to promote the six-cylinder M3. BMW Motorsport supported mod-

These 1994 M3s had a pretty strange specification, covering bits of the Group N production racer and some sterner stuff like the 340-bhp/7,800-rpm 3-liter motors. The latter offered a slight torque bonus over 1993's ADAC-winning GTR specification (350 Nm at 4,750 rpm versus 1993's 340 Nm at 5,500 rpm).

Dream Team M3s had the full-size 2-liter race brakes, 75 percent preloaded limited-slip differential, and an excellent 1,200-kg minimum weight target, which meant they had a much better power-to-weight ratio than the 1993 GTR Cup winner: some 283 bhp/ton versus 250 bhp/ton. Yet these 1994 M3s were clothed in two-door showroom M3 cues, right down to the color-coded white road wheels.

Neither of those two M3s finished that 24 Hours, but that motor and associated technology

At Daytona 1996, the #06 M3 lost its class lead and a wheel but still finished third in class, ninth overall. Drivers included Pete Halsmer, David Donohue, Javier Quiros, and John Paul Jr.

Photo: Klaus Schnitzer, Florida, US, 1996

an immediate (class) pole position.

The M3s had wet-sump lubrication on their debut, and Daytona's bankings destroyed two engines before the need for a dry-sump system was accepted. Another PTG priority was to slash weight from the monocoque in a category where flyweight tube-frame cars were the outright pace-setting norm.

arrived in the US for a 1995 debut with Tom Milner's Virginia-based PTG.

When the 240-bhp American version of the M3 was released, competitive interest was almost as strong as ferocious M3 sales rates. For seasons, BMW North America's Erik Wensberg and the enormous BMW CCA club (over 53,000 members today) had been telling Munich that they needed another race program. This was a subject that made the men of Munich flinch in remembrance of the aborted IMSA GTPs .

Back in winter 1994–95, BMW NA supported Milner's PTG as it strove to sort out its first racing M3s. The cars arrived (just) in time to contest February 1995's Daytona 24 Hours. Expectations were sky-high as the M3 recorded

Having put the M3 on a savage diet, PTG also adjusted handling, because it is easier to adjust a tubular-chassis car to each track than it is for a machine that started life on the production line. It's the difference between creating a competition car that looks like a street machine and converting a street car that only looks like a competition car.

That PTG diet returned a 2,300-lb (1,045-kg) M3 as the lightest of four cars fielded at Daytona 1996, the remaining trio averaging out around 2,450 lbs (1,114 kg). With the stated 380 bhp from 3.2 liters, the lightweight 07 First Union/ Valvoline example had the best power-to-weight ratio for a 3 Series since the old McLaren turbo days at 390 bhp/ton.

The PTG Bimmer gang in full flight at Lime Rock in 1997.

Photo: Klaus Schnitzer, US, 1997

Here is the engine bay, at 1997 specification, with a larger percentage of production parts employed than some rivals field for endurance events.

Photo: Klaus Schnitzer, Laguna Seca, California, US, 1997

Another huge transatlantic difference was the availability of 100-plus racing gas octanes in the US, where 98-octane pump fuel and catalytic converters featured in most recent BMW 3 Series experience.

PTG redeveloped the engine around American conditions and reckoned to have added a reliable 60 bhp to the original output. The resulting 380 bhp engine would run cleanly from pit-lane speeds and happily pull from 4,500 rpm upward.

When it came to carving up the coupe and designing a proper roll cage, Munich's two-door coupe data went back to the 3-liter 1993 ADAC M3, or the 1992 British 2-liters. Overcoming such basic difficulties took time, but BMW was committed to seeing the M3 succeed.

In 1999, the same 380 bhp, along with higher (2,535 lbs, or 1,152 kg) weight figures, were officially quoted, but PTG went through a 1998 season of weight increases from organizers to punish its winning record.

European and American racing conditions are different enough to cause much development heartache. BMW Motorsport in Munich had most data for four-door, 2-liter cars of different dimensions and weights to the PTG M3s.

PTG won its first Daytona in 1997, but this #07 car lost its class lead with an infield collision that delayed it more than hour. In the early hours, it was taken off track permanently in a second collision.

Photo: Klaus Schnitzer, Daytona, Florida, US, 1997

Tom Milner, the driving force of PTG, really knows how to get things done, *fast*.

The 1998 season was a good one, with the M3s scoring more individual class victories (15) than ever.

Photo: Klaus Schnitzer, US, 1998

The #10 M3 GT3 shared by Bill Auberlen and Mark Simo during the 1998 season delivered titles, including the Sports Car GT3 Manufacturer's title, for both the PTG team and driver Simo.

Photo: Klaus Schnitzer, US, 1998

Here's how the M3 shaped up technically for its fifth race season:

Body	E36 M3 in 2-door coupe or 4-door sedan formats. Official figures relay street dimensions but note 56-inch front and rear track and race weight of 2,535 lbs given over 1997-99 seasons
Motor	PTG- built 3.2-liter of 86.35 mm x 91 mm (3,196 cc) with EFI HS3.3 (listed as Bosch Motronic 3.3 in 1997–99), or EFI 3.1 electronic engine management with Bosch surface gap plugs
Power	380 bhp @ 8,200 rpm
Torque	290 lb ft @ 6,000 rpm
Transmission	Five-speed Hewland. Have used Holinger five-speed at Daytona 24 Hours. Differential set from 75% pre-load with 3.89:1 most common final-drive ratio
Brakes	Brembo/PFC with four vented discs having 8-piston front calipers and 4-piston rears
Wheels & Tires	Front and rear BBS cast-magnesium 11 x 18-inch with Yokohama racing 290/640 fronts and 290/680 rears
Suspension & Steering	Showroom-principle MacPherson strut front, center-link rear. Eibach coil springs, JRZ strut inserts/telescopic dampers. Production components for power-assisted rack and pinion

M3 Technical details

On July 14, 1996 at Sears Point in Northern California, PTG M3s scored their first IMSA GTS-2 win, sweeping the three podium spots and vanquishing the Porsches that provided BMW's principal opposition to winning their first IMSA title since the 1981 M1.

There were three straight victories to record before a quartet of PTG M3s lined up at Daytona 1996 as part of a World Sports Car Championship round, held in heavy Floridian rain. The driving teams behind Halsmer included Bill Auberlen, Javier Quiros, Boris Said and veteran Dieter Quester.

Since Pete Halsmer had scored three consecutive wins on the way to Daytona, it was hoped that he would do the job again at Daytona, even if the odds read Porsche 15, BMW 4 entries. For much of the race, it looked as if Halsmer's number-four win was on the way, but seven minutes from the end, an oil line was severed and Halsmer's hopes were shattered. Still, BMW's honor was saved by lanky Javier Quiros who, with five minutes remaining, surged past the remaining Porsche to secure the 1996 IMSA GTS-2 title for BMW.

The PTG M3s were still winning in 1–2–3 order within the revamped 1997 IMSA series at Lime Rock, and took first, third, and fourth places at Watkins Glen in June 1997. The 1997 season of eleven races yielded seven category pole positions, nine race wins and four sweeps of the top three in class. Bill Auberlen won the GTS-3 category of the Exxon Supreme GT series and PTG also secured the Constructor's title again.

Opposition was not as fierce as in the later 1990s, but the first national driver's title for PTG and their M3s was a fitting reward for so much hard work and disappointment.

The 1998 season saw the PTG M3 continue to race in its familiar 380-bhp wide-body format, but the power battle to run American

M3s are raced at every level in the US. Here are Texan Paul Torre and ex-pat Briton Tim Probert, who ranked sixth and seventh, respectively, in the BMW CCA Club racing series of 1999. The author is tagging along behind in his luxury 635CSi, a loaner courtesy of Rick Meinig.

Photo: Marilyn Walton, PPIR, Colorado, US, 1999

sports and GT racing between Professional Sports Car and USRCC (United States Road Racing Championship) went to court and prevented prompt announcement of Ross Bentley's GTS-3 Drivers title. This occurred after an autumn 1998 Watkins Glen third-in-class result (shared with co-pilots Marc Duez of Belgium and Peter Cunningham) had secured the series, in which PTG BMWs had seized 16 pole positions and taken 15 wins.

Unfortunately, the results from 1999 were the worst since that initial 1995 season, but there were wins (four), a scattering of pole positions (two), a lap records, and top three/ten finishing consistency was better than you'd think from simply scanning the Stuck catalogue of driveshaft termination.

When even a multiple Le Mans winner like Hans Stuck—who has been a familiar racing sight in the US with BMW (1975–85), Porsche, and Audi (1988–89)—cannot find the pace and durability to consistently win, then PTG and BMW needed to go back to the drawing board. For 2000, they found a better E46 format to tackle those pesky Porsches.

Next, we see what the rest of the planet achieved with their 2-liter motors panting away at an 8,500-rpm limit. For Bimmer 3'ers battled their way to many more world titles.

25 Global Gladiator

Away from the M3 limelight of America, the E36 Bimmer seized over thirty national championship titles in eight world-wide seasons.

Closing the BMW 3 Series official factory racing career on November 25, 1998, BMW Motorsport commented, "The BMW 320i is the most successful Super Touring Car in the World." BMW had beaten up to nine other factory teams during split-second global action. The 3'er also raced successfully with 2-liters as a "318i" or "318is" and enjoyed a solitary successful season as a 2-liter E36 coupe in the UK.

That coupe debut formed a winning probe in 1992 that allowed BMW to capture the bump-and-grind British (BTCC) title. The E36 sedan 320i continued its winning streak after the factory withdrew direct support, taking national 1999 titles in Australia, New Zealand, and even Russia! BMW Threes garnered at least 31 international/ national titles, and there are surely many more at grassroots levels.

Looking back to Germany in 1992, BMW Motorsport fought its last season with the obsolete E30 M3 in the 1992 German Championship, and argued over regulations for their planned 1993 assault on the German title with a 2.5-liter six-cylinder Three. Even then, some new E36 coupe bodies were being built for the 2-liter British Touring Car Championship.

The British series, governed by expat Australian Alan Gow, was reputedly the toughest sedan title to win outside of NASCAR. It certainly attracted the extensive television coverage and competiton between rival manufacturers in the mid-1990s. BMW Motorsport contested many other international 2-liter championships between 1992–98, and privateers kept on winning through 1999.

The factory Bimmers were usually operated by subcontractors with BMW Motorsport support. The most wins came via Schnitzer out of Freilassing on the German-Austrian border, but there were the effective and Italian Championship-winning efforts from Bigazzi and Cibiemme, plus Warthofer and Isert in Germany.

"Smokin' Jo" Winkelhock blasts the opposition, including John Cleland's GM Cavalier and the unusual Mazda Xedos 6 of Patrick Watts away from the line at Donington Park with his Schnitzer 318i, in round 4 of the 1993 British Championship. Teammate Steve Soper heads the pack.

Photo: John Colley Photographic, courtesy BMW GB, 1993

BMW 3'ers met and usually beat the best. Fierce opposition came from Audi (armed with the trick 4x4 quattro A4), Opel/Vauxhall (Cavalier/Vectra), Ford (Mondeo-Cosworth V6), Volvo-TWR (Tom Walkinshaw Racing 5-cylinders), Toyota, Honda, and more.

Some opposing 2-liter race brands, such as Alfa Romeo and Peugeot, are now unavailable in the US. The French "Pugs" beat both BMW and Audi on home ground in 1997 and were close to 320i in 1998. Then there was Renault, which teamed up with Grand Prix World Champions Williams Engineering (now BMW's Grand Prix team) and won only in the UK.

The UK's Vic Lee Motorsport (VLM) earned that debut season of championship glory for the 318is coupe. Prodrive—best known for rallying—was the second UK M-team that received coupe bodies. The bodies, which were designed by BMW Motorsport and prepared by Matter GmbH, were stiffened a massive 25 percent over E30's race-strength body via an integrated chrome-moly-steel roll cage.

Raced in the UK as 318is coupes, VLM maintained BMW's 1991–93 British Championship monopoly with Tim Harvey's five wins. The British Touring Car Series delivered highly competitive and tightly regulated racing in near-one-ton four-door autos of less than 300 bhp that were rpm-limited to 8,500 revs.

The specification for a winning VLM E36 in 1992 embraced the old M3 dry sump-pan motor cut down to a 2-liter. Prodrive quoted a BMW Motorsport figure of 93.4 mm versus an ultra short 72.6-mm stroke for 1,989 cc. VLM reported only 1,991 cc and undeclared internal dimensions. BMW Motorsport developed their own 90.6 mm x 77.4 mm for 1,996 cc, when they released their first E36 customer cars (all four-doors) in 1993.

Whatever the bore and stroke, some 270–275 bhp was harvested before the mandatory 8,500-rpm limiter interceded. Torque was scarce, at less than 180 lb-ft at around 7,000 rpm, but factory-engined BMWs exhibited very honest horsepower. A trick six-speed H-pattern gearbox from Holinger in Australia and ABS braking from Teves in Germany completed the 1992 UK race specification.

Prodrive ran Pirelli tires on 19-inch wheels, versus 18-inch rollers and more durable Yokohamas at VLM. A former Prodrive employee revealed, "That was a nightmare season for us. We had a lap speed deficit you could measure in 1- to 1.5-second chunks; we were lucky if the Pirellis did five laps."

Tim Harvey with the garland of victory that was not his until the closing crash fest at Silverstone.

Photo: John Colley Photographic, courtesy BMW GB, 1992

Tim Harvey's 1992 VLM teammate was internationally-rated Steve Soper, and the new BMWs were the most difficult to drive yet. They displayed a twitching over bumps that was never fully eliminated, even with subsequent assistance from McLaren.

However, E36 dominated late-season 1992. Its key attributes were: sleek shape, a rear-drive layout, wide power band, and divine braking through 14-inch fronts and 12.6-inch rears, all clamped by multiple carbon-fiber pads. By round seven, Tim Harvey and VLM started a winning roll. In fact, Harvey only failed to win three of the remaining eight events. Finishing fourth in a

Silverstone crash-fest of a final was enough to decide a three- way Championship fight in Harvey's favor, maintaining BMW's succession of BTCC winners. That edgy Silverstone finale featured seven rivals in a 7-second band with two laps to go. All three championship challengers occupied consecutive 4–5–6 positions.

1993: Four-Door Pioneers

For 1993, BMW Motorsport delivered "an all-new racing car—the BMW 318i based on the current 3 Series." This 2-liter 318i contested events from Britain to Australia, via the Asia Pacific rim. The new car was based on the shell of the four-door 1.8-liter, after the coupe—and ABS—was banned from 2-liter racing.

Initially, teams were not allowed additional spoilers, but this ruling collapsed in 1994. Alfa Romeo squeezed through a unique tall rear wing and front splitter set and humiliated most of the opposition. BMW adopted a recognized wing set starting July 1, 1994, along with a new motor. At that race, the four-cylinder Bimmer officially became a 318is. Using the front and rear aerodynamic package, the four-door 318is raced with yearly Evolutions. From 1996 on, it was re-homologated as a 320i, although it retained the 16-valve (M42) four-cylinder redeveloped for racing as the S42.

Alain Menu suffered an injury outside racing and was not able to complete his 1992 season in the Prodrive 318is, but later won the British title twice.

Photo: John Colley Photographic, courtesy BMW GB, 1992

BMW didn't appear to owe braking loyalty to any particular company. Here, we see those monster drilled discs and the box section steel employed to beef up the silvered rear trailing arms on the touring car.

Photo: Sabine Hofmann, Nürburgring, Germany, 1998

Back in 1993, the wing-less 318i looked little different from a street car. The driver sat 3.25 inches (80 mm) further back, and it was over four inches lower at the roof line. Then, 8 x 18-inch wheels kissed the wheel wells, but later Bimmers (1997) featured 8.3 x 19-inch BBS within extended arches. The 318i racer featured pneumatic air jacks and 40 meters (130 ft) of steel tubing in a roll cage which increased torsional strength to what BMW Motorsport reckoned was "seven times" that of the "standard production model."

For 1993, the 318i sedan retained an S14-coded 2-liter M3 motor of the previous season's 1,996 cc. BMW Motorsport revealed that a unique combustion chamber shape was required for an abbreviated 90.6 x 77.4-mm bore and

stroke. The motor employed forged racing pistons (12:1 compression ratio), steel connecting rods, and a forged-steel crankshaft. The 2-liter was now closer to 280 bhp, but was also available with higher torque and lower bhp for tighter circuits. It was mated to the Holinger six-speed gearbox with an H-pattern shift, digital display, data-collecting multi-mode instrumentation, and massive discs. These 14-inch fronts and 12-inch rears were prodded by six- and four-piston calipers, respectively.

Suspension retained the principles of the MacPherson strut front and multi-link rear end, but the components were new. BMW specified a limited-slip ZF differential with 75 percent locking action, but the 1992 British team's 318is sometimes used a solid (spool) differential.

These 1996 Donington season preview photos show the extended rear wheel arch blended ahead of the back doors.

Photo: Marilyn Walton, Donington Park, Derbyshire, UK, 1996

A 1993 ride with Joachim Winkelhock in Britain revealed why Winkelhock's starts during the season verged on sensational. A standing start imposed 65 percent of the vehicle weight over the driven rear wheels, whereas a front-drive car might have half as much traction. This was enough to counter a 1993 BTCC 220-lb BMW

The 2, 200 lb four-door racing 320i was heavily strengthened and featured aerodynamic improvements.

Photos: Author, Donington Park, Derbyshire, UK, 1996

By 1995 the S42 16-valve engine developed more than 310 bhp.

Photo: Author, Donington Park, Derbyshire, UK, 1996

Jo Winkelhock, in traditional British Midland weather, gets a taste of the 1996 Schnitzer-BMW 320i. A new sequential Holinger gearbox for that season allowed the fastest of 8,499-rpm power shifts.

Photo: Author, Donington Park, Derbyshire, UK, 1996

weight penalty (subsequently, BMW 320i carried a minimum 50 lb/25 kg). Joachim won a clutch of 1993 events from the front, running 0–60 mph in a scant four seconds.

The E36 318i racer sold over 40 units globally and seized championships in Britain, Germany and Italy in its 1993 debut season. Such Championship harvests were harder to replicate in the later 1990s. High-tech (electro-hydraulic) differential developments for the front-drive majority produced a big breakthrough in front-drive lap speed. Their pace was further quickened by motors tilted so low—mounted deep within engine bays—that a driver's feet almost rested on rocker covers.

BMW used fine drivers and teams to scoop their 1993 Italian and British titles for Roberto Ravaglia and Joachim Winkelhock. At Monza, Italy, a BMW 318i flotilla was assembled to fight the first FIA 2-liter World Cup in 1993, which drew 43 drivers from 12 countries. BMW and their star fleet drivers failed to beat a pair of Cosworth-engined Mondeo (Contour) V6s. The best BMW—and German manufacturer—result came from Alex Burgstaller, who finished fifth. BMW took a lot of flak for this comparative lack of the success German media demanded.

The rest had to play second fiddle to Radisich and Mondeo again in 1994's FIA shoot-out, held in the UK. It was the 1995 final edition of the FIA World Cup in France that finally saw German

Audis and BMWs take revenge and monopolize the front rows of the grids. They went unchallenged by Ford and the rest of the front drivers. BMW was awarded a unique FIA Cup for its winning record with racing 3'ers at the close of its illustrious career.

BMW Motorsport started 1994 with a machine that looked much like the 1993 318i, but it was reworked from the much stiffer roll cage outward. The 1994 race 318i featured revised aerodynamics and a new motor. Much of the rest of the running gear was replaced for 1994 too, including front and rear suspension layout as well as a sequential version of the BMW-Holinger-engineered six-speed gearbox.

BMW Motorsport could build a 318i at 2,200 lbs (1,000 kg) or less, but the FIA rules at the beginning of the season put them at 2,310 lbs (1,050 kg), versus 2,090 lbs (950 kg) for the front-drive majority. That changed on July 1, 1994, when a 2,145-lb (975 kg) minimum for front drive arrived. Then BMW was allowed to drop to 2,255 lbs (1,025 kg).

Despite assorted weight penalties, the 1994 results were rewarding. BMW scored a remarkable 1–2–3–4 result in the Belgian Spa 24 hours (one of four Spa wins for various E36s), and snatched National Championships in Australia, Belgium, and South Africa. BMW was also the FIA World Championship Manufacturer's team. Nationally, BMW won the German 2-liter title

Road and track. The author's most prized assignment of 1998 was access to the 225-bhp competition and 136-bhp production versions of BMW's turbocharged 320d.

Photo: Sabine Hofmann, Nürburgring, Germany, 1998

(ONS/ADAC TourenWagen Cup) for Johnny Cecotto, and Steve Soper won four races in the All-Japan series to finish third overall. He would return to beat the local Toyota/Honda giants with a Schnitzer Three in 1995.

During 1994, a homologation run of four-door 318is sedans appeared on the German market. The base (M42) 16-valve, DOHC unit was accepted for motorsports in a variation coded S42. With cooperation from long-standing partners at Heini Mader in Switzerland, BMW Motorsport gradually redeveloped this new unit into an 8,500-rpm racer. Equipped with slide throttles,

dry-sump lubrication and a new steel crankshaft, the race motor had dimensiions of 86.5 mm x 85 mm for 1,998 cc, rather than the 1,796-cc and 84 x 81-mm street dimensions. Compression was set around 12:1, but escalated to over 13:1 in later 1990s racing.

The German market 318is street replica had the front and rear wing kit, plus that M42/S42 base 16-valve motor, which started racing in the 1994 German 2-liter Cup cars of Johnny Cecotto and Alex Burgstaller.

Under the hood, the new S42 motor was distinguished by its vertical stance, rather than the traditional BMW slant installation. In pre-season trials, power was reported to be 280 bhp by 8,500 rpm. The big benefit was torque (a claimed 180 lb-ft at 7,000) and—after a lot of hard development work—a comparatively wide power band.

Cockpit-adjustable roll bars worked their cable-linkage and solid-joint magic in the trunk of a racing BMW from the later 1990s. Penske remote reservoir shock absorbers were popular with BMW Motorsport at that time.

Photo: Sabine Hofmann, Nürburgring, Germany, 1998

Extracting an 89-bhp bonus from the tough 2-liter turbo-diesel with plenty of production parts was a task similar to that faced by PTG with the early racing M3s.

Photo: Sabine Hofmann, Nürburgring, Germany, 1998

The Diesel that Dared to Race

Motorsports and diesel engines have an honorable pedigree that stretches back to pre-war America. Post-war international interest has only been sparked by the spark-less engine in turbocharged four-cylinder format in Germany in the 1990s.

Both Volkswagen and BMW have enjoyed competition success in the last three years, Volkswagen tackling rallying and a variety of Continental European races. BMW stuck to long distance racing with better international results.

In June 1998, BMW Motorsport's two factory entries took pole position on their home track of Nürburgring. A single surviving 320d won the 24-hour race outright, the first time the overall win of an international sedan race had fallen to diesel motivation.

Deploying an E36 3 Series body in SuperTouring race trim, and pre-production versions of the new 1,950-cc M47D turbo diesel unit, BMW Motorsport worked with the Austrian Steyr engine production facility. Together, they created a formidable 225-bhp diesel capable of winning, partially because of its near-300-lb-ft pulling power, but also owing to its parsimonious fuel consumption.

Under racing conditions, BMW recorded 13.5 mpg—virtually twice what would be expected for a normally-aspirated gasoline racing motor in similar conditions.

Engine modifications were minimal compared to those of an equivalently powerful gasoline power unit. The cost of competition could be significantly reduced, eliminating the 500-mile routine rebuilds that are commonplace on a 2-liter SuperTouring motor.

On the shorter Nürburgring GP circuit, driving a rare 320d was a blast. With braking and handling from the 1990s, the torque was so accessible, you'd swear there was a 1960s Detroit iron V8 installed, especially when the back wheels stepped out so smartly under 3,000-rpm turbo boost.

The 2,000–4,000-rpm torque was amazing, carrying us along every straight with an unstressed rush. It was a complete contrast to the usual 8,000-rpm raucous soundtrack of a SuperTouring Car in full flight. It was only the imploding scenery that reminded you to apply big brakes...NOW!

For 1994, Traditional British event winners BMW and Ford were thrashed by Williams Renault and TWR Volvo. BMW would not win the BTCC again, abandoning the British series at the close of 1996.

1995: Bad-News Britain

Headline success for the racing E36 in 1995 centered on Steve Soper's first international title, the All-Japan 2-liter series, plus a successful home-title run for Joachim Winkelhock in Germany.

Altogether, the company won five touring car titles in 1995, including far-flung Australia, but the bumpy tracks of Britain and white-hot front-drive opposition were bad news for BMW in 1995. A GM Cavalier for John Cleland clasped the championship's shiniest rewards. The

Günther Warthofer/BMW Team Motorsport outfit languished in sixth place.

The biggest 1995 routine change was that the S42 2-liter was now the regular customer engine. Running 12.5:1 compression, the S42 was now rated at 285 bhp by 8,300 rpm with 184 lb-ft of torque at the 7,000-rpm peak. It featured many major modifications that made it hard to transplant to earlier racing Bimmers.

BMW Motorsport reported a roofline 110 mm (4.5 inches) lower than a production 3 Series and the racer began to pull its wheels within the arches. The biggest body change, though was a new roll cage that hiked body torsional rigidity to a value ten times that of a production four-door E36.

The 145-mph hybrid E36 touring-car chassis and prototype 320d turbo-diesel engine from BMW's Austrian Steyr subsidiary was driven by an all-star team and attracted enormous media attention at the 1998 Nürburgring 24-hours.

Photos: Sabine Hofmann, Nürburgring, Germany, 1998

The 1995 factory racer nibbled at chassis weight by 10 kg (22 lbs). The composite Keiper Recaro seat went rearward again, but BMW did not go for the near-central driving position adopted by rivals until 1997.

Updates to the suspension involved the use of lighter and stronger aluminum or magnesium parts. The factory race wheel was an 18- or 19-inch diameter BBS Magnesium item; customer cars also came on Speedline rims.

Bimmers always raced on Bilstein gas dampers, right? Not beyond 1995, for the factory recommended Penske products from Tamworth, England. Meanwhile, there were a wide choice of anti-roll bars, eventually resulting in both front and rear components that could be adjusted from the cockpit.

By 1995, the disc brakes expanded again at the front, but were smaller for the rear. The vented units were specified at 342 mm and 283 mm (13.5 inches and 11.1 inches) and ran swing caliper designs of six-piston layout for fronts, twin piston for rears. The official 1995 supplier was Brembo, but BMW Motorsport used a number of brake component suppliers, including AP Racing in 1997.

Winning the 2-liter series at home (re-christened the STW, or Super Touring Wagen Cup) was particularly sweet for BMW in 1995, because there was a season-long battle with Audi. The A4 quattro had to race at an even heavier weight than BMW (1,040 kg versus 1,025 kg) but the 4x4 element soaked up the wet races. The Championship was in doubt until the Nürburgring GP circuit final, when great teamwork from their 2–3–4 placed drivers clinched it for BMW despite another Audi win.

Soper had also won the Japanese title with Schnitzer in 1995, so BMW was happy, especially as Yvan Muller took the 1995 French Supertourisme Championship in the Oreca-run 320i.

The effective trio of Kox, Winkelhock and Soper also hauled home the Spa 24 hour spoils (BMW were also second in this 1995 edition). Steve Soper had also given Audi a good run (second and third) in the two FIA World Cup races at Paul Ricard, France.

The (Günther) Warthofer team, established in 1992 at a Nürburgring base, were winners of the 1994 German 2-liter title with the S42 motor development program. Now they had settled at Silverstone for the 1995 British assault, but it was not enough to offset the increasing speed of the now all-winged front-drive brigade.

British-based 1995 race BMWs only progressed in terms of power-to-weight ratio because their 285 bhp was now harnessed to a 1,000-kg (2200 lb) minimum, whereas 1,025 kg was their international norm. In Germany, they changed their aerodynamic package mid-season, a possibility not allowed in the UK.

Pole position and race leader at 6 hours, but no win for the second 320d of multinational driving squad Hans Stuck, Steve Soper (UK) and former motorcycle ace Didier Radrigues.

Photo: Bock, courtesy BMW AG Presse, Germany, 1998

Perhaps the most photogenic racing liveries in BMW history are those from Jägermeister. This is the 1998 BMW Team Isert factory-backed 320i in German 2-liter action for Christian Menzel.

Photo: BMW AG Presse, Germany, 1998

The results for ace Johnny Cecotto and hard-trying David Brabham were so dire in the UK that the factory importer pleaded with Munich to withdraw the cars, a request that was refused. By the close of 1995, BMW had slumped to their worst ever UK race performances to finish sixth in the Manufacturer's 8-team league and place their drivers a dismal 12 and 13th.

BMW Motorsport Great Britain, Ltd.

December 1995's icy European winter and one of many BMW satellite offices in Munich were the backdrop for the next startling development. While the adjacent massive marquee

filled up with BMW Motorsport evening guests, the media heard BMW management—headed by Karl Heinz Kalbfell and Paul Rosche—announce that BMW Motorsport was to sub-contract all but the racing engine business to British specialists!

All hardcore work outside the engine bay for the touring car program was to be run in the UK, ostensibly via a small office at BMW GB. Later, a purpose-built British BMW Motorsport department and buildings were established. First, Anglo-German non-F1 cooperation came at McLaren, and later, alongside Williams Grand Prix in Oxfordshire.

BMW Motorsport's commercial M-branded operations were not affected, nor were Paul

This side view of the 1998 E36 racing 2-liter 3 Series emphasizes the 19-inch wheel diameters, ever-changing aerodynamic front and rear spoilers/splitters, the marked negative camber angles used on the (non-power-assist) steering, rear wheel fairings for increased high speed ability, catalytic converter exhaust tailpipe and a driving position alongside the center pillar.

Photo: BMW AG Presse, Germany, 1998

Fitting farewell. A multiple champion for BMW, expat Venezuelan Johnny Cecotto took the final factory-backed Championship title in the 1998 German Super Touring Wagen (STW) series.

Photo: BMW AG Presse, Germany, 1998

Rosche's engine building men. No layoffs were incurred, and recruitment actually increased on the run into Formula 1.

BMW Motorsport and BMW AG wanted a higher international profile than 2-liter race sedans brought. Initially, BMW extended the link with McLaren. The relationship had blossomed into GT racing and Le Mans-winning success with the fabled triple-seater F1 BMW V12.

First came GT racing with McLaren, then international sports prototype racing—plus Grand Prix—with Williams. At Williams, there was no touring car link, but the higher profile 1998–2000 BMW V12 LMR/LMP programs, which won Le Mans and all but two of six events contested in the US in 1999.

Since BMW was about to climb into a Grand Prix double bed with McLaren rivals Williams, and McLaren was linked with Mercedes in GP racing, the 1996 McLaren alliance was interim; by the end of 1997, it was all over.

McLaren manager Jeff Hazell recalled, "We examined the 1995 touring cars in November 1995. There was not much time to make a major input for the 1996 season, but we did construct two test 320s for both 1996 and 1997. We worked in partnership with Schnitzer to boost their 1996 assault on the BTCC, running a full test program whilst they got with the business of racing. Our changes were not just for Britain, but fed into BMW factory cars, wherever they appeared."

What was done to the 1996 320s? The German Matter roll cages lost seven percent of overall weight and the race Threes mutated.

They squatted on the ground, with rear haunches featuring flared wheelarches. The 320i benefited from a new wing set, now biased toward slower British circuits.

The 1996 motor pushed the power-to-weight ratio up to 304 bhp a ton, compared with the 1993 debut year at 262 bhp per ton, so the 320 snapped up to pace quicker than the 318i of 1993. Official output on 98-octane unleaded gasoline was now just short of 150 bhp a liter in emission-controlled form, with a metallic (rather than ceramic) catalytic converter, for German racing. The result was 298 bhp at 8,300 rpm with torque at a record 192 lb-ft by 7,000 rpm.

The new six-speed sequential gearbox from Holinger was dropped in the frame to provide a lowline stance in association with new front- and rear-axle suspension layouts. A sprint 50-liter (9.2 US gal, or 11 UK gal) fuel tank was used in place of earlier, larger reservoirs.

BMW's 1996 record was a vast improvement with 1993 British Champion Joachim Winkelhock and Robert Ravaglia. Winkelhock took seven pole positions in 1996, but these converted into just four early-season wins. Ravaglia won the race of the year, the British Grand Prix supporter at Silverstone. He also took another pole position, so BMW accrued eight poles and five wins between the two drivers, a fine recovery from 1995's win-less misery.

In Germany in 1996, the 320s, fielded by Bigazzi for top BMW points-scorer Steve Soper, succeeded in winning against Audi, Honda and Peugeot three times. Soper—who preferred

German racing to that in his native UK—looked to be a possible German champion until he was pushed off by teammate Alex Burgstaller, who was on his way to the pits! Johnny Cecotto equaled that result in Italy, and the dream-team combo of Winkelhock and Ravaglia came back from the UK with fifth and sixth to show for the Schnitzer-McLaren race alliance.

The US witnessed the birth of its own SuperTouring (NATCC) 2-liter contest in 1996, but only Chrysler, with the Reynard-created Stratus, fielded factory 2.0 sedans. The grids were thin, but were uplifted by some excellent racing. An ex-BTCC Honda took the inaugural US series and there was no sign of BMW NA wanting more of the 2-liter action in 1997. However, with 1996 Champion Randy Pobst in a BMW, there had been hope for better Bimmer results in 1997. The US 2-liter series was abandoned in 1998.

1997–98 E36 End Game

The touring-car technical liaison with McLaren continued in 1997, but BMW had withdrawn from Britain. On the Continent, BMW Motorsport had its hands full fighting Peugeot in Germany (lost in 1997, won with Schnitzer in 1998) and Alfa Romeo in Italy.

E36 Bimmers proved competitive in the 1998 and 1999 seasons, but the Italian 2-liter series, like the German and British series, suffered from waning manufacturer support. For 2000, German and Italian 2-liter series were set to link, but by then BMW had announced that the E46 was not to be developed into a full-blooded 2-liter tourer, a decision reversed, rapidly, for the 2002–2005 European and World Championships.

Instead, the factory supported development of a customer-only E46 320i for less-radical Deutsche Touring Car Challenge (DTC) rules. A 320i/E46 won in 1999 in Holland, but even in Germany, the 1998–99 seasons saw only a second and fourth overall from the privateers.

Paul Rosche's team overhauled the S42 motor—and the rest of the power train—to reduce friction in 1997. The motor sported twin injector nozzles for each intake manifold cylinder feed, while the now-traditional carbon-fiber air collector was joined by an equally high-tech, light drive shaft in the same material.

The motor operated with a 13.2:1 compression (on pump unleaded gasoline!). Details included low-friction crankshaft/bearings, reprogrammed BMW Motorsport engine management for the ECU, and revised valve timing.

Maximum power was now quoted as 305 bhp at 8,300 rpm and 195 lb-ft of torque by 7,000 rpm. Rival teams thought up to 315 bhp was actually available to BMW for sprint racing. This was certainly the case by 1998, but BMW still quoted a 310-bhp maximum.

At 305 bhp, the 1,000-kg (2,200-lb) BMW punched up a power-to-weight ratio of 311 bhp a ton. Good, but it was exceeded by front-drive outfits such as Honda, whose equally powerful Neil Brown motors carried only 975 racing kg (2,145 lbs).

The 1997 German series would be a struggle between Peugeot's factory 406 and Johnny Cecotto's Bigazzi BMW. Their winning scorelines were 4–2 at mid-season, but the BMWs were more numerous and had finished 1–2 (Cecotto, Winkelhock) on their winning runs. Finally, Peugeot's front-drive 406 with Laurent Aiello was too much for the aging Bimmers.

In 1997 in Australia and Belgium, the 320s were winning, the Italian series was a runaway for BMW and more titles were logged in Finland, Holland, and Southeast Asia. Paul Morris was the championship winner for BMW in Australia, and his teammate and runner-up was Geoff Brabham. BMW also won the first 2-liter edition of the classic Bathurst "Great Race" to compliment BMW's historic twentieth Spa 24-hour race victory.

BMW's world-wide haul of 1997 was completed with an FIA World Cup (given to the most

Top BMW sporting trio. Left to right are Jo Winkelhock, legendary Schnitzer team manager Charly Lamm, and Johnny Cecotto.

Photo: BMW AG Presse, Germany, 1998

successful Manufacturer in SuperTouring) and a dominant win for Steve Soper in the season-closing Macao Grand Prix.

The 1998 season provided a fitting swansong for the factory E36, which became obsolete with the introduction of the E46. Johnny Cecotto and Joachim Winkelhock fought a season-long battle against Audis, Peugeots, and a horde of Opel Vectras. Cecotto came home German Champion with five wins.

On the technical side, upgraded suspension, increased traction differential, and an aerodynamic package for 1998 complemented new motor components. These included replacement pistons, exhaust system, air box, and associated intakes to provide the quickest 2-liter yet.

Bimmer's racing power-to-weight ratio that final season was up to a best of 297 bhp per Imperial ton, assuming they managed to extract 315 bhp rather than the official 310 bhp at 8,300 by the end of the season. Torque now nudged a reported 270 Nm (199 lb-ft) by the usual 7,000 revs.

To complete an excellent E36 final season, Joachim Winkelhock out-paced Audi ace Frank Biela in the Macao street races. It was BMW's tenth win at that colony since 1980.

We can conclude that, even without the PTG M3s, the E36 BMW 3 Series was one hell of a tin-top racer!

"Ultimate Driving Machines" Revisited

While Audi promises "Progress through Technology" (Vorsprung durch Technik), there are two primary BMW slogans: Freude am Fahren, or sheer driving pleasure, in Germany, and The Ultimate Driving Machine, now used in major English-language markets. Are they justified?

To help us answer that, in a 1993 interview, former *Autosport* Grand Prix Editor Joe Saward described the rides of several lifetimes squeezed into the schedule of a young Austrian called Gerhard Berger. In hectic 3 Series action, Berger, a former Grand Prix winner and later Herr Motorsport at BMW, proved the product.

Berger subsequently became a Grand Prix winner for the best, right up to Ferrari, McLaren and Benetton-BMW, for whom he scored the last BMW Turbo engine's victory (Mexico 1986). The versatile Berger has been BMW Motorsport director since 1998 and was a key player in both the Le Mans 1999 winning team and the 2000 Grand Prix move to Williams.

In 1984, four years before Berger achieved fame as a Ferrari GP star, our tale of the hardest-driven E30 BMW 325i begins. Saward recounted the following story,

I will always remember one particular ride in a BMW 325i. I can even recall the number plate of the car ... S for Salzburg 14611. The driver of the S14611 was a young racing hero called Gerhard Berger.

At the time, I was a struggling free-lance reporter, trekking around Europe, sleeping in tents, trucks, and stations, dependent on the kindness of strangers. Necessity meant I had to cover the European Touring Car Championship, amongst others.

This schedule matched that of Berger, so we saw a great deal of each other, and had several adventures in BMW #S14611. I developed a defensive psychology for driving with Gerhard. If you accepted that you were dead before you climbed aboard, the rest didn't matter. It became fun.

The most memorable drive was within the weekend of the Spa 24-hour touring car race. Gerhard was a factory BMW driver. He was sharing one of the Schnitzer team's factory-backed BMW 635CSi's with Roberto Ravaglia and the late Manfred Winkelhock. The latter was (we spoke of such things in awe) a Grand Prix driver!

Qualifying at Spa started on the Tuesday and ran for two days. By Wednesday evening, everyone was getting fed up. I was standing in the pit lane, waiting for the final session to begin at 9 p.m., when I was tapped on the shoulder.

'In ten minutes you are going Holland,' said a voice.

'No I'm not, I have to report this,' I replied grumpily.

'There is something better to report in Holland.'

'Like what?'

'I'm doing my first Formula 1 test,' said Gerhard.

'So what?' I replied uncharitably.

'I want you to come....'

I could not refuse. I suppose he wanted moral support. We would be back, he said, in time for the start of the 24-hour race. Around 11 p.m., we crossed the Dutch border and began to run out of gas. I had no money and Gerhard only had German Marks. We could not find any garage that took credit cards. The situation became critical. So we drove into the first garage we saw and offered

Gerhard Berger, in his ATS-BMW and 635CSi season.

Photo: John Townsend, BMW Pressefoto, 1985

a passing Dutchman a one-to-one swap, Marks for Guilders. He looked suspiciously at us: you don't get something for nothing. He did.

The next stop was Schipol airport, where we picked up an Austrian mechanic who was coming to help Gerhard. We reached Amsterdam in the small hours, found a hotel room into which we all three crammed, and slept.

For much of the following day, we waited. Gerhard would not test until Saturday. When the testing was finished for the day, as dusk fell, Gerhard and I headed out onto the track in the abused 325i.

'To begin with,' Gerhard said, 'we go very slow.'

It did not seem that slow. As we came steaming out of Bos Uit curve, I thought that I had survived. I also remember the sinking feeling as we went past the pits, with Gerhard muttering about 'going a little quicker this time.' We did, tires screeching and chassis twisting. Schlievlak, the diving right-hander out amongst the dunes, was simply horrifying. We made it to Bos Uit again and I relaxed. For a second.

'Now we trying going fast,' said Gerhard. Gulp. As we arrived at Schlievlak, I remember quite clearly thinking that if I survived, it would be something to tell my grandchildren about.

The next morning, Gerhard was like an excited kid when he climbed into the turbocharged ATS-BMW and did a few tentative laps. 'You cannot believe the power,' he said, bug-eyed.

This is the Schnitzer 635 that Gerhard shared with Italian champions Roberto Ravaglia and Emanuele Pirro for third place at the Belgian 24-hour classic in 1984.

Photo: BMW Archiv, re-released 1998

It was after three o'clock when I first realized that we should get moving to be back at Spa. I thrust a watch in front of Gerhard's helmet in the pits, and he nodded, then drove out of the pits again. It was at about 4:30 p.m. that I had a horrifying thought.

The Spa 24 hours began at 5 p.m.. I figured we could miss an hour or so, no problem. It would probably take three hours to get back, but Ravaglia could always hand the Schnitzer 635 on to Manfred at the first pit stop.

It was then that Manfred Winkelhock drove by me ... in Holland! He was also there, testing the ATS. I tapped Gerhard on the helmet and explained the problem. He shrugged. Finally, I think something broke on the car, because he gave up and came running towards me, waving at the mechanics and thanking everyone as he ran. In full overalls he climbed into the BMW 325 and off we went.

The Dutch Highway Code has never been so abused. We went straight through red lights without thinking; we overtook cars on the grass between the fast lane and the central barriers; we dodged and weaved. It was a race against the clock.

Once, and I don't remember why, we stopped at a traffic light. Alongside was a local petrolhead in a souped-up something or other. He looked across at me and revved his engine. I smiled back and

then sat back, to let him see the driver in racing overalls. The man's jaw dropped and, at the same moment, the lights changed. We did not see him again.

As we went into Belgium, it started to rain. Life became infinitely more interesting. Finally, after getting lost in the lanes around Spa, and several handbrake spin-turns later, Gerhard slithered to a soggy halt in the paddock at Spa and ran off, yelling, 'Park the car!' A few moments later, he was out on the track in a Schnitzer 635 CSi.

'Not bad for an afternoon,' Gerhard said later. 'I drove three BMWs: one with 1000 bhp, one with 350 bhp, and the other with 150 bhp!'

A fortnight later, Gerhard made his Formula 1 debut with ATS. Within three months he and BMW registration #S14611 had gone off a cliff in Austria ... when he was hit from behind. Gerhard broke his neck, and was lucky to live. Within a few weeks he discharged himself from hospital and went off to England to sign a contract with Arrows GP.

A year after our adventures, Gerhard and Roberto won the Spa 24 hours for BMW.... As for S14611, I expect it can still be found at the bottom of a remote Austrian ravine," concluded Joe Saward of a rare insight into race driver psychology, and 3 Series integrity.

26 Engineering and Designing an Icon

A distinctly desirable 3 Series retains its icon status and inspires fierce owner loyalty.

Thanks to record US sales, BMW synchronized their production act for 1998, debuting the new 3 Series in Europe, America, and Britain. This classy 3'er swept into showrooms for all major markets under the E46 factory coding. It was a big critical and commercial hit with all but the pickiest critics and previous E36-performance-biased customers.

After 18 months on the market, the initially cool reception ("A better BMW; will anybody notice?" queried BMW CCA's *Roundel* in October 1998) was replaced by renewed loyalty to the new BMW 3 Series as a worthy successor of hidden attractions. Its advantages only became obvious after a longer acquaintance.

That same *Roundel* magazine, bible to over 53,000 American BMW owners, stated in its February 2000 introduction to the E46 coupe, "From the moment you lay eyes on its shape, you can't help but feel passion. You can't help but look back over your shoulder as you walk away. You can't help but fall in love—to the point of obsession."

Car and Driver stated, "The BMW 3 Series closes out the century with its ninth successive selection on our best 10 list. The reason is simple: an unusually accurate correlation between 3 Series virtues and the desires of committed car enthusiasts.

"Foremost credit goes to the inline six-cylinder engines that power all 3 Series models [in the US]. Although they do not possess huge horsepower ratings, these turbine smooth sixes deliver terrific performance without ever breaking a sweat. And thanks to their variable valve timing systems, they combine abundant mid-range with energetic high-rpm surge.

"The 3 Series' effortless competence also manifests itself in responsive handling, consistent and powerful brakes, and notably linear and progressive controls. These virtues are enhanced by the compact body

Press cars at the 1998 launch of the current 3 Series went through a dusty Italian demonstration like this BMW NA 323i is enduring. It was intended to emphasize the difference between having the active electronic safety systems switched on or off.

Photo: Klaus Schnitzer, US, 1998

that fosters agility while still packing considerable space for four occupants and their luggage."

Consumer Digest simply acknowledged the latest 323i as "Best Buy of the Year." And American consumers agreed: in its first five months on the American market, the six-cylinder newcomers recorded over 14,000 sales and accounted for more than half of all 3 Series sales. Registrations of the E36-bodied 3 Series had fallen after a record 64,000-plus figure in 1996, recovering ground but breaking no more records. Through 1997 and 1998, the 3 Series accounted for 43 and 44 percent, respectively, of all US sales; but from July 1998, the new E46 3 Series put that percentage up beyond 50 percent of all US sales.

The 1998 US sales saw a record 131,559 BMWs flee the showrooms, but 1999 beat both

overall and 3 Series sales records. Some 154,970 American-specification Bimmers were sold in BMW's biggest export market. But the important US statistic was that a staggering 77,138 units were Threes. The introduction of E46 alongside the surviving E36s (primarily Compacts and Convertibles) energized 3 Series sales by a substantial 34 percent, the biggest BMW gain in a sensational global sales year in which the UK accounted for 70,932 right-drive BMWs, the bulk (52,121) of them 3 Series.

In media briefs, BMW stated that the E46 was the fifth generation of a range that encompassed the 1966–75 legends of 02, thus extending the Three pedigree beyond the 1975 introduction of the first (E21) 3 Series. BMW's reckoning allowed the company to quote an impressive total of some seven million small sports BMW sedan owners (it's just over six million if you stick to 3 Series) in launch publicity. That was obviously some act to follow, as contemporary American BMW Design chief Chris Bangle acknowledged: "In the sports sedan segment, the 3 Series is absolutely the icon."

Ancestors: left to right we have the 02 and an E21 example of the 2-door only E21 breed. Center stage is, the current E46, flanked by the versatile E30 plus the 1990–98 E36, the first of the aerodynamically advantaged 3 Series.

Photo: BMW Press, Germany/UK, 1998

Factory cutaways record the comparatively conventional front-engine, rear-drive layout of the current 3 Series in six-cylinder format. The second cross section illustration records the extensive protection zones offered by six standard European specification airbags and the optional rear side bags.

Photos: BMW Press, Germany/UK, 1998

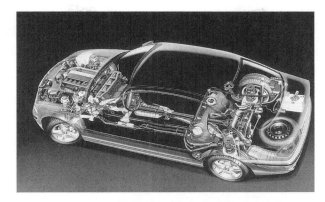

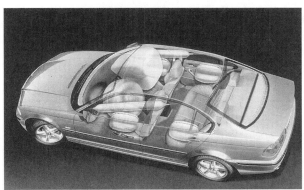

There was an increased spread of the anti-corrosion galvanization process, now reckoned to count for 85 percent of all panels. The obvious new safety stuff was the global showroom fitment of a six-airbag system: passenger, driver, ITS (Inflatable Tubular Structure headbags trickled down from 5 and 7), and the established side air bags, leaving only rear side bags on the options list.

But the bigger story was hidden in that bulging body, reportedly delivering "60 percent greater rigidity and stability," thanks to manufacturing techniques as basic as welding method improvements, and a 50 percent increase in the use of high-tensile sheet steel.

The diagonal door bars that, in BMW's briefing words, "lock in the sideframes, turning the doors and body into one single unit for extra strength," were a comfort in heavy side-impact accidents. Another ingenious accident/practicality feature was the twin-chamber plastic fuel tank looped over the propeller shaft, located under the back seat floorpan. That tank offered service protection against corrosion as well as a capacity of 63 liters (13.9 Imperial/11.6 US gallons).

BMW was intent on keeping the 3 Series from crowding into 5 Series territory, so there were restrictions on how big the smaller car could grow. The E46 gained 1.5 inches in length and 1.6 in exterior width, while the wheelbase was up virtually an inch (25 mm). Inside, rear knee

Bangle, and a truly international team of 200 at Designworks in California—as well as in Germany—approached an all-new 3 Series, Bangle said, in the spirit of "maintaining honesty, truthfulness and the integrity of what made that icon great. Not abandoning that and trying to do everything all over again. That's not the BMW approach."

Mechanically speaking, the teams were led by Dr. Wolfgang Ziebart in a reported three-and-a-half-year development process, with quality as the first priority at the top of a very long list of objectives. Although BMW has an excellent safety record for constructing cars that lead or meet the best in all their primary 3–5–7 ranges, the company bested themselves with the current 3 Series. BMW set new standards of crash and torsional rigidity that were supported by innovative changes in manufacturing at Regensberg and by all BMW primary suppliers.

room grew 0.8 inch, which made it better, but still tight for a six-footer, even though headroom was up almost half an inch and BMW claimed to have found almost 4 inches (actually 3.9 inches, or 100 mm) across the cabin.

The first official preview photos of the E46 BMW 3 Series made many wonder if anything had changed?

Photos: BMW Press, Germany/UK, November 1997

That taut, stretched look of the sheet metal reflected that the track was widened by 2.4 inches (60 mm) in front and nearly as much in the rear. Less-welcome gains were at the curb. Despite lower declared poundage for engine and suspension components, curb weights were declared up by 130 to 165 lbs, depending on the model and options, but some testers reported gains under 70 lbs.

To get the best perspective on how BMW developed the 3 Series to meet consumer demands, let's rewind 23 years, back to the first 323i, and compare its key figure progress with today's 323i counterpart (see page 286).

It is fascinating comparing the 1970s to 2000, but what those comparisons don't tell us about is the civilization, enhanced safety, and capability of superior current cars. It is a wonder that we are still talking about a conventional internal combustion engine car, one laid out along established front-engine, rear-drive parameters. Automotive development limps along at a self-satisfied snail's pace compared to postwar computer progress and pricing.

A clue to the current Bimmer's prowess is given by the massive boost in top speed, which is mostly a by-product of an aerodynamic body. This sleek body comes with a far more efficient engine to propel the extra weight of safety and power-assist comfort items that customers—particularly in the US—demand as a basic right in the 21st century.

The new 3 Series may not have looked substantially different, nor did its basic BMW design parameters reveal radical revisions "on paper." For here was the familiar slant-mounted front-engine and rear-drive formula established in the 1960s four-cylinder BMWs, from 1500/1800 onward. The E46 has MacPherson strut front suspension, multi-link central-axle rear, and its trailing arm principles—but not its major alloy location components—remaining from its immediate (E36) predecessor. So where was the change to take us forward into the new millennium with the benchmark BMW four-door?

From an American stance, the first thing to realize was that four-cylinders were now history. Yes, the Compact hatchback design remained with US specification four-cylinders—as did the Z3 Roadster line out of Spartanburg—but the main two-door and four-door line in Stateside trim began with the 323i (actually a 2.5-liter, as in E36) and escalated to 328i.

These 24-valve sixes of 150 and 193 bhp continued to have the same alloy-block M52 engine family specification, whether complying with European or American specifications. The only major exceptions included OBD (On Board Diagnostics), a US requirement that was deleted in Europe for fears of unreliability (the earlier float sensors could prompt a warning signal that made drivers abandon a perfectly healthy automobile). The second major trans-Atlantic powertrain difference came in the use of an air pump to preserve catalytic converter standards to Low Emission Vehicle (LEV) standards.

Relevant to the aural comfort of every E46 customer were the intensive steps BMW development engineers took to combat acoustic rowdiness, but the biggest benefits were reserved for two four-cylinder power plants that were not offered in the US line-up.

Senior BMW R&D engineer Martin Kolk—who served time on the mid-1980s BMW-McLaren IMSA GT racer project earlier in his BMW career—commented, "We knew Volkswagen and especially Audi in the A3 would come with a double front bulkhead design: one that would take much of the engine noise from the interior. We had to have an answer to this in our new 3 Series and we needed most help with the four-cylinder engines.

"That is why we took the single overhead camshaft engine family that started life as the 1.8-liter M40 in 1987, then M43, and now with balancer

New York allows a wonderful backdrop for the 328i sedan. This four-door rode on the optional 17x 8-inch wheels, with Dunlop rather than Michelin tires.

Photo: Klaus Schnitzer, US, 1998

shafts and other important changes as the M43/E46 at 1.9 liters. It was not that the original four-cylinder M43 was rough—it had always been praised for smoothness. It was just that customer expectations would be higher and we must be better than our rivals with four cylinders," concluded Kolk.

BMW took an old British balancer-shaft principle and incorporated it within the M43/E46. The vibration-abating qualities of such shafts dated back to the British Lanchester of the 1920s, but had been effectively reworked by current patent holder Mitsubishi in Japan during the 1980s. Contra-rotating shafts, driven at twice crankshaft speed, were implanted in the sump pan of the European BMW 318i to avoid making even more expensive alterations to the cylinder block.

The shafts were driven from the crankshaft via cogs, and the results were deeply impressive, eliminating many of the low speed vibrations that haunt four-cylinder motors under acceleration and over-run. The European 318i also

Some key controls, such as the radio volume/channel selection (left), optional telephone, and cruise control (right) have button controls on the SRS airbag three-spoke steering wheel for the 323i/328i. This example is from a right-drive 323i.

Photo: Author, UK, 1999

gained long-life spark plugs, dependence on synthetic multigrade 5W40 oils, and a secondary air admission system to pass all immediately forthcoming European emission levels.

Although the 318, as for every other BMW of the late 1990s, utilized the Service Interval Indicator to prompt garage oil-change services, these intervals were averaged up by BMW engineers and reportedly boosted intervals from 15,000 km (9,315 miles) to 25,000 km (15,525 miles).

The 136-bhp European four-cylinder turbo-diesel engine was all-new and designed to be built on a modular base as part of a program that also contained a 240-bhp diesel V8, which BMW premiered in the 7 Series during May 1999. Both were deeply impressive units, but let's cut to the chase and talk about the six-cylinders, as that was the entry point for US E46 variants of 1998 onward.

These inline 24-valve sixes with their chain-drive overhead camshafts were referred to as M52 units, but they were significantly improved, perhaps even more than at any time in their extensive history dating back to the May 1990 520i and 525i. Then, they were coded M50, and followed the M42 fours in introducing quad-valve technology outside the M-brands of BMW.

For the latest-generation 3 Series, the alloy-block M52 sixes took on revised crankcases featuring cast-in liners and reinforcement frames for enhanced rigidity. Behind that move was the fact that during 1995, BMW decided against Europe's all-alloy sixes for American cars, which retained cast-iron blocks. Good call.

The alloy sixes developed a reputation for premature failure caused by high sulfur levels in US fuel. For the current 3 Series, BMW fitted steel cylinder liners to the alloy block to prevent excessive bore wear, and those engines were sold in the US. Even with the steel liners, the new engines were 70 lbs lighter than the previous iron blocks which, together with the aluminum lightweight suspension components, could only help both handling and operating economy.

There was also a new cylinder head based on "lost foam" castings; and the cooling system

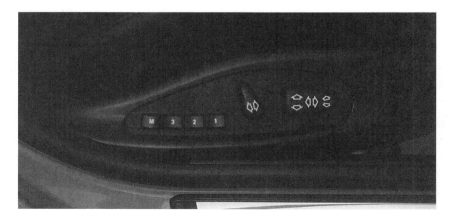

Seat 3-memory and power assist package is clearly labeled, but you naturally find the backrest and height adjusters through shape rather than labeling.

Photo: Author, UK, 1999

The first official factory photo of the latest 3 Series coupe was issued late in 1998, with volume sales around the world by the summer of 1999.

Photo: BMW AG Presse, November 1998

was overhauled, with reduced crankcase circulation and a computer-controlled map for more accurate thermostat operation. The 3-way catalytic converter could now be found right under the hood, rather than lurking under the floor. The BMW's variable valve/cam timing device (VANOS, or Variable Nockenwellen Stererung) was applied to both inlet and exhaust valve set timing, and an electric throttle valve was installed.

The customer benefits of these changes included a claimed 5 percent fuel consumption reduction. Far better response to full throttle demands at 3,500 of the available 6,500 rpm came from double VANOS. Steady speed economy was boosted by even better aerodynamic drag values (even the 328 was below 0.30 Cd), and the total E46 range was in a tight 0.28–0.29-Cd range.

Since weight was up and horsepower was practically the same as the previous E36, so far as the US market was concerned, theoretical performance tended to be slightly slower for equivalent six-cylinder comparisons. Independent European figures report 323i and 328i sedans at 141- and 148-mph maximums with 0–60 mph times of 7.6 and 7.3 sec and overall economy returns in the

23–24 Imperial (19.2 to 20 US) mpg range. *Car and Driver* went for the quickest times again and reported 6.4 sec as their launch-pad 0–60 mph scorch marker.

The 318i starter four-cylinder for Europe still managed 125 mph on 118 bhp, but you had to work hard to row from 0–60 mph in less than 10 seconds. The compensation was a fuel economy of close to 30 Imperial (25 US) mpg.

Your author's experience with the 323i in the US over 1,882 miles in 1999 saw 25.4 mpg at average speeds around 75 mph, and nearer 30 US mpg on more restricted roads.

Beneath Sheet-Metal Muscles

Although weight was up as a result of enhanced basic safety and quality construction, unsprung excess in the suspension and other key chassis elements were put on a serious diet. The company recorded a loss of 8 kg (17.6 lbs). That loss was owed to light-alloy construction of nine suspension or steering elements, including forged-aluminum front-suspension track control arms, brake guard plates, steering column and its casing, strut support bearing, upper rear-axle control arms, and the rear-axle compression rod.

1977 versus 2000 BMW 323i sedans: German Market

Model	E21 323i	E46 323i
Years made	1977–82	1998–2000
Base Prices	$20,000 US (1981)*; £6,249 UK (1977)	$27,560 US (2000); £24,895 UK (2000)
Bodies	2-dr sedan, Baur cabriolets	4-door sedan, 2-door coupe, Convertible, Compact, Touring 5-door
Aero drag factor	0.45 Cd	0.29 Cd
Length	4,355 mm/171.5 in	4,471 mm/176.0 in
Width	1,610 mm/63.4 in	1,739 mm/66.5 in
Height	1,380 mm/54.3 in	1,415 mm/55.7 in
Front track	1,388 mm/54.7 in	1,481 mm/58.3 in
Rear track	1,401 mm/55.1 in	1,488 mm/58.6 in
Wheelbase	2,563 mm/100.9 in	2,725 mm/107.3 in
Trunk space	404 (VDA, liters)	440 (VDA, liters)
Curb weight	1,110 kg/2,442 lbs	1,370 kg/3,014 lbs**
Engine	SOHC 6-cyl,12v, iron/alloy 2.3 liters	DOHC 6-cyl, 24v, aluminum 2.5 liters
Induction	Bosch K-Jetronic	DME Siemens-BMW MS 42.0
Power	143 bhp	170 bhp
Transmission	4-speed manual, ZF HP 22 3-speed automatic	5-speed Getrag or 5-speed ZF 5HP19
Final drive	3.45:1	3.07:1
Steering	ZF rack & pinion, 21:1 ratio	Hydraulic power-assisted rack & pinion, 15.5:1 ratio
Suspension	Inclined & upgraded MacPherson struts, 23.5 mm anti-roll bar	MacPherson struts, roll bar linked to Lower forged L-shape track control arm
Rear	Trailing arms at 20-degree swept angles, concentric coil springs/dampers;	Central arm axle with trailing arms and double track control links, plus anti-roll bar
17-mm diameter roll bar		
Brakes	9-in Mastervac & HP pump	Hydraulic assist, Teves ABS
Front	10.04-in vented discs	11.25-in vented discs
Rear	10.2-in solid discs	10.8-in vented discs
Wheels	5.5 x 13-in steel	6.5 x 15-in aluminum
Tire size	185/70 HR13	195/65 R15
Fuel	58 liters***/12.8 Imp. gal	63 liters/13.9 Imp. gal
Max. speed	119 mph	143 mph
0–62 mph	9.5 sec	8.0 sec
Urban mpg	20.9 (Imperial)	22.6 (Imperial)

*Gray Import via Hardy & Beck CA for *Road & Track*, 1981. UK price is an unmodified car without extras; most were £8,000 [over $15,000 at prevailing rates].

**DIN weight quoted for 23-year comparison purposes: Current standard EU weights—used throughout chapter texts— include 75 kg/165 lbs for a driver; by EU measurement, current 323i is 1,445 kg/3,179 lbs.

***52 liters to September 1977, then 58 liters adopted, all under rear seats.

"You can't help but fall in love—to the point of obsession," said *Roundel*'s Bob Roemer of the 1999 BMW 3 Series coupe.

Photo: Author, France, May 1999

One really neat suspension move was widely echoed in racing, but was confined to European four-cylinders (316/318i). BMW delivered a patented hollow-tube front roll bar from aerospace technology that saved 1.7 kg (3.7 lbs). The company stated that this was achieved through "a 40% higher tension level compared to previous pipe stabilizers—a level previously unattainable in the automotive industry."

Braking was substantially enhanced, even though 3 Series had always been at the top of the class. The Three was one of the best performers for 60–0 mph as well as 0–60 mph. All models gained vented discs on all four wheels; BMW's 50–50 weight distribution, as well as deliberate rearward brake bias, supported the adoption of yet larger and thicker discs.

The entire line-up of 316i to 323i four-cylinders and six-cylinders (plus the 320 diesel) gained vented front discs of 286 x 22-mm dimensions (11.25 in by 0.87 in), backed up by solid discs at the back. A 328i took on monster 300-mm vented units up front and 294-mm units at the rear (11.8 in and 11.6 in). All were supported by the best in Teves ABS braking and

an array of electronic handling aids that is currently unparalleled.

Developed in association with ITT-AE Corporation in Germany, there were four major electronic dynamic-assist systems available on the most recent 3 Series. They were: upgraded ABS anti-lock braking, Automatic Stability Control (ASC), CBC (Cornering Brake Control), and Dynamic Stability Control (DSC). All offered improved safety levels through electronic intervention of braking/engine throttle opening.

Since BMW NA often used differing marketing expressions for traction controls—and fitted such systems as AST (All Season Traction) across their range by 1997—some confusion can result. The European ASC+T layouts have the same technology.

All of these electronic systems depend on computer-monitored and controlled millisecond commands via sensors that prompt enhanced braking control limiting, excess acceleration, or restoring cornering grip. They are mostly developments of the ABS anti- lock commands—sometimes using the ABS

This is the Bimmer workhorse, a 320d turbodiesel of 45-mpg capability, cruising comfortably at 100 mph. But neither the US or UK governments seem happy to encourage the frugal habits of diesel, and the medical evidence of a cancerous health hazard is confusing.

Photo: BMW GB, 1999

Elongated one-piece side panels frame the 3 Series Touring and provide the giant machine tool presses of Regensburg with some serious stamping duties. How well it all fitted together can be seen in the side view of the five-door.

Photos: Author, Regensberg, Germany, 1999; BMW GB, 1999

fluid-return pumps—that will also brake each wheel individually. Another addition is the ability to modulate/ reduce power when wheel spin is detected.

MSR, translated as motor drag torque control, was important in the US market, with its heavy take on automatic transmissions. MSR prevents the rear wheels from locking when the accelerator is lifted too sharply on a slimy surface (particularly valuable downhill) or when the clutch is clumsily operated. In the US, such systems are usually sub-sections within AST.

New to the 3 Series was CBC (Cornering Brake Control) seen previously on the 5 and 7 Series. This system guarded against running out of control when the electronic sensors detected the combination of either excess braking or speed mid-corner, redistributing braking to comparatively unladen wheels in an effort to restore stability before a full emergency onset.

CBC is usually employed as a support to DSC, or Dynamic Stability Control: DSC III was a 328i option only in Europe. DSC is the umbrella for systems that sense sideways as well as longitudinal forces, and was available in Europe on the 5, 7, and 8 Series from September 1997. DSC adds another dimension to ABS and AST/ASC+T, sensing those side forces against steering angles. It reacts by braking individual wheels—the principle found on some sledges—or by using a combination of reduced engine power and spurts of ABS braking to regain control whenever sensors report an unsafe cornering attitude.

Developing the Line

Full technical specifications were issued in Munich as of February 1998 and cars were available in the LHD showrooms of Continental Europe starting in May 1998. It was July of 1998 before the latest 323i and 328i arrived in America, while RHD Britain took the 318i and 328i starting in September of that year, followed by the 323i in December 1998.

Some of the E36 predecessors—-principally, derivatives such as the Convertible, M3 derivatives, Tourer and Compact— stayed on in production in the BMW tradition, post-E46. However, the four-door sedan line replacements were all E46 in 1998, and the two-door coupe arrived the following summer in all markets, to the warmest reception of any variant...yet.

The second-generation coupe was another restrained stretch of the E36/E46 theme. Initially, you don't see much difference aside from two fewer doors and a price span of $27,560 to $33,970 Base for 323is and 328is respectively. But on closer inspection, there is not a panel in common for this slightly (less than an inch) longer

Good news for the snow belt: BMW decided to return 4x4 as an option on 3 Series for the first time since the time of the E30 325iX. The first show cars were touring models with diesel engines, but gasoline motors with sedan four-door bodies were scheduled for US sales in 2000.

Photo: BMW AG Presse, Geneva Show, Switzerland, March 2000

Just in time for summer 2000 sales around the world, BMW brought the Convertible back into the 3 Series line.

The landscape is brightened by the usual clean drop-top line and an aluminum hardtop option.

Photos: BMW AG, 2000

Like the contemporary M5, the new M3 has a more aggressive "face." It also shares the usual European electronic limiter set at 155 mph and is expected to be the fastest accelerating BMW production model, with an official 5.3-second clip for 0–60 mph, 0–100 mph in 11.4 seconds, and a standing quarter-mile anticipated around 13.5 seconds.

Photo: BMW AG Presse, February 2000

BMW M engineers constructed V8 prototype M3s, but logically redeveloped the 24-valve inline six for the late 2000/early 2001 showroom debut at a new bhp-per-liter benchmark of 105.7. A 0.6-mm overbore allowed just a 44-cc increase in capacity (now 3,245 cc from 87 x 91 mm).

Photo: BMW AG Presse, February 2000

and wider E46 variant. It does ride over an inch lower at the roofline and is a superb drive.

Your author was privileged to discover this in test track routines for BMW GB with 323is and also ran three 328is of varying wheel (16- to 18-inch) and suspension formats in France, including the annual outing to Le Mans. Such experiences—especially the track stuff with electronic assists off and a demand for spectacular action—revealed that there was true dynamic worth beneath these flowing lines. That track mileage restored faith in BMW's ability to supply driving pleasure through to the edges of sanity. Simultaneously, the company was being criticized in Europe and the US for taming the 3'er a step too far.

US prices for the four-door BMW 323i sedan through the 328is coupe two-door were $27,560 to $34,560 in 1999, compared to 1998 introductory price tags of $26,970 for the 323i and $33,370 for the E36 coupe. These 1998 Base prices represented increases of around 5 percent over the previous (E36) models. You could expect to actually pay around $37,245 for a Sports Pack 328i, and the same car cost $36,870 with the Premium/Luxury Pack in October 1998.

The Regensberg-made 5-door Touring E46 arrived in late 1999 in Europe and was slated for US sale in 2000. The further Good Touring

News was that BMW was scheduled to display a 4x4 Touring/Sedan 3-liter [330xi] variant of significance to the snow belt customers, countering the only really serious basic flaw found in the front-engine, rear-drive design. It is the worst of layouts for slippy surface traction. Even with the anti-skid electronics and mechanical limited-slip differentials Bimmer has developed, simple rear-drive cannot be as effective on the slippery stuff as the majority of most basic front-drive designs. The all-wheel-drive 4x4 traction is better yet...unless the engine is placed over the rear wheels as per Porsche, or you have a mid-engined exotic, but you wouldn't normally choose these as commuter hacks for snowbelt use.

Why does BMW persist with front-engine rear-drive? Because it is the best-balanced system for performance/track use in higher-grip conditions, providing affordable driving pleasure at more accessible prices and lower curb weights than the complexities of all-wheel-drive. Even so, we'd like to see 4x4 spread wider in the BMW 3 and 5 ranges, not just as part of the X5 or higher-priced body combinations. As this book was readied, it looked like Jaguar would have 4x4 in their Ford-financed smaller-car/bigger-volume assault on Planet Three.

If you like your M-motoring with a leather and luxury power-assist twist, the new M3 will provide it all. Here we see the sprawling switchgear for three spoke wheel and curvaceous 3-memory seat, plus the M5 influence in the chrome-ringed instrumentation including the warm-up warning light sequence in the 5000 to 8000 rpm yellow band.

Photos: BMW AG Presse, February 2000

The only obvious missing elements to a full 3 Series line at press time were the E46 convertible (displayed and pictured but not available for driving until spring 2000), the M3 warriors (slated for September 2000 press introduction, on sale in the first quarter of 2001), and a successor to the E36/E30 Compact hybrid hatchbacks. BMW plans to have these ready for market in mid-2001.

Thus the 3'er line remains a class benchmark, an icon of our time. It reigns supreme for the immediate future, with a 2 Series starter model in 2004 that allowed the 3 Series increasing upmarket sophistication as it grew from E46 to E90 fifth generation in 2005.

Appendix 1
Production

Official BMW AG 3 Series Production Records, May 1966–December 1997: Highlights

'02 (1502, 1602, 1802, and 2002):
- 861,940 units manufactured from May 1966–July 1976
- 382,740 units were 2002s
- 112,524 of all 02 series were exported to the US
- 13,162 were 1602s of 1967-1971 for the US
- Plus 99,362 (11.5 per cent) US 2002s, Feb 1968 to July 1976

E21 3 Series:
- 1,364,038 units manufactured from June 1975–Sept 1983
- 186,039 four-cylinders made to US specification
- 270,445 carburetted six-cylinder 320 units made, not for US
- 137,107 fuel-injected 323i units made, not for US
- 30 percent (407,552) of all first-generation 3'ers were six-cylinders

E30 3 Series:
- 2,339,250 units manufactured from 1982–January 1994
- 1,058,562 two-door units and 908,789 four-door units made
- 17,970 of the first E30 M3 made

E36, all models, 1990–99:
- By December 1998, 2,373,463 units made: E36 variants (Convertible/Touring) continued into 1999
- 1,449,809 four-door sedans made
- 430,000 two-door coupes made (includes M3)
- 280,000 three-door Compact E36/30 hatchbacks made
- 150,000 two-door convertibles made
- 130,000 (production estimate) five-door Touring (not for US) made by July 1999

E36 M3:

- 71,279 E36 M3 units declared for production period 1992–2000
- By December 1997, BMW reported all M-car production since 1978 at 105,260. The M3 represented over 70 percent of all M-sales!
- 89,249 M3 units made
- 28,285 E36 European M3 3-liters made (E36 and E30 combined)
- Among low-production E36 M3s were 50 RHD M3 GT Individual coupes built in 1995
- The lowest-volume US M3 model was the M3L Lightweight, with 122 units registered

M3 Production 1985–93

Total production figures are for the M3 sedan only, excluding Motorsport prototypes, all from the Munich 1.1 plant. These totals have been overhauled since the publication of *Unbeatable BMW*, using yearly sales totals researched and supplied by BMW NA in 1999. See also the text and table notes in Chapter 13.

E30 (first-edition) M3 annual production

Year	M3 Sedans	M3 Cabriolet (Convertible)
1985	1	—
1986	2396	—
1987	6396	—
1988	3426	130
1989	2541	180
1990	2424	176
1991	—	300
Totals	17,184	786

Grand Total E30 M3 production from 1985–1991 was 17,970 units. The rarest E30 M3 sedan was the Europemeister 88 (150 units). Evolutions were next, with total Evo I production at 505 units and Evo II at just 501units. Production of Cecotto and Ravaglia special editions in Europe totaled 508 units. Final 2.5-liter M3 Sport Evolution production totaled 600 units. The E30 M3 continued to be sold in the US in 1992 and 1993 in very limited numbers (see Appendix 2).

The subsequent E36 M3 smashed all sales and export records for M3 in the 1990s.

M3 Buyer's Guide: Model Codes (MC) and VINs

Model	Model Code (MC)	VIN
Official US import M3	1003	AK03
200-bhp European non-cat original	1001	AK01
195-bhp European cat sedan	1005	AK05
238-bhp European Sport Evolution	1007	AK07
200-bhp European non-cat Convertible	BB01	BB01
215-bhp European cat Convertible	BB05	BB05

All M-Production

Model	Units manufactured	Production span
M1	450	1978–81
M3(first edition)	17,970	1986–90
E36 M3 (second edition)	71,279	1992–2000
M535i (all models)	11,113	1980–87
M5 (all models)	14,394	1984–95
M635 CSi/M6	5,855	1984–89
M5 V8	7,186	1999–5/2000
Z3 M Roadster	12,654	1997–5/2000
Z3 M Coupe	4,816	1998–5/2000
Totals	**145,481**	**1978–5/2000**

Yearly 3 Series Statistics, 1975–98, Germany

These figures are from German production records retained by BMW (GB) Ltd. Note that the first 3 Series came only in the two-door body, while the second generation included a four-door and five-door option. Dates refer to a mass-production line from start to finish; pilot rarities are noted for collector interest and in the relevant chapter.

E21 3 Series production analysis

Year	315	316	318	318i	320i/4-cyl	320/M60 6-cyl	323i/M60 6-cyl	Yearly total
1975	—	10,629	10,446	—	1,851	—	—	443,349
1976	—	42,166	14,618	—	20,477	—	—	130,821
1977	—	52,834	20,369	—	32,322	18,203	337	166,758
1978	—	53,513	20,897	—	26,775	61,402	18,467	183,377
1979	—	45,914	16,388	9,401	17,474	65,369	31,123	188,809
1980	2	54,794	10,491	43,264	—	59,383	36,424	206,326
1981	33,115	44,019	—	71,739	—	44,882	33,205	228,832
1982	47,112	28,727	—	66,358	—	21,206	17,851	182,010
1983	27,069	4,438	—	1,302	—	—	—	33,757
Totals	**107,538**	**337,034**	**93,209**	**192,561**	**98,899**	**270,445**	**137,107**	**1,364,038**

E30 3 Series Production

Year	Units produced	Year	Units produced
1982	15,580	1989	257,307
1983	218,201	1990	246,818
1984	285,134	1991	56,363
1985	297,886	1992	26,913
1986	329,460	1993	18,440
1987	316,075	1994	1,997
1988	269,074	**Total**	**2,339,251**

E30 Production analysis by key model, 1982–1994

E30 variants of the Touring and Cabriolet continued in production alongside the E36 generations of the 1990s, so BMW AG's definitive analysis figures for the E30 were not released until the late 1990s, thus the final totals are higher than previously reported, amounting to 2,339,251. These figures are the final ones, including thousands of CKD (Completely Knocked Down) kits supplied in more remote overseas territories and not accounted for in public print until now. Diesels and the smallest (316-badged) gasoline-engine line have not been individually quoted.

E30 Production totals, by model

Model	Production span	Units made
318i/M40	1987–91	89,637
All 318is	1989–91	41,234
320i/2dr	1982–91	198,559
320i/4dr	1982–86	182,210
323i/2dr	1983–86	64,076
323i/4dr	1983–90	26,700
325i/2dr	1985–91	113,906
325i/4dr	1985–91	83,030
325iX 2-dr only	1985–91	12,557
All 325iX 4x4	1985–91	29,589
325e 2-dr	1983–88	114,498
325e 4-dr	1983–88	74,789
All 325e 2/ 4dr	1983–88	189,287
M3 2-dr sedan	1986–90	17,184
M3 2-dr Cabrio	1988–91	786
318i Cabrio	1990–93	24,706
320i Cabrio	1986–93	32,687
325i Cabrio	1985–93	85,246
All Touring	1987–1994	103,704
All Cabrios	1985–1994	143,425
All 2-dr	1982–1991	1,058,562
All 4-dr	1983–1991	908,789

E36 Production, Model Year 1990–1998

Year	Units made	Year	Units made
1989	3	1994	387,811
1990	8,335	1995	428,800
1991	265,527	1996	386,869
1992	362,845	1997	385,393*
1993	339,791	1998	193,509
		Total	**2,373,463****

*Estimate: UK/D sources say 338,889 units were made during this final full year for E36

**This is a working total only to this point, as Convertible and Touring production continued into the new millennium.

E36 Key collectibles

Production span	Body type	Units made
1990–98	Coupes, incl. M3	459,835
1992–98	Convertibles, incl. M3	154,669
1994–98	Touring 5-dr	122,503
1993–98	Compact 3-dr	330,967
1992–98	All M3 types	71,279

E36 M3 production

Year	M3 Coupes, all types	Cabrio/Convertible M3, Regensberg only	Sedan 4-dr M3, Regensberg only	Total M3 output, including all CKD and SKD kits
1992	470	—	—	520
1993	6,080	3	—	6,712
1994	9,289	1,118	288	9,355
1995	9,828	860	1,282	9,828
1996	6,896	1,248	3,639	11,591
1997	5,873*	1,135**	4,468	12,205
1998	—	—	—	6,118
Totals	**38,436**	**4,364**	**9,677**	**56,329******

*Estimate: There is also a separate 1992–95 record of 748 right-drive M3 coupes assembled from CKD kits outside of Munich. Some could have also been sold in the UK, as were E36 318is derivatives at various run-out dates. These are included in E36 M3 production totals.

**Estimate

***South Africa made 272 4-dr M3s from CKD assembly in 1997 and another 168 in 1996 from a four-door kits supplied via Munich.

****The last E36 M3 was not made until Summer 2000, when BMW dedeclared a total of 71,279 assembled.

Appendix 2
Sales Statistics and UK Rarities

Here is how BMW NA and BMW GB reported sales growth of the company's most popular product. We also cover some deviations of the most collectible 3'er on either side of the Atlantic. Our particular thanks go to BMW staffers Andrew Cutler, Jay Binneweg in the US, and Frank Sutton in the UK.

US Sales Records

US sales records, 1976–99

Year*	3 Series sales	Total	Year*	3 Series sales	Total
1976	1,763	26,040	1988	38,346	N/A
1977	19,159	28,776	1989	32,153	N/A
1978	22,164	31,439	1990	29,583	N/A
1979	23,604	34,520	1991	29,002	53,343
1980	25,786	37,017	1992	38,040	N/A
1981	31,902	41,761	1993	45,595	N/A
1982	36,462	51,707	1994	49,255	N/A
1983	34,619	59,243	1995	54,720	N/A
1984	44,433	70,898	1996	64,745**	N/A
1985	53,905	87,832	1997	52,470**	105,761
1986	61,822	96,759	1998	57,520	131,559
1987	58,896	N/A	1999	77,138	153,658

* Individual model and annual totals are given by calendar year, not model year.

**Not including Z3 derivatives. We regard these model lines as separate from the 3 Series.

US E30 and E36 M3 sales, 1987–99

Year	Units sold	Year	Units sold
1987	1,113	1994	2,953 (US 240 bhp E36 available)
1988	1,675	1995	5,806 (Includes 43 Lightweights and 1,311 automatic M3s)
1989	979	1996	3,175 (Includes 79 Lightweights and 299 automatic M3s)
1990	764	1997	7,940 (New 4-door M3 sedan 4,535; coupe 3,405)
1991	384	1998	8,762 (4-door 3,225; Convertible 2,876; coupe 2,661)
1992	76	1999	3,161 (only the Convertible, at 3,335 units, was fully available)
1993	5 (only the 1990 and 1991 E30 available)		

All 4-cylinder sales	4,996
All 6-cylinder sales	35,193
All M3 sales	40,189

US: Individual model sales totals, E30

Year	318i	325e	325i	325iX	Convertible
1983	19,198	—	—	—	—
1984	27,782	20,846	—	—	—
1985	12,842	29,036	—	—	—
1986	907	60,895	—	—	—
1987	18	41,299	16,143	297	11,609
1988	—	9,364	16,286	310	11,021
1989	—	282	21,854	844	8,194
1990	—	20	20,914	699	7,186
1991	—	—	24,422	454	3,742
1992	—	—	—	41	5,256
1993	—	—	—	2	1,391
1994	—	—	—	—	13
Totals	**60,747**	**161,742**	**99,619**	**2,647**	**48,412**

US: Individual model sales totals, E36 4-door sedans

Year	325i	318i	328i	Total
1992	17,062	3,350	—	20,412
1993	17,977	5,936	—	23,913
1994	14,027	7,071	—	21,098
1995	13,555	8,485	341	22,381
1996	571	4,712	13,810	19,093
1997	11	7,608	14,039	21,658
1998	—	—	10,316	10,316
1999	—	—	286	286
Totals	**63,203**	**37,162**	**38,792**	**139,157**

US: Collectible model sales totals, E36 2-door coupes

Year	325i	318is	328is	Total
1992	7,980	2,817	—	10,797
1993	10,315	5,892	—	16,207
1994	8,693	5,562	—	14,255
1995	6,359	4,131	6,359	16,849
1996	248	2,274	6,375	8,897
1997	−2(!)	1,298	4,382	5,678
1998	—	171	2,283	2,454
1999	—	13	1,538	1,551
Totals	**33,593**	**22,158**	**20,937**	**76,688**

US E36 Convertible sales, collectible models

Year	325iC	318iC	328iC	323 iC	Total
1993	4,038	—	—	—	4,038
1994	7,778	3,156	—	—	10,934
1995	7,204	3,383	149	—	10,736
1996	762	2,876	7583	—	11,221
1997	6	1,629	8815	963	11,413
1998	—	57	4467	N/A	4,524+
1999	—	4	2892	N/A	2,896+
Total	**19,788**	**11,105**	**23,906**	**963+**	**55,762+**

BMW 318ti Compact/3-door sales

Calendar Year	BMW NA sales
1995	5119
1996	7238
1997	4622
1998	3735
1999	656
Total	**21,370**

UK Sales Records

E30 3-series sales versus overall BMW (GB) total sales

Year	3-series	Total	Year	3-series	Total
1980	6,463	13,450	1986	24,125	35,896
1981	10,330	17,088	1987	24,883	N/A
1982	13,776	22,977	1988	26,441	42,761
1983	14,214	25,178	1989	29,072	48,910
1984	16,25S	25,785	1990	25,119	43,004
1985	20,793	33,448			

UK Rarities

As an official special-order import for Britain, the M3 was a comparatively rare sight on British roads. Just 55 of the original M3 saloons were brought in for 1987 registration, and 58 were sold in 1988. The peak UK E30 M3 sales year was 1989, with just 62 M3 saloons. By then, however, the importers also had the 2.5 Evolution for 1988 and a convertible for 1989 (19 units sold that year). At the close of 1990, just 211 of the 2.3-liter saloons, 32 convertibles and 38 of the 2.5-liter saloons had been officially imported.

Of the rarer Evolutionary models, the official UK importation documentation shows only 7 Evolution I units, 51 Evolution II units, and none of the 1988 EuropaMeister 88 models, which were handled by BMW GB. The official Roberto Ravaglia (Cecotto on the Continent) model reached 25 UK copies, and approximately 51 of the final Evolution Sport 2.5-liters were ordered, though 1990 sales figures recorded 38 sales to August 1991.

The initial German price was £18,500, but British special-order M3s always exceeded £20,000 from the official network. They held their value, even in LHD, until the 1990s recession took prices of older models down to less than £15,000.

The first M3s came to Britain via the official importers in April 1987, nearly a year after their LHD announcement. The initial price on a D-plate was £23,550, and that was maintained until the 1988 E-plate examples. Standard equipment included the 7J x 15-inch alloy wheels, limited-slip differential, power steering, sports seats, and electronic ABS anti-lock braking. Options included power roof and windows, on-board computer, and, on later M3s, EDC (Electronic Damper Control).

For 1988, the standard 200-bhp M3 was supplanted for UK purposes by the Evolution models of 220 bhp that retailed for £26,960. Showroom features centered upon the upgraded engine and revised aerodynamics, identified by additional tail spoiler flap and brake ducting to the front device. Similarly priced, but officially 5 bhp less, was the Roberto Ravaglia edition (25 for UK); these cost £26,850 in July 1989. At this point, all imported BMW M3s went into 3-way catalytic converter form only in UK specification.

The 2.5-liter Evolution (Evo III to the Germans) was sold in the UK. Launched in Germany at the equivalent price of £29,820, it cost £34,500 when it arrived in Britain. Only 38 were shifted during the early 1990's recession.

The retail price in June 1990 was £34,500, but that did not include an electric sliding roof (£745), front electric windows (£413), electronic damper control (EDC) (£1,494), venting rear windows (£119), air conditioning (£1,341), on-board computer (£363), anti-theft locking (£3,397), headlight wash-wipe (£310), and electronic heating control (£160). The seats were normally finished in anthracite cloths, and wore Motorsport striping, but an additional £1,310 bought black leather in Britain. Air conditioning was on one demonstration model we tried (the engine of which did not run cleanly when the air conditioning cut in)and cost an extra £1,341.

The following figures are the official totals of approved imports via BMW (GB). Expect many more original M3 saloons to be present in UK via unofficial/personal imports, a practice as popular in the late 1990s as it was when the E30 M3 was new.

UK M3 collectible model sales

Year	M3	M3 Cabrio	M3 Evo
1987	55	—	—
1988	58	—	—
1989	62	19	—
1990	36	13	38
Total	211	32	38

UK 323i and 325i sales

Year	323i	325i
1983	2,095	—
1984	1,858	—
1985	2,093	—
1986	87	5,038

Year	323i	325i
1987	81	5,592
1988	—	5,964
1989	—	6,597
1990	—	4,203
Totals	4,119	27,394

UK 325i Sport sales figures

Year	Manual	Automatic
1986	352	30
1987	1,320	106
1988	208	29
1989	1,236	199
1990	812	110

UK 320 SE sales

Year	320 SE/2dr		320 SE/4dr		Total
	Manual	Automatic	Manual	Automatic	
1988	518	167	416	202	1,303
1989	828	200	580	247	1,055
1990	654	186	565	240	1,645
Totals	2,000	553	1,561	689	4,803

UK 325i SE sales

Year	325i SE 2dr		325i SE/4 dr		Total
	Manual	Automatic	Manual	Automatic	
1988	729	240	551	293	1,813
1989	409	193	660	303	1,565
1990	225	120	388	216	949
Totals	663	553	1,599	812	4,327

UK E36 M3 sales

Year	Coupes*	Sedans**	Convertibles***	Total
1993	270	—	—	270
1994	789	—	210	999
1995	687	389	333	1,409
1996	737	411	470	1,618
1997	708	231	470	1,409
1998	683	18	513	1,214
Totals	3,874	1,049	1,996	6,919

Appendix 3
The 3 Series Spotter's Guide

The following pages contain a detailed breakdown of all the statistics for all the 3 Series models distributed in the US. Credit goes to Phil Marx for the hard work that went into collecting and organizing all this material. Also included at the end of this section is a breakdown of all the optional equipment and packages for all of the E46 models. All photos in this section are courtesy of BMW of North America.

Technical Data BMW 1977-1979 320i (E21)—US Model

General

Manufacturer's suggested retail price at introduction: $7,775 ($7,875 West Coast)
Air Conditioning: $550
Metallic Paint: $255
Recaro Seats: $300
Sport St.Wheel: $40
Manual sunroof: $310
Light Alloy Rims: $225
Dealer Prep: $150
Federal Excise Tax:
  Std. Wheels: $10.50
  Alloy Wheels: $10.90

Base price
1977: $7,990
1978: $9,315
1979: $9,735
Production:
1977 7/76 to 8/77
(California only) 9/76 to 9/77
1978 9/77 to 7/78
1979 9/78 to 7/79
Curb weight: 2650 lbs.
Wheelbase: 100.9 in.
Weight distribution: Front/Rear % 51/49
Fuel capacity: 15.9 gal.
Fuel requirement: 87 octane (91 RON)
Front Engine, rear wheel drive

Engine

Type 2.0 liter 4-cylinder in-line water cooled, longitudinally mounted, inclined, single chain-driven overhead camshaft, forged crankshaft with 5 main bearings and 8 counterweights.
Bore/Stroke: 89/80 mm
Displacement: 1990 cc
Compression Ratio: 8.1:1
Fuel injected Bosch K-Jetronic fuel injection
Exhaust emission control: Manairox system with air injection (Thermal Reactor on California version only)
Horsepower:

110hp (SAE net) @ 5,800 rpm
105hp (SAE net) @ 5,800 rpm (California version)
Torque: 112 ft-lb (SAE) @ 3,750 rpm
108.5 ft-lb (SAE) @ 3,750 rpm (California version)
Ignition distributor with vacuum retard and centrifugal advance, mechanical breaker points. 55 amp alternator, 12-volt 55 amp hrs. battery. Hydraulic shock damper at left engine mount

Chassis and Drivetrain

Transmission:
4-speed manual (Getrag)
  Gear ratios I/II/III/IV/R:
  3.764/2.022/1.320/1.000/4.096
Optional 3-speed automatic (ZF)
  Gear ratios I/II/III//R:
  2.478/1.478/1.000/2.090
Steering: rack and pinion (non-assisted), with hydraulic damper
Steering ratio: 21.1:1
Front Suspension: MacPherson struts, off-center mounted coil springs & torsion bar stabilizer (22mm) acting as tension strut

Rear Suspension: independent semi-trailing arms, shock absorber mounted inside coil springs & torsion bar stabilizer
Final drive ratio: 3.64:1
Braking:
  Front 255 mm discs, (vented 1977 only)
  Rear 250 mm rear twin-shoe drums incorporating handbrake; rear axle brake pressure regulator
Wheels: styled steel rims 5 1/2J x 13
  (Optional light alloy wheels)
Offset: 18mm
Tires: 185/70HR-13

Interior

Front reclining bucket seats (manually operated) with height-adjustable head rests, cloth or leatherette upholstery, full carpeting, carpet on rear shelf, storage pockets in front doors, lockable (and lighted) glove compartment with flashlight socket, anti-glare mirror, heated rear window, 3-point automatic seat belts front and rear with 2-point lap belt in center rear, 120 mph speedometer with 6-digit odometer and trip odometer,

tachometer, analog clock, orange instrument and ventilation control lighting, flow-through ventilation, manually operated front windows with pop-out rear windows, tinted glass all around with dark green border on top of windshield, four spoke padded steering wheel with horn buttons in each spoke, tool kit in trunk lid.

Exterior

Unit body with impact and roll over protection, integrated roll bar in center pillar for safety, energy absorbing 5 mph bumpers, full-frame doors, hood safety catch, polished stainless

door, mounted rear view mirror driver side only, twin saddle-type fuel tanks mounted forward of the rear axle.

Technical Data BMW 1977-1979 320i (E21)—US Model

Optional Equipment	Automatic transmission, limited slip differential (25%), sport steering wheel (15"), Recaro front seats in black cloth or leatherette, air-conditioning, dual operation mechanical sunroof, light alloy wheels, metallic paint, radios

Performance	Acceleration, 0-60 mph: 10.5 sec
	Top Speed, mph:
	  106 standard
	  104 automatic transmission
	Lateral Acceleration (g's) .757
	  (.761 for 1978 model)
	1977 Fuel economy EPA (Hwy/city), mpg
	  Standard transmission 29/20
	  Automatic transmission 25/19
	
	1978 Fuel economy EPA (Hwy/city/combined), mpg
	  Standard transmission 28/19/22
	  Automatic transmission 26/18/21
	Stopping distance from 60 mph 156 ft.
	Noise level at 70 mph: 74 dbA

Changes for 1978	Front springs stiffer by 10% Front stabilizer bar diameter reduced by 1mm to 21mm Rear stabilizer bar deleted Increased dampening from revalved shock absorbers Solid front rotors Size changed on front axle spindle/bearings Lower temperature operating range rear brake linings Top gear ignition advance switch added Reduced height in front seats Improved cloth upholstery Aluminum heater core Deletion of plastic engine compartment headlight covers (improved air flow) Additional exhaust hanger between front and rear muffler Improved heat shield/protection for fuel tanks connection tube Gas filler cap holder added inside fuel filler door	
Changes for 1979	Improvements to front seat spring core upholstery, backrest spring set deeper in seat, seat cushion upholstery thickened. Restyled steering column levers and symbols to match 733i Enlarged rear-view mirror and modified sun-visor opening Seat belt receptacle moved from floor to seat Seat front/back adjustment lever moved to beneath seat Narrower slot at seat belt tongue to prevent twist Lip removed from door storage bins Head rests flared at sides Aluminum radiator core with plastic tank Brake pad wear indicator warning lamp added (sensor in left front pad) Low fuel level warning lamp incorporated into fuel gauge Position of turn signal indicator and handrake/fluid level warning lights reversed in instrument cluster Radio antenna, wiring and front speakers become standard License plate lamps move from side to top of mounting plate Exhaust pipe shorter and straight now near left corner Modified front sway-bar thrust bushing	

Technical Data BMW 1980-1983 320i (E21)—US Model

General

Manufacturer's suggested retail prices for 1982:
Base Price: $13,290
Automatic Transmission: $620
Metallic Paint: $420
Dual Position Sunroof: $555
Limited Slip Differential: $370
Light Alloy Rims: $500
Luxus Touring Group: $1,685
"S" Package: $2,620
Dealer Preparation Charge: $150
Destination and Handling: $245
Federal Excise Tax on Tires: $10.20
Wheelbase: 100.9 in.
Weight distribution, front/rear (%): 51/49

Base price
1980: $11,810
1981: $12,895
1982: $13,290
1983: $13,290
Production:
1980: 9/79 to 7/80
1981: 9/80 to 7/81
1982: 9/81 to 7/82
1983: 9/82 to 12/82
Curb weight: 2500 lbs.
Fuel capacity: 15.9 gal.
Fuel requirement: Unleaded 87 octane (91 RON)
Front engine, rear wheel drive

Engine

Type: 1.8 liter (M10) 4-cylinder in-line water cooled, longitudinally mounted, inclined, single chain-driven overhead camshaft, cast crankshaft with 5 main-bearings and 4 counterweights.
Bore/Stroke: 89/70 mm
Displacement: 1766 cc
Compression Ratio: 8.8:1
Fuel injected Bosch K-Jetronic fuel injection modified with pulse valve for Lambda-control

Exhaust emission control: 3-way catalyst with Lambda-sensor (50 state version)
Horsepower: 101hp (SAE net) @ 5,800 rpm
Torque: 100 ft-lb (SAE) @ 4,500 rpm
Breakerless electronic Ignition system (reverse rotation from previous years)
65 amp alternator, 12-volt 55 amp hrs. battery
Hydraulic shock damper at left engine mount

Chassis and Drivetrain

Transmission:
5-speed manual (Getrag) 245
  Gear ratios I/II/III/IV/V/R:
  3.682/2.002/1.330/1.000/0.806/4.096
Optional 3-speed automatic (ZF)
  Gear ratios I/II/III//R:
  2.730/1.560/1.000/2.090
Steering: rack and pinion (non-assisted), with hydraulic damper
Steering ratio: 21.1:1
Front Suspension: MacPherson struts, off-center mounted coil springs & torsion bar stabilizer acting as tension strut

Rear Suspension: independent semi-trailing arms, shock absorber mounted inside coil springs (anti-roll bar stabilizer S-package only)
Final drive ratio: 3.91:1 Manual transmission; 3.64:1 Automatic transmission
Braking:
  Front 255 mm discs
  Rear 250 mm rear twin-shoe drums incorporating handbrake; rear axle brake pressure regulator
Wheels: styled steel rims 5 1/2J x 13 (Optional light alloy wheels)
Offset: 18mm
Tires: 185/70SR-13

Interior

Front reclining bucket seats (manually operated) with height-adjustable head rests, cloth or leatherette upholstery, full carpeting, carpet on rear shelf, storage pockets in front doors, lockable (and lighted) glove compartment with flashlight socket, anti-glare mirror, heated rear window, 3-point automatic seat belts front and rear with 2-point lap belt in center rear, 85 mph speedometer with 6-digit odometer and trip odometer,

tachometer, digital clock, orange instrument and ventilation control lighting, radio antenna and four speakers and fader control, flow-through ventilation, manually operated front windows with pop-out rear vents, tinted glass all around with dark green border on top of windshield, four-spoke padded steering wheel with horn buttons in each spoke, tool kit in trunk lid.

Exterior

Unit body with impact and roll-over protection, integrated roll bar in center pillar for safety, energy absorbing 5 mph bumpers, full-frame doors, hood safety catch, electrically

controlled window frame mounted plastic housing rear view mirror driver side only, twin saddle-type fuel tanks mounted forward of the rear axle.

Technical Data BMW 1980-1983 320i (E21)—US Model

Optional Equipment	Automatic transmission, limited slip differential (25%), air-conditioning, dual operation mechanical sunroof, light alloy wheels, metallic paint, radios Luxus Touring Group (320i) includes: Air Conditioning, Electronic AM/FM Stereo Cassette Radio, Fog Lights Sport Package (320iS) includes: Recaro front seats in black cloth or leatherette, leather wrapped smaller diameter sport steering wheel, leather shift knob, electric passenger side rear view mirror, halogen high beams, front air dam, larger diameter front anti-roll bar, rear anti-roll bar, limited slip differential, special cross-spoke (BBS-style) wheels, AM-FM stero cassette radio, fog lights, deluxe tool kit, Recaro front seats in black cloth or leatherette, model designation deleted. Not available with automatic transmission or air conditioning. Availability limited to three exterior colors: Schwarz (black), Alpine white, Polaris silver.

Performance	Acceleration, 0-60 mph: 11.1 sec
	Top Speed, mph:
	105 manual, 102 automatic transmission
	Lateral Acceleration (g's) .743
	Fuel economy EPA (Hwy/city), mpg
	   Manual transmission 25/36
	   Automatic transmission 27/31
	Stopping distance from 60 mph 169 ft.
	Noise level at 70 mph: 75 dbA

Changes for 1980	1.8 liter engine, three-way catalytic converter with Lambda-sensor, cast crankshaft with single counterbalance weight per cylinder, redesigned combustion chamber, breakerless electronic ignition, standard 5-speed manual transmission with changed final drive ratio, lower ratios in first and second gears for automatic transmission, reduced diameter filler neck for unleaded gasoline, Digital quartz clock, 85mph speedometer, Oxygen sensor service light, electrically controlled driver side rear view mirror standard, new hood and trunk emblems with smooth plastic finish, standard four radio speakers and fader control, increased oil filter capacity, extended oil change interval (7500 miles), new long-life spark plugs (WR9DS) allow 30,000 replacement interval. New dashboard appearance accommodates: LED quartz clock (integrated into tachometer face), oxygen sensor warning light, rotary heating and ventilation controls, and addition of four adjustable fresh air and air conditioning vents. Models compatible with port or dealer installed air conditioning pre-wired from factory (except 320iA with sunroof and all "S" packages). Weight reduction by use of aluminum in fuel lines, disc brake shields, master brake cylinder housing, brake pistons and clutch operating cylinder. Reduction in thickness and weight of window glass, body panels and insulation. Solid pedal arms replaced with lighter three-sided design.
Changes for 1982	Increased loudspeaker handling capacity, gearshift pattern inscribed on shift knob, electrically operated rear-view mirrors on both driver and passenger side now standard, trunk light and switch now standard. New colors: Lapis Blue, Baltic Blue and Opal Green
Changes for 1983	Introduction of lightweight 5-speed transmission with single main section housing. Deletion of sound deadening surface finish inside trunk
Available Colors	Standard Paint: Phoenix Orange, Chamonix White, Pastel Blue, Golf, Henna Red, Black, Biscay Blue, Sepia, Alpine White, Sierra Beige, Safari Beige, Corona Yellow, Lapis Blue Metallic Paint: Polaris, Fjord, Anthracite, Graphite, Cashmere, Sapphire Blue, Stratos, Ascot Grey, Cypress Green, Chestnut Red, Opal Green, Baltic Blue

Technical Data BMW 1984-85 318i (E30)—US Model

General	Manufacturer's suggested retail prices:
	  1984: $16,430
	  1985: $16,430 (2dr)
	  $16,925 4dr
	Curb weight:
	  1984 intro. 2360 lbs.
	  (2380 lbs. w/automatic transmission)
	  1985: 2395 lbs. (2dr)
	  2450 lbs. (4dr)

Wheelbase: 101.2 in.
Weight distribution, front/rear (%):53/47
Fuel capacity: 14.5 gal.
Fuel requirement: 87 AKI/91 RON unleaded
Front engine, rear wheel drive
Production:
  1984 12/82 to 9/84
  1985 9/84 to 9/85

Engine

Type: 1.8 liter (M10) 4-cylinder in-line water cooled, longitudinally mounted, inclined, single chain-driven overhead camshaft, cast crankshaft with 5 main bearings and 4 counter weights.
Bore/Stroke: 89/70 mm
Displacement: 1766 cc
Compression Ratio: 9.3:1
Fuel injected: Bosch L-Jetronic electronic fuel injection

Exhaust emission control: 3-way catalytic converter, Lambda sensor
Electronic Idle Control
Horsepower: 101hp (SAE net) @ 5800 rpm
Torque: 103 ft-lb @ 4500 rpm
Breakerless electronic ignition
80 amp alternator, 12-volt 50 amp hrs. battery

Chassis and Drivetrain

Transmission:
5-speed manual (Getrag)
  Gear ratios I/II/III/IV/R:
  3.72/2.02/1.32/1.0/0.81/3.45:1
Optional 3-speed automatic (ZF)
  Gear ratios I/II/III/R:
  2.73/1.56/1.0/2.09:1
Final drive ratio: 3.64: 1 Manual and automatic transmission (3.91:1 after approximately 11/83 production)
Steering: variable power assisted rack and pinion, with hydraulic damper
Steering ratio: 20.5:1

Front Suspension: MacPherson struts, coil springs, sickle-shaped lower control arms & anti-roll bar
Rear Suspension: independent with 15° semi-trailing arms, separate progressive rate coil springs and telescopic shocks, anti-roll bar
Braking:
  Front 260mm discs
  Rear 230mm rear twin-shoe drums (self adjusting) incorporating mechanically operated handbrake
Lifetime lubricated wheel bearings
Wheels: 6 J x 14 light alloy
Offset: 35mm
Tires: 195/60HR-14

Interior

Front reclining bucket seats with height adjustment (manually operated), height and tilt-adjustable head rests, cloth or leatherette upholstery, full carpeting, carpet on rear shelf, storage pockets in front doors, lockable (and lighted) glove compartment with flashlight socket, anti-glare mirror, heated rear window, 3-point automatic seat belts front and rear with 2-point lap belt in center rear, 140 mph speedometer with 6-digit odometer and trip odometer, tachometer, digital clock, fuel-economy indicator, Service Interval indicator, orange instrument and ventilation control lighting, heating/ventilating system with integrated air conditioning, manually operated front windows (with pop-out rear vents from 11/83), tinted glass all around with dark green border on top of windshield, four-spoke padded steering wheel with horn buttons in each spoke, tool kit in trunk lid.

Exterior

Unit body with impact and roll over protection, integrated roof reinforcement, energy absorbing 5mph bumpers, full-frame doors, hood safety catch, electrically controlled exterior rear view mirrors on driver and passenger sides, integrated front spoiler, halogen headlamps, halogen fog lamps (phased-in).

Technical Data BMW 1984-85 318i (E30) — US Model

Optional Equipment	Automatic transmission, limited slip differential (25%), air-conditioning, dual position manual sunroof, metallic paint, AM/	FM stereo cassette radio with 4 speakers, fader control and automatic antenna, power windows, central locking, leather upholstery
Performance	Acceleration, 0-60 mph: 11.4 sec (manual) Top Speed: 113 mph Lateral Acceleration (g's) .743	1984 Fuel economy EPA (Hwy/city), mpg: Standard transmission 27/38 Automatic transmission 27/34
Changes for 1984	Mid year 1984: Opening swing-out rear windows phased-in, power windows available, central locking available, shorter final drive	ratio (better acceleration), 4-speed blower fan phased-in.
Changes for 1985	4dr model available	
Available Colors	Standard Paint: Henna Red, Black, Alpine White, Savanna Beige, Safari Beige, Lapis Blue, Gazelle Beige, Cinnabar Red	Metallic Paint: Polaris, Graphite, Sapphire Blue, Baltic Blue, Bronzit Beige, Bahama Beige, Delphin, Opal Green, Agate Green, Graphite, Burgundy Red, Diamond Black, Arctic Blue, Cosmos Blue

Technical Data BMW 1984-85 325e (E30) — US Model

General

Manufacturer's suggested retail :
  1984: $20,970
  1985: $20,970 2dr
    $21,105 4dr
Production:
  1984 12/83 to 9/84
  1985 9/84 to 9/85

Curb weight:
  1984: 2654 lbs. (2698 lbs. w/automatic transmission)
  1985: 2710 lbs. (2dr)
    2765 lbs. (4dr)
Wheelbase: 101.2 in.
Weight distribution, front/rear (%): 53/47
Fuel capacity: 14.5 gal.
Fuel requirement: 87 AKI/91 RON unleaded
Front engine, rear wheel drive

Engine

Type: 2.7 liter (M20) 6-cylinder in-line eta concept, water cooled, longitudinally mounted, inclined, single belt-driven overhead camshaft, 7 main-bearing crankshaft.
Bore/Stroke: 84/81 mm
Displacement: 2693 cc
Compression Ratio: 9.0:1
Fuel Injected: Bosch Motronic electronic fuel injection

Engine management system: Digital Motor Electronics (DME)
Exhaust emission control: 3-way catalytic converter, Lambda sensor
Electronic Idle Control
Horsepower: 121hp (SAE net) @ 4250 rpm
Torque: 170 ft-lb @ 3250 rpm
80 amp alternator, 12-volt 50 amp hrs. battery (trunk mounted)

Chassis and Drivetrain

Transmission:
5-speed manual (Getrag 260/5)
  Gear ratios I/II/III/IV/R:
  3.822/2.202/1.398/1.00/0.813/3.705:1
Optional 4-speed automatic (ZF 4 HP 22)
  Gear ratios I/II/III/IV/R: 2.478 /1.478/1.00/0.730/2.090:1
Final drive ratio: 2.78: 1 Manual and automatic transmission
Steering: engine speed proportional power assisted rack and pinion, with hydraulic damper
Steering ratio: 20.5:1

Front Suspension: MacPherson struts, coil springs, sickle-shaped lower control arms & anti-roll bar
Rear Suspension: independent with 15° semi-trailing arms, separate progressive rate coil springs and telescopic shocks, anti-roll bar
Braking:
  Front 264mm ventilated discs
  Rear 264mm solid discs, mechanically operated handbrake
Lifetime lubricated wheel bearings
Wheels: 6 J x 14 light alloy
Offset: 35mm
Tires: 195/60 HR-14

Interior

Front reclining sports seats with height and tilt adjustment (manually operated), height-adjustable and tilting head rests, cloth or leatherette upholstery, full carpeting, carpet on rear shelf, storage pockets in front doors, lockable (and lighted) glove compartment with flashlight, anti-glare mirror, heated rear window, 3-point automatic seat belts front and rear with 2-point lap belt in center rear, 140 mph speedometer with 6-digit odometer and trip odometer, tachometer, digital clock, fuel-economy indicator, Service Interval indicator, On-Board Computer, Active Check Control,

orange instrument and ventilation control lighting, climate control air-conditioning with electronic temperature control, power operated front windows with pop-out rear windows, BMW-Alpine 4-speaker stereo system with automatic antenna, two-way electric sunroof, electric central locking with lighted master key, tinted glass all around with dark green border on top of windshield, three-spoke padded leather steering wheel, leather shift knob, tool kit in trunk lid.

Exterior

Unit body with impact and roll over protection, integrated roof reinforcement, energy absorbing 5 mph bumpers, full-frame doors, hood safety catch, electrically

controlled exterior rear view mirrors on driver and passenger sides, integrated front spoiler, halogen headlamps, halogen fog lamps.

Technical Data BMW 1984-85 325e (E30) — US Model

Optional Equipment	4-speed automatic transmission, limited slip differential (25%), air-conditioning, metallic paint, leather upholstery	

Performance	Acceleration, 0-60 mph: 11.4 sec (manual)
	Top Speed: 113 mph
	Lateral Acceleration (g's) .743
		Fuel economy EPA (Hwy/city), mpg:
		   Standard transmission 27/38
		   Automatic transmission 27/34

Changes for 1985	4dr model available	
Available Colors	Standard Paint: Black, Alpine White, Savanna Beige, Safari Beige, Lapis Blue, Gazelle Beige, Cinnabar Red,	Metallic Paint: Polaris, Graphite, Sapphire Blue, Baltic Blue, Bronzit Beige, Bahama Beige, Delphin, Opal Green, Agate Green, Graphite, Burgundy Red, Diamond Black, Arctic Blue, Cosmos Blue

Technical Data BMW 1986-87 325, 325es, 325e (E30)—US Model

General

Manufacturer's suggested retail price:
1986
   325 2dr: $19,560
   325 4dr: $20,055
   325es 2dr: $21,950
   325e 4dr: $22,650
1987
   325 2dr: $21,475
   325 4dr: $22,015
   325es 2dr: $24,370
   325e 4dr: $25,150
Production:
   1986: 9/85 to 7/86
   1987: 9/86 to 9/87

Curb weight:
   325 2dr: 2723 lbs.
   325 4dr: 2767 lbs.
   325es: 2778 lbs.
   325e: 2789 lbs.
Wheelbase: 101.2 in.
Weight distribution, front/rear (%): 53/47
Fuel capacity: 14.5 gal.
Fuel requirement: 87 AKI/91 RON unleaded
Front engine, rear wheel drive

Engine

Type: 2.7 liter (M20) 6-cylinder in-line "eta" concept, water cooled, longitudinally mounted, inclined, single belt-driven overhead camshaft, 7 main-bearing crankshaft.
Bore/Stroke: 84/81 mm
Displacement: 2693 cc
Compression Ratio: 9.0:1
Fuel Injected: Bosch Motronic electronic fuel injection

Engine management system: Digital Motor Electronics (DME)
Exhaust emission control: 3-way catalytic converter, Lambda sensor
Horsepower: 121hp (SAE net) @ 4250 rpm
Torque: 170 ft-lb @ 3250 rpm
80 amp alternator, 12-volt 50 amp hrs. battery (trunk mounted)

Chassis and Drivetrain

Transmission: 5-speed manual (Getrag 260/5)
   Gear ratios I/II/III/IV/VR:
   3.83/2.20/1.40/1.00/0.81/3.46:1
Optional 4-speed automatic (ZF 4 HP 22)
   Gear ratios I/II/III/IV/R:
   2.48/1.48/1.00/0.73/2.09:1
Final drive ratio: 2.93:1 Manual and automatic transmission
Steering: engine speed proportional power assisted rack and pinion, with hydraulic damper
Steering ratio: 20.5:1

Front Suspension: MacPherson struts, coil springs, sickle-shaped lower control arms & anti-roll bar
Rear Suspension: independent with 15° semi-trailing arms, separate progressive rate coil springs and telescopic shocks, anti-roll bar
Braking:
   Front 260 mm ventilated discs
   Rear 260 mm solid discs, mechanically operated handbrake
Anti-lock brakes (ABS) standard on all models
Wheels: 6 J x 14 light alloy
Offset: 35 mm
Tires: 195/65R-14H

Interior

Front reclining seats w/height adjustment (manually operated), height-adjustable and tilting head rests, cloth or leatherette upholstery, full carpeting, carpet on rear shelf, storage pockets in front doors, lockable (and lighted) glove compartment with flashlight socket, anti-glare mirror, heated rear window, 3-point automatic seat belts front and rear with 2-point lap belt in center rear, 140 mph speedometer with 6-digit odometer and trip odometer, tachometer, digital clock, fuel-economy indicator, Service Interval indicator, multi-function digital clock, Active Check Control, orange instrument and ventilation control lighting, climate control air-conditioning with electronic temperature control, power operated front windows with pop-out rear windows, Anti-theft AM/FM stereo radio/cassette player with four speaker and automatic antenna, two-way manual sunroof, electric central locking with lighted master key, tinted glass all around with dark green border on top of windshield, three spoke padded leather steering wheel, leather shift knob, tool kit in trunk lid Standard Center High Mounted Signal Light (CHMSL) third brake light.

Technical Data BMW 1986-87 325, 325es, 325e (E30)—US Model

Exterior	Unit body with impact and roll-over protection, integrated roof reinforcement, energy absorbing 5mph bumpers, full-frame doors, hood safety catch, dual electrically controlled exterior rear view mirrors, integrated front spoiler, halogen headlamps, halogen fog lamps	Canadian models: Cruise control, ABS, alloy wheels, leather seating, electric windows, on-board computer, air conditioning, premium sound system and electric sunroof optional on 325.

Additional Equipment	325es compared to 325 M-Technic sports suspension with gas-pressure shock absorbers, limited slip differential, deep front spoiler with integrated fog lights, rear-deck spoiler, M-Technic leather sports steering wheel, front sports seats with height/cushion angle and thigh-support adjustments, On-Board computer. Available in 2-door only. 325e compared to 325	On-Board computer, leather steering wheel, rear head restraints, leather seating, rear center armrest. Available in 4-door only.
Optional Equipment	Four speed automatic transmission, limited slip differential (325, 325e), metallic paint, leather upholstery (325, 325es), premium sound system: power amplifier, custom	contoured equalizer, eight speakers (325e, 325es)

Performance	Acceleration, 0-60 mph: 10.0 sec (11.7 automatic)
	Top Speed, mph: 116 (112 automatic)
	Lateral Acceleration (g's) .79
		1986 Fuel economy EPA (city/hwy), mpg
		    Standard transmission: 21/28
		    Automatic transmission: 20/27

Changes for 1987	325e and 325es replaced mid-year by 325i and 325is (See next section); twin-tube low-	pressure gas shocks introduced on non-"s" models.
Available Colors	Standard Paint: Black, Alpine White, Savanna Beige, Safari Beige, Lapis Blue, Gazelle Beige, Cinnabar Red,	Metallic Paint: Polaris, Graphite, Sapphire Blue, Baltic Blue, Bronzit Beige, Bahama Beige, Delphin, Opal Green, Agate Green, Graphite, Burgundy Red, Diamond Black, Arctic Blue, Cosmos Blue

Technical Data BMW (E30)—U.S. Models 1987-1991 325is, 325i

General

Manufacturer's suggested retail prices (US$):
325is 2dr
  1987: $26,990
  1988: $28,400
  1989-90: $28,950
325i 2dr
  1989-90: $24,650
  1991: $25,600
325i 4dr
  1987: $26,990
  1988: $28,400
  1989-90: $25,450
  1991: $26,400
Curb weight (lbs.):
325is
  1987: 2813 lbs.
  1988: 2865 lbs.
  1989-90: 2844 lbs.

Curb weight (continued):
325i 2dr
  1989-91: 2811 lbs.
325i 4dr
  1987: 2850 lbs.
  1988: 2895 lbs.
  1989-91: 2844 lbs.
Wheelbase: 101.2 in.
Weight distribution, front/rear (%): 53/47
Fuel capacity: 14.5 gal. (1988: 16.4 gals.)
Fuel requirement: 87 AKI/91 RON unleaded
Front engine, rear wheel drive
Production: 11/86-4/91

Engine

Type: 2.5 liter (M20) 6-cylinder in-line, water cooled, longitudinally mounted, inclined, single belt-driven overhead camshaft, 7 main bearing crankshaft.
Bore/Stroke: 84x75
Displacement: 2494 cc
Compression Ratio: 8.8:1
Horsepower: 168hp (SAE net) @ 5800 rpm
Torque: 164 ft-lb @ 4300 rpm

Fuel Injected: Bosch Motronic electronic fuel injection
Engine management system: Digital Motor Electronics (Motronic 1.1) now with adaptive control, self-diagnosis capability and knock sensing system
Exhaust emission control: 3-way catalytic converter, Lambda sensor
90 amp alternator, 12-volt 66 amp hrs. battery (trunk mounted)

Chassis and Drivetrain

Transmission:
5-speed manual (Getrag 280/5)
  Gear ratios I/II/III/IV/V:
  3.83/2.20/1.40/1.00/0.81:1
Optional 4-speed automatic (ZF 4 HP 22)
  Gear ratios I/II/III/IV:
  2.48/1.48/1.00/0.73:1
Final drive ratio: 3.73:1 Manual and automatic transmission
Steering: engine speed proportional power assisted rack and pinion, with hydraulic damper
Steering ratio: 20.5:1
Front Suspension: Independent with struts, coil springs, sickle-shaped lower control arms,

twin-tube gas-pressure shocks ('87 325is: single-tube), anti-roll bar
Rear Suspension: Independent with 15° semi-trailing arms, separate progressive rate coil springs and telescopic shocks, 13.5 mm anti-roll bar
Braking:
  Front 260 mm ventilated discs
  Rear 260 mm solid discs, mechanically operated handbrake
Anti-lock brakes (ABS) standard on all models
Wheels: 6 J x 14 light alloy; (6.5J x 14 cross-spoke styling for 325is)
Offset: 35mm (30mm for 6.5Jx14 325is wheel)
Tires: 195/65VR-14

Interior

Front reclining seats w/height adjustment (manually operated), height-adjustable and tilting head rests, cloth or leatherette upholstery, full carpeting, carpet on rear shelf, storage pockets in front doors, lockable (and lighted) glove compartment with flashlight socket, anti-glare mirror, heated rear window, 3-point automatic seat belts front and rear with 2-point lap belt in center rear, 150 mph speedometer with 6-digit odometer and trip odometer, tachometer, digital clock, fuel-economy indicator, Service Interval indicator,

multi-function digital clock, Active Check Control, orange instrument and ventilation control lighting, climate control air-conditioning with electronic temperature control, power operated windows with pop-out rear windows on two-door, Anti-theft AM/FM stereo radio/cassette player with four speaker and automatic antenna, two-way manual sunroof, electric central locking with lighted master key, tinted glass all around with dark green border on top of windshield, drop-down tool kit in trunk lid.

Technical Data BMW (E30)—U.S. Models 1987-1991 325is, 325i

Exterior	Unit body with impact and roll-over protection, integrated roof reinforcement (sedans), energy absorbing 5 mph bumpers, full-frame doors (sedans), hood safety catch,	dual electrically controlled exterior rear view mirrors, integrated front spoiler, halogen headlamps, halogen fog lamps.
Additional Equipment	325is: M-Technic sports suspension with gas-pressure shock absorbers (single tube Bilstein '87 only), progressive rate springs, limited slip differential, deep front spoiler with integrated fog lights, rear-deck spoiler, M-Technic leather sports steering wheel, leather shift knob, front leather sports seats with height/cushion angle and thigh-support adjustments, On-Board computer, limited slip differential, 6.5x14" cross-spoke alloy wheels with VR-rated tires, electric two-way sunroof. Premium sound	system with power amplifier, equalizer and eight speakers. Available in 2-door only. 325i: On-Board computer, leather steering wheel and shift knob, rear head restraints, leather seating, rear center armrest, electric two-way sunroof, VR-rated tires. Premium sound system with power amplifier, equalizer and eight speakers. Available in 4-door only.
Optional Equipment	Four speed automatic transmission, limited slip differential (standard 325is), metallic paint.	Canadian models: Fog lights standard only on 325is. Ski bag standard. Heated front seats. Heated outside mirrors and driver's door lock standard in all models. Rear headrests optional.

Performance	Acceleration, 0-60 mph: 8.5 sec (10.3 auto.)
	Car and Driver: 7.4 sec (325is)
	Fuel economy EPA (city/hwy), mpg:
	  Manual transmission: 18/23
	  Automatic transmission: 18/23
		Top Speed, mph
		  325i: 130 (126 auto.)
		  325is: 133 (130 auto.)
		  All from 1989:122 (electronically limited)
		Lateral Acceleration (g's): 0.79

Changes for 1988	All: revised front-end structure to improve crash absorbtion by 35% and simplify repairs; standard ellipsoid low-beam headlights. All restyled front valance panel with integrated fog lights and brake ducts; new design front spoiler (slightly extended on 325is); better integration of front and rear bumpers; chrome-less side trim, larger taillights; larger fuel tank, dual electric heated outside mirrors now standard; twin-tube low-pressure gas shocks introduced on 325is model. Rear quarter panel wheel arches lowered to match Convertible.	Canadian models: Cruise control, alloy wheels, air conditioning and premium sound system available as separate options. Fog lights standard only on 325is. Ski bag standard. Heated front seats optional. Heated driver's door lock standard in all models. Rear headrests optional in 325i. Leather seats optional. Sports seats optional in 325i.
Changes for 1989	Smaller, European style body-color bumper system standard. Eta engine 325 replaced by	similarly equipped base model 325i using same engine as previous 325i and 325is models.
Changes for 1990	Driver's air bag standard, pre-wired for BMW CD changer, leather upholstery available for base model 325i. Two-stage heated front seats	and ski-sack available in 325is. Four-season glass sunroof available as option.
Changes for 1991	All models: Free Form (sealed beam) headlights and fog lights replace previous ellipsoid units. Premium sound system now standard on 325i. Optional Sports package ($1,920), available on two and four door 325i, replaces discontinued 325is; adds M-style rocker panel covers to "is" equipment, deletes	limited slip differential, and rear seat armrest (four-door only). Optional Touring package ($1,665) includes: leather seating, leather covered steering wheel, map reading lights, rear center armrest (four-door only), and Four Season glass sunroof.
Available Colors	Standard Paint: Black, Alpine White, Cinnabar Red, Brilliant Red, Metallic Paint: Salmon Silver, Bronzit Beige, Bahama Beige, Delphin Grey, Agate Green, Burgundy Red, Diamond Black, Arctic Blue,	Lagoon Green, Mauritius Blue, Glacier Blue, Sterling Silver, Calypso Red, Granite Silver, Kashmir Beige

Technical Data BMW (E30)—U.S. Models
1987-1993 325i Convertible and 1988 325

General	Manufacturer's suggested retail prices (US$): 325i Conv.: 1987 $28,875; 1988 $32,500; 1989-90 $33,850; 1991 $35,700; 1992 $36,320; 1993 $36,320 325 2dr $23,750; 325 4dr $24,400 Curb weight (lbs.): 325i Conv.: 1987 3015 lbs.; 1988-90 3055 lbs.; 1991 2988 lbs; 1992 2990 lbs.; 1993 2988 lbs. 325 2dr: 2765 lbs.; 325 4dr 2809 lbs.	Wheelbase: 101.2 in. Weight distribution, front/rear (%): 53/47 Fuel capacity: 14.5 gal. (1988: 16.4 gals.) Fuel requirement: 87 AKI/91 RON unleaded Front engine, rear wheel drive Production: 325i Convertible: 10/86-12/92 325: 9/87-7/88

Engine	325i Convertible: Type: 2.5 liter (M20) 6-cylinder in-line, water cooled, longitudinally mounted, inclined, single belt-driven overhead camshaft, 7 main bearing crankshaft. Bore/Stroke: 84x75 mm Displacement: 2494 cc Compression Ratio: 8.8:1 Horsepower: 168hp (SAE net) @ 5800 rpm Torque: 164 ft-lb @ 4300 rpm 325: Type: 2.7 liter(M20) 6-cylinder in-line improved "eta" concept, water cooled, longitudinally mounted, inclined, single	belt-driven overhead camshaft, 7 main-bearing crankshaft. Bore/Stroke: 84x81 mm Displacement: 2693 cc Compression Ratio: 8.5:1 Horsepower: 127 (SAE net) @ 4800 rpm Torque: 170 ft-lb @ 3200 rpm Both models: Fuel Injected: Bosch Motronic electronic fuel injection Engine management system: Digital Motor Electronics (Motronic 1.1) now with adaptive control, self-diagnosis capability and knock sensing system Exhaust emission control: 3-way catalytic converter, Lambda sensor

Chassis and Drivetrain	Transmission: 5-speed manual (Getrag 280/5) Gear ratios I/II/III/IV/V: 3.83/2.20/1.40/1.00/0.81:1 Optional 4-speed automatic (ZF 4 HP 22) Gear ratios I/II/III/IV: 2.48/1.48/1.00/0.73:1 Final drive ratio: 325i Conv.: 3.73:1 325: 2.93:1 Steering: engine speed proportional power assisted rack and pinion, with hydraulic damper Steering ratio: 20.5:1 Front Suspension: Independent with struts, coil springs, sickle-shaped lower control arms, twin-tube gas-pressure shocks, anti-roll bar	Rear Suspension: Independent with 15° semi-trailing arms, separate progressive rate coil springs and telescopic shocks, 13.5 mm anti-roll bar Braking: Front 260 mm ventilated discs Rear 260 mm solid discs, mechanically operated handbrake Anti-lock brakes (ABS) standard on all models Wheels: 6 J x 14 light alloy Offset: 35mm (30mm for 6.5Jx14 325is wheel) Tires: 325I Conv.: 195/65VR-14; 325: 195/65R-14H

Interior	Front reclining seats w/height adjustment (manually operated), height-adjustable and tilting head rests, cloth or leatherette upholstery, full carpeting, carpet on rear shelf, storage pockets in front doors, lockable (and lighted) glove compartment with flashlight socket, anti-glare mirror, heated rear window, 3-point automatic seat belts front and rear with 2-point lap belt in center rear, 150 mph speedometer with 6-digit odometer and trip odometer, tachometer, digital clock, fuel-economy indicator, Service Interval indicator, multi-function digital clock, Active Check	Control, orange instrument and ventilation control lighting, climate control air-conditioning with electronic temperature control, power operated windows with pop-out rear windows on two-door, Anti-theft AM/FM stereo radio/cassette player with four speaker and automatic antenna, two-way manual sunroof (not on Convertible), electric central locking with lighted master key, tinted glass all around with dark green border on top of windshield, drop-down tool kit in trunk lid.

Exterior	Unit body with impact and roll-over protection, integrated roof reinforcement (sedans), energy absorbing 5 mph bumpers, full-frame doors (sedans), hood safety catch,	dual electrically controlled exterior rear view mirrors, integrated front spoiler, halogen headlamps, halogen fog lamps.

Technical Data BMW (E30)—U.S. Models
1987-1993 325i Convertible and 1988 325

Additional Equipment	325i Convertible only: Manually operated convertible top, leather steering wheel and shift knob, leather sports seats, distinctively contoured individual rear seating for two, electric rear	windows lower completely into body, specially tuned suspension. Premium sound system with power amplifier, equalizer and six speakers. Bumper surrounds in body color.
Optional Equipment	Four speed automatic transmission, limited slip differential, metallic paint. Hardtop available for 325i Convertible.	Canadian models: Convertible is called Cabriolet. Heated front seats standard on Cabriolet. Heated outside mirrors and driver's door lock standard in all models. Rear headrests optional in 325.

Performance	Acceleration, 0-60 mph:
	  325I Conv. : 8.6 sec (10.5 auto.)
	  325 1988: 8.8 sec (10.2 auto.)
	  Car and Driver (manual Conv.):7.7 sec
	Fuel economy EPA (city/hwy), mpg:
	  Manual transmission:
	  325I Conv. : 18/23
	  325 1988: 21/28
		Automatic transmission:
		  325I Conv. : 18/23
		  325 1988: 20/27
		Top Speed, mph:
		  325I Conv.: 130 (126 auto.)
		  325: 119 (117 auto.)
		Lateral Acceleration (g's): 0.79

Changes for 1988	Revised front-end structure to improve crash absorbtion by 35% and simplify repairs; standard ellipsoid low-beam headlights. 325: restyled front valance panel with integrated fog lights and brake ducts; new design front spoiler; better integration of front and rear bumpers; chrome-less side trim, larger taillights; larger fuel tank, dual electric heated outside mirrors now standard. Rear quarter panel wheel arches lowered. Convertible: heated seats now an available option. Third brake light (CHMSL) shorter profile.	Canadian models: Convertible is called Cabriolet. ABS, Alloy wheels, electric windows, air conditioning, premium sound system and electric sunroof optional on 325 as Luxus Package. Cruise control, alloy wheels, air conditioning and premium sound system available as separate options. Heated front seats standard on Cabriolet. Heated driver's door lock standard in all models. Rear headrests, leather seats, or sports seats optional in Cabriolet. Hardtop standard on Cabriolet.
Changes for 1989	Eta engine 325 replaced by similarly equipped base model 325i using same engine as previous 325i and 325is models.	
Changes for 1990	Driver's air bag standard, pre-wired for BMW CD changer, leather upholstery available for base model. Additional gas strut added to	trunk lid and cross-spoke wheels available as option.
Changes for 1991	Free Form (sealed beam) headlights and fog lights replace previous ellipsoid units. Premium sound system now standard. Optional Sports package ($1,920), replaces discontinued 325is; adds M-style rocker panel covers to "is" equipment, deletes limited slip differential. Optional Touring package ($1,665) includes:	leather seating, leather covered steering wheel, map reading lights. Power top, new body color bumpers and larger taillights as in sedans and cross-spoke alloy wheels now standard after mid-year introduction in 1990.
Changes for 1992	Automatic (pyrotechnic) right front seat belt tensioner improves occupant restraint. Limited Edition appearance packages (M-style) available in Alpine white with Lotus white leather and Diamond black with black	leather versions complete with aerodynamic body modifications, leather handbrake handle and boot, leather shift boot, color-matched cross-spoke wheels.
Changes for 1993	CFC-free refrigerant in air-conditioning system. Automatic transmission not available. Limited Edition appearance packages discontinued.	
Available Colors	Standard Paint: Black, Alpine White, Cinnabar Red, Brilliant Red, Metallic Paint: Salmon Silver, Bronzit Beige, Bahama Beige, Delphin Grey, Agate Green,	Burgundy Red, Diamond Black, Arctic Blue, Lagoon Green, Mauritius Blue, Glacier Blue, Sterling Silver, Calypso Red, Granite Silver, Kashmir Beige

Technical Data BMW (E30)—U.S. Models 1988-1991 325ix

General

Manufacturer's suggested retail prices (US$):
325ix 2dr:
1988: $32,800
1989-90: $29,950
1991: $31,100
325ix 4dr:
1989-90: $30,750
1991: $31,900
Curb weight (lbs.):
325ix 2dr:
1988-90: 3010 lbs.
1991: 2955 lbs.

Curb weight (continued):
325ix 4dr:
1989: 3054 lbs.
1990: 3050 lbs.
1991: 2999 lbs.
Wheelbase: 101.2 in.
Weight distribution, front/rear (%): 55.2/44.8
Fuel capacity: 16.4 gals.
Fuel requirement: 87 AKI/91 RON unleaded

Engine

Type: 2.5 liter (M20) 6-cylinder in-line, water cooled, longitudinally mounted, inclined, single belt-driven overhead camshaft, 7 main bearing crankshaft.
Bore/Stroke: 84x75 mm
Displacement: 2494 cc
Compression Ratio: 8.8:1
Horsepower: 168hp (SAE net) @ 5800 rpm
Torque: 164 ft-lb @ 4300 rpm

Fuel Injected: Bosch Motronic electronic fuel injection
Engine management system: Digital Motor Electronics (Motronics 1.1) includes adaptive controls, self-diagnosis capability and knock sensing system
Exhaust emission control: 3-way catalytic converter, Lambda sensor
90 amp alternator, 12-volt 66 amp hrs. battery

Chassis and Drivetrain

Transmission:
5-speed manual (Getrag 280/5)
Gear ratios I/II/III/IV/V:
3.83/2.20/1.40/1.00/0.81:1
Final drive ratio: 3.91:1
Optional 4-speed automatic (ZF 4 HP 22) (From 1989 on)
Gear ratios I/II/III/IV:
2.48/1.48/1.00/0.73:1
Final drive ratio: 4.10:1
Center differential with viscous coupling and 27/63%, front/rear torque split
Rear differential with viscous coupling
Steering: engine speed proportional power assisted rack and pinion, with hydraulic damper

Steering ratio: 20.5:1
Front Suspension: Independent with struts, coil springs, sickle-shaped lower control arms, twin-tube gas-pressure shocks ('87 325is: single-tube), anti-roll bar
Rear Suspension: Independent with 15° semi-trailing arms, separate progressive rate coil springs and telescopic shocks, anti-roll bar
Braking:
Front 260mm ventilated discs
Rear 260mm solid discs, mechanically operated handbrake
Anti-lock brakes (ABS) standard on all models
Wheels: Cross-spoke style 7J x 15 light alloy
Offset: 45mm
Tires: 205/55VR-15

Interior

M-Technic leather sports steering wheel, leather shift knob, front leather sports seats with height/cushion angle and thigh-support adjustments (manually operated), height-adjustable and tilting head rests, leather upholstery, full carpeting, carpet on rear shelf, storage pockets in front doors, lockable (and lighted) glove compartment with flashlight socket, anti-glare mirror, heated rear window, 3-point automatic seat belts front and rear with 2-point lap belt in center rear, 150 mph speedometer with 6-digit odometer and trip odometer, tachometer, fuel-economy indicator, Service Interval indicator, On-

Board computer, Active Check Control, orange instrument and ventilation control lighting, climate control air-conditioning with electronic temperature control, power operated windows with pop-out rear windows on two-door, Anti-theft AM/FM stereo radio/cassette player premium sound system with power amplifier, equalizer, eight speakers and automatic antenna, two-way electric sunroof, electric central locking with lighted master key, tinted glass all around with dark green border on top of windshield, drop-down tool kit in trunk lid. fog lights, ski sack standard.

Exterior

Unit body with impact and roll-over protection, integrated roof reinforcement, energy absorbing 5 mph bumpers, full-frame doors, hood safety catch, dual electrically heated and controlled exterior rear view

mirrors, deep front spoiler with integrated halogen fog lamps, rear-deck spoiler, halogen headlamps, special wheel-well flares and rocker panel extensions.

Technical Data BMW (E30)—U.S. Models 1988-1991 325ix

Optional Equipment	Metallic paint.	Canadian models: Ski bag standard. Heated front seats optional. Heated driver's door lock standard. Leather seats optional. Sports seats optional.
Performance	Acceleration, 0-60 mph: 9.1 sec (10.4 auto.) *Car and Driver*: 7.8 sec. (manual) Fuel economy EPA (city/hwy), mpg Manual transmission: 17/23 Automatic trans.: 18/23	Top Speed, mph: 127 (electronically limited to 122 mph from 1989) Lateral Acceleration (g's): 0.77
Changes for 1989	4-door model added. Smaller, European style body-color bumper system. Sports equipment deleted producing an equipment level equivalent to the 325i of the same year at a substantial price reduction. Deleted	equipment includes: sport seats, leather interior, leather steering wheel and shift knob, premium sound system, electric operation of sunroof, on-board computer.
Changes for 1990	Driver's air bag standard, pre-wired for BMW CD changer, leather upholstery available as option. Two-stage heated front seats available.	BMW premium sound system available as option at $250
Changes for 1991	Free Form (sealed beam) headlights and fog lights replace previous ellipsoid units. Premium sound system now standard.	
Available Colors	Standard Paints: Alpine White, Cinnabar Red, Black, Brilliant Red	Optional Metallic Paints: Diamond Black Metallic, Salmon Silver Metallic, Sterling Silver Metallic

Technical Data BMW (E30)—U.S. Models 1988-1991 M3

General

Manufacturer's suggested retail prices (US$)

M3 2dr
  1988: $34,000
  1989-90: $34,950
  1991: $35,900
Curb weight (lbs.): M3 2dr: 2865 lbs.

Wheelbase: 100.9 in.
Weight distribution, front/rear, %: 53/47
Fuel capacity: 14.5 gals.
Fuel requirement: 91 AKI/95 RON unleaded
Front engine, rear wheel drive
Production: 12/86-12/90

Engine

Type: 2.3 liter (S14) 4-cylinder, 16 valve, in-line, water cooled, longitudinally mounted, inclined, double chain-driven overhead camshafts, five main-bearing crankshaft with eight counter-weights.
Bore/Stroke: 93.4x84.0 mm
Displacement: 2305 cc
Compression Ratio: 10,5:1
Horsepower: 192hp (SAE net) @ 6750 rpm
Torque: 170 ft-lb @ 4750 rpm

Fuel Injected: Bosch Motronic electronic fuel injection with four individual throttle plates. Engine management system: Digital Motor Electronics (ML-3)
Exhaust emission control: 3-way catalytic converter, Lambda sensor
Hydraulic engine mounts
80 amp alternator, 12-volt 50 amp hrs. battery (trunk mounted except convertible)

Chassis and Drivetrain

Transmission: 5-speed manual (Getrag 260)
  Gear ratios I/II/III/IV/V:
  3.83/2.20/1.40/1.00/0.81:1
Final drive ratio: 4.10:1
Rear differential with limited slip
Steering: engine speed proportional power assisted rack and pinion, with hydraulic damper
Steering ratio: 19.6:1
Front Suspension: Independent with struts, coil springs, sickle-shaped lower control arms, twin-tube gas-pressure shocks, anti-roll bar

Rear Suspension: Independent with 15° semi-trailing arms, separate progressive rate coil springs and telescopic shocks, 14,5 mm anti-roll bar
Braking:
  Front 280 mm ventilated discs
  Rear 282 mm solid discs, mechanically operated handbrake
Anti-lock brakes (ABS) standard
Wheels: Cross-spoke style 7J x 15 light alloy, 5-bolt
Offset: 30 mm
Tires: 205/55VR-15

Interior

M-Technic leather sports steering wheel, leather shift knob and boot, front leather sports seats with height/cushion angle and thigh-support adjustments (manually operated), height-adjustable and tilting head rests, leather upholstery, full carpeting, carpet on rear shelf, storage pockets in front doors, lockable (and lighted) glove compartment with flashlight socket, anti-glare mirror, heated rear window, 3-point automatic seat belts front and rear, 170 mph speedometer with 6-digit odometer and trip odometer, 8000 rpm tachometer, oil temperature gauge, red gauge needles, Service Interval indicator,

On-Board computer, Active Check Control, orange instrument and ventilation control lighting, climate control air-conditioning with electronic temperature control, power operated windows with pop-out rear windows, Anti-theft AM/FM stereo radio/cassette player premium sound system with power amplifier, equalizer, eight speakers and roof mounted antenna, two-way electric sunroof, electric central locking with lighted master key, tinted glass all around with dark green border on top of windshield, drop-down tool kit in trunk lid, fog lights standard.

Exterior

Unit body with impact and roll-over protection, integrated roof reinforcement, energy absorbing 2.5 mph bumpers, full-frame doors, hood safety catch, dual electrically heated and controlled exterior rear view mirrors, deep fiberglass front spoiler

with integrated halogen fog lamps, rear-deck wing and bumper spoiler, widened front and rear fenders and rocker panel extensions, halogen headlamps, bonded windshield and rear window.

Optional Equipment

Metallic paint.

Performance

Acceleration, 0-60 mph: 7.6 sec
Car and Driver: 6.9 sec.
Fuel economy EPA (city/hwy), mpg: 17/29

Top Speed (mph): 143
Lateral Acceleration (g's): 0.82

Technical Data BMW (E30)—U.S. Models 1988-1991 M3

Changes for 1989	Mid-year changes include: Offset control arm bushings, Free-form (sealed beam) headlights, larger airbox.	
Changes for 1990	Driver's air bag phased-in, pre-wired for BMW CD changer; two-stage heated front seats and Four-season glass sunroof available as options. Rear windows now non-opening.	Aluminum lower control arms from 9/89 production.
Changes for 1991	Free Form (sealed beam) headlights replace previous ellipsoid units. M3 not available for sale in California.	
Available Colors	Standard Paints: Alpine White, Henna Red, Cinnabar Red, Brilliant Red,	Optional Metallic Paints: Diamond Black Metallic, Salmon Silver Metallic, Sterling Silver Metallic

Technical Data BMW (E30) — U.S. Models 1991 318is, 318i and 1991-1992 318i Convertible

General	Manufacturer's suggested retail prices (US $):
	 318is 2dr: $21,500
	 318i 4dr: $19,900
	 318i Conv.
	     1991: $28,500
	     1992: $28,870
	 Curb weight (lbs.):
	 318is 2dr: 2602 lbs.
	 318i 4dr: 2657 lbs.
	
	 318i Conv.: 2867 lbs.
	 Wheelbase: 101.2 in.
	 Weight distribution, front/rear (%): 54/46
	 Fuel capacity: 14.5 gal.
	 Fuel requirement: Premium unleaded
	 Front engine, rear wheel drive
	 Production:
	 318is: 11/96-4/91
	 318i: 3/90-4/91
	 318i Convertible: 7/90-12/92

Engine	Type: 1.8 liter (M42) 4-cylinder in-line, 16 valve, water cooled, longitudinally mounted, inclined, double overhead chain-driven camshafts, hydraulic lifters, 5 main-bearing forged crankshaft, hydraulic engine mounts. Bore/Stroke: 84x81 mm Displacement: 796 cc Compression Ratio: 10.0:1 Horsepower: 134hp (SAE net) @ 6000 rpm Torque: 127 ft-lb @ 4600 rpm Fuel Injected: Bosch Motronic electronic fuel injection Engine management system: Digital Motor Electronics (Motronics 1.7), RSV solid state ignition distribution. Exhaust emission control: 3-way catalytic converter, Lambda sensor 80 amp alternator, 12-volt 65 amp hrs. battery

Chassis and Drivetrain	Transmission: 5-speed manual (Getrag 260/5)
	     Gear ratios I/II/III/IV/V:
	     3.72/2.02/1.32/1.00/0.80:1
	 Automatic transmission not available
	 Final drive ratio: 4:10:
	 Steering: engine speed proportional power assisted rack and pinion, with hydraulic damper
	 Steering ratio: 20.5:1
	 Front Suspension: Independent with struts, coil springs, sickle-shaped lower control arms, twin-tube gas-pressure shocks, anti-roll bar (larger diameter on 318is)
	
	 Rear Suspension: Independent with 15° semi-trailing arms, separate progressive rate coil springs and telescopic shocks, anti-roll bar (larger diameter on 318is)
	 Braking:
	     Front 260 mm ventilated discs
	     Rear 260 mm solid discs, mechanically operated handbrake
	 Anti-lock brakes (ABS) standard on all models
	 Wheels: Steel 6J x 14 (318); light alloy 6Jx14 (318iC); 6.5J x 14 cross-spoke styling (318is)
	 Offset: 35mm (30mm for 6.5Jx14 318is wheel)
	 Tires: 195/65R-14H

Interior	Front reclining seats w/height adjustment (manually operated), height-adjustable and tilting head rests, cloth or leatherette upholstery, full carpeting, carpet on rear shelf, storage pockets in front doors, lockable (and lighted) glove compartment with flashlight socket, anti-glare mirror, heated rear window, 3-point automatic seat belts front and rear with 2-point lap belt in center rear, 150 mph speedometer with 6-digit odometer and trip odometer, 7000 rpm tachometer, multi-function digital clock, fuel-economy indicator, Service Interval indicator, multi-function digital clock, Active Check Control, orange instrument and ventilation control lighting, climate control air-conditioning with electronic temperature control, power operated windows with pop-out rear windows on two-door, Anti-theft AM/FM stereo radio/cassette player with four speaker and automatic antenna, tinted glass all around with dark green border on top of windshield, drop-down tool kit in trunk lid.

Exterior	Unit body with impact and roll-over protection, integrated roof reinforcement (sedans), energy absorbing 2.5mph bumpers, full-frame doors (sedans), hood safety catch, dual body-colored electrically controlled exterior rear view mirrors, integrated front spoiler, halogen headlamps.

Additional Equipment	318is: M-Technic sports suspension with gas-pressure shock absorbers progressive rate springs, deep front spoiler, rear-deck spoiler, leather steering wheel, leather shift knob, front sports seats with height/cushion angle and thigh-support adjustments, 6.5x14" cross-spoke alloy (available in 2-door only). 325i Convertible: Manually operated convertible top, sports seats, distinctively contoured individual rear seating for two, electric rear windows lower completely into body, specially tuned suspension. Premium sound system with power amplifier, equalizer and six speakers, 6Jx14" alloy wheels.

Technical Data BMW (E30)—U.S. Models 1991 318is, 318i and 1991-1992 318i Convertible

Optional Equipment	Two-way manual sunroof (except convertible), fog lights, limited slip differential, metallic paint. Hardtop available for Convertible.	
Performance	Acceleration, 0-60 mph: 318is: 9.8 sec. 318i: 10.0 sec. 318i Convertible: 10.4 sec.	Fuel economy EPA (city/hwy), mpg (all): 21/27 Top Speed, mph (all): 122 (electronically limited)
Changes for 1991	Electric central locking with deadbolt feature and lighted master key phased-in. Automatic (pyrotechnic) right front seat belt tensioner improves occupant restraint.	
Changes for 1992	(Convertible the only remaining E30 model) 318iC: Automatic (pyrotechnic) right front seat belt tensioner improves occupant restraint.	
Available Colors	Standard Paint: Alpine White, Brilliant Red,	Metallic Paint: Diamond Black, Sterling Silver. (Additionally for Convertible only: Granite Silver, Calypso Red, Lagoon Green, Glacier Blue, Mauritius Blue, Cashmere Beige.)

Technical Data BMW (E36)—U.S. Model 1992-1995 325is, 325i, and 1994-1995 325i Convertible

General

Manufacturer's suggested retail prices (US $):
325is Coupe: $29,100 (1992), $30,950 (1993), 32,200 (1994), $32,750 (1995)
325i 4-door: $27,990 (1992), $29,650 (1993), $30,850 (1994), $31,450 (1995)
325i Convertible: $38,800 (1994), $39,600 (1995)
Curb weight (lbs.):
325is Coupe Manual: 3020 (1992), 3087 (1993), 3086 (1994), 3087 (1995)
325is Coupe Automatic: 3097 (1992), 3164 (1993-1995)
325i 4-door Manual: 3020 (1992), 3087(1993), 3086 (1994), 3087 (1995)
325i 4-door Automatic: 3097 (1992), 3164 (1993-1995)
325i Convertible Manual: 3351 (1994), 3352 (1995)
325i Convertible Automatic: 3428 (1994), 3429 (1995)
Wheelbase: 106.3 in.
Weight distribution, front/rear (%): 51/49
Fuel capacity: 17.2 gal
Fuel requirement: Premium unleaded
Front engine, rear wheel drive
Production:
325is: 12/91-N/A
325i: 3/91-N/A
325iC: 5/93-9/95

Engine

Type: 2.5 liter (M50) 6-cylinder in-line, 24 valve, chain-driven dual overhead camshaft, hydraulic lifters, water cooled, longitudinally mounted, inclined, 7 main bearings.
Bore/Stroke: 84x75 mm

Displacement: 2494 cc
Compression Ratio: 10.0:1
Horsepower: 189hp (SAE net) @ 5900 rpm
Torque: 181 ft-lb @ 4700 rpm

Fuel Injected: Bosch M 3.1 Motronic with hot-wire air-mass meter
Engine management system: Digital Motor Electronics (MH-Motronic) with direct ignition, adaptive control, self-diagnosis capability
Exhaust emission control: dual 3-way catalytic converters, Lambda sensor
90 amp alternator (105 anp w/auto.trans), 12-volt 75 amp hrs. battery (trunk mounted)

Chassis and Drivetrain

Transmission: 5-speed manual (Getrag type-C)
Gear ratios I/II/III/IV/V:
4.23/2.52/1.67/1.22/1.00:1
Final drive ratio: 3.15:1
Optional 4-speed automatic (THM R1)
Gear ratios I/II/III/IV:
2.40/1.47/1.00/0.72:1
(2.86/1.62/1.00/0.72 from 1994)
Final drive ratio: 3.91:1
Steering: engine speed sensitive power assisted rack and pinion
Steering ratio: 16.8:1
Front Suspension: Independent with MacPherson struts, coil springs, arc-shaped lower control arms, twin-tube gas-pressure shocks, anti-roll bar
Rear Suspension: Independent Multi-link with Central links, separate coil springs and twin-tube gas-pressure shocks, anti-roll bar
Braking:
Front 287mm ventilated discs
Rear 279mm solid discs, mechanically operated handbrake
Anti-lock brakes (Teves Mark IV ABS) standard on all models
Wheels: 7 J x 15 light alloy; 5-bolt
Offset: 47mm
Tires: 205/60R-15

Interior

Front reclining seats w/height adjustment (manually operated), height-adjustable and tilting head rests, cloth, leatherette, or optional leather upholstery, SRS (supplemental restraint system) with driver's airbag and knee bolster, dual lighted visor vanity mirrors, two map reading lights, full carpeting, carpet on rear shelf, storage pockets in front doors, lockable (and lighted) glove compartment with flashlight socket, anti-glare mirror, heated rear window, 3-point automatic seat belts with mechanical tensioners (front) and 3-point ergonomic rear belts with buckles at outside and 2-point lap belt in center, 160 mph speedometer with 6-digit LCD odometer and trip odometer, tachometer, fuel-economy indicator, Service Interval indicator, LCD dot matrix Multi-Information Display (MID) including digital clock, Check/Control, and outside temperature indicator. Orange instrument and ventilation control lighting, air-conditioning with separate right-left electronic temperature control, separate recirculation control, rear seat heater duct, air-intake microfilter, power operated windows w/one-touch driver's and key-off operation, BMW Sound System Anti-theft AM/FM stereo radio/cassette player with 4x25 watt power amplifier, custom contoured equalizer with ten speakers and integrated antenna, two-way electric sunroof with one-touch function, electric central locking with lighted master key, tinted glass all around with dark green border on top of windshield, drop-down tool kit in trunk lid.

Technical Data BMW (E36)—U.S. Model 1992-1995 325is, 325i, and 1994-1995 325i Convertible

Exterior	Impact zones and integrated roof crossbar (except Convertible), energy absorbing 2.5 mph bumpers with replaceable slide-over elements protecting up to 9 mph, full-frame doors (sedan), hood safety catch, dual electric side mirrors, integrated front spoiler, halogen headlights and fog lamps.
Additional Equipment	325is coupe: Alloy wheels; frameless doors with automatic sealing windows; body color bumpers, height-adjustable steering wheel; leather seats, steering wheel, shift knob, handbrake grip and boot; fold-down rear seatbacks; swing-out side windows; one-touch passenger window operation. 325i Convertible: Electrically operated lined convertible top, leather seats, steering wheel, shift knob, handbrake grip and boot, contoured rear seating with removable armrest, automatic sealing windows plus electric rear and one-touch operation of all windows, specially tuned suspension, alloy wheels, central locking glove box, height adjustable steering wheel. Premium sound system with power amplifier, equalizer and six speakers. Bumper surrounds in body color.
Optional Equipment	All: Four speed automatic transmission, limited slip differential, heated seats, On-board computer, metallic paint.
Performance	Acceleration, 0-60 mph (sec): 1992 325i/is: 7.8 sec (9.3 auto.) 1993-94 325i/is: 7.8 sec (8.8 auto.) 1994-95 325iC: 8.3 sec (8.9 auto.) Fuel economy EPA (city/hwy), mpg: 1992 325i/is: 19/28 manual, 20/28 auto 1993-94 325i/is: 19/28 manual, 20/28 auto 1994-95 325iC: 19/27 manual, 20/28 auto Top Speed, mph: 128 (electronically limited)
Changes during 1992	Refined front suspension, improved central locking can be engaged from passenger door, redesign of outside mirrors for noise reduction, alarm system pre-wiring, improved sound insulation, upper dash surfaces in color, one-touch driver's window operation, CD changer pre-wiring. 325is Coupe introduced with improvements above. CFC-free refrigerant introduced for air conditioning systems very late in production.
Changes for 1993	Standard: Extensively improved engine (M50 TU) with variable valve timing and knock control; electrically adjustable front seats; CFC-free refrigerant introduced for air conditioning; improved material for dashboard, center console, door panels, front seatbacks. Body color bumpers and center armrest on 325i 4dr. Optional: Sports Package introduced including sport seats, cross-spoke wheels, sports suspension. Inclement Weather Package introduced including limited-slip differential, heated mirrors and seats. Split fold-down rear seats available for 325i 4dr.
Changes for 1994	Standard: Wide-ratio automatic transmission for improved acceleration. Lighted mode switch for automatic. All-season tires standard. Revised front spoiler design. Redesigned dual airbag and glovebox. Flashlight standard. Storage nets on front seat back. Dual-diversity antenna system (except convertible). Driveaway protection on double-locking. Window operation from driver's side outside door lock. Both front windows now one-touch operation (4dr). 10x25 watt audio system. Optional: Color-keyed aluminum hardtop and pop-up roll-over protection for Convertible. Inclement weather package discontinued. All Season Traction Control. Limited Slip phased out. Heated seats, mirrors, washer jets and driver's door lock. Limited production M-Design 325is available. Approximately 150 produced for U.S. with no special badging. (Also knows as "M-Technic" 325is.)
Changes for 1995	Standard: New seat belt and air bag systems (phased in beginning 9/94). Side directionals in front fenders (earlier phase-in). Free-wheeling door locks. New steering wheel and front seat design. Temperature control with 8°F increments. Coded driveaway protection phased-in 1/95 production. Optional: Wood trim and On-board computer. 16" wheels. Leather and height-adjustable steering wheel on 4dr.
Available Colors	Standard Paint: Black, Jet Black, Alpine White, Brilliant Red, Bright Red Metallic Paint: Sterling Silver, Cashmere Beige, Granite Silver, Lagoon Green, Mauritius Blue, Glacier Blue, Calypso Red, Arctic Gray, Boston Green, Samana Beige, Morea Green, Samoa Blue, Montreal Blue

Technical Data BMW (E36) — U.S. Model 1992-1997 318is Coupe

General	Manufacturer's suggested retail prices (US $): 1992: $23,600 1993: $24,810 1994: $25,800 1995: $26,675 1996: $27,700 1997: $27,700 Curb weight (lbs.): Manual: 2866 (1992-1994), 2933 (1995), 2976 (1996-1997) Automatic: 2955 (1993), 2954 (1994), 3021 (1995), 3064 (1996-1997) Wheelbase: 106.3 in. Weight distribution, front/rear (%): 49/51 Fuel capacity: 17.2 gal (16.4 gal. from 1996) Fuel requirement: Premium unleaded Front engine, rear wheel drive Production: 3/92-N/A
Engine	Type: (1992-1995) 1.8 liter (M42) 4-cylinder in-line, 16 valve, chain-driven dual overhead camshaft, hydraulic lifters, water cooled, longitudinally mounted, inclined, 5 main bearings. Bore/Stroke: 84x81 mm (85x83.5 from 1996, M44 engine) Displacement: 1796 cc (1895 cc from 1996) Compression Ratio: 10.0:1 Horsepower: 138hp (SAE net) @ 6000 rpm Torque: 129 ft-lb @ 4500 rpm (133 ft-lb @ 4300 rpm from 1996) Fuel Injected: Bosch ML-Motronic Engine management system: Digital Motor Electronics (ML-Motronic) with direct ignition, adaptive control, self-diagnosis capability Type: (From 1996) 1.9 liter (M44) 4-cylinder in-line, 16 valve, chain-driven dual overhead camshaft, hydraulic lifters, water cooled, longitudinally mounted, inclined, 5 main bearings. Bore/Stroke: 85x83.5 Displacement: 1895 cc Compression Ratio: 10.0:1 Horsepower: 138hp (SAE net) @ 6000 rpm Torque: 133 ft-lb @ 4300 rpm Fuel Injected: Bosch HFM-Motronic 5.2 with hot-wire air-mass meter Engine management system: Digital Motor Electronics (HFM-Motronic) with direct ignition, adaptive control, self-diagnosis capability Exhaust emission control: 3-way catalytic converter, Lambda sensor, 105 amp alternator, 12-volt 65 amp hrs. battery (trunk mounted)
Chassis and Drivetrain	Transmission: 5-speed manual, Getrag type-C Gear ratios I/II/III/IV/V: 4.23/2.52/1.67/1.22/1.00:1 Final drive ratio: 3.45:1 Optional 4-speed automatic (THM R1) Gear ratios I/II/III/IV: 2.40/1.47/1.00/0.72:1 (2.86/1.62/1.00/0.72 from 1/94) Final drive ratio: 4.45:1 (4.44:1 from 1996) Steering: engine speed sensitive power assisted rack and pinion Steering ratio: 16.8:1 Front Suspension: Independent with MacPherson struts, coil springs, arc-shaped lower control arms, twin-tube gas-pressure shocks, anti-roll bar Rear Suspension: Independent Multi-link with Central links, separate coil springs and twin-tube gas-pressure shocks, anti-roll bar Braking: Front 287mm ventilated discs Rear 279mm solid discs, mechanically operated handbrake Anti-lock brakes (Teves Mark IV ABS) standard on all models Wheels: 7 J x 15 light alloy; 5-bolt Offset: 47mm Tires: 205/60R-15
Interior	Front reclining seats w/height adjustment (manually operated), height-adjustable and tilting head rests, cloth or leatherette upholstery, SRS (supplemental restraint system) with driver's airbag and knee bolster, dual lighted visor vanity mirrors, two map reading lights, full carpeting, carpet on rear shelf, storage pockets in front doors, lockable (and lighted) glove compartment with flashlight socket, anti-glare mirror, heated rear window, 3-point automatic seat belts with mechanical tensioners (front) and 3-point ergonomic rear belts with buckles at outside and 2-point lap belt in center, fold down rear seats, 160 mph speedometer with 6-digit LCD odometer and trip odometer, tachometer, fuel-economy indicator, Service Interval indicator, LCD dot matrix multi-function digital clock and outside temperature indicator with freeze warning. Orange instrument and ventilation control lighting, air-conditioning with separate right-left electronic temperature control, separate recirculation control, rear seat heater duct, air-intake microfilter, power operated windows w/key-off and one-touch driver's and passenger's operation, swing-out side windows, Anti-theft AM/FM stereo radio/cassette player with four speakers and integrated antenna, two-way electric sunroof, electric central locking with lighted master key, tinted glass all around with dark green border on top of windshield, drop-down tool kit in trunk lid.

Technical Data BMW (E36)—U.S. Model 1992-1997 318is Coupe

Exterior	2-door, impact zones and integrated roof crossbar, specially designed alloy wheels, frameless doors with automatic sealing windows, body colored energy absorbing	2.5 mph bumpers with replaceable slide-over elements protecting up to 9 mph, hood safety catch, electrically controlled side mirrors, integrated front spoiler, halogen headlamps.
Optional Equipment	Limited slip differential, heated seats, metallic paint.	

Performance	Acceleration, 0-60 mph (sec):
	  Manual: 9.9 (1992-1995), 8.5 (1996)
	  Automatic: 11.4 (1993), 10.9 (1994-1995),
	  10.6 (1996), 9.8 (1997)
		Fuel economy EPA (city/hwy), mpg :
		  Manual: 22/30 (1992-1994),
		  22/32 (1995-1997)
		  Automatic: 22/30 (1992-1994)
		Top Speed: 128 mph (electronically limited),
		  (116 mph beginning 1994)

Changes during 1992	Introduced after the E36 325i. CFC-free refrigerant introduced for air conditioning	systems very late in production.
Changes for 1993	Standard: Increased headroom for driver though increased seat height adjustment range. CFC-free refrigerant introduced for air conditioning; improved material for	dashboard, center console, door panels, front seatbacks. Optional: Automatic Transmission, cruise control, sports suspension, fog lights
Changes for 1994	Standard: Wide-ratio automatic transmission for improved acceleration (phased in 1/94 production). Lighted mode switch for automatic transmission. All-season tires standard (phased in 1/94 production). Revised front spoiler design. Dual airbag. Redesigned and upgraded airbag and glovebox area. Rechargeable flashlight standard. Storage nets on front seat back. Pre-wiring for CD	changer. Dual-diversity antenna system. Driveaway protection on double-locking. Window operation from driver's side outside door lock. Optional: Inclement weather package discontinued. All Season Traction Control available. Limited Slip phased out. Heated seats, mirrors, washer jets and driver's door lock available as a group.
Changes for 1995	Standard: New seat belt tensioners and air bags (phased in 9/94 production). Side directionals in front fenders (earlier phase-in). Freewheeling door locks (phased in 7/95). New steering wheel and front seat design. Temperature control with 8°F increments.	Cruise Control. Fog lights. Coded driveway protection phased-in 1/95 production. Optional: Leather, premium audio, height adjustable steering wheel, sports suspension, and limited slip differential.
Changes for 1996	Standard: New 1.9 liter engine (M44), improved cylinder head with roller rocker arms, Bosch DME with hot-film air mass sensor, dual resonance intake system switches over 600 rpm earlier, fabricated stainless steel headers, central locking switch on console, seat belts accommodate child safety seats, new 10-speaker 200 watt audio system with weather band, one-touch exterior door lock	and sunroof operation, automatic climate control. Radial 15-spoke design wheels standard. Optional: AST phased in, Limited Slip phased out; 320 watt Harman/Kardon audio system; ski-bag; sports and premium packages include leather steering wheel, shift knob, handbrake knob and shift and handbrake boots.
Changes for 1997	Standard: All Season Traction; clutch interlock (manual); revised front end/grills; new side-marker lights; heated outside mirrors; leather shift knob for automatics in 8 series style; new center console with integrated cupholders,	ashtray and coinholder; side compartments in trunk, side-impact airbags in front doors (phased-in 1/97 production) Optional: Premium Packages deleted; sunroof now optional
Available Colors	Standard Paint: Black, Jet Black, Alpine White, Brilliant Red, Bright Red Metallic Paint: Sterling Silver, Cashmere Beige, Granite Silver, Lagoon Green, Mauritius Blue,	Glacier Blue, Calypso Red, Arctic Gray, Boston Green, Samana Beige, Morea Green, Samoa Blue, Montreal Blue, Arctic Silver, Cosmos Black, Avus Blue, Ascot Green, Sierra Red.

Technical Data BMW (E36)—U.S. Model 1992-1998 318i 4-door Sedan

General

Manufacturer's suggested retail prices (US $):
  1992: $19,990
  1993: $23,710
  1994: $24,675
  1995: $24,975
  1996 and 1997: $25,950
  1998: $26,150
Curb weight (lbs.): Manual: 2866 (1992 1994), 2933 (1995), 2976 (1996-1998)
Automatic: 2955 (1993), 2954 (1994),
  3021 (1995), 3064 (1996-1998)
Wheelbase: 106.3 in.
Weight distribution, front/rear (%): 49/51
Fuel capacity: 17.2 gal (16.4 gal. from 1996)
Fuel requirement: Premium unleaded
Front engine, rear wheel drive
Production: 2/92-N/A

Engine

Type: (1992-1995) 1.8 liter (M42) 4-cylinder in-line, 16 valve, chain-driven dual overhead camshaft, hydraulic lifters, water cooled, longitudinally mounted, inclined, 5 main bearings.
Bore/Stroke: 84x81 mm
  (85x83.5 from 1996, M44 engine)
Displacement: 1796 cc (1895 cc from 1996)
Compression Ratio: 10.0:1
Horsepower: 138hp (SAE net) @ 6000 rpm
Torque: 129 ft-lb @ 4500 rpm
  (133 ft-lb @ 4300 rpm from 1996)
Fuel Injected: Bosch ML-Motronic
Engine management system: Digital Motor Electronics (ML-Motronic) with direct ignition, adaptive control, self-diagnosis capability

Type: (From 1996) 1.9 liter (M44) 4-cylinder in-line, 16 valve, chain-driven dual overhead camshaft, hydraulic lifters, water cooled, longitudinally mounted, inclined, 5 main bearings.
Bore/Stroke: 85x83.5
Displacement: 1895 cc
Compression Ratio: 10.0:1
Horsepower: 138hp (SAE net) @ 6000 rpm
Torque: 133 ft-lb @ 4300 rpm
Fuel Injected: Bosch HFM-Motronic 5.2 with hot-wire air-mass meter
Engine management system: Digital Motor Electronics (HFM-Motronic) with direct ignition, adaptive control, self-diagnosis capability
Exhaust emission control: 3-way catalytic converter, Lambda sensor, 105 amp alternator, 12-volt 65 amp hrs. battery (trunk mounted)

Chassis and Drivetrain

Transmission: 5-speed manual, Getrag type-C
  Gear ratios I/II/III/IV/V:
  4.23/2.52/1.67/1.22/1.00:1
  Final drive ratio: 3.45:1
Optional 4-speed automatic (THM R1)
  Gear ratios I/II/III/IV:
  2.40/1.47/1.00/0.72:1
  (2.86/1.62/1.00/0.72 from 1/94)
  Final drive ratio: 4.45:1 (4.44:1 from 1996)
Steering: engine speed sensitive power assisted rack and pinion
Steering ratio: 16.8:1
Front Suspension: Independent with MacPherson struts, coil springs, arc-shaped lower control arms, twin-tube gas-pressure shocks, anti-roll bar
Rear Suspension: Independent Multi-link with Central links, separate coil springs and twin-tube gas-pressure shocks, anti-roll bar
Braking:
  Front 287mm ventilated discs
  Rear 279mm solid discs, mechanically operated handbrake
Anti-lock brakes (Teves Mark IV ABS) standard on all models
Wheels: 6 J x 15 steel; 5-bolt
Offset: 47mm
Tires: 185/65R-15

Interior

Front reclining seats w/height adjustment (manually operated), height-adjustable and tilting head rests, cloth or leatherette upholstery, SRS (supplemental restraint system) with driver's airbag and knee bolster, dual lighted visor vanity mirrors, two map reading lights, full carpeting, carpet on rear shelf, storage pockets in front doors, lockable (and lighted) glove compartment with flashlight socket, anti-glare mirror, heated rear window, 3-point automatic seat belts with mechanical tensioners (front) and 3-point ergonomic rear belts with buckles at outside and 2-point lap belt in center, 160 mph speedometer with 6-digit LCD odometer and trip odometer, tachometer, fuel-economy indicator, Service Interval indicator, LCD dot matrix multi-function digital clock and outside temperature indicator with freeze warning. Orange instrument and ventilation control lighting, air-conditioning with separate right-left electronic temperature control, separate recirculation control, rear seat heater duct, air-intake microfilter, power operated windows w/one-touch driver's and key-off operation, Anti-theft AM/FM stereo radio/cassette player with four speakers and integrated antenna, two-way electric sunroof, electric central locking with lighted master key, tinted glass all around with dark green border on top of windshield, drop-down tool kit in trunk lid

Technical Data BMW (E36) — U.S. Model 1992-1998 318i 4-door Sedan

Exterior	Impact zones and integrated roof crossbar, energy absorbing 2.5 mph bumpers with replaceable slide-over elements protecting up to 9 mph, full-frame doors, hood safety catch,	dual electrically controlled exterior rear view mirrors, integrated front spoiler, halogen headlamps.
Optional Equipment	Limited slip differential, heated seats, metallic paint.	

Performance	Acceleration, 0-60 mph (sec):
	    Manual: 9.9 (1992-1995), 8.5 (1996),
	    9.9 (1997)
	    Automatic: 11.4 (1993), 10.9 (1994-1995),
	    10.6 (1996), 9.8 (1997), 10.8 (1998)
		Fuel economy EPA (city/hwy), mpg :
		    Manual: 22/30 (1992-1994),
		    22/32 (1995-1997)
		    Automatic: 22/30 (1992-1994)
		Top Speed: 128 mph (electronically limited),
		    (116 mph beginning 1994)

Changes during 1992	Introduced after the E36 325i and included mid-year 325i updates. CFC-free refrigerant	introduced for air conditioning systems very late in production.
Changes for 1993	Standard: Increased headroom for driver through increased seat height adjustment range. CFC-free refrigerant introduced for air conditioning; improved material for	dashboard, center console, door panels, front seatbacks. Optional: Automatic Transmission, cruise control, sports suspension, fog lights, split fold-down rear seats
Changes for 1994	Standard: Wide-ratio automatic transmission for improved acceleration (phased in 1/94 production). Lighted mode switch for automatic transmission. All-season tires standard (phased in 1/94 production). Revised front spoiler design. Dual airbag. Redesigned and upgraded airbag and glovebox area. Rechargeable flashlight standard. Storage nets	on front seat back. Pre-wiring for CD changer. Dual-diversity antenna system. Driveaway protection on double-locking. Optional: Inclement weather package discontinued. All Season Traction Control available. Limited Slip phased out. Heated seats, mirrors, washer jets and driver's door lock available as a group. 
Changes for 1995	Standard: New seat belt tensioners and air bags (phased in 9/94 production). Side directionals in front fenders (earlier phase-in). Freewheeling door locks (phased in 7/95). New steering wheel and front seat design. Temperature control with 8°F increments.	Body color bumpers and exterior mirrors. Cruise Control. Coded driveway protection phased-in 1/95 production. Optional: Leather, alloy wheels, fog lights, premium audio, height adjustable steering wheel, and sports suspension.
Changes for 1996	Standard: New 1.9 liter engine (M44), improved cylinder head with roller rocker arms, Bosch DME with hot-film air mass sensor, dual resonance intake system switches over 600 rpm earlier, fabricated stainless steel headers, central locking switch on console, seat belts accommodate child safety seats, new 10-speaker 200 watt audio system with	weather band, one-touch exterior door lock and sunroof operation, automatic climate control. Optional: AST phased in, Limited Slip phased out; 320 watt Harman/Kardon audio system; ski-bag; full body color front and rear bumpers and rocker panels, leather steering wheel, shift knob, handbrake knob and shift and handbrake boots. 
Changes for 1997	Standard: All Season Traction; clutch interlock (manual); revised front end/grills; new side-marker lights; heated outside mirrors; leather shift knob for automatics in 8 series style; new center console with integrated cupholders,	ashtray and coinholder; side compartments in trunk, new wheel covers, full body color bumpers, side-impact airbags in front doors (phased-in 1/97 production) Optional: Premium Packages deleted; sunroof now optional, 10-spoke alloy
Changes for 1998	Optional: sunroof, alloy wheels, remote keyless-entry security system, front-center	armrest, leather steering wheel, shift knob and handbrake boot.
Available Colors	Standard Paint: Black, Jet Black, Alpine White, Brilliant Red, Bright Red Metallic Paint: Sterling Silver, Cashmere Beige, Granite Silver, Lagoon Green, Mauritius Blue,	Glacier Blue, Calypso Red, Arctic Gray, Boston Green, Samana Beige, Morea Green, Samoa Blue, Montreal Blue, Arctic Silver, Cosmos Black, Avus Blue, Ascot Green, Sierra Red.

Technical Data BMW (E36) — U.S. Model 1994-1997 318i Convertible

General	Manufacturer's suggested retail prices (US $): 1994: $29,900, 1995: $31,505, 1996: $32,900, 1997: $33,150. Curb weight (lbs.): Manual 3120 (1994-1995), 3131 (1996-1997)	Automatic: 3208 (1994-1995), 3219 (1996-1997). Wheelbase: 106.3 in. Weight distribution, front/rear (%): Manual 49/5, Automatic 48/52. Fuel capacity: 17.2 gal (16.4 gal. from 1996). Fuel requirement: Premium unleaded. Front engine, rear wheel drive. Production: 2/94-N/A

General

Manufacturer's suggested retail prices (US $):
  1994: $29,900
  1995: $31,505
  1996: $32,900
  1997: $33,150
Curb weight (lbs.): Manual: 3120 (1994-1995), 3131 (1996-1997)

Automatic: 3208 (1994-1995), 3219 (1996-1997)
Wheelbase: 106.3 in.
Weight distribution, front/rear (%):
  Manual 49/5, Automatic 48/52
Fuel capacity: 17.2 gal (16.4 gal. from 1996)
Fuel requirement: Premium unleaded
Front engine, rear wheel drive
Production: 2/94-N/A

Engine

Type: (1992-1995) 1.8 liter (M42) 4-cylinder in-line, 16 valve, chain-driven dual overhead camshaft, hydraulic lifters, water cooled, longitudinally mounted, inclined, 5 main bearings.
Bore/Stroke: 84x81 mm
  (85x83.5 from 1996, M44 engine)
Displacement: 1796 cc (1895 cc from 1996)
Compression Ratio: 10.0:1
Horsepower: 138hp (SAE net) @ 6000 rpm
Torque: 129 ft-lb @ 4500 rpm
  (133 ft-lb @ 4300 rpm from 1996)
Fuel Injected: Bosch ML-Motronic
Engine management system: Digital Motor Electronics (ML-Motronic) with direct ignition, adaptive control, self-diagnosis capability

Type: (From 1996) 1.9 liter (M44) 4-cylinder in-line, 16 valve, chain-driven dual overhead camshaft, hydraulic lifters, water cooled, longitudinally mounted, inclined, 5 main bearings.
Bore/Stroke: 85x83.5
Displacement: 1895 cc
Compression Ratio: 10.0:1
Horsepower: 138hp (SAE net) @ 6000 rpm
Torque: 133 ft-lb @ 4300 rpm
Fuel Injected: Bosch HFM-Motronic 5.2 with hot-wire air-mass meter
Engine management system: Digital Motor Electronics (HFM-Motronic) with direct ignition, adaptive control, self-diagnosis capability
Exhaust emission control: 3-way catalytic converter, Lambda sensor, 105 amp alternator, 12-volt 65 amp hrs. battery (trunk mounted)

Chassis and Drivetrain

Transmission: 5-speed manual, Getrag type-C
  Gear ratios I/II/III/IV/V:
  4.23/2.52/1.67/1.22/1.00:1
  Final drive ratio: 3.45:1
Optional 4-speed automatic (THM R1)
  Gear ratios I/II/III/IV:
  2.40/1.47/1.00/0.72:1
  (2.86/1.62/1.00/0.72 from 1/94)
  Final drive ratio: 4.45:1 (4.44:1 from 1996)
Steering: engine speed sensitive power assisted rack and pinion
Steering ratio: 16.8:1
Front Suspension: Independent with MacPherson struts, coil springs, arc-shaped

lower control arms, twin-tube gas-pressure shocks, anti-roll bar
Rear Suspension: Independent Multi-link with Central links, separate coil springs and twin-tube gas-pressure shocks, anti-roll bar
Braking:
  Front 287mm ventilated discs
  Rear 279mm solid discs, mechanically operated handbrake
Anti-lock brakes (Teves Mark IV ABS) standard on all models
Wheels: 7 J x 15 light alloy; 5-bolt
Offset: 47mm
Tires: 205/60R-15

Interior

Front reclining seats w/height adjustment (manually operated), height-adjustable and tilting head rests with storage nets, cloth or leatherette upholstery, adjustable steering wheel, SRS (supplemental restraint system) with dual airbag and knee bolster, dual lighted visor vanity mirrors, two map reading lights, full carpeting, carpet on rear shelf, storage pockets in front doors, lockable (and lighted) glove compartment with flashlight, anti-glare mirror, heated rear window, 3-point automatic seat belts with mechanical tensioners (front) and 3-point ergonomic rear belts with buckles at outside and 2-point lap belt in center, contoured rear seats with removable arm rest, 160 mph speedometer with 6-digit LCD odometer and trip odometer, tachometer, fuel-economy indicator, Service Interval indicator,

LCD dot matrix multi-function digital clock and outside temperature indicator with freeze warning. Orange instrument and ventilation control lighting, air-conditioning with separate right-left electronic temperature control, separate recirculation control, rear seat heater duct, air-intake microfilter, automatic sealing power operated windows w/key-off and one-touch driver's operation, Anti-theft AM/FM stereo radio/cassette player with six speakers, prewired for CD player, electric central locking (including glovebox) with lighted master key, tinted glass all around with dark green border on top of windshield, drop-down tool kit in trunk lid.

Technical Data BMW (E36) — U.S. Model 1994-1997 318i Convertible

Exterior	Impact zones and fully-lined manual top, specially designed alloy wheels, revised front spoiler, frameless doors with automatic sealing windows, body colored energy absorbing 2.5 mph bumpers with replaceable slide-over	elements protecting up to 9 mph, driveaway protection on double-locking, hood safety catch, electrically controlled side mirrors, integrated front spoiler, halogen headlamps.
Optional Equipment	Heated seats, mirrors, washer jets, metallic paint, color keyed aluminum hardtop, all season traction control,	

Performance	Acceleration, 0-60 mph (sec):
	  Manual: 10.6 (1994-1995),
	  10.2 (1996-1997)
	  Automatic: 11.6 (1994-1995),
	  11.5 (1996-1997),
	Fuel economy EPA (city/hwy), mpg :
		Manual: 22/30 (1992-1994),
		  22/31 (1995), 22/32 (1996-1997)
		  Automatic: 22/30 (1992-1994)
		Top Speed: 128 mph (electronically limited),
		  (116 mph beginning 1994)

Changes during 1994	Standard: Wide-ratio automatic transmission for improved acceleration (phased in 1/94 production). Lighted mode switch for automatic transmission. All-season tires standard (phased in 1/94 production).	
Changes for 1995	Standard: New seat belt tensioners and air bags (phased in 9/94 production). Side directionals in front fenders (earlier phase-in). Freewheeling door locks (phased in 7/95). New steering wheel and front seat design. Temperature control with 8°F increments.	Cruise Control. Fog lights. Coded driveway protection phased-in 1/95 production. Optional: Leather, premium audio and height adjustable steering wheel available. Sports Package available including: sports suspension, height-adjustable steering wheel and limited slip differential.
Changes for 1996	Standard: New 1.9 liter engine (M44), improved cylinder head with roller rocker arms, Bosch DME with hot-film air mass sensor, dual resonance intake system switches over 600 rpm earlier, fabricated stainless steel headers, central locking switch on console, seat belts accommodate child safety seats, new 10-speaker 200 watt audio system with	weather band, one-touch and exterior door lock sunroof operation, automatic climate control. Optional: AST phased in, Limited Slip phased out; 320 watt Harman/Kardon audio system; ski-bag; sports and premium packages and leather steering wheel, shift knob, handbrake knob and shift and handbrake boots.
Changes for 1997	Standard: All Season Traction; clutch interlock (manual); revised front end/grills; new side-marker lights; heated outside mirrors; leather shift knob for automatics in 8 series style; new center console with integrated cupholders,	ashtray and coinholder; side compartments in trunk, side-impact airbags in front doors (phased-in 1/97 production) Optional: Premium Packages deleted
Available Colors	Standard Paint: Black, Jet Black, Alpine White, Brilliant Red, Bright Red. Metallic Paint: Sterling Silver, Cashmere Beige, Granite Silver, Lagoon Green, Mauritius Blue,	Glacier Blue, Calypso Red, Arctic Gray, Boston Green, Samana Beige, Morea Green, Samoa Blue, Montreal Blue, Arctic Silver, Cosmos Black, Avus Blue, Ascot Green, Sierra Red.

Technical Data BMW (E36)—U.S. Model 1995 M3 Coupe

General	Manufacturer's suggested retail prices (US $):
	 Coupe: $35,800
	    Lightweight: $49,000
	 Curb weight (lbs.):
	    Coupe: 3175 lbs.
	    Coupe (automatic): 3241 lbs
	    Lightweight: 3125 lbs
	 Wheelbase: 106.3 in.
	 Weight distribution, front/rear (%): 50/50
		Fuel capacity: 17.2 gal.
		 Fuel requirement: Premium unleaded
		 Front engine, rear wheel drive
		 Production:
		    5 speed from 3/94
		 Automatic from 2/95

Engine	Type: 3.0 liter (S50US) 6-cylinder in-line, 24 valve, chain-driven dual overhead camshafts, VANOS variable valve timing, hydraulic lifters, water cooled, longitudinally mounted, inclined, 7 main bearings. Bore/Stroke: 86x85.8 mm Displacement: 2900 cc Compression Ratio: 10.5:1	Horsepower: 240hp (SAE net) @ 6000 rpm Torque: 225 ft-lb @ 4250 rpm Fuel Injected Engine management system: Digital Motor Electronics (Bosch HFM Motronic) with direct ignition, adaptive control, self-diagnosis capability, dual knock sensors Exhaust emission control: dual 3-way catalytic converters, Lambda sensor

Chassis and Drivetrain	Transmission: 5-speed manual (ZF 50)
	    Gear ratios I/II/III/IV/V:
	    4.20/2.49/1.66/1.24/1.00:1
	 Final drive ratio: 2.93:1 (Lightweight: 3.23:1)
	 Optional 5-speed automatic (ZF 5 HP 18)
	    Gear ratios I/II/III/IV:
	    3.67/2.00/1.41/1.00/0.74:1
	 Final drive ratio: 3.23:1
	 Steering: variable ratio and variable power assisted rack and pinion
	 Steering ratio: 15.4 – 19.8:1 (variable)
	 Front Suspension: M-sport independent with MacPherson struts, coil springs, arc-shaped
		lower control arms, twin-tube gas-pressure shocks, anti-roll bar
		 Rear Suspension: M-sport independent Multi-link with Central links, separate coil springs and reinforced spring mounting plates, twin-tube gas-pressure shocks, anti-roll bar
		 Braking:
		    Front 315mm ventilated discs
		    Rear 312mm vented discs, mechanically operated handbrake
		 Anti-lock brakes standard
		 Wheels: 7.5 J x 17 light 10-spoke alloy; 5-bolt
		 Tires: 235/40ZR-17

Interior	M sport front seats, 12-way manual adjustment with thigh support and height-adjustable upper section including shoulder and head support; suede/cloth or leather upholstery; leather M-Technic steering wheel with M-color stitching and shift knob; height adjustable steering column; SRS (supplemental restraint system) for driver and passenger; dual lighted visor vanity mirrors; two map reading lights; full carpeting, carpet on rear shelf, storage pockets in front doors; lockable (and lighted) glove compartment with removable flashlight; anti-glare mirror; heated rear window; 3-point automatic seat belts with mechanical tensioners (front) and 3-point ergonomic belts with buckles at outside and 2-point lap belt in center rear; red-pointered instuments with 6-digit LCD odometer and trip odometer, tachometer, fuel-economy indicator; Service	Interval indicator, LCD dot matrix Multi-Information Display (MID) including digital clock, Check Control, and outside temperature indicator. Orange instrument and ventilation control lighting; air conditioning with separate right-left automatic electronic temperature control, separate recirculation control; rear seat heater duct, air-intake microfilter; power operated windows w/one-touch and key-off operation, BMW Sound System Anti-theft AM/FM stereo radio/cassette player with 10x20 watt power amplifier, custom contoured equalizer with ten speakers and integrated antenna, electric central locking with lighted master key, tinted glass all around with dark green border on top of windshield, drop-down tool kit in trunk lid. Limited slip differential and M badging standard.
Exterior	Unit body with impact zones and integrated roof crossbar, energy absorbing 2.5 mph bumpers with replaceable slide-over elements protecting up to 9 mph, hood safety catch,	dual electrically controlled M-design exterior rear view mirrors, integrated front spoiler, halogen headlamps, halogen fog lamps; heated mirrors and washer jets.

Technical Data BMW (E36) — U.S. Model 1995 M3 Coupe

Optional Equipment	Two-way electric sunroof with one-touch function; sunroof and cruise control as package; heated seats; On-board computer.	
Performance	Acceleration, 0-60 mph: 6.1 sec. Automatic: 6.9 Fuel economy EPA (city/hwy), mpg : 19/27 Automatic: 19/28	Top Speed: 137 mph (electronically limited)
Changes during 1995	Standard: Height adjustable steering column deleted. Coded driveaway protection phased-in 1/95 production. Port-installed center console cupholder phased-in. Optional: 5-speed automatic transmission with adaptive control available as of 12/94 production. Rear spoiler with integrated third brake light available as of 1/95. Luxury Package includes: M-Contour II alloy wheels, cruise control, shorter front spoiler and rocker panel covers, 8-way leather power sport seats and center arm rest, hazelnut wood trim, Onboard computer, chrome interior door handle surrounds, Nappa leather trim including door and rear-side panels, availability of Boston Green and Arctic Silver paint and Mulberry, black and Champagne interior colors. Forged 5-spoke "star" wheels available (wider 8.5" rear normally included). M-Contour II wheels.	Lightweight model introduced: approximately 120 produced for 1995 only. Special equipment included: Alpine White paint with Motorsport flag graphic decals, individually selected engines, 3.23:1 final drive ratio, special sports suspension, larger oil pan, reinforcement braces, aluminum door skins, carbon fiber interior trim, forged wheels, rear wing and extended rear wing. Deleted equipment: sound system, air conditioner, leather, M sport seats, soundproofing, speed limiter, and tool kit. Weight saving approximated 150 lbs.
Available Colors	Standard Paint: Alpine White, Mugello Red, Bright Red,	Metallic Paint: Daytona Violet, Boston Green, Arctic Silver, Imola Red, Cosmos Black, Avus Blue, Techno Violet, Estoril Blue, Byzanz (1997 sedan only), Fern Green, Titanium Silver

Technical Data BMW (E36)—U.S. Model 1996-1999 M3 Coupe, 1997-1998 M3 Sedan 4-door, and 1998-1999 M3 Convertible

General

Manufacturer's suggested retail prices (US $): Coupe:
- 1996: $38,960
- 1997: $39,380
- 1998: $39,700
- 1999: $39,700

4dr:
- 1996: N/A
- 1997: N/A
- 1998: $39,700
- 1999: N/A

Convertible:
- 1996: N/A
- 1997: N/A
- 1998: $45,900
- 1999: $45,900

Curb weight (lbs.):
- Coupe: 3175 (manual), automatic N/A
- 4dr: 3175 (manual), 3241 (automatic)
- Convertible: 3494

Wheelbase: 106.3 in.
Weight distribution, front/rear (%): 50/50
Fuel capacity: 16.4 gal.
Fuel requirement: Premium unleaded
Front engine, rear wheel drive
Production:
- Coupe: 3/96- N/A
- Sedan: 4/96- N/A
- Convertible: 3/98-8/99

Engine

Type: 3.2 liter (S52US) 6-cylinder in-line, 24 valve, chain-driven dual overhead camshafts, VANOS variable valve timing, hydraulic lifters, water cooled, longitudinally mounted, inclined, 7 main bearings.
Bore/Stroke: 86.4x91 mm
Displacement: 3201 cc
Compression Ratio: 10.5:1
Horsepower: 240hp (SAE net) @ 6000 rpm

Torque: 236 ft-lb @ 3800 rpm (225 ft-lb with automatic transmission)
Fuel Injected
Engine management system: Digital Motor Electronics (Siemens MS 41.1) with direct ignition, adaptive control, self-diagnosis capability, dual knock sensors
Exhaust emission control: dual 3-way catalytic converters, Lambda sensor

Chassis and Drivetrain

Transmission: 5-speed manual (ZF 50)
   Gear ratios I/II/III/IV/V:
   4.20/2.49/1.66/1.24/1.00:1
Final drive ratio: 1996 - 2.93, 1997 on - 13.23:1
Optional 5-speed automatic (ZF 5 HP 18)
   Gear ratios I/II/III/IV:
   3.67/2.00/1.41/1.00/0.74:1
Final drive ratio: 1996 - 3.23:1,
   1997 on - 3.38:1
Steering: variable ratio and variable power assisted rack and pinion
Steering ratio: 15.4 – 19.8:1 (variable)
Front Suspension: M-sport independent with MacPherson struts, coil springs, arc-shaped

lower control arms, twin-tube gas-pressure shocks, anti-roll bar
Rear Suspension: M-sport independent Multi-link with Central links, separate coil springs and reinforced spring mounting plates, twin-tube gas-pressure shocks, anti-roll bar
Braking:
   Front 315mm ventilated discs
   Rear 312mm vented discs, mechanically operated handbrake
Anti-lock brakes standard
Wheels: Front 7.5 J x 17; Rear 8.5J x 15
Tires: Front 225/45ZR-15; Rear 245/40ZR-15

Interior

M sport front seats, 12-way manual adjustment with thigh support and height-adjustable upper section including shoulder and head support; revised cloth upholstery colors, leather upholstery now includes door inserts and new colors; leather M-Technic steering wheel with M-color stitching and shift knob; height adjustable steering column; SRS (supplemental restraint system) for driver and passenger; dual lighted visor vanity mirrors; two map reading lights; full carpeting, carpet on rear shelf, storage pockets in front doors; lockable (and lighted) glove compartment with removable flashlight; anti-glare mirror; heated rear window; 3-point automatic seat belts with mechanical tensioners (front) and 3-point ergonomic belts with buckles at outside and 2-point lap belt in center rear; red-pointered instuments with 6-digit LCD odometer and trip odometer, tachometer, fuel-economy

indicator; Service Interval indicator, OBD update, LCD dot matrix Multi-Information Display (MID) including digital clock, Check Control, and outside temperature indicator. Orange instrument and ventilation control lighting; air conditioning with separate right-left automatic climate control, separate recirculation control; rear seat heater duct, air-intake microfilter; power operated windows w/one-touch and key-off operation, BMW Sound System Anti-theft AM/FM stereo radio/cassette player with 10x20 watt power amplifier, custom contoured equalizer with ten speakers and integrated antenna, electric central locking with lighted master key, tinted glass all around with dark green border on top of windshield, drop-down tool kit in trunk lid. Limited slip differential and M badging standard.

Technical Data BMW (E36) — U.S. Model 1996-1999 M3 Coupe, 1997-1998 M3 Sedan 4dr, and 1998-1999 M3 Convertible

Exterior	Unit body with impact zones and integrated roof crossbar (except Convertible), center front grill now black on all models, energy absorbing 2.5 mph bumpers with replaceable slide-over elements protecting up to 9 mph, hood safety catch, dual electrically controlled M-design exterior rear view mirrors, integrated front spoiler, halogen headlamps, halogen fog lamps; heated mirrors and washer jets.
Optional Equipment	Two-way electric sunroof with one-touch function; sunroof and cruise control as package; heated seats; leather seat backs; on-board computer, Harman Kardon 320-watt sound system.
Performance	Acceleration, 0-60 mph (sec): Coupe and Sedan — Manual: 5.9 (1996), 5.7 (1997-1999); Automatic: 6.4 (1997-1998). Convertible — Manual: 5.8 (1998-1999); Automatic: 6.6 (1998-1999). Fuel economy EPA (city/hwy), mpg: Manual: 20/28 (1997-1998), 19/26 (1999); Automatic: 19/28 (1997-1998), 17/25 (1999). Top Speed: 137 mph (electronically limited)
Changes for 1997	Standard: clutch interlock on manual transmissions; new side-marker lights; new center console with integrated cupholders, ashtray and coinholder; side compartments in trunk; side-impact airbags in front doors (phased-in 1/97 production, sedan only); soft lighting in front footwell; switches on rear reading lights. 8-way manual sport seats, front and rear power windows with one-touch operation (sedan only). Optional: 5-speed automatic transmission with adaptive control (sedan only). Split-foldown rear seat backs (sedan). Power front seat option phased-in. 4dr sedan now available
Changes for 1998	Standard: side-impact airbags in front doors; front center armrest; illuminated shift pattern knob; Magma and Mulberry interiors now available as standard; manual sport seats for sedan and convertible. Optional: Harman Kardon audio option includes port-installed CD changer. Luxury Package discontinued. Automatic transmission not available for coupe. Removable aluminum hardtop for Convertible. M3 Convertible introduced.
Changes for 1999	Standard: depowered front impact airbags; Modena Natur interior color discontinued. Optional: M three-spoke steering wheel, aerodynamic body components and M side molding on Sports Package. Automatic transmission available only for convertible. 4dr sedan discontinued
Available Colors	Standard Paint: Alpine White, Mugello Red, Bright Red, Metallic Paint: Daytona Violet, Boston Green, Arctic Silver, Imola Red, Cosmos Black, Avus Blue, Techno Violet, Estoril Blue, Byzanz (1997 sedan only), Fern Green, Titanium Silver

Technical Data BMW (E36)—U.S. Model 1995-1999 318ti (E36/5 Compact)

General

Manufacturer's suggested retail prices (US$):
318ti 3-door Coupe:
  1995: $19,900
  1996: $20,560
  1997: $21,390
  1998: $21,390
  1999: $23,300
Curb weight (lbs.):
  1995: Manual 2734, Automatic 2822
  1996: Manual 2745, Automatic 2833
  1997: Manual 2745, Automatic 2833
  1998: Manual 2778, Automatic 2866
  1999: Manual 2778, Automatic 2866
Wheelbase: 106.3 in.
Weight distribution, front/rear (%): 51/49
Fuel capacity: 13.7 gal. (14.5 from 1998)
Fuel requirement: unleaded premium
Front engine, rear wheel drive
Production: from 2/95

Engine

Type: (1995) 1.8 liter (M42) 4-cylinder in-line, 16 valve, chain-driven dual overhead camshaft, hydraulic lifters, water cooled, longitudinally mounted, inclined, 5 main bearings.
Bore/Stroke: 84x81 mm

Displacement: 1796 cc
Compression Ratio: 10.0:1
Horsepower: 138hp (SAE net) @ 6000 rpm
Torque: 129 ft-lb @ 4500 rpm

Fuel Injected: Bosch ML-Motronic
Engine management system: Digital Motor Electronics (ML-Motronic) with direct ignition, dual knock sensors, adaptive control, self-diagnosis capability
Type: (From 1996) 1.9 liter (M44) 4-cylinder in-line, 16 valve, chain-driven dual overhead camshaft, hydraulic lifters, water cooled, longitudinally mounted, inclined, 5 main bearings.
Bore/Stroke: 85x83.5
Displacement: 1895 cc
Compression Ratio: 10.0:1
Horsepower: 138hp (SAE net) @ 6000 rpm
Torque: 133 ft-lb @ 4300 rpm
Fuel Injected: Bosch HFM-Motronic 5.2 with hot-wire air-mass meter
Engine management system: Digital Motor Electronics (HFM-Motronic) with direct ignition, adaptive control, self-diagnosis capability and dual knock sensors.
Exhaust emission control: 3-way catalytic converter, Lambda sensor
105 amp alternator, 12-volt 65 amp hrs. battery (under hood)

Chassis and Drivetrain

Transmission: 5-speed manual (Getrag type-C)
  Gear ratios I/II/III/IV/V:
  4.23/2.52/1.67/1.22/1.00:1
  Final drive ratio: 3.45:1
Optional 4-speed automatic (THM R1)
  Gear ratios I/II/III/IV:
  2.40/1.47/1.00/0.72:1
  (2.86/1.62/1.00/0.72 from 1/96)
Final drive ratio: 4.45:1 (4.44:1 from 1996)
Steering: engine speed sensitive power assisted rack and pinion
Steering ratio: 16.8:1
Front Suspension: Independent with MacPherson struts, coil springs, arc-shaped lower control arms, twin-tube gas-pressure shocks, anti-roll bar
Rear Suspension: Semi trailing arms, coil springs, twin-tube gas-pressure shocks and anti-roll bar
Braking:
  Front 287mm solid discs
  Rear 272mm solid discs, mechanically operated handbrake
Anti-lock brakes (Teves Mark IV ABS) standard on all models
Wheels: 6Jx15 steel wheels and covers standard
Offset: 47mm
Tires: 185/65R-15

Interior

Front reclining seats (manual) w/height adjustment on driver's side, height-adjustable and tilting head rests, cloth upholstery, SRS (supplemental restraint system) with dual airbags, dual lighted visor vanity mirrors , two map reading lights, full carpeting, carpet on rear shelf, storage pockets in front doors, lockable (and lighted) glove compartment with flashlight socket, anti-glare mirror, heated rear window, 3-point automatic seat belts with mechanical tensioners (front) and 3-point ergonomic rear belts with buckles at outside and 2-point lap belt in center, split fold-down rear seats, 155 mph speedometer with 6-digit LCD odometer and trip odometer, tachometer, fuel-economy indicator, Service Interval indicator, LCD dot matrix multi-function digital clock. Orange instrument lighting, air-conditioning (without separate right-left temperature control), separate recirculation control, rear seat heater duct, air-intake microfilter, power operated windows w/one-touch driver's and key-off operation, Anti-theft AM/FM stereo radio/cassette player with six speakers and integrated antenna, dual cupholders, electric central locking of doors, gas filler and hatch with lighted master key and coded driveaway protection, tinted glass all around with dark green border on top of windshield, space-saving drop-down spare tire in trunk, tool kit under cargo compartment floor. Rear hatch design with rear window wiper/washer.

Technical Data BMW (E36) — U.S. Model 1995-1999 318ti (E36/5 Compact)

Exterior	Three door design hatchback. Impact zones and integrated roof crossbar energy absorbing 2.5 mph bumpers painted in body color with replaceable slide-over elements protecting up	to 9 mph, full-frame doors, hood safety catch, dual electrically controlled heated exterior rear view mirrors, integrated front spoiler, halogen headlamps.

Optional Equipment	4-speed automatic transmission and metallic paint. Active Package: Alloy wheel 15x7 in. with 205/60R-15 tires; keyless remote entry alarm system; leather steering wheel, shift knob and handbrake grip; Onboard computer with outside temperature, average fuel economy, range, average speed and freeze warning; 2-way power sunroof. Optional with package was a 10-speaker premium audio system, leather upholstery, and limited slip differential. Sports Package: Sports suspension with firmer springs, shocks and anti-roll bars; alloy wheels and tires as Active Package, front and rear fog	lights, sport front seats with adjustable thigh support, leather and cloth upholstery, leather steering wheel, shift knob and handbrake grip. Optional with package was a 10-speaker premium audio system, limited slip differential, and 2-way power sunroof. Club Sport Package: Limited edition model for 1995 only: included 16" wheels, M-Technic body panels and suspension, M-badging and special interior trim. Approximately 300 imported into U.S.

Performance	Acceleration, 0-60 mph (sec): 1995: Manual 9.6, Automatic, 10.3 1996: Manual 9.3, Automatic, 10.3 1997: Manual 9.3, Automatic, 10.3 1998: Manual 9.9, Automatic, 10.8 1999: Manual 8.3, Automatic, 9.6	Fuel economy EPA mpg (city/highway): 1995: Manual 22/32, Automatic, 22/29 1996: Manual 23/31, Automatic, 23/31 1997: Manual 23/31, Automatic, 22/31 1998: Manual 23/32, Automatic, 22/31 1999: Manual 23/32, Automatic, 22/31 Top Speed (electronically limited): 116 mph

Changes for 1996	Standard: New 1.9 liter engine (M44) includes improved cylinder head with roller rocker arms, Bosch DME with hot-film air mass sensor, dual resonance intake system now switches over 600 rpm earlier, fabricated stainless steel headers replace previous cast iron units. Central locking switch on console, freewheeling door locks (phased-in 7/95), seat belts accommodate child safety seats, central locking via trunk lock (phased-in 9/95), 10-speaker 200-watt sound system.	Optional: All Season Traction (AST), one-touch sunroof, full body-color bumpers with all option packages. California Package: automatic convertible roof, cruise control, 15x7" alloy wheels with 205/60R-15 tires, leather steering wheel. Leather, Onboard computer, and metallic paint also available. Sports Package: modeled on Club Sport with 16" wheels and tires added. Onboard computer and metallic paint also available.

Changes for 1997	Standard: All Season Traction; clutch interlock on manual transmissions; revised front end/grills; new side-marker lights; leather shift knob for automatics in 8 series style; new wheel covers; full body-color bumpers, side skirts; new in-dash audio system with weather	band; locking glove compartment; upgraded cloth upholstery. Optional: heated seats; leather upholstery; Open-Air roof stand alone option as of 2/97 production (California package deleted); sunroof deleted from Active Package, now stand-alone option.

Changes for 1998	Standard: Side impact airbags (1/98). Leatherette interior on base and Active Package models. 14.5 gal. fuel tank capacity.	Optional: Open-Air roof renamed California roof. Active Package includes round-spoke design 15x7 in. alloy wheel.

Changes for 1999	318ti Sport only model available: Sports Package now standard, including M three-	spoke steering wheel. New upholstery cloth as of 1/99 production.

Available Colors	Standard Paint: Jet Black, Alpine White, Bright Red	Metallic Paint: Boston Green, Morea Green, Cordoba Red, Alaska Blue, Calypso Red, Arctic Silver, Cosmos Black, Avus Blue, Ascot Green, Montreal Blue, Titanium Silver.

Technical Data BMW (E36)—U.S. Model 1996-1998 328i, 1996-1999 328is, and 328i Convertible

General

Manufacturer's suggested retail prices (US$):
328is Coupe:
  1996-1997: $32,990
  1998-1999: $33,200
328i 4-door:
  1996-1997: $32,900
  1998: $33,100
328is Coupe:
  1996-1997: $41,390
  1998-1999: $41,500
Curb weight (lbs.):
328is Coupe:
  1996-1997: Manual 3120, Automatic 3197
  1998-1999: Manual 3142, Automatic 3230

328i 4-door:
  1996-1997: Manual 3120, Automatic 3197
  1998: Manual 3131, Automatic 3208
328i Convertible:
  1996-1997: Manual 3362, Automatic 3439
  1998-1999: Manual 3395, Automatic 3472
Wheelbase: 106.3 in.
Weight distribution, front/rear (%): 50/50
  (1998: 328i 51/49; 328is (automatic) 51/49)
Fuel capacity: 16.4 gal.
Fuel requirement: Unleaded premium
Front engine, rear wheel drive
Production: N/A

Engine

Type: 2.8 liter (M52) 6-cylinder in-line, 24 valve, chain-driven dual overhead camshafts, dual VANOS stepless variable valve timing, hydraulic lifters, water cooled, longitudinally mounted, inclined, 7 main bearings.
Bore/Stroke: 84x84 mm
Displacement: 2793 cc
Compression Ratio: 10.2:1
Horsepower: 190hp (SAE net) @ 5300 rpm

Torque: 207 ft-lb @ 3950 rpm
Fuel Injected
Engine management system: Digital Motor Electronics (Siemens MS 41.0) with direct ignition, adaptive control, self-diagnosis capability, dual knock sensors
Exhaust emission control: dual 3-way catalytic converters, Lambda sensor

Chassis and Drivetrain

Transmission: 5-speed manual (ZF type-C)
  Gear ratios I/II/III/IV/V:
  4.20/2.49/1.67/1.24/1.00:1
  Final drive ratio: 2.93:1
Optional 4-speed automatic (THM R1)
  Gear ratios I/II/III/IV:
  2.86/1.62/1.00/0.72:1
  Final drive ratio: 3.91:1
Steering: engine speed sensitive power assisted rack and pinion
Steering ratio: 16.8:1
Front Suspension: Independent with MacPherson struts, coil springs, arc-shaped lower control arms, twin-tube gas-pressure shocks, anti-roll bar

Rear Suspension: Independent Multi-link with Central links, separate coil springs and twin-tube gas-pressure shocks, anti-roll bar
Braking:
  Front 287mm ventilated discs
  Rear 279mm solid discs, mechanically operated handbrake
Anti-lock brakes (Teves Mark IV ABS) standard on all models
Wheels: 7 J x 15 light alloy; 5-bolt
Offset: 47mm
Tires: 205/60R-15

Interior

8-way power front seats; height-adjustable and tilting head rests; leatherette, or optional leather upholstery (standard on Convertible); leather steering wheel and shift knob, SRS (supplemental restraint system) for driver and passenger, dual lighted visor vanity mirrors , two map reading lights, full carpeting, carpet on rear shelf, storage pockets in front doors, lockable (and lighted) glove compartment with removable flashlight, anti-glare mirror, heated rear window, 3-point automatic seat belts with mechanical tensioners (front) and 3-point ergonomic rear belts with buckles at outside and 2-point lap belt in center, 160 mph speedometer with 6-digit LCD odometer and trip odometer, tachometer, fuel-economy indicator, Service Interval indicator, LCD dot matrix Multi-Information Display (MID)

including digital clock, Check Control, and outside temperature indicator. Orange instrument and ventilation control lighting; automatic climate control with separate right-left electronic temperature control and LCD display, separate recirculation control; rear seat heater duct, air-intake microfilter, power operated windows w/one-touch and key-off operation, BMW Sound System Anti-theft AM/FM stereo radio/cassette player with 10x20 watt power amplifier, custom contoured equalizer with ten speakers and integrated antenna, two-way electric sunroof with one-touch function, electric central locking with lighted master key, tinted glass all around with dark green border on top of windshield, drop-down tool kit in trunk lid.

Technical Data BMW (E36) — U.S. Model 1996-1998 328i, 1996-1999 328is, and 328i Convertible

Exterior	Impact zones and integrated roof crossbar (except Convertible), energy absorbing 2.5 mph bumpers with replaceable slide-over elements protecting up to 9 mph, full-frame	doors (sedan), hood safety catch, dual electrically controlled exterior rear view mirrors, integrated front spoiler, halogen headlights and fog lamps.
Additional Equipment	328is coupe: Alloy wheel; frameless doors with automatic sealing windows; fold-down rear seatbacks; swing-out side windows; one-touch passenger window up-operation. 328i Convertible: Electric, lined convertible top, leather seats; contoured rear seating with removable armrest, automatic sealing	windows plus electric rear and one-touch operation of all windows, specially tuned suspension, alloy wheel design as Coupe, central locking glove box, height adjustable steering wheel. Premium sound system with power amplifier, equalizer and six speakers. Bumper surrounds in body color.
Optional Equipment	All: Four speed automatic transmission; All Season Traction control; heated seats; heated windshield washer jets, driver's door lock and side mirrors. On-board computer, metallic paint. Sports Package: sports suspension (except Convertible), 16x7"double-spoke alloy wheels with 225/50ZR-16 tires, leather upholstery	(standard on Convertible), power front sport seats, Onboard computer. Premium Package: leather upholstery (standard on Convertible), wood interior trim, Onboard computer. Harman/Kardon audio system with upgraded speaker and 8x40 watt amplifiers. Ski bag and split folding rear seat for sedan.

Performance	Acceleration, 0-60 mph (sec):
	328i/s:
	  1996: Manual 7.0, Automatic 7.7
	  1997-1999: Manual 6.6, Automatic 7.2
	328i Convertible:
	  1996: Manual 7.3, Automatic 8.2
	  1997-1999: Manual 6.9, Automatic 7.5
		Fuel economy EPA (city/hwy), mpg
		
		  Manual transmission: 20/29
		
		  Automatic transmission: 20/27
		Top Speed, mph (All models):128
		  (electronically limited)

Changes for 1997	Standard: All Season Traction; clutch interlock on manual transmissions; revised front end/grills; new side-marker lights; heated side mirrors; leather shift knob for automatics in 8 series style; new center console with cupholders, ashtray and coinholder; side compartments in trunk; side-impact airbags in front doors (phased-in 1/97 production, sedan only); door sill trim with chrome inserts; soft lighting in front footwell; switches on	rear reading lights; 10-spoke wheels on 328i; beefed-up manual transmission. Convertible: Fully automatic top now includes latching and unlatching. Leather upholstery now optional, leatherette standard. Optional: Available Premium Package discontinued. Onboard computer now standalone option. Leather option includes wood trim. Sunroof.

Changes for 1998	Standard: side-impact airbags in front doors, adjustable rear headrests; Harman/Kardon audio option includes port-installed CD changer; new standard wheels for sedan.	Optional: Port-installed keyless entry security system now standard with Sports and Premium packages. Premium Package includes leather, electric sunroof, wood trim and remote keyless entry.
Changes for 1999	Standard: Coupe and Convertible wheels as on '98 sedan. Convertible: leather upholstery standard. Premium Package: walnut replaced by Yew hardwood trim .	Optional: M three-spoke steering wheel, aerodynamic body components and M side molding on Sports Package. E36 328i 4dr discontinued, replaced by new E46 model.
Available Colors	Standard Paint: Jet Black, Alpine White, Bright Red	Metallic Paint: Calypso Red, Samoa Blue, Montreal Blue, Boston Green, Arctic Silver, Morea Green, Cosmos Black, Avus Blue, Ascot Green, Sierra Red.

Technical Data BMW (E36) — U.S. Model 1998-1999 323is and 1998-1999 323i Convertible

General

Manufacturer's suggested retail prices (US$):
323is Coupe: $28,700
323i Convertible: $34,700
Curb weight (lbs.):
323is Coupe:
  Manual 3075
  Automatic 3175
323i Convertible:
  Manual 3296
  Automatic 3373

Wheelbase: 106.3 in.
Weight distribution, front/rear (%): 50/50 (coupe w/automatic transmission – 51/49)
Fuel capacity: 16.4 gal.
Fuel requirement: unleaded premium
Front engine, rear wheel drive
Production:
  323is: 9/97-N/A
  323iC: 9/97-N/A

Engine

Type: 2.5 liter (M52) 6-cylinder in-line, 24 valve, chain-driven dual overhead camshafts with double VANOS stepless variable valve timing, hydraulic lifters, water cooled, longitudinally mounted, inclined, 7 main bearings.
Bore/Stroke: 84x75 mm
Displacement: 2494 cc
Compression Ratio: 10.5:1
Horsepower: 168hp (SAE net) @ 5500 rpm

Torque: 181 ft-lb @ 3950 rpm
Fuel Injected
Engine management system: Digital Motor Electronics (Siemens MS 41.1) with direct ignition, adaptive control, self-diagnosis capability, twin knock control sensors
Exhaust emission control: 3-way catalytic converter, dual Lambda sensors
105 amp alternator, 12-volt 65 amp hrs. battery (Convertible 70 amp hrs.)

Chassis and Drivetrain

Transmission: 5-speed manual (Getrag type-C)
  Gear ratios I/II/III/IV/V:
  4.23/2.52/1.66/1.22/1.00:1
  Final drive ratio: 2.93:1
Optional 4-speed automatic (THM R1)
  Gear ratios I/II/III/IV:
  2.86/1.62/1.00/0.72:1
  Final drive ratio: 3.91:1
Steering: engine speed sensitive power assisted rack and pinion
Steering ratio: 15.4:1
Front Suspension: Independent with MacPherson struts, coil springs, arc-shaped lower control arms, twin-tube gas-pressure shocks, anti-roll bar

Rear Suspension: Independent Multi-link with Central links, separate coil springs and twin-tube gas-pressure shocks, anti-roll bar
Braking:
  Front 287mm ventilated discs
  Rear 279mm solid discs (vented on Convertible)
  Mechanically operated handbrake
Anti-lock brakes standard on all models
Wheels: 7 J x 15 light alloy; 5-bolt
Offset: 47mm
Tires: 205/60R-15

Interior

Front reclining seats w/height adjustment (manually operated), front and rear height-adjustable and tilting head rests, leatherette upholstery, leather steering wheel and shift knob, SRS (supplemental restraint system) for driver and passenger, side-impact airbags in front door panels, dual lighted visor vanity mirror, two map reading lights, full carpeting, carpet on rear shelf, storage pockets in front doors, lockable (and lighted) glove compartment with flashlight socket, anti-glare mirror, heated rear window, 3-point automatic seat belts with mechanical tensioners (front) and 3-point ergonomic rear belts with buckles at outside and 2-point lap belt in center, 160 mph speedometer with 6-digit LCD odometer and trip odometer, tachometer, fuel-economy indicator, Service Interval indicator, LCD dot matrix multi-function digital clock and

outside temperature indicator with freeze warning. Orange instrument and ventilation control lighting, automatic climate control with separate right-left temperature controls and digital LED read out, rear seat heater duct, air-intake microfilter, power operated windows w/one-touch and key-off operation (manual swing-out rear windows on Coupe), Anti-theft AM/FM stereo radio/cassette player with ten speakers and integrated antenna (mast on Convertible), central locking with lighted master key (included glovebox on Convertible), tinted glass all around with dark green border on top of windshield, drop-down tool kit in trunk lid. Fold-down rear seats standard in Coupe.

Technical Data BMW (E36)—U.S. Model 1998-1999 323is and 1998-1999 323i Convertible

Exterior	Impact zones and integrated roof crossbar (except Convertible), energy absorbing 2.5 mph bumpers with replaceable slide-over elements protecting up to 9 mph, hood safety	catch, dual electrically controlled side mirrors, integrated front spoiler, halogen headlamps.
Additional Equipment	323i Convertible: Manually operated fully lined convertible top, contoured rear seating with removable armrest, automatic sealing windows plus electric rear and one-touch	simultaneous operation of all windows, specially tuned suspension, alloy wheel design as Coupe, glove box included in central locking.
Optional Equipment	All: 4-speed electronically controlled automatic transmission; Harman//Kardon audio system with upgraded speakers and amplifier, CD changer (and subwoofer on Convertible); metallic paint; front foglights; leather upholstery; heated front seats, driver's door lock and windshield washer jets; power two-way sunroof (Coupe); Onboard computer; roll-over protection system (Convertible).	Sports Package includes: sport suspension (Coupe only), 16x7" cross-spoke alloy wheels with 225/50ZR-16 performance tires, front foglights. Premium Package includes: leather seat upholstery, two-way power sunroof (fully automatic top on Convertible), remote keyless-entry security system, front center armrest.

Performance	Acceleration, 0-60 mph:
	323is:
	    Manual: 7.1 sec.
	    Automatic: 8.2 sec.
	323i Convertible:
	    Manual: 7.7 sec
	    Automatic: 8.8 sec.
		Fuel economy EPA (city/highway) mpg:
		    Manual: 21/31
		    Automatic: 19/27
		Top Speed (electronically limited): 128 mph

Changes for 1999	Aerodynamic body components, M side moldings, M three-spoke steering wheel and double spoke wheels standard in Sports Package	
Available Colors	Standard Paint: Jet Black, Alpine White, Bright Red	Metallic Paint: Boston Green, Morea Green, Arctic Silver, Cosmos Black, Avus Blue, Ascot Green, Sierra Red.

Technical Data BMW (E46) — U.S. Model 1999-2000
323i, 323Ci and 323Ci Convertible

General	Manufacturer's suggested retail prices (US$):
	 1999 323i Sedan: $26,970
	 2000
	     323i Sedan: $27,560
	     323i Sportwagon: $29,770
	     323Ci Coupe: $29,560
	     323Ci Convertible: $35,560
		Wheelbase: 107.3 in.
		 Fuel capacity: 16.6 gal. (62.8 liters)
		 Fuel requirement: 92 AKI

Engine

Type: 2.5 liter (M52TU) 6-cylinder in-line, water cooled, longitudinally mounted, inclined, double vanos variable timing chain-driven dual-overhead camshafts, 7 main bearing crankshaft.
Bore / Stroke: 84.0 x 75.0 / 3.31 x 2.95
Displacement: 2494cc / 152ci

Compression Ratio: 10.5:1
Horsepower (SAE net): 170 @ 5500
Torque (SAE net): 181 @ 3500
Management System: Seimens MS 42
Alternator: 80 amps / 1120 watts
Battery: 80 amp/hrs.

Chassis and Drivetrain

Transmission: 5 Speed manual
   Gear Ratios 1, 2, 3, 4, 5, R
   4.23/2.25/1.66/1.22/1.00/4.04
   Final Drive: 3.07:1
Transmission: 5 Speed Automatic
   Gear Ratios 1, 2, 3, 4, 5, R
   (1999) 3.45/2.21/1.59/1.00/0.76/3.19
   (2000) 3.67/2.00/1.41/1.00/0.74/4.10
   Final drive ratio: 3.46:1
Steering: Vehicle speed proportional, power assisted rack and pinion.
Steering Ratio: 15.5:1
Braking:

Front discs: 300 mm / 11.8" vented discs
Rear discs: 295 mm / 11.6" vented discs
Front Suspension: Struts, arc-shaped forged aluminum lower control arms with hydraulic rear cushion, coil springs, twin tube gas pressurized shock absorbers, anti-roll bar.   Rear Suspension: Multi-link system with central links, upper and lower transverse links, coil springs, twin tube gas pressurized shock absorbers, anti roll bar
Wheels/Tires:
   (1999) 15" x 6.5" steel 195/65R-15
   (2000) 16" x 7" alloy 205/55R-16

Optional Equipment

Sport Package: on the Sedan & Wagon includes Sport Suspension, 17" Alloy wheels and tires (2000 only), Sport seats, fog lights, heated mirrors and washer jets, sport multi-function steering wheel with cruise control. On the Coupe & Convertible it includes Sport suspension, 17" Alloy wheels and tires, Sport seats.
Premium Package: on the Sedan & Wagon includes a Moonroof, auto-dimming mirror, power seats, front armrest, multi-function steering wheel with cruise control, on-board computer, upgraded interior lighting, memory for driver's seat and exterior mirrors, auto-dipping passenger side mirror when reverse is engaged, wood trim. On the Coupe it

includes a Moonroof, auto-dimming mirror, power seats, wood trim. On the Convertible it includes a fully automatic soft top, auto-dimming mirror, integrated garage door opener, wood trim.
Sport-Premium Package: (Sedan & Wagon only) includes a Moonroof, auto-dimming mirror, power seats, front armrest, multi-function steering wheel with cruise control, on-board computer, upgraded interior lighting, memory for driver's seat and exterior mirrors, auto-dipping passenger side mirror when reverse is engaged, wood trim, sport Suspension, 17" Alloy wheels and tires, fog lights, heated mirrors and washer jets.

Performance

Acceleration, 0-60 mph (sedan):
   Manual: 7.6 sec
   Automatic: 8.8 sec

Fuel Economy (city/highway) mpg (sedan):
   Manual: 20/29
   Automatic: 19/27
Top Speed: 128 mph

Technical Data BMW (E46) — U.S. Model 1999-2000 328i and 2000 328Ci

General	Manufacturer's suggested retail prices (US$):
	1999 328i Sedan: $33,970
	2000
	    328i Sedan: $33,970
	    328Ci Coupe: $34,560
		Wheelbase: 107.3"
		Fuel Capacity: 16.6 gallons (62.8 liters)
		Fuel Requirement: 92 AKI

Engine	Type: 2.7 liter (M52TU) 6-cylinder in-line, water cooled, longitudinally mounted, inclined, double vanos variable timing chain-driven dual-overhead camshafts, 7 main bearing crankshaft. Bore / Stroke:84.0 x 84.0 / 3.31 x 3.31 Displacement:2792cc / 170ci Compression Ratio: 10.2:1	Horsepower (SAE net): 193 @ 5500 Torque (SAE net): 206 @ 3500 Management System: Seimens MS 42 Alternator: 80 amps / 1120 watts Battery: 80 amp/hrs.

Chassis and Drivetrain	Transmission: 5 Speed manual
	    Gear Ratios: 1, 2, 3, 4, 5, R
	    4.21/2.49/1.66/1.24/1.00/3.85
	    Final Drive Ratio: 2.93:1
	Transmission: 5 Speed Automatic
	    Gear Ratios: 1, 2, 3, 4, 5, R
	    3.45/2.21/1.59/1.00/0.74/3.19
	    Final Drive Ratio: 3.46:1
	Steering: Vechicle speed proportional, power assisted rack and pinion.
	Steering Ratio: 15.5:1
		Braking:
		    Front discs: 300 mm / 11.8" vented discs
		    Rear discs: 294 mm / 11.6" vented discs
		Front Suspension: Struts, arc-shaped forged aluminum lower control arms with hydraulic rear cushion, coil springs, twin tube gas pressurized shock absorbers, anti-roll bar.
		Rear Suspension: Multi-link system with central links, upper and lower transverse links, coil springs, twin tube gas pressurized shock absorbers, anti roll bar
		Wheels/Tires: 16" x 7" Alloy 205/55HR 16

Optional Equipment	Sport Package includes a Sport suspension, 17" Alloy wheels and tires, sport seats, and sport steering wheel	Premium Package includes a Moonroof, auto-dimming mirror, leather upholstery, and power lumbar support wood trim.

Performance	Acceleration, 0-60 mph:
	    Manual (sedan): 6.5 sec
	Fuel Economy (city/highway) mph:
	    Manual (sedan): 20/29
	    Automatic (sedan): 19/27
	Top Speed: 128 mph	

Technical Data BMW (E46)—U.S. Model 2001 325i, 325xi, 325Ci, and 325Ci Convertible

General	Manufacturer's suggested retail prices (US$): 325i Sedan: $27,560 325xi Sedan: $29,310 325i Sportwagon: $29,970 325xi Sportwagon: $31,720	325Ci Coupe: $29,560 325Ci Convertible: $36,560 Wheelbase: 107.3" Fuel Capacity: 16.6 gallons (62.8 liters) Fuel Requirement: 92 AKI

Engine	Type: 2.5 liter (M54) 6-cylinder in-line, water cooled, longitudinally mounted, inclined, double vanos variable timing chain-driven dual-overhead camshafts, 7 main bearing crankshaft. Bore /Stroke: 84.0mm x 75.0mm /3.31" 2.95"	Displacement: 2494cc /152ci Compression Ratio: 10.5:1 Horsepower (SAE net): 184 @ 6000 rpm Torque (SAE net): 175 @ 3500 rpm Management System: Seimens MS 43mp Alternator: 120 amps / 1680 watts Battery: 80 Amp hours

**Chassis
and
Drivetrain**
	Transmission: 5 Speed manual
	  Gear Ratios 1, 2, 3, 4, 5, R
	  (325i and Ci) 4.23/2.25/1.66/1.22/1.00/4.04
	(325 xi) 4.21/2.44/1.66/1.24/1.00/3.85
	  Final Drive Ratio:
	  (325i and 325Ci) 3.15:1
	  (325Ci Convertible) 3.41:1
	  (325xi) 3.23:1
	Transmission: 5 Speed Automatic
	  Gear Ratios 1, 2, 3, 4, 5, R
	  (325i and Ci) 3.67/2.00/1.41/1.00/0.74/4.10
	  (325xi) 3.45/2.21/1.54/1.00/0.76/3.17
	  Final Drive Ratio: 3.46:1
		Steering: Vehicle speed proportional, power assisted rack and pinion.
		Steering Ratio: 15.5:1
		Brakes:
		  Front: 300 mm /11.8" vented discs
		  Rear: 294 mm /11.6" vented discs
		Front Suspension: Struts, arc-shaped forged aluminum lower control arms with hydraulic rear cushion, coil springs, twin tube gas pressurized shock absorbers, anti-roll bar.
		Rear Suspension: Multi-link system with central links, upper and lower transverse links, coil springs, twin tube gas pressurized shock absorbers, anti roll bar.
		Wheels/Tires: 16" x 7" alloy 205/55HR 16

Optional Equipment	Sport Package includes (Sedan and Wagon) a Sport Suspension, 17" Alloy wheels and tires, Sport seats, fog lights, sport multi-function steering wheel with cruise control. On the Coupe and Convertible the package includes 17" Alloy wheels and tires, and Sport seats. All Wheel Drive package is available for the xi Sedan and Wagon only, and includes the Sport package, with17" Alloy wheels and tires, Sport seats, fog lights, sport multi-function steering wheel with cruise control. Premium Package includes (Sedan and Wagon) a Moonroof, auto-dimming mirror, power seats, front armrest, multi-function steering wheel with cruise control, on-board computer, upgraded interior lighting, memory for	driver's seat and exterior mirrors, automatic climate control, wood trim. On the Coupe, the package includes a Moonroof, auto-dimming mirror, power seats,, memory for driver's seat and exterior mirrors, wood trim. On the Convertible, the package includes a fully automatic soft-top, auto-dimming mirror, auto-dimming mirror, automatic climate control, integrated garage door opener, wood trim. Cold Weather Package includes (Sedan and Wagon) fold down rear seats with ski bag, heated front seats, and heated mirrors and washer jets. On the Coupe and Convertible, the package includes heated front seats, ski bag, heated mirrors and washer jets.

Performance	Acceleration, 0-60 mph
	(325i Sedan):
	  Manual: 7.1 sec
	  Automatic: 8.1 sec
	(325xi Sedan):
	  Manual: 7.6 sec
	  Automatic: 8.8 sec
		Fuel Economy (city/highway) mpg
		(325i Sedan):
		  Manual: 20/29
		  Automatic: 19/27
		(325xi Sedan):
		  Manual: 19/27
		  Automatic: 18/25
		Top Speed: 128 mph

Technical Data BMW (E46)—U.S. Model 2001 330i, 330xi, 330Ci, and 330Ci Convertible

General

Manufacturer's suggested retail prices (US$):
330i Sedan: $34,560
330xi Sedan: $36,310
330Ci Coupe: $35,560
330Ci Convertible: $42,970

Wheelbase: 107.3"
Fuel Capacity: 16.6 gallons (62.8 liters)
Fuel Requirement: 92 AKI

Engine

Type: 3.0 liter (M54) 6-cylinder in-line, water cooled, longitudinally mounted, inclined, double vanos variable timing chain-driven dual-overhead camshafts, 7 main bearing crankshaft.
Bore / Stroke: 84.0 x 89.6/3.31 x 3.53
Displacement: 2979cc/182ci

Compression Ratio: 10.2:1
Horsepower (SAE net): 225 @ 5900
Torque (SAE net): 214 @ 3500
Management System: Seimens MS 43
Alternator: 120 amps /1680watts
Battery: 80 amp/hrs.

Chassis and Drivetrain

Transmission: 5 Speed manual
Gear Ratios 1, 2, 3, 4, 5, R
(330i) 4.21/2.49/1.66/1.24/1.00/3.85
(330Ci and 330Xi)
Final Drive Ratio:
(330i) 2.93:1
(330xi) 3.07:1
Transmission: 5 Speed Automatic
Gear Ratios 1, 2, 3, 4, 5, R
(330i) 3.67/2.00/1.41/1.00/0.74/4.10
(330xi) 3.42/2.22/1.60/1.00/0.75/3.03
Final Drive Ratio: 3.46:1

Steering: Vehicle speed proportional, power assisted rack and pinion.
Steering Ratio: 15.5:1
Braking:
    Front discs: 325 mm / 12.8" vented discs
    Rear discs: 320 mm / 12.6" vented discs
Front Suspension: Struts, arc-shaped forged aluminum lower control arms with hydraulic rear cushion, coil springs, twin tube gas pressurized shock absorbers, anti-roll bar.
Rear Suspension: Multi-link system with central links, upper and lower transverse links, coil springs, twin tube gas pressurized shock absorbers, anti roll bar.
Wheels/Tires: 17" x 7" Alloy 205/50HR 17

Optional Equipment

Sport Package includes (Sedan) a Sport Suspension, 17" Alloy wheels and tires, Sport seats, aerodynamic package, fog lights,and a sport multi-function steering wheel with cruise control. In the Coupe and Convertible the package includes a Sport Suspension, 17" Alloy wheels and tires, and Sport seats.
All Wheel Drive Sport package includes (330xi Sedan) 17" Alloy wheels and tires, Sport seats, sport steering wheel, and an aerodynamic package.

Premium Package includes (Sedan and Coupe) a Moonroof, auto-dimming mirror, power seats, lumbar support, rain sensing wipers, leather upholstery, wood trim. In the Convertible the package includes an Auto dimming mirror, wood trim, lumbar support, rain sensing wipers, and an integrated garage door opener.
Cold Weather Package includes fold down rear seats with ski bag, rear armrest, heated front seats, and heated mirrors and washer jets.

Performance

Acceleration, 0-60 mph
(330i Sedan):
    Manual: 6.4 sec
    Automatic: 7.0 sec
(330xi Sedan):
    Manual: 6.9 sec
    Automatic: 7.5 sec

Fuel Economy (city/highway) mpg
(330i Sedan):
    Manual: 21/30
    Automatic: 19/27
(330xi Sedan):
    Manual: 20/27
    Automatic: 17/25
Top Speed: 128 mph

BMW E46 Technical Data—Optional Equipment Overview

Options	323i	323Ci	323iC	323iT	328i	328Ci	325i
All Wheel Drive	No	No	No	No	No	No	OPT
All Season Traction	STD	STD	STD	STD	STD	STD	STD
Automatic transmission	OPT	No	No	No	OPT	No	No
Automatic transmission w/Steptronic	OPT	OPT	OPT	OPT	OPT	OPT	OPT
Cruise control	PP/SP	STD	OPT	OPT	STD	STD	OPT
Front seat armrest	PP	STD	STD	OPT	STD	STD	OPT
Leather wrapped steering wheel with cruise control	OPT/PP	STD	STD	OPT/PP	STD	STD	OPT
Fog lights (and heated mirrors and washer jets)	SP	STD	STD	OPT/ SP/PP	STD	STD	OPT/SP/ AWD
Fold down rear seats	OPT	STD	No	STD	OPT	STD	OPT
Ski bag	OPT	OPT	OPT	OPT	OPT	OPT	OPT/CWP
Full size spare tire	PP/SP	STD	STD	OPT	STD	STD	STD
Onboard computer	OPT/PP	STD	STD	OPT/PP/SPP	STD	STD	OPT
Onboard navigation system	OPT	OPT	OPT	OPT	OPT	OPT	OPT
Park distance control	No	No	No	OPT	OPT	OPT	No
Power glass moonroof	OPT/ PP/SPP	OPT/ PP/SPP	No	OPT/ PP/SPP	OPT/ PP/SPP	OPT/ PP/SPP	OPT/ PP/SPP
Power convertible top	No	No	PP	No	No	No	No
Rear seat side impact airbags	OPT	No	No	OPT	OPT	No	OPT
Xenon headlights	OPT	OPT	OPT	OPT	OPT	OPT	OPT
Heated front seats	OPT	OPT	OPT	OPT	OPT	OPT	OPT/CWP
In dash cd player	OPT	OPT	OPT	OPT	OPT	OPT	OPT
Harmon Kardon sound system	OPT	OPT	OPT	OPT	OPT	OPT	OPT
Leather upholstery	OPT	OPT	OPT	OPT	OPT	OPT	OPT
Metallic paint	OPT	OPT	OPT	OPT	OPT	OPT	OPT
Power front seats with driver memory	OPT/ PP/SPP	OPT/ PP/SPP	STD	OPT/ PP/SPP	STD	STD	OPT/PP
Wood trim	OPT/PP/SPP	OPT/PP	OPT/PP	OPT/PP/SPP	OPT/PP	OPT/PP	OPT/PP
Sport suspension	SP	STD	No	SP	SP	STD	OPT i only
M Aerodynomic package	OPT	No	No	No	OPT	No	No
Premium package	$3,500	$2,100	$2,900	$2,900	$2,900	$2,900	$3,500
Sport package	$2,400	$1,000	$1,700	$1,700	$1,350	$1,200	$1,500
Sport Premium package	$4,300	No	No	$4,200	No	No	No
All Wheel Drive Sport package	No	No	No	No	No	No	$1,200
Cold Weather package	No	No	No	No	No	No	$700

OPT—optional with standard model   PP—included in Premium package   CWP—included in Cold Weather package
STD—standard with purchase   SP—included in Sport package   AWD—included in All Wheel Drive Sport package

Options	325Ci	325iC	325iT	330i	330Ci	330iC
All Wheel Drive	No	No	OPT	OPT	No	No
All Season Traction	STD	STD	STD	STD	STD	STD
Automatic transmission	No	No	No	No	No	No
Automatic transmission w/Steptronic	OPT	OPT	OPT	OPT	OPT	OPT
Cruise control	OPT	OPT	OPT	STD	STD	STD
Front seat armrest	STD	STD	OPT	STD	STD	STD
Leather wrapped steering wheel with cruise control	STD	STD	OPT	STD	STD	STD
Fog lights (and heated mirrors and washer jets)	STD	STD	OPT/ SP/AWD	STD	STD	STD
Fold down rear seats	STD	No	STD	OPT	STD	No
Ski bag	OPT	OPT	OPT	OPT/ CWP	OPT	OPT
Full size spare tire	STD	No	$250	STD	STD	No
Onboard computer	3STD	STD	OPT	STD	STD	STD
Onboard navigation system	OPT	OPT	OPT	OPT	OPT	OPT
Park distance control	No	No	OPT	OPT	OPT	OPT
Power glass moonroof	OPT/ PP/SPP	No	OPT/ PP/SPP	OPT/ PP/SPP	OPT/ PP/SPP	No
Power convertible top	No	PP	No	No	No	STD
Rear seat side impact airbags	No	No	OPT	OPT	No	No
Xenon headlights	OPT	OPT	OPT	OPT	OPT	OPT
Heated front seats	OPT/CWP	OPT/CWP	OPT/CWP	OPT/CWP	OPT/CWP	OPT/CWP
In dash cd player	OPT	OPT	OPT	OPT	OPT	OPT
Harmon Kardon sound system	OPT	OPT	OPT	OPT	OPT	OPT
Leather upholstery	OPT	OPT	OPT	OPT	OPT	OPT
Metallic paint	OPT	OPT	OPT	OPT	OPT	OPT
Power front seats with driver memory	OPT/PP	STD	OPT/PP	OPT/PP	STD	STD
Wood trim	OPT/PP	OPT/PP	OPT/PP	OPT/PP	OPT/PP	OPT/PP
Sport suspension	STD	SP	SP	OPT i only	STD	SP
M Aerodynomic package	No	No	No	OPT/ STD on Xi	No	No
Premium package	$2,100	$1,900	$3,500	$3,850	$2,900	$800
Sport package	$1,000	$1,200	$1,500	$1,200	$600	$800
Sport Premium package	No	No	No	No	No	No
All Wheel Drive Sport package	No	No	$1,200	$900	No	No
Cold Weather package	$700	$700	$700	$1,000	$700	$700

Appendix 4
Buyer's Guide

This buyer's guide encompasses four generations of BMW 3 Series from 1977 to 2001. It is a collection of information gleaned from knowledgeable repair professionals, avid BMW owners, historical literature, and other informational sources. Special credit goes to Paul "Doc" Provenza of Doc's Bimmer Shop in Oxford, Mississippi and Jimmy Albright of Mighty Motors in Cambridge, Massachusetts for their help in gathering the information in this Buyer's Guide. The objective of the guide is to educate the prospective BMW buyer by pointing out well-known differences, attributes, and possible trouble areas for E21 (1977-1983), E30 (1984-1991), E36 (1992-1998), and E46 (1999–on) BMW 3 Series cars.

Answers to questions such as "what's the difference between a 325e and a 325i," or "why is one model better for me than another," can be answered using this guide. It is in no way intended to cover everything you'll need to know about buying a used 3 Series. But it may serve as an additional resource in the sea of BMW material available to you in this information age. It should be used as information only and it is your responsibility to evaluate the accuracy and completeness of all information and opinions in this guide.

No matter which pre-owned 3er you buy, a pre-purchase inspection of your final selection is highly recommended. These inspections are done by professional repair technicians and can range from inexpensive to relatively expensive, depending on the extent and scope of the examination. If you're buy-

ing a newer E46 car, buying it through an authorized BMW dealer under the certified pre-owned program will give you peace of mind knowing that it has been fully reconditioned and that it carries an extended warranty.

Most importantly, be sure the car you buy is safe to drive. If you're thinking of buying a high mileage car or if the maintenance history is unknown, you owe it to yourself to have a professional look at the wheels, tires, suspension, steering, and other systems that could affect the safety of the vehicle and its passengers.

E21 Cars (320i: 1977-1983)

The first 3 series car, known as the E21 chassis, was introduced to the US market for the 1977 model year as the successor to the legendary 2002. Over 180,000 E21s were officially sent to the US until production end in 1982. The E21 was 18-percent stiffer than its predecessor and was a much more modern car than the '02. The E21 received mixed reviews, partly because it was heavier than the 2002 and couldn't match its predecessor's sporty performance.

The US market received only the 320i, although a full range of engines and options were offered to other markets. These included the 316, 318, 320, 320i, 320/6, and 323i. Some of these models did find their way to the States through the "gray mar-

The underhood appearance has always been a priority of BMW, as shown by this early example of the 2-liter fuel injected 320i motor.

Photo: BMW of NA

ket," including the highly sought-after 6-cylinder 323i cars. European tuners such as Alpina produced modified E21s that included the B6 and 333i.

The 1977-1979 models used a 2-liter Bosch fuel-injected engine—which produced 110 hp at 5,800 rpm—mated to a 4-speed manual or a 3-speed automatic transmission. In 1980, the engine displacement was reduced to 1.8 liters, although the 320i badge was retained. Mated to a 5-speed manual or a 3-speed automatic transmission, power output was 101 hp at 5,800 rpm.

The limited edition 320iS (sport package), offered from 1980 through 1983, added a rear stabilizer bar, a bigger front stabilizer bar, special light alloy wheels, an integrated front spoiler, and Recaro sport seats, among other special 'S' equipment. (See Appendix 3 for a complete equipment listing.)

The 320iS is easily identified by its Recaro sports seats.

Photo: BMW of NA

Buying an E21

When looking to purchase an E21, keep in mind that these cars haven't been made for two decades or more. Most have served a long hard life. Many others have simply rusted away like other cars of that era. If you find one that appears to be rust-free, have it checked by a good body shop to evaluate the extent and quality of any rust repair.

Check under the carpets for structural rust damage. A rusty or rotted out floor pan indicates windshield and rear glass water leaks. The front and rear shock towers, wheel arches, and inner fenders are also suspect for terminal rust. Check for cracking

and structural rust damage at the B-pillars, below the glass. Look for accident damage by examining the fit of the doors and lids. Strong fluorescent lighting is a good aid in picking up differences in paint color and quality.

Pre-1980 models had a history of cracked cylinder heads. Timing chain service and cylinder head reconditioning are often required on high mileage versions. If the car is structurally sound, check for oil leaks, body and suspension rattles, or a rough running or noisy engine. Watch for blue smoke when starting, and on deceleration. Expect the engine to use some oil if there are many miles on the clock.

Look under the hood for shoddy repair work and examine the electrical system for sloppy wiring repairs. Check for worn bushings on the alternator by tugging on the V-belt. Drive the car from stone cold to full warm to make sure everything feels "normal." If you're still unsure after a thorough self-inspection, a pre-purchase inspection by a professional will help you make the decision. A car this old may look good, but may not be safe to drive.

Although there are still nice examples to be had, they may be hard to find. Is affordability driving the purchase, or are you enamored by the styling of the E21? If you're interested in good BMW performance, try to find a 323i gray market model, a limited edition 320iS, or better yet, a 6-cylinder E30 car. Replacement parts and service are still readily available for the E21, and in general, the bang for the buck can't be beat.

E30 Cars (1984-1993 3 Series)

Introduced in 1984, the E30 was the successor to the popular E21 320i. The E30 was more of an upgraded E21 than an all-new car. Major changes included improved front and rear suspensions, more contemporary interior design, and a larger front spoiler. The coupes and sedans lasted through

1991, when the E36 4-door sedan replaced them. The E30 convertible models survived until 1993, when superceded by the E36 convertible in 1994.

The 1984 through 1991 3 Series cars can be grouped into 5 broad categories:

- 318i (1984, 1985 4-cylinder)

- 325e, 325es. 325 (eta-powered 6-cylinder, 1984-1988)

- 325i, 325is (i-powered 6-cylinder, 1987-1993)

- 318i, 318is (M42 4-cylinder, 1991)

- Specialty segment (325iC, 325iX, M3)

318i (1984, 1985 4-cylinder)

The single-cam E30 318i model was short-lived owing to heavy criticism for inadequate performance. The 101-hp engine lacked the necessary horsepower and low-end torque inherent in most other BMW powerplants. Although 1984 models were only available in the two-door variant, a four-door model was introduced for 1985.

There was little help in the way of available performance modifications. Adding Bilstein sport shocks increased sportiness and replacing the rear drums with rear disc brakes from a 325e gave it better stopping power, but in the end it was still a weakling. If what you want is performance from a 318i, you're going to have to swap in a bigger engine.

The 1.8 liter M10 engine uses a dependable Bosch L-Jetronic fuel injection system and a break-erless electronic ignition system. The camshaft is chain driven. This end result is dependability and longevity. Probably the best thing to say about the 318i is that it's an E30 car–a well made, good handling chassis that really stands up to the test of time. If you can find one that's structurally and mechanically sound, the 318i is an economical daily driver for BMW buyer with a small allowance.

325e, 325es, 325 (eta-powered 6-cylinder, 1984-1988)

Based on its performance numbers on paper, the 325e came under heavy criticism when introduced late in the '84 model year. "Eta," for the Greek letter E, was used to represent efficiency. This was a long stroke engine with single valve springs and a low 4,700 rpm redline. Although the 121-hp M20 engine lacked the necessary horsepower, it was tuned to produce good low-end torque (170 ft-lb @ 3,250 rpm). Disc brakes at all four corners and the torquey six-cylinder power plant made this one lots more fun to drive than the 318i. By the time the 325e (later badged 325) was discontinued in 1988, it had become a big success in the United States.

Some important features found on most 6-cylinder models include ABS braking from the '86 model year, a 9-function on-board computer (optional on some models), power windows, a power two-way sunroof, and leather upholstery (325e Luxus). Just as in the case of the 318i, the 4-door body was not introduced until the 1985 model year.

For the 1988 model year, the eta engine was retuned for improved performance and dubbed by the enthusiast community

The 318i was the entry level model of the new E30 sports sedan in 1984.

Photo: BMW of NA

The 2.7 liter engine in the 325e was the first 6-cylinder engine installed in the Series. The eta engine delivered good torque, but lacked horsepower.

Photo: BMW of NA

as the super-eta. This engine used the 325i cylinder head (eta camshaft retained) with an upgraded Motronic 1.1 engine management system. Power went up to 127 hp, while the torque remained the same. Unfortunately, this car retained the same sluggish final drive gearing so the horsepower gain was difficult to detect.

Note: In an attempt to increase market share in 1987, BMW offered an affordable 3er. These models had a manual sunroof and lacked the on-board computer and other niceties.

If you're on a quest for BMW performance, keep in mind that the basic "efficiency" design of the eta engine significantly limits its potential. A chip for the Motronic fuel injection control unit will yield little improvement. The suspension can always be enhanced, but it's probably going to cost more to upgrade the suspension than it will to find a good 325es. This limited edition sport version can be spotted by its body colored front air dam with integrated fog lights and a rear deck lid spoiler. Sports seats, sport suspension (gas pressure shocks, pro-

gressive rate springs, reinforced front and rear stabilizer bar), a limited-slip differential, and an M-Technic steering wheel make this one of the best 325e cars out there. Probably the best way to increase the performance of an eta car is to replace the final drive with a shorter geared unit.

With its tall gearing and rear end ratio (2.79 on early cars, 2.93 on '86 and later cars), the eta-engined 325e is masterful in conserving fuel and delivering good seat-of-the-pants daily driving torque. The 325e is very affordable, the supply is abundant, and there doesn't seem to be an end to miles this model can handle.

325i, 325is (6-cylinder 'i' cars, 1987-1991)

The 325i is a spirited performer with ample room for the kids and groceries. At 168hp and 164 ft-lb torque, the 'i' power plant is right at home in the E30 chassis. Sporting aggressive final drive gearing (3.73:1) and a five speed transmission, its 0-60 time is an impressive 8.5 seconds. The sport suspension, VR-rated tires, and large front ventilated and solid rear brake rotors translate into the BMW experience. Drive one and you'll understand why this is the choice of the BMW enthusiast.

Most 325i models came standard with many luxury features such as cross spoke alloy wheels, sport seats, cruise control, on-board computer, 8-speaker sound system, ABS braking, and ellipsoid

Body-colored bumpers with integrated fog lights and redesigned headlights gave the '89 and later E30s an updated look.

Photo: BMW of NA

The 1.8 liter "near zero maintenance" engine was only available in the E30 for one year.

Photo: BMW of NA

technology low beams (later models only). The last of the 325i cars even received an SRS airbag on the driver's side. The 2-door 325is models can be recognized by their deep front spoiler with integrated fog lights, body-colored rear spoiler, and leather BMW sport seats. The fuel injection system is the first self-diagnostic system that BMW used, known as Motronic 1.1. The trouble codes can be read out through a series of flash codes through the Check Engine light in the instrument cluster. Consult your service manual for diagnostic code listings and code activation.

In 1989, the E30 cars received an overdue face-lift and a more contemporary look. The bumpers were neatly integrated into the body and painted in body color, much like their European equivalents. Esthetically, there's a big difference between the early cars and the 89 and later cars, and it shows in the higher prices. In addition, 1989 and later had a CD-ready radio.

318i/is (4-cylinder M42, 1991)

The 318is was offered during the last year of the E30 coupe and sedan production. The 134 hp M42 engine was a completely new twin-cam, multi-valve, four-cylinder engine for BMW and perfectly suited for the E30. This engine has a very flexible power band and excellent torque in relation to its small 1.8-liter displacement.

The M42 engine is considered to be one of BMWs low maintenance engines. Hydraulic lifters, separate ignition coil for each cylinder, adaptive Bosch Motronic 1.7 engine management, and long-life platinum electrode spark plugs are some of the modern techniques employed.

The one chronic problem with this engine as that the cylinder head profile gasket didn't hold up. Be sure to get the service history on the particular car you're considering. If the gasket hasn't been replaced, there's a high probability it is going to need it. (See Buying an E30 below for more on this subject.)

One thing to know about the 318i is that it was a sold as a price leader. Don't expect leather upholstery or a long list of creature comforts. In summary, the 318i is a lot of fun to drive considering it's a four-cylinder car. As it was only offered for one year, finding a used one may prove difficult. With the restyled bumper and the last of a very proven chassis, many people consider it BMW's best E30s.

Specialty cars (M3, 325iC, 325iX)

M3

Although the M3 looked like the 325i, it was a very different car. The flared body panels, the 192 hp twin-cam 16-valve Motorsport engine, and the 205/55 VR 15 tires are some of the cues that the E30 M3 is in a league of its own. Larger brakes, bigger wheel bearings, bonded front and rear glass, structural chassis enhancements, larger fuel tank, and its one-off suspension geometry, are just a few in a long list of special treatments the M3 received.

If you want to learn more about the M3, there are numerous websites dedicated to this unique car. Stay away from clapped out examples, no matter how attractive the price. M3 replacement parts and service are very costly and can quickly turn a good buy into a bad judgment call. M3s are considered to be collectible and are pricey to buy second hand. They also require a certain amount of regular attention.

325iC

Introduced in 1987 and lasting until the 1993 model year, the E30 soft-top is an attractive convertible by most standards.

The 325iC is much the same as the two-door 325is model except that the convertible was a high line model; leather upholstery, heated seats, and other luxury comfort features were added as standard equipment. The convertible model weighed in heavier than the coupe, so performance suffered a bit. This was especially true for the late 4-cylinder 318iC models.

The structure was significantly reinforced to minimize the body flex and shake that is traditionally inherent in convertibles. Thicker rocker panel metal with internal strengthening members, a stronger floor pan, a beefed up windshield frame, and numerous welded-in steel members were some of the stiffening techniques employed.

The triple-layer convertible top is well designed, seals out water and noise well, and is easy to raise and lower. Models from 1991 on received a power-assisted top. When looking to buy this model, check that the top functions correctly. The power top is a complicated matrix of microswitches and few technicians—dealer trained or otherwise—know the system well enough to service it properly. Note that the top will eventually need replacing. When purchasing a 325iC with a rough top, make sure you know its full replacement cost.

325iX

The iX is a special car and with it comes many special parts. Aside from all the four- wheel drive components, the front cross member, the front control arms, and the engine oil pan are some of the 325iX-only parts. Should things break, this exclusivity can increase the cost of ownership over a two-wheel drive car.

The Ferguson-based drive system is very robust given proper maintenance. Transfer case problems can be avoided by regularly replacing the lubricant. Strange noises coming from the transfer case and drive system signal imminent trouble. Leaky front drive seals are one of more the common ailments.

As the 325iX received a good amount of extra hardware, it was heavier than it's two-wheel drive equivalent. This combined with the energy losses through the additional drivetrain components gave the two-wheel drive cars a significant performance edge.

The 325iX is relatively rare with only four years of production. They can be had in two and four door versions, but the 4-door, automatic transmission configuration seems to be most common. When put up for sale the iX demands a premium price, but their owners tend to treat them with respect and proper care–something that's hard to put a price tag on. They will no doubt become collectable in the near future. If the 4-wheel drive feature appeals to you, buy one now while they're still affordable.

Buying an E30

The E30 chassis seems to be holding up to the elements and rust doesn't seem to be the problem it was on the E21 cars. Be it a four- or six-cylinder model, the E30 is an easy car to understand and service. Replacement parts are affordable and readily available, both new and used. Barring any unforeseen structural or mechanical damage, the E30 is a good used car to buy, even with lots of miles on the clock provided it has had the proper care.

Note: The specialty cars (M3, 325iX in particular) have known problems and trouble spots, so some research may be in order before setting your sites on a particular vehicle. There are well-organized and knowledgeable special interest groups for each of these cars. A good starting place would be the BMW Car Club of America (http://bmwcca.org).

Start with a thorough inspection by taking a slow walk around the car. Check for loose, damaged, or missing body moldings, emblems or wheel centers. The faded front and rear window trim moldings can be easily replaced with black or silver trim. Inspect the paint finish and metallic clear coat for fade, dulling, or crazing. Early examples had problems with the clear coat failing.

Exterior plastic and rubber body trim deteriorates with age and exposure. Although considered normal wear and tear, these replacement parts tend to be very expensive and probably not worth the investment. Be sure you can live with the car if some of the expensive trim parts don't get replaced. Check the glove box lock operation, and replace any broken parts before the glove box locks and stays locked. Check for accident damage by examining the fit of the doors and lids. Strong fluorescent lighting is a good aid in picking up differences in paint color and quality.

Note: On 1987 and later cars, all major body panels and parts are labeled with the VIN during manufacture. This can be invaluable when trying to determine if the car is original. Bumpers, fenders, engine, transmission, doors, and lids all have this label affixed to them. The labels are tamper proof and tear apart when removal is attempted. If a body panel was replaced, it should carry a 'DOT-R' label without the VIN.

Check for a soggy trunk. If the trunk is damp, the taillight gaskets probably need replacing. Other common water entry spots include the sunroof drains, the trunk lid seal, and the front and rear glass rubber gaskets.

Open the hood and check for engine oil leaks, especially at main front crank seals. This is best done with the car in the air. Look carefully at the seam where the cylinder head meets the cylinder block. Seepage/wetness along this area indicates a leaking head gasket, which is a rather costly repair. The 6-cylinder cars also had a history of cracked cylinder heads. Pull the dipstick and make sure the oil is not milky or muddy. Ask the owner if he has

to add coolant on a regular basis. As a final test, blip the throttle with the engine running and look for billowing white steam from the exhaust.

On 6-cylinder models, find out when the timing belt was last replaced. The camshaft is driven by a toothed belt that must be replaced every 50k. If it breaks while underway, you'll have bent valves, possible cylinder head replacement, and a very large repair bill. When replacing the belt, always replace the belt tensioner and strongly consider a new water pump and V-belts if they have 50k or more miles on them.

If the car has driveability problems, look for cracked or dry-rotted vacuum and intake hoses causing lean running.

On 1984 through most 1987 cars, a high idle speed is a sign that the idle control system is no longer working. It's a good practice to replace the idle control valve when replacing the idle control unit. Plan on putting aside a few hundred dollars for this repair. Be sure to check the idle control fuse before replacing parts.

Note: The 1987 325i model and all 1988 and later cars integrated the idle control function into the Motronic 1.1 control unit, which proved to be a longer lasting solution. When this idle valve starts to go, the idle speed usually becomes intermittently erratic.

The late 318i models (M42 engines) were known for profile gasket failure. The gasket is at the front of the cylinder head and when it goes, coolant mixes with the oil. If not caught in time, it can easily destroy the engine. It's a big job to replace the gasket; the cylinder head needs to come off. Ask the owner if he knows anything about this subject and ask to see the maintenance records. High mileage M42s also suffered from timing chain and chain guide wear. This is indicated by chain noise in the timing chain case.

Ball joints in the lower control arm require frequent replacement. Move the front tire in and out while it's unloaded; noticeable play indicates worn joints. Rear shock upper mounts break regularly, causing rattle and knock over rough road surfaces. Replace the stock rear mounts with those from the E30 Convertible or any E36. The steering rack should be inspected for leaks. Failed racks will fill the end bellows with power steering fluid. Check for leaks in the power steering pump and all power steering hoses. Also examine the power steering pump pulley for cracks. Brake fluid should be clear and clean; murky dark fluid indicates insufficient maintenance.

Additional items to check:

Note: Some of the following items require dis-assembly, special knowledge or tools, and/or that the vehicle be safely raised on a professional auto-motive lift.

• Valve cover gaskets (and rear half-moon plugs in cover), and breather hoses. Leaky gaskets and hoses make a mess and can cause driveability com-plaints.

• Viscous coupling fan clutch. If the engine runs hot while idling, the viscous coupling fan clutch is probably faulty. With the engine off, spin the clutch by hand. If the fan free wheels without resistance, the fluid coupling should be replaced.

• Exhaust system hangers. Missing or worn hangers can lead to a damaged (read expensive) catalytic converter.

• Exhaust manifolds/header pipes. Check for cracking.

• Oxygen sensor. This sensor is threaded into the exhaust system and should be replaced every 100k on 4-wire sensors and every 50k on single wire sensors.

• Wheel bearings. Check by spinning the tires while listening for any gritty or rumbling noise.

• Front and rear sway bar links. Check the links by tugging on them. Worn link ball joints will result in suspension noises on rough road surfaces. Be sure to replace the links with original equip-ment parts. Some aftermarket replacement links aren't worth the metal they're made from.

• Front struts. On older cars, check the front strut spring perch for rot.

• Check that the upper strut bearing dust caps are present. Missing dust caps can cause premature mount wear.

• Alternator mounting bushings. Tug on the drive belt to check bushing wear.

• Check alternator brush length by removing voltage regulator from rear of alternator.

• Engine and transmission mounts. These parts have a high failure rate, especially on cars that are driven hard. Broken mounts will cause knocking sounds on takeoff and driveline judder.

• Driveshaft U-joints and flex disc (Guibo). These parts are subject to lots of loading and abuse. Driveshaft U-joints are not available separately, i.e. only complete driveshafts are available from BMW.

• Instrument cluster. Gauge fluctuation and illuminated service interval lights is an indication that the Ni-Cad batteries on the Service Indicator printed circuit board have failed. Although some have had luck soldering in new batteries, the best solution is to replace the entire SI board inside the instrument cluster.

• Electrical checks. Does the on-board computer illumination work. Even though the "light bar" is a $20 part, it takes two hours of labor to get to it. Check all other electrical systems and functions, such as cruise control, ABS braking, wipers, and check control.

E36 (1992-2000)

The E36 replaced the well-respected E30 in 1992. Both esthetically and technically, the E36 was a very a different car than the E30. In stark contrast to the E30, each model year brought more refinement and technical improvements. So, if you're in the market for an E36, buy the latest one you can afford.

The E36 featured an all-new body with an aerodynamic wedge shape, strong tapered nose, and a distinctive high rear deck lid. Covered headlights, integrated bumpers, bonded front and rear glass, flush side glass, and internal gut-ters enhanced its aerodynamic efficiency.

The high-tech E36, with its clean aerodynamic design, was an evolutionary departure from the E30.

Photo: BMW of NA

Major new features and systems included a roomier interior (especially in the rear seat area), a redesigned rear suspension, the all new lower-maintenance M50 24-valve 6-cylinder 189 hp engine, a new 3-channel Teves anti-lock brake system, new direct-drive manual transmission and GM automatic transmission, sophisticated central body electronics, more advanced self-diagnostics, and SRS airbag(s). The E36 represented a big technological leap above the E30 cars.

The E36 was first introduced as a 4-door sedan, followed by the 2-door coupe. Sharing only its front section with the sedan, almost all of the coupe's body panels were redesigned. A lower roof and trunk lid, longer hood, more steeply raked front and rear glass, flush frameless side windows, and narrower taillight assemblies helped give the coupe a distinctive sleeker design.

E36 offerings continued to expand over the years. The following are some of the highlights of E36 production.

1992: DISA (adaptive two-stage intake runner system) and cylinder-selective knock control was added to M42 engine.

1993: VANOS (Variable Intake Camshaft Timing) integrated into M50 engine. Coded M50TU for Technical Update, it used a Bosch 3.3.1 engine management system with knock detection. This updated engine boasted improved mid-range torque and engine response, lower emissions, and lower fuel consumption.

1994: The E36 convertible (325iC/318iC) joined the E36 lineup. From 1/94, the M42 engine was updated to optimize noise levels and comply with emission regulations. Some of the key changes of this update included: new DME 1.7.2 system, air shrouded injectors, poly-ribbed drive belts, one-piece ignition coil design, and 80-amp alternator.

1995: 318ti Compact (E36/5) introduced. The 3-door coupe with its short rear body section was a full 9 in. shorter and 200 pounds lighter than the E36 sedan.

EWS II (anti-theft system with electronically coded key) installed as of January '95 production.

1996: On-Board Diagnostics–Generation II (OBD II), a sophisticated fault monitoring and self-diagnostic engine management program implemented for all models.

• Z3 Roadster (E36/7) introduced.

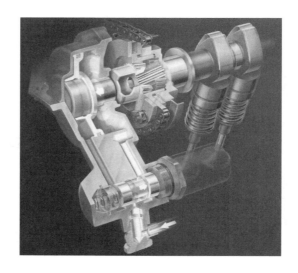

VANOS, a system that varies valve timing to optimize engine torque, is fitted to 1993 and later 6-cylinder engines.

Photo: BMW of NA

• M52 2.8 liter engine with Siemens MS 41.1 engine management system replaces M50TU. Plastic cylinder head cover, 12-percent lighter connecting rods, asymmetrical pistons, smaller hydraulic lifters with single conical springs, and stainless steel exhaust manifolds are some of the updated features. M52 engine was quieter, more efficient and produced more torque than M50TU.

• M44 1.9 liter engine replaces M42 1.8 engine.

1997: E36 line receives redesigned, rounder front end. Pyrotechnic automatic seat belt tensioners and upgraded security system added. Traction control standard equipment.

1998: Side airbags installed as standard equipment across line. New M52 variant 168 hp 2.5 liter installed in 323is/323iC to displace 4-cylinder models.

Note: Certain E36 cars have known problems and trouble spots, so some research may be in order before setting your sites on a particular model. There are well-organized and knowledgeable special interest groups for most of these cars. A good starting place would be the BMW Car Club of America (http://bmwcca.org).

Start with a thorough inspection by taking a slow walk around the car. Check for loose, damaged, or missing body moldings, emblems or wheel centers. Inspect the paint finish and metallic clear coat for fade, dulling, or crazing.

Exterior plastic trim can deteriorate with age and exposure to the elements. Although considered normal wear and tear, these replacement parts are expensive. Painted plastic pieces (bumper covers, front grille parts) are also expensive to replace. Check for accident damage by examining the fit of the doors and lids. Strong fluorescent lighting is a good aid in picking up differences in paint color and quality.

Note: Since 1987, all major body panels and parts are labeled with the VIN during manufacture.

The E36 M3 was available with four doors beginning in 1997. Other options included an automatic transmission and luxury package.

Photo: Jonathan Stein

This can be invaluable when trying to determine if the car is original. Fenders, engine, transmission, doors, lids, and major body parts all have this label affixed to them. The labels are tamper proof and tear apart when removal is attempted. If a body panel was replaced, it should carry a 'DOT-R' label without the VIN.

Open the hood and check for engine oil leaks, especially at main front crank seals. This is best done with the car in the air. Look carefully as the seam where the cylinder head meets the cylinder block. Seepage/wetness along this area indicates a leaking head gasket. Check four cylinder engines for leaky valve cover gaskets. Pull the dipstick and make sure the oil is not milky or muddy. If the engine uses coolant, it's best to have it checked by a professional.

E36 4- and 6-cylinder engines use chain driven camshafts, as opposed to a rubber drive belt. Under normal conditions, timing chain service should not be necessary for the life of the engine.

All E36 models incorporated some level of engine management self-diagnostics. The Check Engine Light will come on, indicating that a fault is present. On 1992 through 1995 cars, quickly flooring the accelerator pedal 5 times will initiate the fault read out. The fault is displayed as a series of check engine light flashes. Consult your repair manual for additional fault code information. Other systems, such as ABS, SRS, and automatic transmission can also be diagnosed using a scan tool.

Some additional known areas of concern include:

Note: Checking some items may require disassembly, special knowledge or tools, and/or the vehicle be safely raised on a professional automotive lift.

• Early M50 water pumps had a plastic impeller that didn't seem to last. Be sure to replace it with a metal impeller pump when the original fails. It's a good idea to replace the thermostat when doing a water pump, especially if the engine was overheated.

• 318i/is models (M42 engine in particular) had a history of profile gasket failure. The gasket is at the front of the cylinder head and when it goes, coolant mixes with the oil. If not caught in time, it can easily destroy the engine. It's a big job to replace the gasket; the cylinder head needs to come off. Early M42s also suffered from timing chain and chain guide wear.

• Radiator necks are also known to fail, because the plastic in the neck area becomes brittle after many heat cylces and literally breaks off when removing the cap. Plastic thermostat housing were also troublesome.

• Idle speed control (IAC) valve. If the engine idles erratically, the IAC valve may need replacing. This valve is constantly working when the engine is running and it does wear out. On 6-cylinder cars, the valve is nested under the intake manifold and hard to reach.

• An EPROM and idle valve update campaign was done on some later 4-cylinder engines (1-94 through 12-95 build date). Dealer service records will indicate if this update has been performed.

• Ignition coil problems on early M50 6-cylinder motors. Faulty coils would also damage the DME control module if not caught in time.

• Camshaft position sensors in front of the cylinder head had a high failure rate.

• On OBDII cars (1996 and later), multiple oxygen sensor are used: 2 sensors for 4-cylinder engines and 3 or 4 sensors on 6-cylinder engines. The sensors age with time and the OBD II monitoring criteria is very strict. When the oxygen sensors can no longer pass the stringent tests, the Check Engine light comes on.

• A/T transmission problems, (GM transmission). While driving at 50-65 mph, check that the transmission stays in gear (no rpm change). Some transmissions would shift back and forth at speed (known as pendulum shifting). The fix is to replace seals and/or other parts internally. Two separate oil sumps identify this transmission. When doing an ATF fluid service, be sure both sumps are drained and cleaned.

• AC compressor front bearing problems. AC compressor front bearing locks up.

• Front strut problems (Fitchell & Sachs manufacture), shock seals fail and leak oil. The shocks should be replaced (always in pairs) if excessive oil is present on the shock.

• Lower control arm balljoints would separate from their rubber bond.

• Rear wheel bearings failure, mainly right side.

• ABS rear wheel sensors – early E36 models had defective rear wheel speed sensors due to poor solder joints, would trigger fault codes.

• Tailight bulb contacts can be finicky.

• Heater water valves would set fault codes, fault codes left side right side.

• Viscous coupling fan clutch. If the engine runs hot while idling, the viscous coupling fan clutch is probably faulty. With the engine off, spin the clutch by hand. If the fan freewheels without resistance, the fluid coupling should be replaced.

• Exhaust system hangers. Missing or worn hangers can lead to a damaged (read expensive) catalytic converter.

• Front and rear sway bar links. Check the links by tugging on them. Worn link balljoints will result in suspension noises on rough road surfaces. Be sure to replace the links with original equipment parts.

• Driveshaft U-joints and flex disc (Guibo). These parts are subject to lots of loading and abuse. Driveshaft U-joints are not available separately, i.e. only complete driveshafts are available from BMW.

• Electrical checks. Does the on-board computer work (if applicable)? Do all the instrument gauges work? Check all other electrical systems and functions, such as cruise control, ABS braking, wipers, and check control.

• Alternator problems – Valeo brand alternators would fluctuate up to 16 volts, and spike AC voltage.

• Early sunroof design was problematic.

E46 (1999–)

The E46 cars were introduced for the 1999 model year. The 4-door sedan came first, followed by the 2-door Coupe and Convertible in model year 2000. The initial offerings, 328i and 323i, were discontinued in model year 2000. In 2001MY, the 325i and 330i were born. The sport wagon and the all-wheel drive 325Xi/330Xi were also offered. As of this writing, the E346 M3 press reviews were just being released to the public.

Extra interior room, improved fuel economy, and cleaner emissions are just a few of the improvements in the fourth-generation 3 Series. The interior of the E46 has been completely redesigned with an emphasis on space, convenience, and luxury. As compared to the E36, the overall length of the E46 is 1.5 inches longer and 1.0 inches wider (wheelbase).

The E46 sports wagon.

Photo: BMW of NA

Some the enhanced features of the current 3 Series are:

• Outstanding performance: 328i: 0-60 in 6.6 seconds, 323i: 0-60 in 7.1 seconds .

• Traction Control (Automatic Stability Control/Dynamic Stability Control).

• Superb weight distribution (51% front/49% rear).

• Enhanced front-suspension geometry for improved straight-line tracking.

• Lower unsprung weight with more light-weight aluminum suspension components.

• Increased overall structural rigidity (approximately 50% more rigid) over E36 body.

• Optional five-speed automatic transmission with Adaptive Transmission Control .

• Premium and/or Sport packages available.

• Multi Restraint System (MRS II): passive safety system includes head protection system (ITS) and four airbags (includes dual-threshold front airbags, and safety belt pre-tensioners with force limiters).

• Car & Key Memory to activate individual driver preferences in safety, comfort and convenience.

• High-strength aluminum cylinder block with cast-iron cylinder liners.

• 1999, 2000: M52TU double VANOS (stepless variable valve timing) engines with Siemens MS 42 engine management system (323i, 328i) with electronically controlled engine cooling.

• 2001: M54 engines with Siemens MS 43 engine management system engines for MY2001 (325i, 330i).

• Headlights 30-percent more effective, headlight covers lighter/more resistant to breakage (optional xenon headlights with auto-leveling)

• Larger taillights for better visibility at night.

• Rain-sensing windshield wipers and multi-function steering wheel available on some models.

• Certified Pre-Owned (CPO) extended warranty program for used cars purchased through an authorized BMW dealer.

Buying an E46

At the time of this writing, the E46 cars were still relatively new with the original manufacturer's warranty still in effect. As the E46 cars age, the E36 buying guide given above should be a good template for the E46 cars.

Index

Acknowledgments

That we have managed to encapsulate the sprawling 3 Series story in one book is a credit to all involved, because BMW's biggest seller and its legendary 02 antecedents don't diet easily.

This is the most international BMW tale I've told: no less than four BMW-linked organizations from around the world took the brunt of my research. First, BMW AG, the parent company in Germany, generously accommodated me in the summer of 1999 with a series of intense factory tours and interviews. The people there who made it all happen include Claudia Hoepner-Korinth [Corporate Communications, Head of International Press unit], Theo Melcher [Powertrain Development General Manager], Friedbert Holz [M-brand Public Relations], Jochen Frey, and Dave Carp of the Munich Design team.

At BMW NA, my particular thanks go to Jay Binneweg and Andrew Cutler (now promoting Mini for BMW) for opening their doors, but bosses Rob Mitchell and Jack Pitney were equally generous in allowing me departmental time. Mitchell's unrivaled knowledge of BMW in a US context provided us a unique insight into the US M-branded Bimmers.

Also at BMW NA, then-recently recruited M brand manager Tom Salkowsky injected his personal vigor into valued support for this project, allowing us to make significant late-stage improvements, particularly for E46 M3 content. BMW Manufacturing Corporation at Spartanburg, South Carolina is now best known for the current Z3 and X5 lines, but its first production car was the 318i; and the media relations team there (Bobby Hitt and Bunny Richardson) added Southern hospitality to education over a trio of factory visits.

At BMW GB Ltd., Alun Parry (now at Toyota GB), present PR director Chris Willows, Rosemary Davies, and manager Graham Biggs made sure that I stayed informed on current-production 3 Series progress, backing my BMW access/travel requirements in Europe. Also in England, I would like to thank Bryan Kennedy of Bookspeed for the trade guidance and wisdom he has generously shared with me over the past twenty years.

Back in America, the Massachusetts-based BMW CCA organization, with its 53,000-plus members, was key in the creation of this title. This car club's acclaimed Roundel magazine allowed a regular outlet for my enthusiasm. Michael Bentley and his Enthusiast team at Bentley Publishers in Cambridge, Massachusetts, displayed a strength and depth that was vital to the creation of this book, the most difficult of three successive BMW titles that I have written for this venerable automotive publishing house.

The faces on the Bentley publishing team changed while this book was becoming a reality, but their commitment to a constantly evolving subject was unwavering. Enthusiast Publishing's lead editor, Janet Barnes, combined managerial skills with brisk pace and charm. I'd also like to thank sales and marketing personnel Tom Downing and Maurice Iglesias for their constant cheerful company, even when the odds were stacked against us.

Freelance editor Lee Ann Best found the time to edit this book alongside her more recent role as a first-time mother to her daughter Tali. Legendary lecturer and Roundel photographer Klaus Schnitzer took many of the pictures for this title to our specifications. I would particularly like to thank PTG in Virginia and Bill Cobb (who makes many BMW NA sporting/Mobile Tradition events run smoothly with his tireless background labor) for giving me access to PTG M3s and a supreme example of the early American E21 road car.

For all of you, mentioned and unmentionable, thanks for transforming a scribbled outline into a professionally presented reality.

Jeremy Walton,
December 2000

Selected Books and Repair Information from Bentley Publishers

Driving

Alex Zanardi: My Sweetest Victory
Alex Zanardi with Gianluca Gasparini
ISBN 0-8376-1249-7

The Unfair Advantage
Mark Donohue ISBN 0-8376-0073-1(hc);
0-8376-0069-3(pb)

**Going Faster! Mastering the Art of
Race Driving** *The Skip Barber Racing
School* ISBN 0-8376-0227-0

**A French Kiss With Death: Steve
McQueen and the Making of**
Le Mans *Michael Keyser*
ISBN 0-8376-0234-3

Sports Car and Competition Driving
Paul Frère with foreword by *Phil Hill*
ISBN 0-8376-0202-5

**Driving Forces: The Grand Prix
Racing World Caught in the
Maelstrom of the Third Reich**
Peter Stevenson ISBN 0-8376-0217-3

The Technique of Motor Racing
Piero Taruffi ISBN 0-8376-0228-9

Engineering/Reference

**Supercharged! Design, Testing, and
Installation of Supercharger Systems**
Corky Bell ISBN 0-8376-0168-1

**Maximum Boost: Designing, Testing,
and Installing Turbocharger Systems**
Corky Bell ISBN 0-8376-0160-6

**Bosch Fuel Injection and Engine
Management** *Charles O. Probst, SAE*
ISBN 0-8376-0300-5

Race Car Aerodynamics
Joseph Katz ISBN 0-8376-0142-8

**Scientific Design of Exhaust and
Intake Systems** *Philip H. Smith and
John C. Morrison* ISBN 0-8376-0309-9

**Road & Track Illustrated Automotive
Dictionary** *John Dinkel*
ISBN 0-8376-0143-6

Audi

**Audi A4 Repair Manual: 1996–2001,
1.8L turbo, 2.8L, including Avant and
quattro** *Bentley Publishers*
ISBN 0-8376-0371-4

**Audi TT Coupe: 2000–2005, TT
Roadster: 2001–2005 Official Factory
Repair Manual on CD-ROM**
Bentley Publishers
ISBN 978-0-8376-1261-4

**Audi A6: 1998–2004 Official Factory
Repair Manual on CD-ROM**
Bentley Publishers
ISBN 978-0-8376-1257-7

BMW

BMW Enthusiast's Companion™
BMW Car Club of America
ISBN 0-8376-0321-8

**BMW 6 Series Enthusiast's
Companion™** *Jeremy Walton*
ISBN 0-8376-0193-2

**Unbeatable BMW: Eighty Years of
Engineering and Motorsport Success**
Jeremy Walton ISBN 0-8376-0206-8

**BMW 3 Series (E46) Service Manual:
1999–2005 including Sedan, Coupe,
Convertible, Sport Wagon**
Bentley Publishers ISBN 0-8376-1277-2

**BMW 3 Series (E36) Service Manual:
1992–1998 including Sedan, Coupe,
Convertible** *Bentley Publishers*
ISBN 0-8376-0326-9

**BMW 5 Series (E39) Service Manual:
1997–2002 525i, 528i, 530i, 540i, Sedan,
Sport Wagon** *Bentley Publishers*
ISBN 0-8376-0317-X

**BMW 5 Series (E34) Service Manual:
1989–1995 525i, 530i, 535i, 540i
including Touring** *Bentley Publishers*
ISBN 0-8376-0317-X

**BMW 7 Series (E32) Service Manual:
1988–1994, 735i, 735iL, 740i, 740iL,
750iL** *Bentley Publishers*
ISBN 0-8376-0328-5

**BMW Z3 Service Manual: 1996–2002,
including Z3 Roadster, Z3 Coupe, M
Roadster, M Coupe** *Bentley Publishers*
ISBN 0-8376-1250-0

Harley-Davidson

**Harley-Davidson Evolution V-Twin
Owner's Bible™** *Moses Ludel*
ISBN 0-8376-0146-0

Jeep

Jeep Owner's Bible™ - Third Edition
Moses Ludel ISBN 0-8376-1117-2

**Jeep CJ Rebuilder's Manual: 1946–
1971** *Moses Ludel* ISBN 0-8376-1037-0

**Jeep CJ Rebuilder's Manual: 1972–
1986** *Moses Ludel* ISBN 0-8376-0151-7

Mercedes-Benz

**Mercedes-Benz Technical
Companion** *the staff of The Star and
members of the Mercedes-Benz Club of
America* ISBN 0-8376-1033-8

**Mercedes-Benz E-Class Owner's
Bible™** *Bentley Publishers*
ISBN 0-8376-0230-0

MINI Cooper

**MINI Cooper Service Manual: 2002–
2004, including MINI Cooper, MINI
Cooper S** *Bentley Publishers*
ISBN 0-8376-1068-0

Porsche

Porsche: Excellence Was Expected
Karl Ludvigsen ISBN 0-8376-0235-1

**Porsche 911 (964) Enthusiast's
Companion: Carrera 2, Carrera 4 and
Turbo, 1989–1994** *Adrian Streather*
ISBN 0-8376-0293-9

**Porsche 911 Carrera Service Manual:
1984–1989** *Bentley Publishers*
ISBN 0-8376-0291-2

**Porsche 911 SC Service Manual:
1978–1983** *Bentley Publishers*
ISBN 0-8376-0290-4

**Porsche 911 Carrera (964) 1989–
1994 Technical Data—Without
Guesswork™** *Bentley Publishers*
ISBN 0-8376-0292-0

SAAB

**SAAB 900 16-Valve Official Service
Manual 1985–1993** *Bentley Publishers*
ISBN 0-8376-0313-7

**SAAB 900 8-Valve Official Service
Manual: 1981–1988** *Bentley Publishers*
ISBN 0-8376-0310-2

Volkswagen

**Volkswagen Sport Tuning for Street
and Competition** *Per Schroeder*
ISBN 0-8376-0161-4

**Jetta, Golf, GTI: 1999–2005 Service
Manual, 1.8L turbo, 1.9L TDI diesel,
PD diesel, 2.0L gasoline, 2.8L VR6**
Bentley Publishers ISBN 0-8376-1251-9

**Passat, Passat Wagon 1998–2005:
Official Factory Repair Manual on
CD-ROM** *Volkswagen of America*
ISBN 978-0-8376-1267-6